LENIN

COLLECTED WORKS

22

THE RUSSIAN EDITION WAS PRINTED
IN ACCORDANCE WITH A DECISION
OF THE NINTH CONGRESS OF THE R.C P.(B).
AND THE SECOND CONGRESS OF SOVIETS
OF THE U.S.S.R.

ИНСТИТУТ МАРКСИЗМА-ЛЕНИНИЗМА ПРИ ЦК КПСС

В. И. ЛЕНИН

СОЧИНЕНИЯ

Издание четвертое

ГОСУДАРСТВЕННОЕ ИЗДАТЕЛЬСТВО
ПОЛИТИЧЕСКОЙ ЛИТЕРАТУРЫ
МОСКВА

V. I. LENIN

COLLECTED WORKS

VOLUME
22

December 1915 - July 1916

PROGRESS PUBLISHERS
MOSCOW 1964

TRANSLATED BY YURI SDOBNIKOV

EDITED BY GEORGE HANNA

CONTENTS

1916

ILLUSTRATIONS

PREFACE

Volume 22 contains works written by Lenin between December 1915 and July 1916. They include his paper, *New Data on the Laws Governing the Development of Capitalism in Agriculture. Part One. Capitalism and Agriculture in the United States of America*, a critique of the non-Marxist theory of the non-capitalist evolution of agriculture under capitalism.

A considerable part of the volume consists of articles substantiating and explaining Bolshevik slogans and the tasks of the proletariat during the imperialist world war of 1914-18, and exposing the avowed social-chauvinists, and also the Centrists, who were actually social-chauvinists. Among them are "Opportunism and the Collapse of the Second International", "The Tasks of the Opposition in France", "Peace Without Annexations and the Independence of Poland as Slogans of the Day in Russia", "Wilhelm Kolb and Georgy Plekhanov", "The Peace Programme", "Proposals Submitted by the Central Committee of the R.S.D.L.P. to the Second Socialist Conference", "German and Non-German Chauvinism", etc.

The present volume includes Lenin's famous work, *Imperialism, the Highest Stage of Capitalism*, which gives a Marxist analysis of imperialism, as the final stage of capitalism, and shows that "imperialism is the eve of the social revolution of the proletariat". On the strength of this analysis, Lenin put forward the new theoretical proposition that initially socialism could triumph in one single capitalist country, and could not triumph in all at once. Lenin formulated his brilliant proposition in two articles: "Slogan for a United States of Europe", written in August 1915, and "The Military Programme of the Proletarian Revolution", written in the autumn of 1916.

This was a new theory of socialist revolution which enriched Marxism and developed it.

In his theses, "The Socialist Revolution and the Right of Nations to Self-Determination", and the article "The Discussion on Self-Determination Summed Up", Lenin elaborated the basic propositions of the Bolshevik programme on the national question. In "The Junius Pamphlet" Lenin criticised the political mistakes of the Left-wing Social-Democrats in Germany.

Documents published for the first time in an edition of Lenin's *Collected Works* are "Draft Resolution on the Convocation of the Second Socialist Conference", "For the Conference to Be Held on April 24, 1916. Proposal of the Delegation", and "Letter from the Committee of Organisations Abroad to the Sections of the R.S.D.L.P."; these are a reflection of Lenin's struggle against Russian and West-European social-chauvinists and his efforts to strengthen the Bolshevik Party and rally the internationalists in the working-class movement of all countries.

NEW DATA ON THE LAWS GOVERNING THE DEVELOPMENT OF CAPITALISM IN AGRICULTURE

PART ONE
CAPITALISM AND AGRICULTURE
IN THE UNITED STATES OF AMERICA[1]

Published in 1915
First published in 1917 as a separate pamphlet
by the *Zhizn i Znaniye* Publishers

Published according
to the manuscript

Книгоиздательство „ЖИЗНЬ и ЗНАНІЕ“.
Петроградъ, Поварской пер., д. 2. кв. 9 и 10. Телефонъ 227-42

Библіотека Обществовѣдѣнія. Кн. 42-ая.

В. ИЛЬИНЪ (Н. Ленинъ).

НОВЫЯ ДАННЫЯ

О ЗАКОНАХЪ РАЗВИТІЯ КАПИТАЛИЗМА

ВЪ ЗЕМЛЕДѢЛІИ.

ВЫПУСКЪ I.

Капитализмъ и земледѣліе въ Соед. Штатахъ Америки.

ПЕТРОГРАДЪ.
1917.

Cover of *New Data on the Laws Governing the Development of Capitalism in Agriculture. Part One. Capitalism and Agriculture in the United States of America.* 1917
Reduced

A leading country of modern capitalism is of especial interest to the study of the socio-economic structure and evolution of present-day agriculture. The U.S.A. is unrivalled either in the rate of development of capitalism at the turn of the century, or in the record level of capitalist development already attained; nor has it any rival in the vastness of the territory developed with the use of the most up-to-date machinery, which is adapted to the remarkable variety of natural and historical conditions, or in the extent of the political liberty and the cultural level of the mass of the population. That country, indeed, is in many respects the model for our bourgeois civilisation and is its ideal.

The study of the forms and laws of agricultural evolution is made easier in the U.S.A. by its decennial censuses of population, which are coupled with remarkably detailed descriptions of all industrial and agricultural enterprises. This yields a wealth of exact information that is unavailable in any other country; it helps to verify many popular notions, most of which are very loosely formulated and repeated without criticism, and usually serve to funnel bourgeois views and prejudices.

Mr. Himmer in the June (1913) issue of *Zavety* [2] gives some data from the latest, Thirteenth (1910) Census, and on this basis reiterates the most popular and thoroughly bourgeois contention—bourgeois both as regards its theoretical basis and political significance—that "the vast majority of farms in the United States employ only family labour"; that "in the more highly developed areas agricultural capitalism is disintegrating"; that "in the great majority of areas... small-scale farming by owner-operators is becoming ever more dominant"; that it is precisely "in the older cultivated

areas with a higher level of economic development" that
"capitalist agriculture is disintegrating and production is
breaking up into smaller units"; that "there are no areas
where colonisation is no longer continuing, or where large-
scale capitalist agriculture is not decaying and is not being
replaced by family-labour farms", and so on and so forth.

All these assertions are monstrously untrue. They are
in direct contradiction to reality. They are a sheer mockery
of the truth. Their incorrectness ought to be explained in
detail for a very good reason: Mr. Himmer is not the man in
the street, he is not a casual contributor of a casual magazine article, but one of the most prominent economists
representing the most democratic, extreme Left-wing *bourgeois*
trend in Russian and European social thinking. That is precisely why Mr. Himmer's views may have, and indeed already
have among some non-proletarian sections of the population,
particularly wide circulation and influence. They are not
merely his personal views, nor his individual mistakes, but
are rather an expression—couched in the most democratic
terms and heavily embellished with pseudo-socialist phraseology—of *general* bourgeois views which in the atmosphere of
a capitalist society are most readily accepted both by the
smug professor, treading the beaten path, and the small
farmer who is more intelligent than millions of his fellows.

The theory of the non-capitalist evolution of agriculture in capitalist society, which Mr. Himmer advocates, is
really the theory of the great majority of bourgeois professors and bourgeois democrats and also of opportunists in the
labour movement of the whole world who are the latest
variety of those selfsame bourgeois democrats. It is no exag-
geration to say that this theory is an illusion, a dream, a
delusion under which the whole of bourgeois society is
labouring. In devoting my further exposition to the refutation of this theory, I shall try to give a complete picture of
capitalism in American agriculture, because one of the main
mistakes made by bourgeois economists is to isolate facts
and figures, major and minor, from the general context of
politico-economic relations. All my data are taken from
official statistical publications of the United States of North
America, including above all the volumes *Five*, devoted to
agriculture, of the Twelfth and Thirteenth censuses taken in

1900 and 1910 respectively,* and also the *Statistical Abstract of the United States for 1911*. Having mentioned these sources, I shall not give references to pages or tables for each separate figure, as this would only burden the reader and needlessly encumber the text; anyone interested enough will easily find the data in question from the tables of contents in these publications.

1. GENERAL CHARACTERISTIC OF THE THREE MAIN SECTIONS. THE HOMESTEAD WEST

The vast area of the United States, which is only slightly smaller than the whole of Europe, and the great diversity of farming conditions in the various parts of the country make absolutely imperative a separate study of the major divisions, each with its peculiar economic status. American statisticians adopted five geographical divisions in 1900, and nine in 1910. (1) New England—six states on the Atlantic coast in the north-east (Maine, New Hampshire, Vermont, Massachusetts, Rhode Island, and Connecticut); (2) Middle Atlantic (New York, New Jersey, and Pennsylvania)—in 1900 these two divisions formed the North Atlantic division; (3) East North Central (Ohio, Indiana, Illinois, Michigan, and Wisconsin); (4) West North Central (Minnesota, Iowa, Missouri, North and South Dakota, Nebraska, and Kansas)—in 1900, the last two made up the North Central division; (5) South Atlantic (Delaware, Maryland, District of Columbia, Virginia, West Virginia, North and South Carolina, Georgia, and Florida)—unchanged from 1900; (6) East South Central (Kentucky, Tennessee, Alabama, and Mississippi); (7) West South Central (Arkansas, Oklahoma, Louisiana, and Texas)—in 1900, the last two made up the South Central division; (8) Mountain (Montana, Idaho, Wyoming, Colorado, New Mexico, Arizona, Utah, and Nevada); and (9) Pacific (Washington, Oregon, and California)—in 1900, the last two made up the Western division.

---

* *Census Reports. Twelfth Census 1900*. Vol. V. Agriculture, Wash. 1902.—*Thirteenth Census of the United States, Taken in the Year 1910*. Vol. V. Agriculture, Wash. 1913.

The excessive patchwork of these divisions prompted American statisticians in 1910 to compress them into three main sections—the North (1-4), the South (5-7) and the West (8-9). We shall presently see that this division into three main sections is really most important and vital, although here, too, as in everything else, there are transitional types, so that on some basic points New England and the Middle Atlantic states will have to be considered separately.

In order to define the fundamental distinction between the three main sections, let us designate them as the *industrial* North, the *former slave-owning* South and the *homestead* West.

Here are the figures on their area, percentage of improved* land, and population:

Sections	Total land area (000,000 acres)	Percentage of improved land	Population (1910) (000,000)
The North	588	49	56
The South	562	27	29
The West	753	5	7
The U.S.A.	1,903	25	92

The North and the South have approximately the same area, while the West is nearly half as large again as either. The population of the North, however, is eight times that of the West, which, one might say, is hardly populated. How rapidly it is being settled is evident from the fact that in the 10 years between 1900 and 1910, the population in the North increased by 18 per cent; the South, by 20 per cent; and the West, by 67 per cent! There is hardly any increase in the number of farms in the North: 2,874,000 in 1900, and 2,891,000 in 1910 (+0.6 per cent); in the South the number increased by 18 per cent, from 2,600,000 to 3,100,000; and in the West, by 54 per cent, i.e., more than half as much again, from 243,000 to 373,000.

---

* The 1910 Census defines farmland as consisting of (1) improved land, (2) woodland, and (3) all other unimproved land. Improved land includes all land regularly tilled or mowed, land pastured and cropped in rotation, land lying fallow, land in gardens, orchards, vineyards, and nurseries, and land occupied by farm buildings.—*Tr.*

How land is being settled in the West is seen from the data on *homesteads*, which are parcels of land, mostly of 160 acres, i.e., about 65 dessiatines, allocated by the government free of charge or at a nominal price. In the 10 years between 1901 and 1910, the area occupied by homesteads in the North was 55.3 million acres (including 54.3 million, i.e., more than 98 per cent, in one division alone, namely the West North Central); the area in the South was 20 million acres (including 17.3 million in one division, the West South Central), and in the West, it was 55.3 million acres spread over both divisions. This means that the West is a solid homestead area, i.e., one where unoccupied land is given away practically free—somewhat similar to the squatter land tenure in the outlying districts of Russia, except that it is not regulated by a feudal state, but in a democratic manner (I very nearly said: in a Narodnik manner; the American Republic has implemented in a capitalist way the "Narodnik" idea of distributing unoccupied land to all applicants). The North and the South, however, *each* have only *one* homestead division, which may be regarded as a transitional type from the unsettled West to the settled North and South. Let us note, by the way, that only in two divisions of the North—the New England and the Middle Atlantic—were there absolutely no homestead grants made in the last decade. We shall later have to return to these two most highly industrialised divisions, where there is no longer any homesteading at all.

The above figures on homesteads refer only to claims that have been staked and not to those actually settled; we have no figures on the latter for the various divisions. But even if these returns are somewhat exaggerated as absolute magnitudes, they are, at any rate, a faithful reflection of the relative importance of homesteads in the various divisions. In the North in 1910 the farms totalled 414 million acres, so that homestead claims in the last 10 years came to about one-eighth of the total; in the South, about one-seventeenth (20 out of 354); and in the West, *one-half* (55 out of 111)! To lump together data on areas with hardly any land ownership at all, and data on areas where all the land is occupied, would be to make nonsense of scientific investigation.

America provides the most graphic confirmation of the truth emphasised by Marx in *Capital*,[3] Volume III, that capitalism in agriculture does not depend on the *form* of land ownership or land tenure. Capital finds the most diverse types of medieval and patriarchal landed property—feudal, "peasant allotments" (i.e., the holdings of bonded peasants); clan, communal, state, and other forms of land ownership. Capital takes hold of all these, employing a variety of ways and methods. For agricultural statistics to be properly and rationally compiled, the methods of investigation, tabulation, etc., would have to be modified to correspond to the *forms* of capitalist penetration into agriculture; for instance, the homesteads would have to be put into a special group and their economic fate traced. Unfortunately, however, the statistics are all too often dominated by routine and meaningless, mechanical repetition of the same old methods.

How extensive agriculture is in the West, as compared with the other sections, is evident, by the way, from the data on expenditures for artificial fertilisers. In 1909, the expenditure per acre of improved land was 13 cents ($0.13) in the North; 50 cents, in the South, and only 6 cents in the West. The South has the highest figure because cotton demands great quantities of fertilisers, and the South is primarily a cotton-growing area: cotton and tobacco account for 46.8 per cent of the total value of all its farm crops; grain, only 29.3 per cent; hay and forage, 5.1 per cent. By contrast, grain leads in the North with 62.6 per cent, followed by 18.8 per cent of hay and forage, most of which is cultivated. In the West, grain accounts for 33.1 per cent of the total value of all farm crops; hay and forage, with wild grasses predominating, 31.7 per cent, while fruits, a special branch of commercial farming rapidly developing on the Pacific coast, account for 15.5 per cent of the total value.

2. THE INDUSTRIAL NORTH

By 1910, the urban population in the North reached 58.6 per cent of the total, as compared with 22.5 per cent in the South and 48.8 per cent in the West. The role of industry is evident from these figures:

	Value of products ($000,000,000)				Workers in industry (000,000)
	Crops	Live-stock	Total	Manufactures less cost of raw materials	
The North	3.1	2.1	5.2	6.9	5.2
The South	1.9	0.7	2.6	1.1	1.1
The West	0.5	0.3	0.8	0.5	0.3
The U.S.A.	5.5	3.1	8.6	8.5	6.6

The total crop value is here overstated because a part of the crops, such as feed, recurs in the value of the live-stock products. But in any case these figures show conclusively that almost five-sixths of American manufacture is concentrated in the North, and that manufacture prevails over agriculture in that section. The South and the West, on the contrary, are predominantly agricultural.

The above table shows that the North differs from the South and the West by a comparatively greater development of industry, which creates a market and makes for the intensification of agriculture. The North—"industrial" in that sense—nevertheless still remains the largest producer of agricultural products. More than one-half, actually about three-fifths, of agricultural production, is concentrated in the North. How much more intensive farming is in the North, as compared with the other sections, will be seen from the following figures on the per-acre value of all farm property—land, buildings, implements and machinery, and livestock. In 1910, it was $66 in the North, as compared with $25 in the South, and $41 in the West. The per-acre value of implements and machinery alone was $2.07 in the North, $0.83 in the South, and $1.04 in the West.

The New England and Middle Atlantic divisions stand out in this picture. As I have already pointed out there is no new homesteading in these parts. From 1900 to 1910, there was an absolute decrease in the number of farms, and in the total and in the improved acreage of the farms. Employment returns show that only 10 per cent of the population there is engaged in farming, as compared with a 33 per cent average for the U.S.A., 25 to 41 per cent for the other divisions of the North, and 51 to 63 per cent for the South. Only 6 to 25 per cent of the improved acreage in these two divisions is under cereal crops (the average for the U.S.A. is 40 per cent, and for the North, 46 per cent); 52 to 29 per cent is under grasses, mostly cultivated (as against 15 per cent and 18 per cent); and 4.6 to 3.8 per cent is under vegetables (as against 1.5 and 1.5 per cent). This is the area of the most intensive agriculture. The average expenditure for fertilisers per acre of improved land in 1909 was $1.30 and $0.62 respectively; the former being the U.S. maximum, and the latter, second only to that of one division in the South. The average value of implements and machinery per acre of improved land was $2.58, and $3.88—the maximum figures for the U.S.A. We shall later see that in these most industrialised divisions of the industrial North, agriculture is the most intensive and has the most pronounced capitalist character.

3. THE FORMER SLAVE-OWNING SOUTH

The United States of America, writes Mr. Himmer, is a "country which has never known feudalism and is free from its economic survivals" (p. 41 of his article). This is the very opposite of the truth, for the economic survivals of *slavery* are not in any way distinguishable from those of feudalism, and in the former slave-owning South of the U.S.A. these survivals *are still very powerful.* It would not be worth while to dwell on Mr. Himmer's mistake if it were merely one in a hastily written article. But all liberal and all Narodnik writings in Russia show that the very same "mistake" is being made regularly and with unusual stubbornness with regard to the Russian *labour-service* system, our own survival of feudalism.

The South of the U.S.A. was slave-owning until slavery was swept away by the Civil War of 1861-65. To this day, the Negroes, who make up no more than from 0.7 to 2.2 per cent of the population in the North and the West, constitute from 22.6 to 33.7 per cent of the population in the South. For the U.S.A. as a whole, the Negroes constitute 10.7 per cent of the population. There is no need to elaborate on the degraded social status of the Negroes: the American bourgeoisie is in no way better in this respect than the bourgeoisie of any other country. Having "freed" the Negroes, it took good care, under "free", republican-democratic capitalism, to restore everything possible, and do everything possible and impossible for the most shameless and despicable oppression of the Negroes. A minor statistical fact will illustrate their cultural level. While the proportion of illiterates in 1900 among the white population of the U.S.A. of 10 years of age and over was 6.2 per cent, among the Negroes it was as high as 44.5 per cent! More than seven times as high! In the North and the West illiteracy amounted from 4 to 6 per cent (1900), while in the South it was from 22.9 to 23.9 per cent! One can easily imagine the complex of legal and social relationships that corresponds to this disgraceful fact from the sphere of popular literacy.

What then is the economic basis that has produced and continues to support this fine "superstructure"?

It is the typically Russian, "purely Russian" *labour-service system*, which is known as *share-cropping*.

In 1910, Negroes owned 920,883 farms, i.e., 14.5 per cent of the total. Of the total number of farmers, 37 per cent were tenants; 62.1 per cent, owners; the remaining 0.9 per cent of the farms were run by managers. But among the whites 39.2 per cent were tenant farmers, and among the Negroes—75.3 per cent! The typical white farmer in America is an owner, the typical Negro farmer is a tenant. The proportion of tenants in the West was only 14 per cent: this section is being settled, with new lands unoccupied, and is an El Dorado (a short-lived and unreliable El Dorado, to be sure) for the small "independent farmer". In the North, the proportion of tenant farmers was 26.5 per cent, and in the South, 49.6 per cent! Half of the Southern farmers were tenants.

But that is not all. These are not even tenants in the European, civilised, modern-capitalist sense of the word. They are chiefly semi-feudal or—which is the same thing in economic terms—semi-slave *share-croppers*. In the "free" West, share-croppers were in the minority (25,000 out of a total of 53,000 tenants). In the old North, which was settled long ago, 483,000 out of 766,000 tenant farmers, i.e., 63 per cent, were share-croppers. In the South, *1,021,000* out of 1,537,000 tenant farmers, *i.e., 66 per cent*, were *share-croppers.*

In 1910, free, republican-democratic America had 1,500,000 share-croppers, of whom *more than 1,000,000 were Negroes*. And the proportion of share-croppers to the total number of farmers is not decreasing, but is on the contrary steadily and rather rapidly increasing. In 1880, 17.5 per cent of the farmers in the U.S.A. were share-croppers; in 1890, 18.4 per cent; in 1900, 22.2 per cent; and in 1910, 24 per cent.

American statisticians draw the following conclusions from the 1910 returns:

"In the South the conditions have at all times been somewhat different from those in the North, and many of the tenant farms are parts of plantations of considerable size which date from before the Civil War." In the South, "the system of operation by tenants—chiefly coloured tenants— has succeeded the system of operation by slave labour.... The development of the tenant system is most conspicuous in the South, where the large plantations formerly operated by slave labour have in many cases been broken up into small parcels or tracts and leased to tenants.... These plantations are in many cases still operated substantially as agricultural units, the tenants being subjected to a degree of supervision more or less similar to that which hired farm labourers are subjected to in the North" (op. cit., Vol. V, pp. 102, 104).

To show what the South is like, it is essential to add that its population is fleeing to other capitalist areas and to the towns, just as the peasantry in Russia is fleeing from the most backward central agricultural gubernias, where the survivals of serfdom have been most greatly preserved, in order to escape the rule of the notorious Markovs, to those areas of Russia which have a higher level of capitalist development, to the metropolitan cities, the industrial gubernias and the South (see *The Development of Capitalism in Russia**). The share-cropping area, both in America and in Russia, is the most stagnant area, where the masses are subjected to the greatest degradation and oppression. Immigrants to America, who have such an outstanding role to play in the country's economy and all its social life, shun the

---

* See present edition, Vol. 3, pp. 585-90.—*Ed.*

South. In 1910, the foreign-born formed 14.5 per cent of the total population of America. But in the South the figure was only 1 to 4 per cent for the several divisions, whereas in the other divisions the proportion of incomers ranged from not less than 13.9 per cent to 27.7 per cent (New England). For the "emancipated" Negroes, the American South is a kind of prison where they are hemmed in, isolated and deprived of fresh air. The South is distinguished by the immobility of its population and by the greatest "attachment to the land": with the exception of that division of the South, which still has considerable homesteading (West South Central), 91 to 92 per cent of the population in the two other divisions of the South resided in the same division where they were born, whereas for the United States as a whole the figure was 72.6 per cent, i.e., the mobility of the population is much greater. In the West, which is a solid homestead area, only 35 to 41 per cent of the population lived in the division of their birth.

Negroes are in full flight from the two Southern divisions where there is no homesteading: in the 10 years between the last two censuses, these two divisions provided other parts of the country with almost 600,000 "black" people. The Negroes flee mainly to the towns: in the South, 77 to 80 per cent of all the Negroes live in rural communities; in other areas, only 8 to 32 per cent. Thus it turns out that there is a startling similarity in the economic status of the Negroes in America and the peasants in the heart of agricultural Russia who *"were formerly landowners' serfs"*.

4. AVERAGE SIZE OF FARMS.
"DISINTEGRATION OF CAPITALISM" IN THE SOUTH

Having examined the chief distinctive features of the three main sections of the U.S.A., as well as the general nature of their economic conditions, we can now proceed to an analysis of the data most commonly referred to. These are primarily data on the average acreage of farms. It is on the basis of these data that a great many economists, including Mr. Himmer, draw the most categorical conclusions.

| | Average acreage per farm in the U.S.A. | |
Years	All farmland	Improved land
1850	202.6	78.0
1860	199.2	79.8
1870	153.3	71.0
1880	133.7	71.0
1890	136.5	78.3
1900	146.2	72.2
1910	138.1	75.2

On the whole, there seems at first glance to be a reduction in the average acreage of all farmland and an uncertain fluctuation—upward and downward—in the average improved acreage. But there is a distinct break in the 1860-70 period and this I have indicated by a line. During that period there was an enormous *decrease* in the average acreage of all farmland by 46 acres (from 199.2 to 153.3) and the greatest change (from 79.8 to 71.0), also a reduction, in the average acreage of improved land.

What was the reason? Obviously, the Civil War of 1861-65 and the abolition of slavery. A decisive blow was dealt at the latifundia of the slave-owners. Further on we shall see repeated confirmation of this fact, but it is so generally known that it is surprising that it needs any proof at all. Let us separate the returns for the North and those for the South.

| | Average acreage per farm | | | |
| | South | | North | |
Years	All farmland	Improved land	All farmland	Improved land
1850	332.1	101.1	127.1	65.4
1860	335.4	101.3	126.4	68.3
1870	214.2	69.2	117.0	69.2
1880	153.4	56.2	114.9	76.6
1890	139.7	58.8	123.7	87.8
1900	138.2	48.1	132.2	90.9
1910	114.4	48.6	143.0	100.3

We find that in the South the average improved acreage per farm between 1860 and 1870 greatly *decreased* (from 101.3 to 69.2), and that in the North it slightly *increased* (from 68.3 to 69.2). This means that the cause lay in the specific conditions of evolution in the South. There we find, even after the abolition of slavery, a reduction in the average acreage of farms, although the process is slow and not continuous.

Mr. Himmer's deduction is that in the South "the small-scale family farms are extending their domination, while capital is leaving agriculture for other spheres of investment.... Agricultural capitalism is rapidly disintegrating in the South Atlantic states...".

This is an amusing assertion likely to be matched only in the arguments of our Narodniks on the "disintegration of capitalism" in Russia after 1861 in consequence of the landlords abandoning corvée for the labour-service (i.e., semi-corvée!) system of economy. The break-up of the slave-worked latifundia is called the "disintegration of capitalism". The transformation of the unimproved land of yesterday's slave-owners into the small farms of Negroes, half of whom are share-croppers (it should be borne in mind that the proportion of share-croppers has been steadily *growing* from census to census!), is called the "disintegration of capitalism". It is hardly possible to go any further in distorting the fundamental concepts of economics!

Chapter Twelve of the 1910 Census supplies information on typical Southern "plantations"—not of the old slave period, but of our own day. On the 39,073 plantations there are 39,073 "landlord farms" and 398,905 tenant farms, or an average of 10 tenants per landlord or "master". Plantations average 724 acres, of which only 405 acres is improved, more than 300 acres being unimproved; not a bad reserve for the gentlemen who were the slave-owners of yesterday to draw on in extending their plans of exploitation....

Land on the average plantation is distributed as follows: "landlord" farm—331 acres, of which 87 is improved. "Tenant" farms, i.e., the parcels of the Negro share-croppers, who continue to work for the master and under his eye, average 38 acres, of which 31 is improved land.

As the population and the demand for cotton increase, the former slave-owners of the South begin to parcel out their vast latifundia, nine-tenths of the land on which is still unimproved, into small tracts which are either sold to the Negroes or, more frequently, leased to them on a half-crop basis. (From 1900 to 1910, the number of farmers in the

South who were full owners of all their farmland increased from 1,237,000 to 1,329,000, i.e., 7.5 per cent, while the number of share-croppers went up from 772,000 to 1,021,000, i.e., 32.2 per cent.) And yet an economist has appeared who says this is "disintegration of capitalism"....

I designate as latifundia farms with an area of 1,000 acres and over. In 1910, the proportion of such farms in the U.S.A. was 0.8 per cent (50,135 farms), and they added up to 167.1 million acres, or 19.0 per cent of the total amount of land. This is an average of 3,332 acres per latifundium. Only 18.7 per cent of their acreage was improved while for all farms the figure was 54.4 per cent. The capitalist North has the *smallest* number of latifundia: 0.5 per cent of the total number of farms accounting for 6.9 per cent of the land, 41.1 per cent of which is improved. The West has the greatest number of latifundia: 3.9 per cent of the total number of farms accounting for 48.3 per cent of the land; 32.3 per cent of the land in the latifundia is improved. But it is in the former slave-owning South that the latifundia have the *highest* proportion of unimproved land: 0.7 per cent of the farms are latifundia; they account for 23.9 per cent of the land; *only 8.5 per cent of the land* in the latifundia is improved! Incidentally, these detailed statistics clearly show that there is really no foundation for the common practice of classifying the latifundia as *capitalist* enterprises, without a detailed analysis of the specific data for each country and each area.

During the 10 years from 1900 to 1910, the total acreage of the latifundia, but only of the latifundia, showed a *decrease*. The reduction was quite substantial: from 197.8 million to 167.1 million acres, i.e., 30.7 million acres. In the South, there was a reduction of 31.8 million acres (in the North, an increase of 2.3 million, and in the West, a reduction of 1.2 million). Consequently, it is in the South, and in the slave-owning South alone, that the latifundia, with their negligible proportion (8.5 per cent) of improved land, are being broken up on a really vast scale.

The inescapable conclusion is that the only exact definition of the economic process under way is —a transition from the slave-holding latifundia, nine-tenths of which remained unimproved, to small *commercial* agriculture. It is a transition to commercial farms and not to farms worked by family labour, as Mr. Himmer and the Narodniks, together with all the bourgeois economists who sing cheap hymns to "labour", love to say. The term "family labour" has no politico-economic meaning and is indirectly misleading. It is devoid of meaning because the small farmer "labours" under any social system of economy, be it slavery, serfdom or capitalism. The term "family labour" is just an empty phrase, pure oratory which serves to cover up the *confusion* of entirely different social forms of economic organisation—a confusion from which the bourgeoisie alone stands to gain. The term "family labour" is misleading and deceives the public, for it creates the impression that *hired* labour is not employed.

Mr. Himmer, like all bourgeois economists, evades just these statistics on hired labour, although they are the most important data on the question of capitalism in agriculture and although they are to be found in the 1900 Census report, as well as in the 1910 *Abstract—Farm Crops, by States*, which Mr. Himmer himself quotes (note on p. 49 of his article).

The nature of the staple crop of the South shows that the growth of small-scale agriculture in the South is nothing but the growth of commercial farming. That crop is cotton. Cereals yield 29.3 per cent of the total crop value in the South; hay and forage, 5.1 per cent; and cotton, 42.7 per cent. From 1870 to 1910, the production of wool in the U.S.A. went up from 162 million lbs. to 321 million lbs., i.e., it doubled; wheat, increased from 236 million to 635 million bushels, i.e., less than threefold; corn, from 1,094 million to 2,886 million bushels, also less than threefold; and cotton, from 4,000,000 bales (of 500 lbs. each) to 12,000,000, i.e., threefold. The growth of the crop that is primarily commercial was faster than that of other, less commercialised, crops. In addition, there was in the main division of the South, the South Atlantic, a rather substantial development of tobacco production (12.1 per cent of the crop value in the State of Virginia); vegetables (20.1 per cent of the total crop value in the State of Delaware, 23.2 per cent in the State of Florida); fruits (21.3 per cent of the total crop value in the State of Florida); etc. The nature of all these crops implies an intensification of farming, a larger scale of operations on smaller acreages, and greater employment of hired labour.

I shall now proceed to a detailed analysis of the returns on hired labour; let us note only that the employment of hired labour is also growing in the South, although in this respect it lags behind the other sections —*less* hired labour is employed because of the *wider* practice of semi-slave share-cropping.

5. THE CAPITALIST NATURE OF AGRICULTURE

Capitalism in agriculture is usually gauged by the data on the size of farms or the number and importance of big farms (in terms of acreage). I have examined some of these data and shall return to the problem later on, but it must be said that all these are, after all, indirect indications, for acreage is not always an indication, and not by any means a direct indication, that a farm is really big as *an economic enterprise*, or that it is capitalist in character.

In this respect the data on hired labour are far more indicative and offer better proof. Agricultural censuses taken in recent years, such as the Austrian of 1902 and the German of 1907, which I shall examine elsewhere, show that the employment of hired labour in present-day agriculture— and especially in small-scale farming —is much greater than is generally believed. Nothing so obviously and categorically refutes the petty-bourgeois myth about small "family" farms as do these figures.

American statisticians have collected very extensive material on this, for each farmer's individual census form asks whether he spends anything on hired labour, and, if he does, exactly how much. In contrast to European statistics — such as those of the two countries just named—no record is made in American statistics of the number of hired labourers employed at the time by each farmer, although that could be easily discovered, and the scientific value of such information, in addition to the returns on the total expenditure on hired labour, would indeed be very great. But the worst thing is the very poor tabulation of these returns in the 1910 Census, which is in general presented much more poorly than the 1900 Census. The 1910 Census groups all farms by acreage (as does the 1900 Census) but, by contrast, it does not give any figures on the employment of hired labour by these groups. This makes it impossible for us to compare the employment of hired labour by farms with small and with large acreages. The Census merely gives the average figures for the states and the sections, i.e., data lumping together capitalist and non-capitalist farms.

I shall make a special point of going into the more elaborate data for 1900 later on; meanwhile, here are the figures for 1910; in fact they relate to 1899 and 1909.

Sections	Percentage of farms hiring labour (1909)	Increase of expenditure on hired labour 1899-1909 (per cent)	Expenditure on hired labour per acre of improved land ($)	
			1909	1899
The North . .	55.1	+ 70.8	1.26	0.82
The South . .	36.6	+ 87.1	1.07	0.69
The West . . .	52.5	+119.0	3.25	2.07
The U.S.A.	45.9	+ 82.3	1.36	0.86

The first thing that is made obvious by these figures is that agriculture is most capitalistic in the North (55.1 per cent of farms employ hired labour); then, follows the West (52.5 per cent) and, lastly, the South (36.6 per cent). That is just as it should be when any densely populated and industrial area is being compared with an area still undergoing colonisation and with an area of share-cropping. It goes without saying that figures on the proportion of farms employing hired labour are more suitable for a precise comparison of the sections than data on the expenditure on hired labour per acre of improved land. For the latter type of data to be comparable, the level of wages in the sections would have to be the same. No information on farm wages in the U.S.A. is available but in the light of the basic distinctions between the sections it is inconceivable that their wage levels are the same.

Thus, in the North and in the West—the two sections which together have two-thirds of the improved land and two-thirds of the livestock—*more than one-half* the farmers cannot manage without hired labour. The proportion is smaller in the South only because there the semi-feudal (alias semi-slave) system of exploitation in the form of share-cropping is still strong. There is no doubt that in America, as in all the other capitalist countries, a part of the handicapped farmers have to sell their labour-power. Unfortunately, American statistics do not contain any information about this, in contrast, for example, to the 1907 German statistics, in which these data have been collected and worked out in detail. According to the German statistics, hiring themselves out as labourers is the *main* occupation of 1,940,867 persons, i.e., over 30 per cent, of the 5,736,082 owners of farms (a total which includes the very small "owners"). To be sure, the mass of these farm-hands and day-labourers with a bit of land of their own belong to the poorest groups of farmers.

Let us assume that in the U.S.A., where the smallest farms (of less than three acres) are as a general rule not registered at all, only 10 per cent of the farmers sell their labour-power. Even then we find that *more than one-third* of the farmers are *directly* exploited by the landlords and capitalists (24 per cent share-croppers who are exploited by former slave-owners in feudal or semi-feudal fashion, plus 10 per cent who are exploited by the capitalists, or altogether 34 per cent). This means that of the total number of farmers a *minority*, hardly more than *one-fifth or one-quarter*, neither hire labourers nor hire themselves out or sell themselves into bondage.

Such is the actual state of affairs in the country of "model and advanced" capitalism, in the country with free distribution of millions of dessiatines of land. Here again the famous non-capitalist, small-scale "family" farming proves to be a myth.

How many hired labourers are engaged in American agriculture? Is their number increasing or decreasing in proportion to the total number of farmers and the total rural population?

It is regrettable that American statistics do not provide a direct answer to these highly important questions. Let us find an approximate answer.

Firstly, we can obtain an approximate answer from the returns on occupations (Volume IV of the Census reports). These statistics are not an American "success". They are compiled in such a routine, mechanical, incongruous manner that they contain no information on the status of the persons employed, i.e., no distinction is made between farmers, family workers, and hired labourers. Instead of making a precise economic classification, the compilers were content to use "popular" terminology, absurdly bracketing members of farmers' families and hired labourers under the head of farm workers. As we know it is *not* only in American statistics that there is complete chaos on this question.

The 1910 Census makes an attempt to bring some order into this chaos, to correct the obvious mistakes and to separate at least a part of the hired labourers (those working out) from members of the family working on the home farm. In a series of calculations the statisticians correct the total number of persons engaged in farming, reducing it by 468,100 (Vol. IV, p. 27). The number of *females* working out is set at 220,048 for 1900, and 337,522 for 1910 (an increase of 53 per cent). The number of males working out in 1910 was 2,299,444. Assuming that in 1900 the proportion of hired labourers to the total number of farm workers was the same as in 1910, the number of males working out in 1900 must have been 1,798,165. We then obtain this picture:

	1900	1910	Increase (per cent)
Total engaged in agriculture	10,381,765	12,099,825	+16
Number of farmers	5,674,875	5,981,522	+ 5
Number of hired labourers	2,018,213	2,566,966	+27

That is, the percentage increase in the number of hired labourers was over five times greater than in that of farmers (27 per cent and 5 per cent). The proportion of farmers in the rural population *decreased*; the proportion of hired labourers *increased*. The proportion of independent farm operators to the total farming population dropped; the number of dependent, exploited persons, increased.

In 1907, hired farm labourers in Germany numbered 4.5 million out of a total of 15 million persons working on the home farm and working out. Consequently, 30 per cent were hired labourers. In America, according to the estimate given above, the figure was 2.5 million out of 12 million, i.e., 21 per cent. It is possible that the availability of vacant land distributed free, and the high percentage of share-cropping tenants tended to lower the percentage of hired labourers in America.

Secondly, an approximate answer may be provided by the figures on expenditure on hired labour in 1899 and 1909. During the same period, the number of industrial wage-workers increased from 4.7 million to 6.6 million, i.e., 40 per cent, and their wages from $2,008 million to $3,427 million, i.e., 70 per cent. (It should be borne in mind that the rise in the cost of living cancelled out this nominal increase in wages.)

On the strength of this we may assume that the 82 per cent increase in expenditure on hired farm labour corresponds to an increase of approximately 48 per cent in the number of hired labourers. Making a similar assumption for the three main sections we obtain the following picture:

Sections	Percentage increase from 1900 to 1910		
	Total rural population	Number of farms	Number of hired labourers
The North	+ 3.9	+ 0.6	+40
The South	+14.8	+18.2	+50
The West	+49.7	+53.7	+66
The U.S.A.	+11.2	+10.9	+48

These figures also show that for the country as a whole the increase in the number of farmers is not keeping pace with the growth of the rural population, while the increase in the number of hired labourers is outstripping the growth of the rural population. In other words: the proportion of independent farm operators is decreasing, and the proportion of dependent farm workers is increasing.

It should be noted that the great difference between the increase in the number of hired labourers obtained in the first estimate (+ 27 per cent) and in the second (+ 48 per cent) is quite possible because in the former only the *professional* farm labourers were enumerated, and in the latter, *every instance* of employment of hired labour was taken into account. In farming, seasonal hired labour is highly important, and it should be the rule, therefore, that it is never enough to determine the number of hired labourers, permanent and seasonal, but that an effort must also be made to determine, as far as possible, the total expenditure on hired labour.

At any rate, both estimates definitely show a *growth* of capitalism in agriculture in the U.S.A., and an *increase* in the employment of hired labour, which is proceeding at a faster pace than the growth of the rural population and of the number of farmers.

6. AREAS OF THE MOST INTENSIVE AGRICULTURE

Having examined the general data on hired labour as the most direct indicator of capitalism in agriculture, we can now go on to a more detailed analysis of the specific *forms* assumed by capitalism in this particular branch of the economy.

We have taken a look at one area with a shrinking average acreage of farms, namely, the South, where the process signifies a transition from latifundia worked by slaves to small-scale commercial farms. There is another area where the average acreage of farms is diminishing—a part of the North: New England and the Middle Atlantic states. Here are the figures for these divisions:

Average acreage per farm (improved land)

	New England	Middle Atlantic states
1850	66.5	70.8
1860	66.4	70.3
1870	66.4	69.2
1880	63.4	68.0
1890	56.5	67.4
1900	42.4	63.4
1910	38.4	62.6

The average farm in New England is smaller than in any other division of the U.S.A. In two Southern divisions the average is 42 to 43 acres, and in the third, the West South Central, where homesteading is still going on, it is 61.8 acres, i.e., almost as much as in the Middle Atlantic states. It is the reduction in the average size of farms in New England and the Middle Atlantic states, "the areas with an older culture and a higher level of economic development" (Mr. Himmer, p. 60), where homesteading is no longer taking place, that has led Mr. Himmer, as it has very many other bourgeois economists, to draw the conclusion that "capitalist agriculture is disintegrating", that "production is breaking up into smaller units", that there are "no areas where colonisation is no longer continuing, or where large-scale capitalist agriculture is not decaying and is not being replaced by family-labour farms".

Mr. Himmer arrived at these conclusions, which are the very opposite of the truth, because he forgot a mere "trifle": the intensification of agriculture! It is incredible, but it is a fact. This matter requires a particularly thorough analysis because quite a few bourgeois economists, almost all in fact, contrive to forget this "trifle" when dealing with small and large-scale production in agriculture, although "in theory" they are all "aware" of and accept the intensification of farming. This is indeed one of the basic sources of all the misadventures of bourgeois (including Narodnik and opportunist) economics on the question of small "family" farms. The "trifle" they forget is this: owing to the technical peculiarities of agriculture, the process of its intensification frequently leads to a *reduction* in the improved acreage on the farm, and at the same time expands it as an *economic unit*, increasing its *output*, and making it more and more of a *capitalist* enterprise.

Let us first see whether or not there is any fundamental difference in farming techniques, in the general character of farming and degree of its intensification between New England and the Middle Atlantic states, on the one hand, and between the rest of the North and the country's other divisions, on the other.

The differences in the crops grown are shown in the following table:

Percentage of the total crop value
(1910)

Divisions	Cereals	Hay and forage	Vegetables, fruits and similar special crops
New England	7.6	41.9	33.5
Middle Atlantic	29.6	31.4	31.8
East North Central	65.4	16.5	11.0
West North Central	75.4	14.6	5.9

The difference in farming conditions is fundamental. In the first two divisions agriculture is highly intensive; in the other two it is extensive. In the latter, cereals account for the bulk of the total crop value; in the former, they contribute not only a minor part, but sometimes a negligible part (7.6 per cent), while the special "commercial" crops (vegetables, fruits, etc.) yield a *greater* part of the crop value than cereals. Extensive agriculture has given way to intensive agriculture. Grass cultivation has become widespread. Of the 3.8 million acres under hay and forage in New England, 3.3 million acres were under *cultivated* grasses. The figures for the Middle Atlantic states are 8.5 and 7.9 million respectively. By contrast, of the 27.4 million acres under hay and forage in the West North Central states (an area of colonisation and extensive agriculture), 14.5 million, i.e., the greater part, were unimproved grasslands, etc.

Yields are considerably higher in the "intensive" states:

Divisions	Per-acre yield in bushels			
	Corn		Wheat	
	1909	1899	1909	1899
New England	45.2	39.4	23.5	18.0
Middle Atlantic	32.2	34.0	18.6	14.9
East North Central	38.6	38.3	17.2	12.9
West North Central	27.7	31.4	14.8	12.2

The same is true of commercial livestock and dairy farming, which are especially highly developed in these divisions:

Divisions	Average number of dairy cows per farm (1900)	Average production of milk per cow (gallons)	
		1909	*1899*
New England	5.8	476	548
Middle Atlantic	6.1	490	514
East North Central	4.0	410	487
West North Central	4.9	325	371
The South (3 divisions)	1.9-3.1	232-286	290-395
The West (2 divisions)	4.7-5.1	339-475	334-470
The U.S.A.	3.8	362	424

This table shows that in the "intensive" states dairy
farming is on a considerably *larger* scale than in all the
others. The areas with the *smallest* farms (in terms of
improved acreage) have the *largest* dairies. This fact is of
tremendous importance, for, as everyone knows, dairy farming develops most rapidly in suburban localities and in
very highly industrialised countries (or areas). Statistics
from Denmark, Germany and Switzerland, which are dealt
with elsewhere,* also show a *growing concentration* of dairy
cattle.

As we have seen, hay and forage in the "intensive" states
constitute a considerably greater proportion of the total
crop value than cereals. Accordingly, livestock farming
there develops largely on the basis of *purchased feed*. Here
are the relevant figures for 1909:

Divisions	Receipts from sale of feed ($000,000)	Outlays on feed	Excess of receipts or outlays
New England	+ 4.3	—34.6	—30.3
Middle Atlantic	+ 21.6	—54.7	—33.1
East North Central	+195.6	—40.6	+155.0
West North Central	+174.4	—76.2	+ 98.2

The extensive states of the North sell feed. The intensive
states buy it. It is clear that if feed is purchased *large-scale*
operations of a highly capitalistic nature can be conducted
on a *small* tract of land.

Let us make a comparison between the two intensive divisions of the North, New England and the Middle Atlantic
states, and the most extensive division of the North, the
West North Central:

Divisions	Improved land (000,000 acres)	Value of livestock ($000,000)	Receipts from sale of feed ($000,000)	Outlays on feed ($000,000)
New England + Middle Atlantic	36.5	447	26	89
West North Central	164.3	1,552	174	76

---

* See present edition, Vol. 5, pp. 205-22, and Vol. 13, pp. 169-
216.—*Ed.*

We find that there is more livestock per acre of improved land in the intensive states (447 : 36=\$12 per acre) than in the extensive states (1,552 : 164= \$9). More capital in the form of livestock is invested in a unit of land area. And the total per-acre turnover of the feed trade (purchases+ +sales) is also very much greater in the intensive states (26+89=\$115 million for 36 million acres) than in the extensive states (174+76= \$250 million for 164 million acres). In the intensive states farming is obviously much more *commercialised* than in the extensive states.

Expenditure on fertilisers and the value of implements and machinery are the most exact statistical expression of the degree of intensification of agriculture. Here are the figures:

	Divisions	Percentage of farms with outlays on fertilisers	Average out-lays per farm (\$)	Average out-lays per acre of improved land (\$)		Average im-proved acre-age per farm
				1909	1899	(1909)
The North	New England	60.9	82	1.30	0.53	38.4
	Middle Atlantic	57.1	68	0.62	0.37	62.6
	East North Central	19.6	37	0.09	0.07	79.2
	West North Central	2.1	41	0.01	0.01	148.0
The South	South Atlantic	69.2	77	1.23	0.49	43.6
	East South Central	33.8	37	0.29	0.13	42.2
	West South Central	6.4	53	0.06	0.03	61.8
The West	Mountain	1.3	67	0.01	0.01	86.8
	Pacific	6.4	189	0.10	0.05	116.1
	The U.S.A.	28.7	63	0.24	0.13	75.2

This fully brings out the difference between the extensive divisions of the North, with an insignificant proportion of farms using purchased fertilisers (2-19 per cent), and with negligible expenditure on fertilisers per acre of improved land (\$0.01- \$0.09) —and the intensive states, where the *majority* of farms (57-60 per cent) use purchased fertilisers and where expenditure on fertilisers is substantial. In New England, for example, the per-acre expenditure is \$1.30— the *maximum* figure for all divisions (once again a case of farms with the smallest acreage and the largest expenditure on fertilisers!), which exceeds the figure for one of the divisions of the South (South Atlantic). It should be noted that in the South especially large quantities of artificial fertilisers are required by cotton, on which, as we have seen, the labour of Negro share-croppers is most widely employed.

In the Pacific states, we find a very small percentage of farms using fertilisers (6.4 per cent) but the maximum average per farm expenditure ($189)—calculated, of course, only for the farms which used fertilisers. Here we have another example of the growth of *large-scale* and capitalist agriculture with a simultaneous *reduction* of the farm acreage. In two of the three Pacific states—Washington and Oregon—the use of fertilisers is quite insignificant, a mere $0.01 per acre. It is only in the third state, California, that the figure is relatively high: $0.08 in 1899, and $0.19 in 1909. In this state, the fruit crop plays a special role, and is expanding at an extremely rapid rate along purely capitalist lines; in 1909, it accounted for 33.1 per cent of the total crop value, as against 18.3 per cent for cereals, and 27.6 per cent for hay and forage. The typical fruit-growing farm has a *smaller-than-average* acreage but the use of fertilisers and hired labour is *much greater* than average. We shall later have occasion to dwell on relationships of this type, which are typical of capitalist countries with an intensive agriculture and which are most stubbornly ignored by statisticians and economists.

But let us return to the "intensive" states of the North. Not only is expenditure on fertilisers— $1.30 per acre—in New England the highest and the average farm acreage the smallest (38.4 acres); expenditure on fertilisers is increasing at an especially rapid rate. In the 10 years between 1899 and 1909, this expenditure increased from $0.53 per acre to $1.30, i.e., two and one-half times. Consequently, here intensification of agriculture, technical progress and improvement of farming techniques are extremely rapid. To get a more graphic picture of what this means let us compare New England, the most intensive division of the North, with West North Central, the most extensive division. In the latter division, scarcely any artificial fertilisers are

used at all (2.1 per cent of the farms and $0.01 per acre);
its farm acreage is larger than that of any other division
of America (148 acres), and is growing at a faster rate. This
particular division is usually taken as the model of capitalism in American agriculture—and this Mr. Himmer
also does. As I shall show in detail later on, this is incorrect.
It is due to the crudest, most primitive form of extensive
agriculture being confused with technically progressive
intensive agriculture. In the West North Central division,
the average farm is four times as big as in New England
(148 acres as against 38.4), while average expenditure on
fertilisers per user is only half as great: $41 as against $82.

Hence, in actual practice there are instances of a substantial *reduction* in farm acreage being accompanied by a
substantial *increase* in expenditure on artificial fertilisers, so that "small" production—if we continue, as a matter
of routine, to regard it as being small in terms of acreage —
turns out to be "large" in terms of the capital invested in
the land. This is not an exception, but the rule for any
country where extensive agriculture is giving way to intensive agriculture. And this applies to *all* capitalist countries, so that when this typical, essential and fundamental
characteristic of agriculture is ignored, the result is the
common error of the votaries of small-scale agriculture who
base their judgement only on farm acreage.

7. MACHINERY AND HIRED LABOUR IN AGRICULTURE

Let us consider another form of capital investment in
land which is technically different from the form examined
above—implements and machinery. All European agricultural statistics provide irrefutable evidence that the larger
the farm acreage, the greater is the proportion of farms
using all types of machines and the greater the number of
machines used. The superiority of big farms in this highly
important respect has been established beyond doubt. In
this field, too, American statisticians have a rather unconven-
tional approach: neither implements nor farm machinery are
recorded separately, only their total value being given.
Such data may, of course, be less exact in each individual
case, but taken as a whole they allow definite comparisons

between divisions and between groups of farms —comparisons which are impossible with other kinds of data.

Below are the figures for farm implements and machinery by divisions:

Divisions	Value of implements and machinery (1909)	
	Average per farm ($)	Average per acre of all farmland ($)
The North { New England	269	2.58
Middle Atlantic	358	3.88
East North Central	239	2.28
West North Central	332	1.59
The South (three divisions)	72-88-127	0.71-0.92-0.95
The West (two divisions)	269-350	0.83-1.29
The U.S.A.	199	1.44

The former slave-owning South, the area of share-cropping, occupies a bottom place in the use of machinery. The value of implements and machinery per acre —for its three divisions —is one-third, one-quarter, one-fifth of the figures for the intensive states of the North. The latter lead the rest and, in particular, are far ahead of the West North Central states, America's most agricultural area and her granary, which superficial observers still frequently regard as a model area of capitalism and of the use of machinery.

It should be noted that the American statistical method of determining the value of machinery, as well as of land, livestock, buildings, etc., per acre of *all* farmland and not per acre of improved land, understates the superiority of the "intensive" areas of the North and cannot, in general, be considered correct. The difference between the divisions in regard to the proportion of improved acreage is very great: in the West, it is as low as 26.7 per cent for the Mountain states, and as high as 75.4 per cent for the East North Central states in the North. For the purposes of economic statistics, improved land is undoubtedly of much greater importance than total acreage. In New England, improved acreage in farms and its proportion of the total has decreased substantially, especially since 1880, probably under the impact of competition from the free lands of the West (i.e., free from ground-rent, from tribute to the land-owning gentry). At the same time, the use of machinery in this division is very extensive and the value of machinery per acre of *improved land* is especially high. In 1910, it amounted to $7 per acre, while in the Middle Atlantic states it was about $5.50 and not more than $2-3 in the other divisions.

Again, the division with the *smallest* farms, in terms of acreage, turns out to have the *largest* capital investments in land in the form of machinery.

Comparing the Middle Atlantic, one of the "intensive" divisions of the North, with the most extensive region of the North, the West North Central, we discover that as far as improved acreage per farm is concerned, that of the former is *less than half that of the latter*—62.6 acres as against 148.0—while the value of machinery used is *greater*— $358 per farm as against $332. The smaller farms are thus larger enterprises in terms of machinery used.

We still have to compare the data on the intensive nature of agriculture with the data on the employment of hired labour. I already gave these figures in brief above, in Chapter 5. We must now examine them in greater detail by divisions.

Divisions	Percentage of farms hiring labour in 1909	Average outlays on hired labour per hiring farm ($)	Outlays on labour per acre of improved land		Increase of outlays from 1899 to 1909 (per cent)
			1909	1899	
The North					
New England	66.0	277	4.76	2.55	+86
Middle Atlantic	65.8	253	2.66	1.64	+62
East North Central	52.7	199	1.33	0.78	+71
West North Central	51.0	240	0.83	0.56	+48
The South					
South Atlantic	42.0	142	1.37	0.80	+71
East South Central	31.6	107	0.80	0.49	+63
West South Central	35.6	178	1.03	0.75	+37
The West					
Mountain	46.8	547	2.95	2.42	+22
Pacific	58.0	694	3.47	1.92	+80
The U.S.A.	45.9	223	1.36	0.86	+58

This shows, firstly, that capitalism is undoubtedly much more developed in the agriculture of the Northern intensive states than in that of the extensive states; secondly, that in the former, capitalism is developing faster than in the latter; thirdly, that the division with the smallest farms, New England, has both the highest level of development of capitalism in agriculture and the highest rate of its development. There the increase of expenditure on hired labour per acre of improved land is 86 per cent; the Pacific states come second in this respect. California, where, as I have said, "small-scale" capitalist fruit-raising is rapidly developing, is also the leader in this respect among the Pacific states.

The West North Central division, with the largest farm acreages (an average of 148 acres in 1910, counting improved land only) and with the most rapid and steady growth of farm acreages since 1850, is commonly regarded as the "model" capitalist region of American agriculture. We have now seen that this contention is profoundly erroneous. The extent to which hired labour is used is certainly the best and most direct indicator of the development of capitalism. And it tells us that America's "granary", the region of the much vaunted "wheat factories", which attract so much attention, is *less* capitalist than the industrial and intensively farmed region, where the indication of agricultural progress is not an increase in improved acreage but an *increase* in capital investments in the land, together with a simultaneous *reduction* of the acreage.

It is quite possible to imagine that with the use of machinery the improvement of the "black soil" or unploughed virgin lands in general can proceed very rapidly despite a small increase in the employment of hired labour. In the West North Central states expenditure on hired labour per acre of improved land was $0.56 in 1899, and $0.83 in 1909, an increase of only 48 per cent. In New England, where the improved area is decreasing and not increasing and where the average size of farms is decreasing and not increasing, expenditure on hired labour was not only very much higher both in 1899 ($2.55 per acre) and in 1909 ($4.76 per acre), but had grown during the period at a much faster rate (+86 per cent).

The average farm in New England is *one-fourth* the size of farms in the West North Central states (38.4 as against 148 acres), yet its average expenditure on hired labour is *greater*: $277 as against $240. Consequently, the reduction in the size of farms means in such cases that a greater amount of capital is invested in agriculture, and that the capitalist nature of agriculture is intensified; it signifies a growth of capitalism and capitalist production.

While the West North Central states, which comprise 34.3 per cent of the total improved acreage in the U.S.A., are the most typical division of "extensive" capitalist agriculture, the *Mountain* states offer an example of similar extensive farming in conditions of the most rapid colonisation. Here less hired labour is employed, in terms of the proportion of farms employing labour, but the average expenditure on hired labour is very much higher than in the West North Central division. But in the former the employment of hired labour increased at a slower rate than in any other division of America (only +22 per cent). This type of evolution was apparently due to the following conditions. In this division, colonisation and the distribution of homesteads are extremely widespread. The area under crops increased more than in any other division: by 89 per cent from 1900 to 1910. The settlers, the owners of the homesteads, naturally employ little hired labour, at any rate when starting their farms. On the other hand, hired labour must be employed on a very large scale, firstly, by some latifundia, which are especially numerous in this division as in the West in general; and secondly, by farms raising special and highly capitalist crops. In some states of this division, for instance, a very high proportion of the total crop value comes from fruits (Arizona—6 per cent, Colorado—10 per cent), and vegetables (Colorado—11.9 per cent, Nevada—11.2 per cent), and so forth.

In summing up, I must say the following: Mr. Himmer's assertion that "there are no areas where colonisation is no longer continuing, or where large-scale capitalist agriculture is not decaying and is not being replaced by family-labour farms", is a mockery of the truth, and entirely contrary to the actual facts. The New England division, where there is no colonisation at all, where farms are smallest, where

farming is most intensive, shows the highest level of capitalism in agriculture and the highest rate of capitalist
development. This conclusion is most essential and basic for
an understanding of the process of capitalist development
in agriculture in general, because the intensification of
agriculture and the reduction in the average farm acreage that
goes with it is not some accidental, local, casual phenomenon, but one that is *common* to all civilised countries. Bourgeois economists of every stripe make a host of mistakes when
considering data on the evolution of agriculture (as in Great
Britain, Denmark, and Germany) because they are not
familiar enough with this general phenomenon, they have
not given it enough thought and have not understood or
analysed it.

8. DISPLACEMENT OF SMALL BY BIG ENTERPRISES. QUANTITY OF IMPROVED LAND

We have examined the major forms of the development
of capitalism in agriculture, and have seen how extremely
varied they are. The most important are: the break-up of
the slave-holding latifundia in the South; the growth of
large-scale extensive farming operations in the extensive
area of the North; the most rapid development of capitalism
in the intensive area of the North, where farms are, on the
average, the smallest. The facts incontrovertibly prove
that in some cases the development of capitalism is indicated by an increase in farm acreage and in others by an
increase in the number of farms. In view of such a state
of affairs we learn nothing from the returns on average
farm acreages summarised for the country as a whole.

What then is the net result of the various local and
agricultural peculiarities? An indication is given by the
data on hired labour. The growing employment of hired
labour is a general process transcending *all* these peculiarities. But in the vast majority of civilised countries agricultural statistics, paying tribute, intentionally or otherwise, to prevailing bourgeois notions and prejudices, either
fail to furnish any systematic information on hired labour
at all, or give it only for the most recent period (e.g., German Agricultural Census of 1907), so that it is impossible

to make a comparison with the past. I shall show in detail
elsewhere that in the elaboration and tabulation of the
returns of hired labour American statistics changed
markedly for the worse between 1900 and 1910.

The most common and most popular method of presenting
statistical summaries in America and most other countries
is to compare big and small farms by acreage. I shall now
proceed to a consideration of these data.

In grouping farms by acreage, American statisticians
take total acreage and not just the improved area, which
w?uld, of course, be the more correct method, and is the one
employed by German statisticians. No reason is given why
seven groups (under 20 acres, 20 to 49, 50 to 99, 100 to
174, 175 to 499, 500 to 999, 1,000 and over) are used to
tabulate the returns of the 1910 Census in the United States.
Statistical routine must apparently have been of paramount
consideration. I shall call the 100-to-174-acre group—
medium, because it consists mostly of homesteads (the official size of a homestead is 160 acres), and also because landholdings of this size usually give the farmer the greatest
degree of "independence" and require the least employment of hired labour. The groups above that I shall call
large or capitalistic because, as a general rule, they do not
manage without hired labour. Farms with 1,000 acres and
over I shall regard as latifundia —of which three-fifths is
unimproved land in the North, nine-tenths, in the South,
and two-thirds, in the West. Small farms are those with
less than 100 acres; how much economic independence they
have is evident from the fact that in three groups, from the
bottom up, 51 per cent, 43 per cent and 23 per cent of the farms
respectively, are recorded as having no horses. It goes without
saying that this characteristic should not be taken in an
absolute sense and should not be applied to all divisions or to
localities with specific conditions without a special
analysis.

I am unable to give here the returns for all the seven groups
in the main sections of the United States, for this would
overload the text with an excessive number of figures.
I shall, therefore, merely outline the basic distinctions
between the North, the South and the West, and give the full
returns only for the United States as a whole. We should

not lose sight of the fact that three-fifths (60.6 per cent) of all the improved land is in the North; less than one-third (31.5 per cent), in the South; and under one-twelfth (7.9 per cent), in the West.

The most striking distinction between the three main sections is that the capitalist North has the *smallest* number of latifundia, although their number, their total acreage, and their improved acreage are on the increase. In 1910, 0.5 per cent of the farms in the North were of 1,000 acres and over; these big farms had 6.9 per cent of all the land and 4.1 per cent of the improved land. The South had 0.7 per cent of such farms, with 23.9 per cent of the total acreage and 4.8 per cent of the improved acreage. In the West there were 3.9 per cent of such farms, owning 48.3 per cent of the total acreage, and 32.3 per cent of the improved acreage. This is a familiar picture: the slave-holding latifundia of the South, and the even vaster latifundia of the West, the latter being partly the foundation of the most extensive stock-raising, and partly reserve tracts of land occupied by "settlers" and resold or (less often) leased to real farmers improving the "Far West".

America demonstrates clearly that it would be imprudent to confuse the latifundia with large-scale capitalist agriculture, and that the latifundia are frequently survivals of pre-capitalist relationships—slave-owning, feudal or patriarchal. A break-up, a parcelling out of the latifundia, is taking place both in the South and in the West. In the North, the total farm acreage increased by 30.7 million acres, of which only 2.3 million is accounted for by latifundia, while 22 million belongs to big, capitalist farms (175 to 999 acres). In the South, the total acreage was reduced by 7.5 million. The latifundia *decreased* by 31.8 million acres. On the small farms there was an increase of 13 million, and on the medium farms, 5 million acres. In the West, the total acreage increased by 17 million; among the latifundia there was a decrease of 1.2 million; on the small farms, an increase of 2 million; medium, 5 million; large, 11 million acres.

The *improved* acreage increased in the latifundia of all three sections: substantially in the North (+3.7 million acres = +47.0 per cent), very slightly in the South (+0.3

million = +5.5 per cent), and more in the West (+2.8 million = +29.6 per cent). But in the North, the maximum increase in the improved acreage occurred on the *large* farms (175 to 999 acres); in the South, on the *small* and *medium*; in the West, on the *large* and *medium*. Hence, it is the large farms that are increasing their *share* of the improved land in the North, and the small and in part the medium farms, in the South and the West. This picture fully corresponds to what we already know about the different conditions in these sections. In the South, there is a growth of small-scale commercial farming at the expense of the disintegrating slave-holding latifundia; the process is similar in the West, except that the break-up of even larger latifundia, which had their origin *not* in slave-holding but in extensive stock ranches and pre-empted tracts, is not as pronounced. Moreover, American statisticians say the following about the Pacific division:

"The great development of small fruit and other farms on the Pacific coast, due, in part at least, to irrigation projects organised in recent years, is reflected in the increase in small farms of less than 50 acres in the Pacific division" (Vol. V, p. 264).

The North has neither slave-holding nor "primitive" latifundia, there is no disintegration of them, no growth of the small farms at the expense of the large.

The process for the United States as a whole appears as follows:

Size group (acres)	Number of farms (000)		Ditto (per cent)		Increase or decrease
	1900	1910	1900	1910	
Nnder 20	674	839	11.7	13.2	+1.5
20 to 49	1,258	1,415	21.9	22.2	+0.3
50 to 99	1,366	1,438	23.8	22.6	—1.2
100 to 174	1,422	1,516	24.8	23.8	—1.0
175 to 499	868	978	15.1	15.4	+0.3
500 to 999	103	125	1.8	2.0	+0.2
1,000 and over . . .	47	50	0.8	0.8	—
Totals	5,738	6,361	100.0	100.0	—

Thus, the number of latifundia in proportion to the total number of farms remains unchanged. The most characteristic change in the relationship between the other groups is the *reduction in the number of medium-size* farms and the

strengthening of the farms at both ends. The medium-size
group (100 to 174 acres) and its smaller neighbour have lost
ground. The smallest and the small farms show the greatest
gains, and are followed by the large-scale capitalist farms
(175 to 999 acres).

Let us take a look at the total acreage.

Size group (acres)	All farmland (000 acres)		Ditto (per cent)		Increase or decrease
	1900	1910	1900	1910	
Under 20	7,181	8,794	0.9	1.0	+0.1
20 to 49	41,536	45,378	5.0	5.2	+0.2
50 to 99	98,592	103,121	11.8	11.7	—0.1
100 to 174	192,680	205,481	23.0	23.4	+0.4
175 to 499	232,955	265,289	27.8	30.2	+2.4
500 to 999	67,864	83,653	8.1	9.5	+1.4
1,000 and over . . .	197,784	167,082	23.6	19.0	—4.6
Totals	838,592	878,798	100.0	100.0	—

Here we find above all a very substantial reduction in
the share of total acreage held by the latifundia. It should
be borne in mind that an absolute reduction is taking place
only in the South and the West, where the proportion of
*un*improved land in the latifundia in 1910 was 91.5 per
cent and 77.1 per cent respectively. There was also an insignificant decrease in the share of the top small group in the
total acreage (—0.1 per cent in the 50-to-99-acre size group).
The greatest increase was shown by the large-scale capitalist
groups, the 175-to-499-acre and the 500-to-999-acre groups.
There was a relatively small increase in the share of the
very small groups in the acreage. The medium group (100
to 174 acres) was practically stagnant (+0.4 per cent).

Let us now take a look at the improved acreage.

Size groups (acres)	Improved land in farms (000 acres)		Ditto (per cent)		Increase or decrease
	1900	1910	1900	1910	
Under 20	6,440	7,992	1.6	1.7	+0.1
20 to 49	33,001	36,596	8.0	7.6	—0.4
50 to 99	67,345	71,155	16.2	14.9	—1.3
100 to 174	118,391	128,854	28.6	26.9	—1.7
175 to 499	135,530	161,775	32.7	33.8	+1.1
500 to 999	29,474	40,817	7.1	8.5	+1.4
1,000 and over . . .	24,317	31,263	5.9	6.5	+0.6
Totals	414,498	478,452	100.0	100.0	—

The size of the *farming enterprise* is indicated with some degree of approximation and allowing for certain exceptions to which I have referred and shall refer again below—only by the improved and not the total acreage. Once again we find that while the share of the total acreage held by the latifundia substantially decreased, their share of the improved acreage *increased*. In general, all the capitalistic groups gained ground, and most of all the 500-to-999-acre group. The largest reduction was in the medium-size group (−1.7 per cent), followed by all the small groups, with the exception of the smallest, the group under 20 acres, which showed a negligible increase (+0.1 per cent).

Let us note in advance that the smallest-size group (under 20 acres) includes farms of less than 3 acres, which are not included in American statistics unless they raise at least $250 worth of products a year. For that reason these tiny farms (of less than 3 acres) have a greater volume of production and a more highly developed capitalist character than the next group up the scale. To illustrate this point here are the returns for 1900—unfortunately the corresponding returns for 1910 are not available:

Average per farm:

Size groups (1900) (acres)	Improved land (acres)	Value of all products ($)	Outlays on hired labour ($)	Value of implements and machinery ($)	Value of livestock ($)
Under 3	1.7	592	77	53	867
3 to 10	5.6	203	18	42	101
10 to 20	12.6	236	16	41	116
20 to 50	26.2	324	18	54	172

Even the 3-to-10-acre farms, to say nothing of farms with less than 3 acres, turn out in some respects to be "larger" (outlays on hired labour, value of implements and machinery) than the 10-to-20-acre farms.* Consequently,

---

* For 1900 we have returns by size groups for the number of high-income farms, i.e., farms with a product valued over $2,500. Here are these figures: among farms of less than 3 acres, the proportion of high-income farms was 5.2 per cent; 3 to 10 acres—0.6 per cent; 10 to 20 acres—0.4 per cent; 20 to 50 acres—0.3 per cent; 50 to 100—0.6 per cent; 100 to 175—1.4 per cent; 175 to 260—5.2 per cent; 260 to 500—12.7 per cent; 500 to 1,000—24.3 per cent; 1,000 and

there is good reason to attribute the increase in the share of the total improved land held by farms under 20 acres to an increase in the improved land of the pronounced capitalist-type farms of the smallest-size group.

On the whole, the returns for 1900 and 1910 on the distribution of improved land in the U.S.A. between small and large farms warrant this absolutely definite and indubitable conclusion: *the large farms are becoming stronger, the medium and the small farms, weaker*. Hence, *insofar* as the capitalist or non-capitalist character of agriculture can be deduced from the data relating to farms grouped by acreage, the United States in the last decade shows, as a general rule, a growth of the large-scale, capitalist farms and the obliteration of small farms.

The statistics on the increase in the number of farms and the improved acreage in each group will confirm this conclusion:

	Increase for 1900-10 (per cent)	
Size groups (acres)	Number of farms	Improved acreage
Under 20	+24.5	+24.1
20 to 49	+12.5	+10.9
50 to 99	+ 5.3	+ 5.7
100 to 174	+ 6.6	+ 8.8
175 to 499	+12.7	+19.4
500 to 999	+22.2	+38.5
1,000 and over	+ 6.3	+28.6
Overall increase	+10.9	+15.4

The largest percentage increase in the improved acreage took place in the two topmost groups. The least increase occurred in the medium-size group and the next smaller group (50 to 99 acres). In the two smallest groups the percentage increase in the improved acreage was less than the percentage increase in the number of farms.

---

over—39.5 per cent. We find the proportion of high-income farms in all the under-20-acre groups to be *greater* than in the 20-to-50-acre group.

9. CONTINUED. STATISTICS ON THE VALUE OF FARMS

American statistics, unlike European statistics, determine, for each farm and each group of farms, the value of the various elements making up the farming enterprise —the land, buildings, implements, livestock and the enterprise as a whole. These data are probably not quite as accurate as the data relating to acreage, but generally speaking they are equally reliable, and in addition give some idea of the general state of capitalism in agriculture.

In order to supplement the above analysis I shall now take the data relating to the total value of farms with all their agricultural property, and also the data on the value of implements and machinery. I single out implements and machinery from among the various elements of the enterprise because they are a direct indication of the agricultural operations being conducted, and of how they are being conducted i.e., whether more or less intensively, and whether they employ technical improvements to a greater or lesser extent. Here are the figures for the U.S.A.:

Size groups (acres)	All property on farms		Increase or decrease	Implements and machinery		Increase or decrease
	1900	1910		1900	1910	
Under 20	3.8	3.7	—0.1	3.8	3.7	—0.1
20 to 49	7.9	7.3	—0.6	9.1	8.5	—0.6
50 to 99	16.7	14.6	—2.1	19.3	17.7	—1.6
100 to 174	28.0	27.1	—0.9	29.3	28.9	—0.4
175 to 499	30.5	33.3	+2.8	27.1	30.2	+3.1
500 to 999	5.9	7.1	+1.2	5.1	6.3	+1.2
1,000 and over . . .	7.3	6.9	—0.4	6.2	4.7	—1.5
Total	100.0	100.0	—	100.0	100.0	—

The caption above the table reads: Percentage distribution of value

The absolute figures show that from 1900 to 1910 the value of all farm property more than doubled; it increased from $20,440 million to $40,991 million, i.e., 100.5 per cent. The rise in the prices of farm products and rents put millions and thousands of millions of dollars into the pockets of the landowners at the expense of the working class. What were the comparative gains of the small and the big farms? The above figures supply the answer. They show that the latifundia declined (their total acreage fell from 23.6

per cent to 19.0 per cent, or 4.6 per cent), and that the *small and medium-size farms are being displaced by the large*, capitalist farms (175 to 999 acres). Adding up the figures for the small and medium farms we find that their share in the total property *decreased* from 56.4 to 52.7 per cent. Adding up the figures for the large farms and the latifundia we find that their share *increased* from 43.7 per cent to 47.3 per cent. There were absolutely identical changes in the distribution of the total value of implements and machinery between the small and large farms.

We also observe the phenomenon noted above in the figures relating to the latifundia. Their decline is limited to two sections: the South and the West. It is a decline, on the one hand, of the slave-holding latifundia, and on the other, of the primitive-squatter and the primitive-extensive latifundia. We find a *growth* of latifundia in the populated industrial North: this applies to the number of farms of this type, their total acreage, their improved acreage, their share in the total value of all farm property (2.5 per cent in 1900; 2.8 per cent in 1910), and their share in the total value of all implements and machinery.

There is moreover a growth of the role of the latifundia not only throughout the North in general but also in *both* the intensive divisions of the North in particular, where there is absolutely no colonisation, namely New England and the Middle Atlantic states. These divisions must be analysed in greater detail because, for one thing, they have misled Mr. Himmer and many others by the particularly small average size of their farms and a reduction of that size, and, for another, these most intensive divisions are most typical of the older, long settled, civilised countries of *Europe*.

Between 1900 and 1910, the number of farms, the total acreage and the improved acreage decreased in both these divisions. In New England, there was an increase only in the number of the *smallest* farms, those under 20 acres, by 22.4 per cent (the improved land on them increased by 15.5 per cent), and in the number of latifundia —by 16.3 per cent, and their improved acreage by 26.8 per cent. In the Middle Atlantic states there was an increase in the *smallest* farms (+7.7 per cent in the number, and +2.5 per cent in the improved acreage) and also in the number of the 175-to-499-

acre farms ($+1.0$ per cent) and the improved land on the 500-to-999-acre farms ($+3.8$ per cent). In both divisions, there was an *increase* in the share of the smallest farms and the share of the latifundia in the total value of all farm property and also of implements and machinery. Here are some figures which give a clearer and fuller picture of each of these divisions:

Percentage increase from 1900 to 1910

| | New England | | Middle Atlantic | |
Size groups (acres)	Value of all farm property	Value of implements and machinery	Value of all farm property	Value of implements and machinery
Under 20 . . .	60.9	48.9	45.8	42.9
20 to 49 . . .	31.4	30.3	28.3	37.0
50 to 99 . . .	27.5	31.2	23.8	39.9
100 to 174 . . .	30.3	38.5	24.9	43.8
175 to 499 . . .	33.0	44.6	29.4	54.7
500 to 999 . . .	53.7	53.7	31.5	50.8
1,000 and over . .	102.7	60.5	74.4	65.2
Totals . .	35.6	39.0	28.1	44.1

This makes it clear that in both divisions *it was the latifundia* that gained most ground, showed the greatest economic gains, and made the greatest technical advance. Here the largest capitalist enterprises are *displacing* the others, the smaller farms. A minimum increase in the value of all property and also of implements and machinery is evident in the medium-size group and in the small group, but not in the smallest. Hence, it is the medium and small farms that mostly lag behind.

As for the smallest farms (under 20 acres), their advance in both divisions is *above the average*, and second only to the latifundia. We already know the reason: 31 to 33 per cent of the crop value in both these intensive divisions comes from the highly capitalist crops (vegetables, and also fruits, flowers, etc.) which yield extremely great values on very small acreages. In these divisions, cereal crops account for only 8 to 30 per cent of the crop value; and hay and forage, 31 to 42 per cent; there is a growth of dairy farming which is characterised by *smaller*-than-average acreages, but a *greater*-than-average value of produce and capital outlays on hired labour.

In the most intensive divisions, there is a decrease in the average improved acreage in farms because the average is obtained by combining the acreage of the latifundia and that of the smallest farms, the number of which is increasing more rapidly than that of the medium-size farms. The smallest farms are increasing in number faster than the latifundia. But there is a dual growth of capitalism: it increases the size of farms worked by old technical methods; and creates new enterprises raising special commercial crops on very small and tiny acreages, with an extremely great volume of production and employment of hired labour.

The net result is the greatest gains by the latifundia and the giant farms, the obliteration of the medium and small farms, and the growth of the smallest highly capitalist enterprises.

We shall presently see how the net result of such contradictory—seemingly contradictory—phenomena of capitalism in agriculture can be expressed in statistical terms.

10. DEFECTS OF CONVENTIONAL METHODS OF ECONOMIC ANALYSIS. MARX ON THE PECULIARITIES OF AGRICULTURE

The grouping of farms by acreage, total or improved, is the only kind of grouping which was used in the American Census reports for 1910, and which is used in the great majority of European countries. Generally speaking, it is indisputable that apart from fiscal, bureaucratic and administrative reasons there are scientific considerations arguing the need and correctness of this kind of grouping. Still it is obviously inadequate for it completely fails to take account of the intensification of agriculture, the increasing expenditure of capital per unit of area in the form of livestock, machinery, improved seeds, better methods of crop cultivation, etc. Meanwhile, with the exception of a very few areas and countries with a primitive or purely extensive agriculture, it is this very process that is most typical for capitalist countries everywhere. For this reason the grouping of farms by acreage in the vast majority of cases gives an oversimplified and entirely inadequate picture of agricultural development in general, and of capitalist development in agriculture in particular.

When the verbose economists and statisticians who express the most popular bourgeois views hold forth on the dissimilarity of conditions in agriculture and industry, the specific nature of the former, and so on and so forth, one is always tempted to say: Gentlemen! You yourselves are most to blame for maintaining and spreading oversimplified and crude notions of evolution in agriculture! Remember Marx's *Capital*. In it you will find references to the extreme variety of forms of land ownership, such as feudal, clan, communal (and primitive-squatter), state, etc., which capitalism encounters when it makes its appearance on the historical scene. Capital subordinates to itself all these varied forms of land ownership and remoulds them after its own fashion, and if one is to understand, evaluate and express this process in statistical terms, one must learn to modify the formulation of the question and the methods of investigation in accordance with the changing *form* of the process. Capitalism subordinates to itself all these forms of land ownership: communal-allotment holdings in Russia; squatter tracts or holdings regulated by free distribution in a democratic or a feudal state, as in Siberia or the American Far West; the slave-holding estates in the American South, and the semi-feudal landholdings of the "purely Russian" gubernias. In all these cases, the development and victory of capitalism is similar, though not identical in form. In order to study and understand the precise nature of the process one must go beyond the trite petty-bourgeois phrases about "family farming" or the routine methods of comparing acreage alone.

You will also find that Marx analyses the origin of the capitalist type of ground-rent and its relationship to its forerunners in history, such as rent in kind, labour service (corvée and its survivals); money-rent (quit-rent, etc.). But who among the bourgeois or petty-bourgeois, Narodnik, economists or statisticians has given any serious thought to applying these theoretical guiding principles of Marx's to an investigation of the rise of capitalism *from* the slave-holding economy of the American South, or *from* the corvée economy in central Russia?

Finally, you will find throughout Marx's analysis of ground-rent systematic references to the varied conditions of

agriculture engendered not only by the differences in quality
and location of the land, but also by the differences in *the
amount of capital invested in it*. Now what does application of
capital to land imply? It implies technical changes in agriculture, its intensification, the transition to higher systems of
field cropping, increased use of artificial fertilisers, the wider
use and improvement of implements and machinery, greater
employment of hired labour, etc. A record of the acreage
alone will not express all these complex and varied processes,
which all combine to make up the general process of the
development of capitalism in agriculture.

Russian Zemstvo statisticians,[4] especially those of the
"good old" pre-revolutionary days, won universal respect
because they avoided the routine approach and took a certain
scientific interest in their business, going beyond its purely
fiscal, bureaucratic and administrative aspects. They were
probably the first statisticians to notice the inadequacy of
grouping farms by acreage alone, and, accordingly, introduced other methods of classification, such as by sown area,
number of draught animals, employment of hired labour,
etc. Unfortunately, the sporadic and scattered operations of
our Zemstvo statistics—in the past ever what you might
call an oasis in the desert of feudal obscurity, bureaucratic
routine, and every kind of stupid red-tapism—have not yielded
any long-term results either for Russian or European economics.

It should be noted that the grouping of the returns canvassed
in modern agricultural censuses is not such a purely
technical or highly specialised question as may appear at
first sight. The returns contain an immense wealth of
complete information on each enterprise as a unit, but due
to the clumsy, thoughtless, routine approach to tabulation
and grouping, this extremely valuable material is all lost,
wasted, and discoloured, which often makes it practically
useless for any study of the laws of agricultural evolution.
The returns make it possible to say quite categorically
whether a farm is a capitalist enterprise, and to what
extent; whether its farming operations are intensive, and to
what degree, etc.; but when data relating to millions of
farms are tabulated the most essential distinctions, features
and characteristics—which ought to be most *effectively*

brought out, determined and taken into account—tend to disappear, so that all the economist gets, instead of a sensible statistical review, is routine, meaningless columns of figures, a kind of statistical "game of digits".

The American Census of 1910 with which we are now concerned is an excellent example of how first-class material of surpassing wealth and completeness has been devalued and spoiled by the routine approach and scientific ignorance of the statisticians. The processing is very much worse than in the 1900 Census, and even the traditional grouping of farms by acreage has not been fully carried out, so that we have no possibility of making a comparison between the enterprises in the various groups, say, as regards their employment of hired labour, the difference in their systems of field cropping, the use of fertilisers, etc.

I am compelled, therefore, to turn to the 1900 Census. It gave, to my knowledge, the world's only example of the use of *three* different methods, instead of one, to group or "classify" (as the Americans say) the great abundance of material on more than five and a half million farms, collected in a single country, at a single time, and under a single programme.

It is true that here, too, no classification gives all the essential characteristics of the type and size of farm. Still the resultant picture of capitalist agriculture and the capitalist evolution of agriculture is, as I hope to show, very much fuller, and reflects the real situation much more correctly than can ever be the case when the conventional, one-sided and inadequate single method of classification is used. Given the opportunity for a fuller study of facts and trends, which may be safely considered common to all the capitalist countries of the world, the most serious errors and dogmas of bourgeois and petty-bourgeois, Narodnik political economy are shown up and exposed.

Since the data in question are so important I shall have to examine them in greater detail and employ statistical tables more frequently than hitherto. Realising fully that statistical tables burden the text and make reading more difficult, I have tried to keep them down to a minimum, and hope the reader will be lenient with me if I now have to increase that minimum, for on the analysis of the points examined here depends not only the general conclusion on the principal question—the trend, type, character and law of evolution of modern agriculture—but also the general assessment of the data furnished by modern agricultural statistics which are so often cited and just as often distorted.

The first grouping—"by acreage"—gives the following picture of American agriculture in 1900:

Size groups (acres)	Percentage of farms	Percentage of total acreage	Improved acreage	Average per farm		
				Outlays on hired labour ($)	Value of produce ** ($)	Value of implements and machinery ($)
Under 3	0.7	—*	1.7	77	592	53
3 to 10	4.0	0.2	5.6	18	203	42
10 to 20	7.1	0.7	12.6	16	236	41
20 to 50	21.9	4.9	26.2	18	324	54
50 to 100	23.8	11.7	49.3	33	503	106
100 to 175	24.8	22.9	83.2	60	721	155
175 to 260	8.5	12.3	129.0	109	1,054	211
260 to 500	6.6	15.4	191.4	166	1,354	263
500 to 1,000	1.8	8.1	287.5	312	1,913	377
1,000 and over	0.8	23.8	520.0	1,059	5,334	1,222
Average for all farms	—	—	72.3	—	656	133

It is safe to say that the statistics of any capitalist country —the inessential particulars apart—would present an absolutely similar picture. This is confirmed by the latest censuses in Germany, Austria, Hungary, Switzerland and Denmark. As total farm acreage increases from group to group, there is also an increase in the average improved acreage, the average value of the produce, the value of implements and machinery, the value of livestock (I have omitted these figures) and the expenditure on hired labour (earlier on I pointed out the significance of the slight exception of the under-3-acre farms and in part of the 3-to-10-acre farms).

It would seem that it could not be otherwise. The increase in expenditure on hired labour appears to confirm beyond any doubt that the division of farms into large and small on

---

* Less than 0.1 per cent.
** Excluding produce used as feed.

the strength of acreage is entirely in accord with their division into capitalist and non-capitalist enterprises. Nine-tenths of the usual arguments about "small-scale" agriculture are based on identification in this way and on such data.

Let us now consider the average per acre of (all) land, instead of per farm:

Per acre of all land in dollars

Size groups (acres)	Outlays on hired labour	Outlays on fertilisers	Value of livestock	Value of implements and machinery
Under 3	40.30	2.36	456.76	27.57
3 to 10	2.95	0.60	16.32	6.71
10 to 20	1.12	0.33	8.30	2.95
20 to 50	0.55	0.20	5.21	1.65
50 to 100	0.46	0.12	4.51	1.47
100 to 175	0.45	0.07	4.09	1.14
175 to 260	0.52	0.07	3.96	1.00
260 to 500	0.48	0.04	3.61	0.77
500 to 1,000	0.47	0.03	3.16	0.57
1,000 and over	0.25	0.02	2.15	0.29

Allowing for some absolutely negligible exceptions we find a uniform decline in the characteristics of intensive farming from the lower groups to the higher.

The conclusion appears to be incontrovertible that "small-scale" production in agriculture is more intensive than large-scale production, that the smaller the "scale" of production, the greater the intensity and productivity of agriculture, and that, "consequently", capitalist production in agriculture is maintained only by the extensive, primitive nature of the economy, etc.

In fact, the same conclusions are being drawn all the time, on every hand, in all bourgeois and petty-bourgeois (opportunist-"Marxist" and Narodnik) writings, for when farms are grouped by acreage (which is not only the most common but practically the only kind of grouping done) the picture will be similar for any capitalist country, that is, it will show the same decline in the characteristics of intensive agriculture from the lower groups to the higher. There is, for instance, the celebrated work of the celebrated Eduard David —*Socialism and Agriculture*—a collection of bourgeois prejudices and bourgeois lies under the cover of quasi-socialist catchwords. It uses just that kind of data to prove the "superiority", "viability", etc., of "small-scale" production.

One factor has especially facilitated such conclusions. It is that data similar to the above are ordinarily available on the quantity of livestock; but practically nowhere are data collected on hired labour—especially in such a summarised form as expenditure on hired labour. But it is precisely the data on hired labour that reveal the incorrectness of all such conclusions. In effect, if the increase, say, in the value of livestock (or the total number of animals, which is the same thing) per unit of area down the scale is taken as evidence of the "superiority" of "small-scale" agriculture, it should be borne in mind that as we go down the scale this "superiority" turns out to be *connected* with *increasing* expenditure on hired labour! But such an increase in the expenditure on hired labour—notice that we have all along been dealing with values per unit of area, per acre, per hectare, per dessiatine—signifies a growth of the *capitalist* nature of the enterprise! But the capitalist nature of the enterprise clashes with the popular notion of "small-scale" production because small-scale production implies enterprise which is *not* based on hired labour.

This seems to create a knot of contradictions. The overall acreage returns for the size groups indicate that the "small" farms are non-capitalist, whereas the big farms are. Yet the very same data show that the "smaller" the enterprise, the more intensive it is, and the larger its expenditure on hired labour per unit of land area!

In order to explain this let us consider another type of grouping.

11. A MORE EXACT COMPARISON OF SMALL AND LARGE ENTERPRISES

As I have already said, American statisticians in this case take the value of the products raised on the farm, less those used as feed. Taken alone, these data, which appear to be available only in American statistics, are, of course, less exact than the figures for acreage or livestock, and the like. But considered as a whole, in relation to several million farms, and especially for the purpose of determining the *relative standing* of the various groups of farms in the country, these data undoubtedly cannot be regarded as less suitable than the rest. At any rate, these data are a much more direct indication than any others of the scale of *production*, especially commercial operations, i.e., the value of the produce raised for the market. It should be borne in mind that any discussion of agricultural evolution and its laws centres on a consideration of small-scale and large-scale *production*.

What is more, in such cases the point is always the evolution of agriculture under capitalism, in connection with capitalism, under its impact, or the like. To evaluate this impact the greatest efforts must above all be made to draw a line of distinction between "natural" and commercial economy in agriculture. It is well known that "natural" economy, i.e., production for consumption on the home farm and not for the market, has a relatively important part to play in agriculture, and is giving way to commercial farming at an extremely slow pace. If the accepted principles of political economy are not to be applied mechanically but intelligently, the law of the displacement of small-scale by large-scale production, for instance, can be applied *only* to commercial agriculture. It is hardly likely that anyone will object to this proposition from the theoretical standpoint. However, it is the rare economist or statistician who will make a special effort to bring out, trace and as far as possible take into account, the characteristics indicative of the transformation of natural into commercial agriculture. A great step towards meeting this most important theoretical requirement is made by the classification of farms according to the money value of produce not used for feed.

Let us note that, when considering the undeniable fact that small-scale production is being displaced by large-scale production in industry, enterprises are always grouped according to the value of their product or the number of wage-workers employed. In industry, due to its technical peculiarities, the matter is much simpler. In agriculture, because relationships are so much more complicated and intertwined, it is a great deal harder to determine the scale of operations, the value of the product and the extent to which hired labour is employed. For the last-named item, it is necessary to take account of the total annual employment of hired labour and not merely the amount on hand when a census is taken, for agricultural operations are of an especially "seasonal" nature; in addition, it is necessary to list not only the permanent hired labourers but also the day-labourers who play a most important part in farming. To say that this is difficult is not to say that it is impossible. Rational methods of investigation adapted to the technical peculiarities of agriculture, including classification by output, the money value of the product, and the frequency and amount of hired labour employed, will have to be used on a much wider scale, in spite of the thick maze of bourgeois and petty-bourgeois prejudices and the efforts to embellish bourgeois realities. And it may be safely said that any step forward in the use of rational methods of investigation will serve to confirm the truth that in capitalist society small-scale production is being displaced by large-scale production both in industry and agriculture.

Let us take the 1900 returns for the groups of farms in America classified according to the value of their product:

Farms classified by value of product ($)	Number of farms (percentage of total)	Acreage	Average per farm		
			Improved acreage	Hired labour ($)	Implements and machinery ($)
0	0.9	1.8	33.4	24	54
1 and under 50	2.9	1.2	18.2	4	24
50 and under 100	5.3	2.1	20.0	4	28
100 and under 250	21.8	10.1	29.2	7	42
250 and under 500	27.9	18.1	48.2	18	78
500 and under 1,000	24.0	23.6	84.0	52	154
1,000 and under 2,500	14.5	23.2	150.5	158	283
Over 2,500	2.7	19.9	322.3	786	781
Average for all farms	—	—	72.3	—	133

The farms reporting no income, i.e., with a $0 value of product, probably consist primarily of newly occupied homesteads on which their owners had not yet had time to erect buildings, acquire livestock or sow and raise a crop. In a country like America, where colonisation is still in progress on such a vast scale, special importance attaches to the question of how long a farmer has been in possession of his farm.

Leaving aside the zero-income farms, we get a picture quite similar to the one obtained above by grouping the same data according to total farm acreage. As the value of the product raised on a farm increases, there is also an increase in the average improved acreage, the average expenditure on hired labour, and the average value of implements and machinery. By and large, the more profitable farms—in terms of gross income, i.e., the value of their total product—turn out to have the larger acreage. It would appear that the new method of grouping has not yielded anything new at all.

But now let us take the averages (the value of livestock and implements, expenditure on hired labour and fertilisers) per acre instead of per farm:

Per acre of all land ($)

Farms classified by value of product ($)	Outlays on hired labour	Outlays on fertilisers	Value of livestock	Value of implements and machinery
0	0.08	0.01	2.97	0.19
1 and under 50	0.06	0.01	1.78	0.38
50 and under 100	0.08	0.03	2.01	0.48
100 and under 250	0.11	0.05	2.46	0.62
250 and under 500	0.19	0.07	3.00	0.82
500 and under 1,000	0.36	0.07	3.75	1.07
1,000 and under 2,500	0.67	0.08	4.63	1.21
Over 2,500	0.72	0.06	3.98	0.72

The exceptions in some respects are the zero-income farms, which in general are in a very special position, and the farms with the highest incomes, which turn out to be less intensive than the next group, judging by three out of the four characteristics we have chosen. But on the whole we find a uniform *increase* in the intensity of agriculture *with the increase* in the value of the farm product.

This result is the very opposite of the one obtained when farms were grouped by acreage.

The same figures yield diametrically different conclusions, depending on the method of grouping.

As the enterprise grows in size the intensity of agriculture *declines*—if the criterion is acreage, and *increases*—if the criterion is the value of the product.

Which of these two conclusions is the correct one?

It is clear that if the land is not being improved, acreage gives *no idea at all* of the scale of agricultural operations (we must not forget that in America farms are grouped not only according to the improved acreage, but also by the total acreage and that in that country the proportion of the improved acreage ranges from 19 to 91 per cent in the farm groups, and from 27 to 75 per cent, in the geographical divisions); it gives *no correct* idea at all if besides this there are so many substantial differences between farms in the methods of cultivation, the intensity of agriculture, the methods of field cropping, quantities of fertilisers, the use of machinery, the character of livestock farming, etc.

This is known to apply to *all* capitalist countries and even to all those whose agriculture is affected by capitalism.

We see here one of the most profound and general reasons why mistaken notions about the "superiority" of small-scale agriculture are so tenacious, and why bourgeois and petty-bourgeois prejudices of this type prove to be compatible with the great progress made in the last few decades by social statistics in general, and agricultural statistics in particular. To be sure, the tenacity of these mistakes and prejudices is also a matter of the *interests* of the bourgeoisie, who seek to cover up the depth of class contradictions in contemporary bourgeois society; and everyone knows that when it comes to interests, the most incontrovertible truths are liable to be questioned.

But we are here concerned only with an examination of the theoretical sources of the erroneous notion of the "superiority" of small-scale agriculture. There is no doubt at all that of all these sources the most important one is the uncritical, routine attitude to the hackneyed methods of comparing enterprises only by their total acreage or the improved acreage.

The U.S.A. is an exception among capitalist countries in that it alone has a great deal of unoccupied, unsettled land, which is given away free. Agriculture still can and indeed does develop here through the occupation of vacant land, through the cultivation of virgin lands never before put to the plough—here it does develop in the form of the most primitive and extensive livestock and crop raising. There is nothing of the kind in the old, civilised countries of capitalist Europe. In these countries, agriculture develops *mainly* through intensive methods, not by increases in the *quantity* of land under cultivation, but by improvement in the *quality* of cultivation, by increases in the amount of capital invested in the original acreage. Those who compare farms by acreage alone lose sight of this principal trend in capitalist agriculture, a trend which is gradually becoming the principal one in the United States as well.

The principal trend in capitalist agriculture is the conversion of *small-scale* enterprise, *which remains small* in terms of acreage, *into large-scale* enterprise in terms of output, in the development of livestock raising, the quantity of fertilisers, the scale on which machinery is used, and the like.

That is why the conclusion drawn from the comparison of the various groups of enterprises by acreage—that the intensity of agriculture declines with the greater size of enterprise—is entirely incorrect. The only correct conclusion, on the contrary, is to be drawn from the comparison of the various farms by the value of their product—the bigger the enterprise, the greater is the intensity of agriculture.

For acreage is only circumstantial evidence of the scale of agricultural operations, and the broader and more rapid the intensification of agriculture, the less authentic is this "evidence". The value of the product of an enterprise is not circumstantial but direct evidence of the scale of its operations. Moreover, it is true in every case. By small-scale agriculture is always meant the kind that is *not* based on hired labour. But the transition to the exploitation of hired labour does not depend only on the extension of the acreage of an enterprise on its old technical basis—this occurs only in primitive, extensive enterprises—but also on an improvement of equipment and techniques and their modernisation, investment in the same acreage of additional capital in the form of, say, new machinery or artificial fertilisers, or of increased and improved livestock, etc.

The classification of farms by the value of their product brings together enterprises which really have *the same scale of production*, regardless of acreage. Accordingly, a highly

intensive enterprise on a small tract of land falls into the
same group as a relatively extensive enterprise on a large
tract; both are actually large-scale in terms of production
and the employment of hired labour.

On the contrary, the classification by acreage throws
together large and small enterprises, because they happen to
have a similar acreage; it puts into the same group enterprises
with an entirely different scale of operations, those in
which family labour predominates, and those in which
hired labour predominates. The result is a picture of *blunted
class contradictions* within capitalism, a picture which is
basically incorrect and entirely misleading as to the actual
state of affairs, but one the bourgeoisie is very fond of.
This leads to an equally fallacious *embellishment of the
condition of the small farmers*, which the bourgeoisie is just
as fond of. The net result is a vindication of capitalism.

In effect, the fundamental and principal trend of capitalism
is the displacement of small-scale by large-scale production,
both in industry and in agriculture. But this displacement
should not be interpreted *merely* as immediate expropriation. Displacement also implies the ruin of the small farmers
and a worsening of conditions on their farms, a process that
may go on for years and decades. This deterioration assumes
a variety of forms, such as the small farmer's overwork or
malnutrition, his heavy debts, worse feed and poorer care
of livestock in general, poorer husbandry—cultivation, fer-
tilisation, and the like—as well as technical stagnation on
the farm, etc. If the researcher is to be absolved from the
charge of wittingly or otherwise playing up to the bourgeoisie by giving a false impression of the condition of the small
farmer, who is being ruined and oppressed, his task is, first
and foremost, to give a precise definition of the symptoms of
this ruination, which are not at all simple or uniform; his
next task is to determine these symptoms, to analyse and, as
far as possible, to define the extent to which they have
spread and how they change with time. But present-day economists and statisticians hardly pay any attention to this
vital aspect of the matter.

Just imagine that to a group of 90 small farmers who have
no capital to improve their farms, who lag behind the times
and are gradually being ruined the statistician adds 10 farm-

ers who have all the capital they need and on equally small tracts of land start large-scale operations based on hired labour. The net result would be an embellished picture of the condition of all the hundred small farmers.

The U.S. Census of 1910 produced just that kind of embellished picture—and one that, objectively, favoured the bourgeoisie—primarily because it discarded the method used in 1900 of comparing the acreage grouping and the value-of-product grouping. We learn, for instance, only that expenditure on fertilisers increased immensely, namely, by 115 per cent, i.e., more than double the previous figure, while the expenditure on hired labour went up by only 82 per cent, and the total crop value by 83 per cent. This is tremendous progress. It is the progress of national agriculture as a whole. And, I dare say, some economist is likely to draw—if indeed has not yet drawn—the conclusion that this is the progress of small-scale family farming, for, generally speaking, the returns for the size groups by acreage indicate that "small-scale" agriculture has a much higher per-acre expenditure on fertilisers.

But we now know that such a conclusion would be fallacious, because the one thing the grouping of farms by acreage does is to lump together farmers on the way to ruin, or at any rate the indigent small farmers who cannot afford to buy fertilisers, and *capitalists* (even if they are small-time capitalists) who, on small tracts of land, start large-scale farming operations with the use of up-to-date, intensive methods and the employment of hired labour.

If small-scale agriculture is being generally displaced by large-scale agriculture, as the figures for the total value of farm property in 1900 and 1910 show; if, as we shall presently see, the raising of highly capitalist crops on small tracts developed at an especially fast rate in this period; if, according to the general statistics on small and large enterprises grouped by the value of their product, expenditures for fertilisers increased proportionately with the scale of the enterprise—then the conclusion inevitably follows that the "progress" in the use of fertilisers from 1900 to 1910 went to increase the preponderance of capitalist agriculture over small agriculture, which was displaced and suppressed to an even greater extent.

12. DIFFERENT TYPES OF ENTERPRISES IN AGRICULTURE

What I have said above about the intensive, large-scale capitalist enterprises on small tracts raises this question: is there any reason to believe that the intensification of agriculture leads to a reduction of farm acreage? In other words, are there any conditions relating to modern farming techniques as such that require smaller farm acreage for greater intensity of farming?

No answer is provided either by general theoretical reasoning or by examples. In each case it is a matter of the concrete technical level of agriculture under a given set of conditions, and the actual amount of capital required by a given system of farming. In theory, any amount of capital can be invested in any acreage in any possible way, but it is obvious that "this depends" on the existing economic, technical, and cultural conditions, etc., and the whole point is the kind of conditions prevalent in a given country at a given time. Examples serve no purpose at all, because in the sphere of such complex, varied, interwoven and contradictory trends in the economics of modern agriculture, any number of examples will be found to support opposite views. What this calls for above all—and more so than in any other sphere— is a picture of the process *as a whole*, with all the trends taken into account and summed up in the form of a resultant.

The third method of grouping used by American statisticians in 1900 helps to find an answer to this question. It is classification according to the *principal source of income*. Accordingly, farms fall into one of the following groups: (1) hay and grain as the principal source of income; (2) miscellaneous; (3) livestock; (4) cotton; (5) vegetable; (6) fruit; (7) dairy produce; (8) tobacco; (9) rice; (10) sugar; (11) flowers and plants; (12) nursery products; (13) taro; and (14) coffee. The last seven groups (8-14) together make up only 2.2 per cent of the total number of farms, i.e., such an insignificant share, that I shall not consider them separately. These groups (8-14) are similar to the preceding three groups (5-7) in economic characteristics and significance and constitute a single type.

Here are the data characterising the various types of farms;

Groups of farms by principal source of income	Percentage of total number of farms	Average acreage per farm Total improved		Average per acre of all land ($)				
				Outlays on labour	Outlays on fertilisers	Value of implements and machinery	Value of livestock	
Hay and grain	23.0	159.3	111.1	0.47	0.04	1.04	3.17	
Miscellaneous	18.5	106.8	46.5	0.35	0.08	0.94	2.73	
Livestock	27.3	226.9	86.1	0.29	0.02	0.66	4.45	
Cotton	18.7	83.6	42.5	0.30	0.14	0.53	2.11	
Vegetables	2.7	65.1	33.8	1.62	0.59	2.12	3.74	
Fruits.	1.4	74.8	41.6	2.46	0.30	2.34	3.35	
Dairy produce	6.2	121.9	63.2	0.86	0.09	1.66	5.58	
Average for all farms . . .	100.0	146.6	72.3	0.43	0.07	0.90	3.66	

It is clear that the first two groups of enterprises (hay and grain, and miscellaneous) may be classified as average both as regards the degree of their capitalist development (their expenditures for hired labour are nearest the average — 0.35 to 0.47, as against an average of 0.43 for the U.S.A.) and the intensiveness of agriculture. All the characteristics of intensive operations—expenditures for fertilisers, the per-acre value of machinery and livestock—are nearest to the general average for the U.S.A.

There is no doubt that these two groups are especially typical of the majority of agricultural enterprises in general. Hay and grain, followed by a combination of various farm products ("miscellaneous" sources of income), are the chief types of agricultural enterprises in all countries. It would be extremely interesting to have more detailed data about these groups, such, for instance, as a breakdown into more and less commercialised enterprises, etc. But, as we have seen, the American Census, having made one step in that direction, did not go forward, but went back.

The next two groups, livestock and cotton, are an example of farms with the least capitalistic development (the expenditures for hired labour: 0.29 to 0.30 as against the average of 0.43), and the least intensive methods of agriculture. Their values of implements and machinery are the lowest and considerably lower than the average (0.66 and 0.53 as against 0.90). Farms whose principal source of income is livestock naturally have more livestock per acre than the average for the U.S.A. (4.45 as against 3.66), but appear to be engaged in extensive livestock raising: their expenditures for fertilisers are the minimum, they have the largest average acreage (226.9 acres) and the smallest proportion of improved acreage (86.1 out of 226.9). The cotton farms have a higher-than-average figure for fertilisers, but other indexes indicative of intensive agriculture (the per-acre value of livestock and machinery) are very low.

Finally, the last three groups—vegetables, fruit, and dairy produce—include farms which are, first, the smallest in acreage (33 to 63 acres of improved land, as against 42 to 86 and 46 to 111 in the other groups); secondly, the most capitalist: they have the heaviest expenditure on hired labour, from 2 to 6 times the average; and thirdly, the most intensive. Almost all the indexes of intensive agriculture are above the average: the expenditure on fertilisers, the value of machinery, the value of livestock (a minor exception are the fruit-growing farms which lag behind the average, but are well ahead of the farms which derive their income chiefly from hay and grain).

Let us now see what is the share of these highly capitalist farms in the country's economy. But we must first examine their intensive character in somewhat greater detail.

Take the farms whose main income is derived from vegetables. It is well known that in all capitalist countries the development of towns, factories, industrial settlements, railway stations, ports, etc., stimulates a demand for this type of product, it pushes up their prices, and increases the number of agricultural enterprises raising them for the market. The average "vegetable" farm has *less than one-third* of the improved acreage of an "ordinary" farm deriving income chiefly from hay and grain: the former is 33.8 acres, and the latter, 111.1. This means that this particular technical level with this particular accumulation of capital in agriculture requires "vegetable" farms of smaller acreage; in other words, if capital invested in agriculture is to yield a not less-than-average profit, a vegetable-raising farm should have, technology being what it is, a *smaller acreage* than a hay-and-grain farm.

But that is not all. The growth of capitalism in agriculture consists above all in a transition from natural agriculture to commercial agriculture. This is being constantly forgotten, and must be brought up again and again. Commercial agriculture, it should be noted, does not develop along the "simple" lines imagined or projected by bourgeois economists, namely, through an ever greater output of *the same* products. Not at all. Commercial agriculture very frequently develops by shifting from one type of product to another, and the shift from hay and grain to vegetables is very common. But what bearing does it have on the question before us, that of farm acreage and the growth of capitalism in agriculture?

Such a shift signifies the *split-up* of a "large" 111.1-acre farm into more than three "small" 33.8-acre farms. The old farm produced a value of $760—the average value of its products, less the feed raised on the farm, whose chief source of income is hay and grain. Each of the new farms produces a value of $665, or a total of $665×3= $1,995, i.e., more than double the original figure.

As large-scale production displaces small-scale production, farm acreage is *reduced*.

The average expenditure on hired labour on the old farm was $76; on the new farm it is $106, or almost half as much again, while acreage is one-third or even less. Expenditure on fertilisers has gone up from $0.04 per acre to $0.59, an increase of almost 15 times; the value of implements and machinery has doubled from $1.04 to $2.12, etc.

There will, of course, be the usual objection that the number of such highly capitalist farms with specialised "commercial" crops is negligible, as compared with the total. The answer is that, first, the number and the *role*, the economic role of such farms, are much greater than is generally realised; and secondly—and this is the most important point— *it is such crops* that are developed *more rapidly* than others in the capitalist countries. That is just why a reduction in farm acreage with the intensification of agriculture so often implies an increase and not a reduction in the scale of operations, an increase and not a decrease in the exploitation of hired labour.

Here are the exact American statistics for the country as a whole. Let us take *all* the special, or "commercial", crops listed above under heads 5-14, namely, vegetables, fruit, dairy produce, tobacco, rice, sugar, flowers, nursery products, taro, and coffee. In 1900, these products were the *principal* source of income for 12.5 per cent of all farms in the U.S.A. This is one-eighth, a very small minority. Their acreage was 8.6 per cent, or one-twelfth, of the total. But to continue. Let us take the total value of the products of American agriculture (less feed). Of this value the farms in question accounted for as much as 16 per cent, i.e., their share of the value was almost double their share of the acreage.

This means that the productivity of labour and land on these farms was almost double the average.

Let us take the sum total of expenditure on hired labour in American agriculture. Of this total, 26.6 per cent, i.e., over one-quarter, fell to the farms in question. This is more than three times their share of the acreage, and more than three times the average. This means that these farms are very much more capitalist than the average.

Their share of the total value of implements and machinery is 20.1 per cent, and of the expenditures for fertilisers, 31.7 per cent, i.e., slightly less than *one-third* of the total, and nearly *four times* the average.

Consequently, an incontrovertible fact is established for the country as a whole. It is that the especially intensive farms have an especially small acreage, especially great employment of hired labour, and especially high productivity of labour; that the economic role of these farms in the nation's agriculture is two, three and more times greater than their proportion of the total number of farms, to say nothing of their share of the total acreage.

As time goes on, does the role of these highly capitalist and highly intensive crops and farms increase or decrease in comparison with other crops and farms?

The answer is provided by a comparison of the last two census reports: their role is unquestionably *increasing*. Let us take the acreage planted to the various crops. From 1900 to 1910, the acreage under grain increased by only 3.5 per cent for the U.S.A.; under beans, peas, and the like, 26.6 per cent; hay and forage, 17.2 per cent; cotton, 32 per cent; vegetables, 25.5 per cent; sugar-beets, sugar-cane, etc., 62.6 per cent.

Let us examine the crop returns. From 1900 to 1910, the grain crop went up only 1.7 per cent; beans, 122.2 per cent; hay and forage, 23 per cent; sugar-beets, 395.7 per cent; sugar-cane, 48.5 per cent; potatoes, 42.4 per cent; grapes, 97.6 per cent; there was a poor crop of berries, apples, etc., in 1910, but the orange and lemon crops, etc., were treble those of 1900.

Thus, the apparently paradoxical but nevertheless proven fact has been shown to apply to U.S. agriculture as a whole that, generally speaking, small-scale production is not only being displaced by large-scale production, but also that this displacement is taking place in the following form:

Small-scale production is being crowded out by large-scale production through the displacement of farms which are "larger" in acreage, but are less productive, less intensive and less capitalist, by farms which are "smaller" in acreage, but are more productive, more intensive, and more capitalist.

13. HOW THE DISPLACEMENT OF SMALL-SCALE BY LARGE-SCALE PRODUCTION IN AGRICULTURE IS MINIMISED

The objection may be raised that if the displacement of small-scale *production* "also" proceeds in the form of the intensification (and "capitalisation") of operations on the smaller-size *farms*, is the grouping by acreage of any use at all? Is this not a case of two contradictory tendencies which make any general conclusion impossible?

This objection can be met by a *complete* picture of American agriculture and its evolution; to meet it we must try to compare all three methods of grouping which present, as it were, the maximum of information social statistics has produced in the sphere of agriculture in recent years.

Such a comparison is possible. All it calls for is a table which may at first sight appear to be so abstract and complex that it may "scare" the reader away. However, it takes only a little bit of concentration to "read", understand and analyse the table.

To compare the three different groupings we need take only their *percentage ratios*. All the necessary calculations are given in the American Census report for 1900. Each grouping is tabulated under *three* main heads. By acreage we have: (1) small farms (under 100 acres); (2) medium (100 to 175 acres), and (3) large (175 and over). By value of product we have: (1) non-capitalist farms (under $500); (2) medium

($500 to 1,000), and (3) capitalist ($1,000 and over). By the principal source of income we take (1) slightly capitalist (livestock, cotton); (2) medium (hay and grain; and miscellaneous), and (3) highly capitalist (the special "commercial" crops listed above, in Chapter 12, under heads 5 to 14).

For every group we first take the percentage of farms, i.e., the number of farms in a given group expressed as a percentage ratio of the total number of farms in the U.S.A. We then take the percentage of all land, i.e., the total acreage in a given group expressed as a percentage ratio of the total acreage of all farms in the U.S.A. The acreage serves as an indicator of the extensive character of the enterprise (unfortunately, the only figures available are for *total* acreage, instead of the improved acreage only, which would have been more exact). If the percentage share of the total acreage is *higher* than the percentage share of the number of farms, for example, if 17.2 per cent of the farms have 43.1 per cent of the land, it is evident that we are dealing with large farms, larger-than-average farms, which are besides more than double the size of the average farm. The reverse is true if the percentage of land is *lower* than the percentage of farms.

Next come the indexes of *intensiveness* of agriculture: the value of implements and machinery, and the total expenditure on fertilisers. Here, too, we take the value and the expenditure in the given group expressed as a percentage share of the totals for the country as a whole. Here again, if the percentage is *higher* than the percentage of *land*, the conclusion is that intensiveness is *above* the average, etc.

Finally, in order to determine exactly the capitalist character of the enterprises, the same method is applied to the total expenditure on hired labour; while in order to determine the scale of production this is done in relation to the total value of the agricultural product for the entire country.

This has produced the following table, which I shall now proceed to explain and analyse:

Comparison of the Three Groupings

(figures are percentages of total, sum total of each horizontal row of three figures = 100)

		By principal source of income			By farm acreage			By value of product			
		Slightly capitalist	Medium	Highly capitalist	Small	Medium	Large	Non-capitalist	Medium	Capitalist	
	Number of farms	46.0	41.5	12.5	57.5	24.8	17.7	58.8	24.0	17.2	Index of extensiveness of agriculture
	Total acreage	52.9	38.5	8.6	17.5	22.9	59.6	33.3	23.6	43.1	
Constant capital	Value of implements and machinery	37.2	42.7	20.1	31.7	28.9	39.4	25.3	28.0	46.7	Index of intensiveness of agriculture
Constant capital	Outlays on fertilisers	36.5	31.8	31.7	41.9	25.7	32.4	29.1	26.1	44.8	
Variable capital	Outlays on hired labour	35.2	38.2	26.6	22.3	23.5	54.2	11.3	19.6	69.1	Index of capitalist character of enterprise
Scale of production	Value of product	45.0	39.0	16.0	33.5	27.3	39.2	22.1	25.6	52.3	

Let us consider the first grouping—according to the principal source of income. Here farms are grouped, so to say, according to their line of farming, which is to some extent similar to the grouping of industrial enterprises by branches of industry. But the picture is immensely more complex in agriculture.

The first column shows the group of slightly capitalist farms. It comprises almost one-half the total number of farms—46 per cent. They own 52.9 per cent of the total acreage, i.e., they are larger than average (this group includes both the very large, extensive, livestock farms and the smaller-than-average cotton farms). Their shares of the value of machinery (37.2 per cent) and the expenditure on fertilisers (36.5 per cent) are lower than their acreage percentages, which means that their intensiveness is lower than the average. The same thing is true of the capitalist character of the enterprise (35.2 per cent) and the value of the product (45 per cent). Hence, their productivity of labour is lower than the average.

The second column shows the medium farms. Because farms which are "medium" in *every* respect fall into the medium group by *all* three methods of grouping, we find here that *all* their percentage ratios are closer to each other than in any of the other groups. The fluctuations are relatively small.

The third column shows the highly capitalist farms. I gave above a detailed analysis of what the figures in this column mean. Be it noted that *only* for this type of farm do we have accurate and comparable data both for 1900 and 1910—data testifying that these highly capitalist crops have a faster-than-average rate of development.

In what way is this more rapid development evident in the ordinary classification in use in most countries? This is shown in the next column: the small farms grouped by acreage.

This group consists of a great number of farms (57.5 per cent of the total). Its acreage is only 17.5 per cent of the total, i.e., less than one-third of the average. Hence, this is the "poorest" group, the most "land-starved" group. But then we find that it has a higher-than-average intensiveness of agriculture (the value of machinery and expenditures for fertilisers); that it is more capitalist (expenditures for hired labour); and that it has a *higher*-than-average productivity of labour (value of product): 22.3 to 41.9 per cent with 17.5 per cent of the acreage.

What is the explanation? Obviously that an especially large number of *highly capitalist* farms—see the preceding vertical column—fall into this "small"-acreage group. A *minority* of rich, capital-owning farmers conducting large-scale capitalist operations on small tracts of land are added to a majority of really small farmers who have little land and little capital. Such farmers make up only 12.5 per cent (=the percentage of highly capitalist farms) of the total in America, which means that even if they were all to be put into this one group of small-acreage farms, 45 per cent of the farmers in that group (57.5 —12.5) would still be short of land and capital. Actually, of course, a part of the highly capitalist farms, even if only a small one, consists of medium and large-acreage farms, so that the figure of 45 per cent in fact *understates* the actual number of farmers who have little land and no capital.

It will be easily seen how the condition of these 45 per cent—a minimum of 45 per cent—of the farmers who are poor in land and capital is *embellished* by the inclusion into the same group of some 12, 10 or so per cent of farmers who are supplied with higher-than-average amounts of capital, machinery, money to buy fertilisers, hire labour, and the rest of it.

I shall not dwell separately on the medium and large farms of this grouping, for this would be to repeat, in slightly different words what has been said about the small farms. For instance, if the data on the small-acreage farms put a better complexion on the oppressed condition of small-scale *production*, the data on the large-acreage farms obviously *minimise* the actual *concentration* of agriculture by large-scale production. We shall presently see an exact statistical expression of this minimised concentration.

We thus arrive at the following general proposition which may be formulated as a law applicable to the grouping of farms by acreage in any capitalist country:

The broader and more rapid the intensification of agriculture, the more the classification by acreage serves to *give*

a rosy picture of the oppressed condition of small-scale production in agriculture, the condition of the small farmer
who is short of *both* land *and* capital; the more it serves to
blunt the real sharpness of the class contradiction between
the prospering large-scale producer and the small-scale producer going to the wall; the more it serves to *minimise* the
concentration of capital in the hands of big operators and the
displacement of the small.

This is graphically confirmed by the third, and last, classification, according to the value of product. The percentage
of non-capitalistic farms (or not very profitable farms in
terms of gross income) is 58.8 per cent, i.e., even somewhat
more than the "small" farms (57.5 per cent). They have much
more land than the group of "small" farmers (33.3 per cent as
against 17.5 per cent). But their share of the total value of
the product is *one-third smaller*: 22.1 per cent as against 33.5
per cent!

What is the explanation? It is that this group does not
include the highly capitalistic farms on small tracts which
have *artificially and falsely* inflated the small farmers' share
of the *capital* in the form of machinery, fertilisers, etc.

Thus, the oppression and dispossession—and hence the
ruin—of the small *producer* in agriculture turn out to be
much more advanced than one would suppose from the data
on small *farms*.

The returns for the small and large farms, grouped by
acreage, take no account of *the role of capital*, and the failure to reckon with this "trifle" in capitalist enterprise dis-
torts the condition of the small producer, puts a false colour
on it, for it "could be" tolerable "but for" the existence of
capital, i.e., the power of money, and the relationship
between the hired labourer and the capitalist, between the
farmer and the merchant and creditor, etc.!

For that reason the concentration of agriculture as shown
by the large farms is much lower than its concentration as
shown by large-scale, *i.e.*, capitalist, production: 39.2 per
cent of the value of the product (slightly more than double
the average) is concentrated on 17.7 per cent of "large"
farms, while 52.3 per cent of the total value of the product,
i.e., more than *three* times the average, is concentrated on
17.2 per cent *capitalist* farms.

4*

In the country which practises the free distribution of
vast tracts of unoccupied land, and which the Manilovs[5]
consider a country of "family" farms, *more than one-half* of
the total agricultural production is concentrated in about
one-sixth of the *capitalist* enterprises, whose expenditure
on hired labour is four times greater than the per-farm average
(69.1 per cent on 17.2 per cent of the total number of
farms), and are half as great again as the per-acre average
(69.1 per cent of the expenditure on hired labour on farms
owning 43.1 per cent of the total amount of land).

At the other pole, more than one-half, almost three-
fifths, of the total number of farms (58.8 per cent) are
non-capitalist. They have one-third of the land (33.3 per
cent) but on it they have less than the average quantity of
machinery (25.3 per cent of the value of machinery); they
use less fertilisers than the average (29.1 per cent of the
expenditures for fertilisers) and so its productivity is only
two-thirds of the average. With one-third of the total acreage,
this immense number of farms, which suffer the greatest oppression under the yoke of capital, produce less than one-quarter
(22.1 per cent) of the total product and of its total value.

Consequently, we arrive at a general conclusion concerning the significance of classification by acreage, namely,
that it is not entirely useless. The one thing that should
never be forgotten is that it understates the displacement of
small-scale by large-scale production, and that the understatement increases with the pace and scope of intensification of agriculture, and with the gap between the amounts of
capital invested by the farms per unit of land. With modern
methods of research, which produce an abundance of sound
information about each farm, it would, for instance, be sufficient to combine two methods of classification—say,
each of the five acreage groups could be broken down into
two or three subgroups according to the employment of hired
labour. If this is not done it is largely because of the fear
of giving a much too naked picture of reality, a much too
striking picture of the oppression, impoverishment, ruin,
expropriation of the mass of small farmers, whose condition
is so "conveniently" and "unnoticeably" made to look better
by the "model" capitalist enterprises, which are also "small"
in acreage and which are a small minority within the mass of

the dispossessed. From the scientific standpoint no one would dare deny that not only land, but also capital has a part to play in modern agriculture. From the standpoint of statistical techniques, or the amount of statistical work involved, a total number of 10 to 15 groups is not at all excessive in comparison, for instance, with the 18 plus 7 groups based on acreage given in the German statistical report of 1907. This report, which classifies an abundance of material about 5,736,082 farms into the above number of acreage groups, is an example of bureaucratic routine, scientific rubbish, a meaningless juggling of figures, for there is *not a shadow* of any reasonable, rational, theoretical or practical ground for accepting such a number of groups as typical.

14. THE EXPROPRIATION OF THE SMALL FARMERS

The question of the expropriation of the small farmers is immensely important to an understanding and assessment of capitalism in agriculture in general, and it is highly characteristic of modern political economy and statistics, which are saturated through and through with bourgeois notions and prejudices, that this question is either practically not considered at all or is given the least attention.

The general statistics in all capitalist countries show that the urban population is growing at the expense of the rural, that the population is abandoning the countryside. In the U.S.A., this process is steadily advancing. The proportion of the urban population increased from 29.5 per cent in 1880, to 36.1 per cent in 1890, 40.5 per cent in 1900, and 46.3 per cent in 1910. In every part of the country the urban population is growing more rapidly than the rural population: from 1900 to 1910, the rural population in the industrial North went up by 3.9 per cent and the urban by 29.8 per cent; in the former slave-holding South, the rural population increased by 14.8 per cent, and the urban, by 41.4 per cent; in the homestead West, the figures were 49.7 and 89.6 per cent, respectively.

One should think that such a universal process would also have to be studied in the taking of agricultural censuses. A most important question from the scientific standpoint naturally arises as to what sections, strata or groups of the rural population provide the fugitives from the countryside and in what circumstances. Since highly detailed information about each agricultural enterprise and about each animal in it is collected every ten years, it would be no trouble at all to include questions as to how many and what kind of farms were sold or rented with an eye to moving into town, and how many members of households abandoned farming temporarily or for good, and in what circumstances. But no such questions are asked: the investigation does not go beyond the official stereotyped statement: "The rural population decreased from 59.5 per cent in 1900 to 53.7 per cent in 1910." The census-takers seem to have no inkling of the mass of misery, oppression and ruin concealed behind these routine figures. As a general rule, bourgeois and petty-bourgeois economists turn a blind eye to the obvious connection between the flight of the population from the countryside and the ruin of the small producers.

There is no alternative, therefore, but to try and bring together the relatively meagre and very badly compiled data on the expropriation of the small farmers gleaned from the 1910 Census report.

There are the figures on the forms of farm tenure: the number of owners, subdivided into *full* and *part* owners; and the number of share-cropping tenants and cash-paying tenants. These figures are tabulated for the various divisions but not the farm groups.

Here is the first picture we get from the totals for 1900 and 1910:

Total rural population increased . . . . 11.2 per cent
Total number of farms increased . . . . 10.9 „ „
Total number of owners increased . . . 8.1 „ „
Total number of *full* owners increased 4.8 „ „

This picture is a clear indication of the growing expropriation of small-scale agriculture. The rural population is increasing more slowly than the urban. The number of farmers is increasing more slowly than the rural population; the number of owners is increasing more slowly than the number of farmers; the number of *full* owners—more slowly than the number of owners in general.

The proportion of owners in the total number of farmers has been decreasing steadily over a period of several decades, as follows:

```
1880    74.0 per cent
1890    71.6   „     „
1900    64.7   „     „
1910    63.0   „     „
```

There is a corresponding growth in the proportion of tenants, with the number of share-cropping tenants going up faster than that of cash-paying tenants. The number of share-cropping tenants was 17.5 per cent in 1880; then it rose to 18.4 per cent and 22.2 per cent, and finally to 24 per cent in 1910.

It is evident from the following figures that the decrease in the proportion of owners and the increase in the proportion of tenants is, on the whole, an indication of the dispossession and displacement of the small farmers:

Class of farm	Percentage of farms owning					
	domestic animals			horses		
	1900	1910	±	1900	1910	±
Owners	96.7	96.1	—0.6	85.0	81.5	—3.5
Tenants	94.2	92.9	—1.3	67.9	60.7	—7.2

According to all the returns for both census years the owners are economically stronger. The condition of the tenants is deteriorating *more rapidly* than that of the owners.

Let us examine separately the figures for the sections.

The greatest number of tenants, as I have already said, is in the South, and there tenancy has the fastest rate of growth: it rose from 47 per cent in 1900, to 49.6 per cent in 1910. Capital defeated slavery half a century ago, merely to *restore* it now in a new form as share tenancy.

In the North, the number of tenants is considerably smaller and is growing at a much slower rate: it went up from 26.2 per cent in 1900, to only 26.5 per cent in 1910. The West has the smallest number of tenants, and it is the *only* section where tenancy, instead of increasing, decreased: it fell from 16.6 per cent in 1900 to 14.0 per cent in 1910. "A very low proportion of tenant farms," says the Census report for 1910, "is also shown for the Mountain and Pacific divisions [the two divisions constituting "The West"]*, where it is

---

* Interpolations in square brackets (within passages quoted by Lenin) have been introduced by Lenin, unless otherwise indicated.— *Ed.*

doubtless attributable mainly to the fact that those divisions
have been only recently settled and that many of the farmers
in them are homesteaders who have obtained their land from
the Government" free or for a very small price (Vol. V,
p. 104).

This is a striking example of the peculiar characteristic
of the U.S.A., to which I have repeatedly referred, namely,
the availability of unoccupied, free land. This explains,
on the one hand, the extremely rapid and extensive development of capitalism in America. The absence of private property in land in some parts of a vast country does not exclude
capitalism—our Narodniks should make a note of this!—
on the contrary, it broadens its base, and accelerates its
development. Upon the other hand, this peculiarity, which is
entirely unknown in the old, long-settled capitalist countries
of Europe, serves in America to *cover up* the expropriation
of the small farmers—a process already under way in the
settled and most industrialised parts of the country.

Let us take the North. We get the following picture:

	1900	1910	+ or — percent
Total rural population (000,000) . .	22.2	23.1	+3.9
Total number of farms (000)	2,874	2,891	+0.6
Total number of owners (000)	2,088	2,091	+0.1
Total number of *full* owners (000). .	1,794	1,749	—2.5

We see not only a relative reduction in the number of
owners, not only a decline in their proportion of the total
number of farmers, etc., but even an *absolute decrease* in the
number of owners, against a background of growing production in the main section of the U.S.A., which embraces 60
per cent of the country's improved acreage!

It should, besides, be borne in mind that in *one* of the
four divisions making up the North, namely, the West North
Central, *the allotment of homesteads continues to this very
day*, and that 54 million acres were allotted in the 10 years
from 1901 to 1910.

The tendency of capitalism to expropriate small-scale
agriculture is so strong that the American "North" shows an
absolute decrease in the number of landowners, *in spite of*
the distribution of tens of millions of acres of unoccupied,
free land.

Only two factors still serve to paralyse this tendency in the U.S.A.: (1) the existence of the still unparcelled slave-holding plantations in the South, with its oppressed and downtrodden Negro population; and (2) the fact that the West is still partly unsettled. Both these factors tend to widen the future base of capitalism, and so prepare the conditions for its even more extensive and more rapid development. The sharpening of contradictions and the displacement of small-scale production are not removed but are transferred to a larger arena. The capitalist fire appears to be "damped down"—but at the price of an even greater accumulation of new and more inflammable material.

Furthermore, on the question of the expropriation of small-scale agriculture, we have the returns for the number of farms owning livestock. Here are the figures for the U.S.A.

Percentage of farms owning	1900	1910	+ or —
Domestic animals in general	95.8	94.9	—0.9
Dairy cows	78.7	80.8	+2.1
Horses	79.0	73.8	—5.2

These figures show, on the whole, a reduction in the number of owners in proportion to the total number of farmers. The increase in the percentage of those who owned dairy cows was smaller than the drop in the percentage of those who owned horses.

Let us now examine the figures for farms grouped in relation to the two major kinds of livestock.

Size groups (acres)	Percentage of farms owning dairy cows		+ or —
	1900	1910	
Under 20	49.5	52.9	+3.4
20 to 49	65.9	71.2	+5.3
50 to 99	84.1	87.1	+3.0
100 to 174	88.9	89.8	+0.9
175 to 499	92.6	93.5	+0.9
500 to 999	90.3	89.6	—0.7
1,000 and over	82.9	86.0	+3.1
Average for the U.S.A. . . .	78.7	80.8	+2.1

We find that the greatest increase was in the number of *small* farms with dairy cows, then came the latifundia, and then the medium-size farms. There was a decrease in the percentage of farms reporting dairy cows among the big owners, with 500 to 999 acres of land.

On the whole, this seems to indicate a gain for small-scale agriculture. Let us recall, however, that in farming the ownership of dairy cattle has a twofold significance: on the one hand, it may generally indicate a higher living standard and better conditions of nutrition. On the other hand, it signifies—and rather more frequently—a development of one branch of commercial farming and cattle-breeding: the production of milk for the market in the towns and industrial centres. We saw above that farms of this type, the "dairy" farms, were classified by American statisticians under a special head, according to the principal source of income. A characteristic of this group is that it has a *smaller*-than-average total and improved acreage, but a *greater*-than-average value of output, and a *double-the-average* employment of hired labour per acre. The increasing importance of small farms in dairy farming may simply mean — and most likely does mean—a growth of *capitalist* dairy farms of the type described, on small tracts of land. For the sake of comparison here are some figures on the *concentration* of dairy cattle in America:

Sections	Average number of dairy cows per farm		Increase
	1900	1910	
The North	4.8	5.3	+0.5
The South	2.3	2.4	+0.1
The West	5.0	5.2	+0.2
Overall average	3.8	4.0	+0.2

We find that the North, which is richest of all in dairy cattle, also showed the greatest increase in wealth. Here is a distribution of this increase among the groups:

The North Size groups (acres)	Percentage increase or decrease in number of dairy cows from 1900 to 1910
Under 20	— 4 (+10.0 in the number of farms)
20 to 49	— 3 (—12.6 „ „ „ „ „)
50 to 99	+ 9 (— 7.3 „ „ „ „ „)
100 to 174	+14 (+ 2.2 „ „ „ „ „)
175 to 499	+18 (+12.7 „ „ „ „ „)
500 to 999	+29 (+40.4 „ „ „ „ „)
1,000 and over	+18 (+16.4 „ „ „ „ „)
Overall increase . . .	+14 (+ 0.6 in the number of farms)

The more rapid growth in the *number* of small farms with dairy cattle did not prevent its more rapid *concentration* in the large enterprises.

Let us now turn to the figures on the number of farms reporting horses. This information about draught animals is an indication of the general pattern of farming and not of any special branch of commercial farming.

Size groups (acres)	Percentage of farms reporting horses		Decrease
	1900	1910	
Under 20	52.4	48.9	—3.5
20 to 49	66.3	57.4	—8.9
50 to 99	82.2	77.6	—4.6
100 to 174	88.6	86.5	—2.1
175 to 499	92.0	91.0	—1.0
500 to 999	93.7	93.2	—0.5
1,000 and over	94.2	94.1	—0.1
Average for the U.S.A.	79.0	73.8	—5.2

We find that as we go down the size-group scale there is a rising number of farms not reporting horses. With the exception of the smallest farms (under 20 acres) which, as we know, include a comparatively greater number of capitalistic farms than the neighbouring groups, we observe a rapid decrease in the number of horseless farms and a much slower increase in their number. The use of steam ploughs and other engines on the rich farms may partly compensate for the reduction in draught animals, but such an assumption is out of the question for the mass of the poorer farms.

Finally, the growth of expropriation is also evident from the returns on the number of mortgaged farms:

Sections	Percentage of mortgaged farms		
	1890	1900	1910
The North . .	40.3	40.9	41.9
The South . . .	5.7	17.2	23.5
The West . . .	23.1	21.7	28.6
Average for the U.S.A.	28.2	31.0	33.6

The percentage of mortgaged farms is on a steady increase in all sections, and it is highest in the most populous industrialised and capitalist North. American statisticians point out (Vol. V, p. 159) that the growth in the number of mortgaged farms in the South is probably due to the "parcelling out" of the plantations, which are sold in lots to Negro and white farmers, who pay only a part of the purchase price, the rest being covered by a mortgage on the property. Consequently a peculiar *buying-up operation* is under way in the slave-holding South. Let us note that in 1910 Negroes in the U.S.A. owned only 920,883 farms, i.e., 14.5 per cent of the total; between 1900 and 1910, the number of white farms increased 9.5 per cent, and that of Negro farms, twice as fast—19.6 per cent. The Negro urge to emancipation from the "plantation owners" half a century after the "victory" over the slave-owners is still marked by an exceptional intensity.

The American statisticians also point out that the mortgaging of a farm does not always indicate lack of prosperity; it is sometimes a way of obtaining capital for land improvement; and the like. This is indisputable, but this indisputable observation should not conceal the fact—as is much too often the case with bourgeois economists—that only a well-to-do minority are in a position to obtain capital for improvements, etc., in this way, and to employ it productively; the majority are further impoverished and fall into the clutches of finance capital assuming this particular form.

Researchers could—and should—have paid much more attention to the dependence of farmers on finance capital. But although this aspect of the matter is immensely important, it has remained in the background.

The growth in the number of mortgaged farms in any case means that the actual control over them is transferred to the capitalists. It stands to reason that apart from officially recorded and notarised mortgages, a considerable number of farms are steeped in private debt, which is not covered by strict legal instruments and is not recorded by the census.

15. A COMPARATIVE PICTURE OF EVOLUTION IN INDUSTRY AND AGRICULTURE

American census statistics, for all their shortcomings, compare favourably with those of other countries because of the completeness and uniformity of the methods used.

This makes it possible to compare the returns for industry and agriculture for 1900 and 1910, and to contrast the overall picture of the structure of both sectors of the economy and the evolution of this structure. One of the most popular ideas in bourgeois economics—an idea, incidentally, which Mr. Himmer repeats—is to *contrast* industry and agriculture. Let us see, in the light of a mass of precise data, what truth there is in such a contrast.

Let us begin with the number of enterprises in industry and in agriculture.

	Number of enterprises (000)		Increase (per cent)	Growth of urban and rural population (per cent)
	1900	1910		
Industry	207.5	268.5	+29.4	+34.8
Agriculture	5,737	6,361	+10.9	+11.2

The enterprises in agriculture are much more numerous and much smaller. That is an expression of its backwardness, parcellisation, and dispersion.

The number of enterprises increases much more slowly in agriculture than in industry. There are two factors in the United States which do not exist in other leading countries, and which greatly intensify and accelerate the growth in the number of enterprises in agriculture. They are, first, the continued parcelling out of the slave-holding latifundia in the South and "buying-up" by Negro and also by white farmers of small parcels from the "planters"; secondly, the availability of an immense quantity of unoccupied, free land, which is distributed by the government to all applicants. Nevertheless the number of enterprises in agriculture is increasing at a slower rate than in industry.

The reason is twofold. On the one hand, agriculture to a rather large extent retains the character of a "natural" economy, and various operations once performed by members of a peasant household are gradually branching off from agriculture—for example, the making and repair of various implements, utensils, etc.—and now constitute separate industries. On the other hand, there is a monopoly which is peculiar to agriculture and unknown to industry, and which cannot be eliminated under capitalism—the monopoly of land ownership. Even when there is no private property in land—in the United States none actually exists on very large areas to this very day—monopoly is created by the ownership of land and its occupation by individual private operators. In the country's most important regions all the land is occupied, and an increase in the number of agricultural enterprises is possible only when existing enterprises are broken up; the free formation of new enterprises alongside the old is impossible. The monopoly of land ownership is a drag on the development of agriculture, and this monopoly retards the development of capitalism in agriculture, which, therefore, is unlike industry in this respect.

We are unable to make an accurate comparison of the amounts of capital invested in industrial and in agricultural enterprises because ground-rent forms a part of the value of the land. Accordingly, we have to compare the capital invested in industry and the value of industrial products with the total value of all farm property and the value of the major farm product. Only the percentages showing increases in the total values on both sides are strictly comparable.

| | | $000,000 | | Increase |
		1900	1910	(per cent)
Industry	Capital of all enterprises..	8,975	18,428	105.3
	Value of products	11,406	20,671	81.2
Agriculture	Value of all farm property	20,440	40,991	100.5
	Value of all cereal crops	1,483	2,665	79.8
	Production of cereals in bushels (000,000)	4,439	4,513	1.7

We find that during the 10 years from 1900 to 1910 the value of capital invested in industry and the value of all farm property have *doubled*. The great and fundamental difference between the two is that in agriculture the major product, cereals, increased by an insignificant 1.7 per cent—while the total population increased 21 per cent.

Agriculture lags behind industry in development; this is a feature of *all* capitalist countries constituting one of the most profound causes of disproportion between the various branches of the economy, of crises and soaring prices.

Capital liberated agriculture from feudalism and drew it into commodity circulation and thereby into world economic development, lifting it from medieval backwardness and patriarchal stagnation. But capital, instead of eliminating the oppression, exploitation and poverty of the masses, produces these calamities in a new guise and restores their old forms on a "modern" basis. The contradiction between industry and agriculture, far from being eliminated by capitalism, is, on the contrary, further extended and sharpened by it. The oppression of capital, seen primarily in the sphere of trade and industry, weighs more and more heavily on agriculture.

The insignificant increase in the quantity of agricultural produce (+1.7 per cent) and the enormous increase in its value (+79.8 per cent) shows clearly, on the one hand, the role of ground-rent, the tribute extorted from society by the landowners. Because of their monopolist position, they are able to take advantage of the backwardness of agriculture, which does not keep pace with industry, and to fill their pockets with millions and millions of dollars. In the 10 years, the value of all farm property increased by $20,500 *million*, of which only $5,000 million constituted the increase in the value of buildings, livestock and equipment. The value of land —capitalised ground-rent —increased in the 10 years by *$15,000 million* (+118.1 per cent).

On the other hand, the difference in the *class* status of the small farmers and the hired labourers is here thrown into especially sharp relief. To be sure, both labour; to be sure, both are subject to exploitation by capital, though in entirely different forms. But only vulgar bourgeois democrats will for this reason put the two different classes together and speak of small-scale operations by family farms. To do so is to cover up and disguise the *social* system of the economy—its bourgeois nature—and push into the foreground a feature common to *all* earlier formations, namely, the necessity for the petty farmer to work, to engage in personal, physical labour, if he is to survive.

Under capitalism, the small farmer—whether he wants to or not, whether he is aware of it or not—becomes a commodity producer. And it is this change that is fundamental, for it alone, even when he does not as yet exploit hired labour, makes him a petty bourgeois and converts him into an antagonist of the proletariat. He sells his product, while the proletarian sells his labour-power. The small farmers, as a class, cannot but seek a rise in the prices of agricultural products, and this is tantamount to their joining the big landowners in sharing the ground-rent, and siding with the landowners against the rest of society. As commodity production develops, the small farmer, in accordance with his *class* status, inevitably becomes a *petty landed proprietor*.

There are cases even among wage-workers when a small part of them side with their masters against the whole class of wage-earners. But this is merely a *small fraction* of a class uniting with its antagonists, against the *entire* class. It is impossible to imagine any improvement of the condition of wage-earners as a class, without an improvement in the living standard of the masses, or without a sharpening of the antagonism between them and capital, which rules contemporary society, the antagonism between them and the entire class of capitalists. But it is quite possible, on the contrary, to imagine a state of affairs—indeed, such a situation is even typical of capitalism—where an improvement in the condition of the small farmers, as a class, results from their alliance with the big landlords, their participation in exacting a higher ground-rent from society as a whole, the contradictions arising between them and the mass of proletarians and semi-proletarians, who depend, entirely or at least mostly, on the sale of their labour-power.

Here is a comparison of American statistics on the number and position of wage-earners and of small farmers:

		1900	1910	Increase (per cent)
Industry	Number of wage-earners (000) . .	4,713	6,615	40.4
	Their wages ($000,000)	2,008	3,427	70.6
Agriculture	Number of wage-earners	?	?	c. 47.1
	Their wages ($000,000)	357	652	82.3
	Number of farmers (000)	5,737	6,361	10.9
	Value of their major product, cereal crops ($000,000)	1,483	2,665	79.8

The workers in industry *lost*, for their wages went up by only 70.6 per cent ("only", because almost the same quantity of cereals, 101.7 per cent of the old quantity, is now 179.8 per cent of the old price!), while the number of workers increased all of 40 per cent.

The small farmers *gained*, in their capacity of petty landowners, at the expense of the proletariat. The number of small farmers increased by only 10.9 per cent (even if the small commercial farms are singled out, the increase is still only 11.9 per cent), and while the quantity of their product hardly increased at all (+1.7 per cent), its value went up 79.8 per cent.

Naturally, commercial and finance capital took the lion's share of this ground-rent, but the class status of the small farmer and the wage-earner, vis-à-vis each other, is entirely akin to the status of petty bourgeois and proletarian.

The numerical growth of wage-earners *outstrips* the growth of population (+40 per cent for the former as against +21 per cent for the latter). There is growing expropriation of the petty producers and small farmers. There is growing proletarisation of the population.*

The increase in the number of farmers—and to an even greater extent, as we already know, in the number of proprietors among them—*lags* behind the growth of the population (10.9 per cent, as against 21 per cent). The small farmers are increasingly converted into monopolists, into petty landed proprietors.

Let us now take a look at the relationship between small-scale and large-scale production in industry and in agriculture. In respect of industry the figures are not for 1900 and 1910, but for 1904 and 1910.

Industrial enterprises are divided into three main groups depending on the value of their products, the small being those with an output of less than $20,000; the medium, from $20,000 to $100,000, and the large $100,000 and over. We have no way of grouping agricultural enterprises except by acreage. Accordingly, small farms are those up to 100 acres; medium, from 100 to 175; and large, 175 and over.

---

* The number of wage-earners in agriculture, or rather the growth in their number, is obtained from the following ratio: 82.3:70.6= =x : 40.4, hence x=47.1.

| Groups | | Number of enterprises (000) | | | Increase |
	1900	per cent	1910	per cent	(per cent)
Industry Small	144	66.6	180	67.2	25.0
Medium	48	22.2	57	21.3	18.7
Large	24	11.2	31	11.5	29.1
Total	216	100.0	268	100.0	24.2
Agriculture Small	3,297	57.5	3,691	58.0	11.9
Medium	1,422	24.8	1,516	23.8	6.6
Large	1,018	17.7	1,154	18.2	13.3
Total	5,737	100.0	6,361	100.0	10.9

The uniformity of evolution proves to be remarkable.

Both in industry and agriculture the proportion of medium establishments is reduced, for their number grows more slowly than that of the small and large enterprises.

Both in industry and agriculture the small enterprises increase in number at a slower rate than the large.

What are the changes in the economic strength or economic role of the various types of enterprises? For the industrial enterprises we have the returns on the value of their products, and for the agricultural, on the total value of all farm property.

| Groups | $000,000 | | $000,000 | | Increase |
	1900	per cent	1910	per cent	(per cent
Industry Small	927	6.3	1,127	5.5	21.5
Medium	2,129	14.4	2,544	12.3	19.5
Large	11,737	79.3	17,000	82.2	44.8
Total	14,793	100.0	20,671	100.0	39.7
Agriculture Small	5,790	28.4	10,499	25.6	81.3
Medium	5,721	28.0	11,089	27.1	93.8
Large	8,929	43.6	19,403	47.3	117.3
Total	20,440	100.0	40,991	100.0	100.5

Once again the uniformity of evolution is remarkable.

Both in industry and agriculture the relative number of small and medium enterprises is decreasing, and only the relative number of the large enterprises is increasing.

In other words, the displacement of small-scale by large-scale production is under way both in industry and in agriculture.

The difference between industry and agriculture in this case is that the proportion of small enterprises in industry increased somewhat more than the proportion of medium enterprises (+21.5 per cent, as against +19.5 per cent), while the reverse was true for agriculture. Of course, this difference is not great, and no general conclusions can be drawn from it. But the fact remains that in the world's leading capitalist country small-scale production in industry gained more ground in the last decade than medium-scale production, whereas the reverse was true for agriculture. This fact shows how little importance is to be attached to the current assertions of bourgeois economists that the law of the displacement of small-scale by large-scale production is confirmed, unconditionally and without any exception, by industry, and refuted by agriculture.

In the agriculture of the U.S.A. the displacement of small-scale by large-scale production is not merely under way, but is proceeding with greater uniformity than in industry.

In considering this, the fact demonstrated above should not be forgotten, namely, that the grouping of farms by acreage *understates* the process of displacement of small-scale by large-scale production.

As for the *degree* of concentration already achieved, agriculture is very far behind. In industry, more than eight-tenths of all production is in the hands of the large enterprises that constitute only 11 per cent of the total number. The role of the small enterprises is insignificant: two-thirds of the total number of enterprises account for only 5.5 per cent of the total production! By comparison, agriculture is still in a state of dispersion: small enterprises, comprising 58 per cent of the total number, account for one-quarter of the total value of all farm property; while 18 per cent large enterprises account for less than one-half (47 per cent). The total number of agricultural enterprises is over 20 times greater than the number in industry.

This confirms the old conclusion—if the evolution of agriculture is compared with that of industry, capitalism in agriculture is at a stage more akin to the manufactory stage than to the stage of large-scale machine industry. Manual labour still prevails in agriculture, and the use of machinery is relatively very limited. But the data given above do not in any way prove the impossibility of socialising agricultural production, even at the present stage of its development. Those who control the banks *directly* control one-third of America's farms, and indirectly dominate the lot. In view of the modern development of associations of every kind and of communications and transport, it is undoubtedly possible to organise production under a single general plan on a million farms raising more than one-half the total value of the product.

16. SUMMARY AND CONCLUSIONS

The agricultural censuses taken in the United States in 1900 and 1910 are the last word in social statistics in this sphere of the economy. It is the best material of any available in the advanced countries, covering millions of farms and allowing precise well-founded conclusions on the evolution of agriculture under capitalism. One other particular reason why this material can be used to study the laws of the evolution is that the U.S.A. has the largest size, the greatest diversity of relationships, and the greatest range of nuances and forms of capitalist agriculture.

We find here, on the one hand, a transition from the slave-holding—or what is in this case the same, from the feudal—structure of agriculture to commercial and capitalist agriculture; and, on the other hand, capitalism developing with unusual breadth and speed in the freest and most advanced bourgeois country. We observe alongside of this remarkably extensive colonisation conducted on democratic-capitalist lines.

We find here areas which have long been settled, highly industrialised, highly intensive, and similar to most of the areas of civilised, old-capitalist Western Europe; as well as areas of primitive, extensive cropping and stock-raising, like some of the outlying areas of Russia or parts of Siberia. We find large and small farms of the most diverse types: great latifundia, plantations of the former slave-holding South, and the homestead West, and the highly capitalist North of the Atlantic seaboard; the small farms of the Negro share-croppers, and the small capitalist farms producing milk and vegetables for the market in the industrial North or fruits on the Pacific coast; "wheat factories" employing hired labour and the *homesteads* of "independent" small farmers, still full of naïve illusions about living by the "labour of their own hands".

This is a remarkable diversity of relationships, embracing both past and future, Europe and Russia. The comparison with Russia is especially instructive, by the way, in regard to the question of the consequences of a possible transfer of all land to the peasants without compensation, a measure that is progressive but undoubtedly capitalist.

The U.S.A. offers the most convenient example for the study of the general laws of capitalist development in agriculture and the variety of forms these laws assume. A study of this kind leads up to conclusions which may be summed up in the following brief propositions.

In agriculture, as compared with industry, manual labour predominates over machinery to an immeasurably greater extent. But the machine is steadily advancing, improving farming techniques, extending the scale of operations and making them more capitalist. In modern agriculture, machinery is used in the capitalist way.

Hired labour is the chief sign and indicator of capitalism in agriculture. The development of hired labour, like the growing use of machinery, is evident in *all* parts of the country, and in every branch of agriculture. The growth in the number of hired labourers outstrips the growth of the country's rural and total population. The growth in the number of farmers lags behind that of the rural population. Class contradictions are intensified and sharpened.

The displacement of small-scale by large-scale production in agriculture is going forward. This is fully proved by a comparison of the returns for 1900 and 1910 on total farm property.

However, this displacement is understated, and the condition of the small farmers is shown in bright colours because statisticians in America in 1910 confined themselves—as in fact they did almost everywhere in Europe—to grouping the farms by acreage. The wider and faster the intensification of agriculture, the higher is the degree of this understatement and the brighter the colours.

Capitalism grows not only by accelerating the development of large-acreage farms in extensive areas, but also by creating in the intensive areas enterprises on smaller tracts whose operations are on a much larger scale and are much more capitalist.

As a result, the concentration of production in the large enterprises is actually much greater—and the displacement of small-scale production actually goes farther and deeper—than is indicated by ordinary data about farms grouped by acreage. The returns of the 1900 Census, compiled with greater care and in greater detail, are more scientific and leave no doubt at all on this score.

The expropriation of small-scale agriculture is advancing. In the last few decades, the proportion of owners to the total number of farmers declined steadily, while the growth in the number of farmers lagged behind population increase. The number of full owners is declining absolutely in the North, the most important section, which yields the largest volume of farm products and has neither any vestiges of slavery nor any extensive homesteading. In the last decade, the proportion of farmers reporting livestock in general decreased; in contrast to the increased proportion of owners reporting dairy cattle there was an even greater increase in the proportion of operators without horses, especially among the small farmers.

On the whole, a comparison of corresponding data on industry and agriculture for the same period shows that although the latter is incomparably more backward, there is a remarkable similarity in the laws of evolution, and that small-scale production is being ousted from both.

PREFACE TO N. BUKHARIN'S PAMPHLET,
IMPERIALISM AND THE WORLD ECONOMY

There is no need for any special explanation to show that the subject dealt with in Bukharin's paper is topical and important. The question of imperialism is not only one of the most essential but is probably *the* most essential question in that sphere of economic science which traces the change in the forms of capitalism in modern times. Anyone interested not only in economics but in any aspect of contemporary social life must certainly acquaint himself with the facts pertaining to this sphere which the author has collected in such abundance from the latest material. It goes without saying that there can be no concrete historical assessment of the current war, unless it is based on a thorough analysis of the nature of imperialism, both in its economic and political aspects. Otherwise, it would be impossible to arrive at a correct understanding of the economic and diplomatic history of the last few decades without which it would be ridiculous to expect to work out a correct view of the war. From the standpoint of Marxism, which states most definitely the requirements of modern science on this question in general, one can merely smile at the "scientific" value of such methods as taking the concrete historical assessment of the war to mean a random selection of facts which the ruling classes of the country find gratifying or convenient, facts taken at random from diplomatic "documents", current political developments, etc. Plekhanov, for instance, must have completely parted with Marxism to substitute the angling after a couple of little facts which delighted Purishkevich as much as Milyukov, for an analysis of the essential properties and tendencies of imperialism, as the system of economic relations of modern highly developed, mature and rotten-ripe capitalism. The scientific concept of imperialism, moreover, is reduced to a sort of term of abuse applied to the immediate competitors, rivals and opponents of the two imperialists mentioned, each of whom holds exactly the same class position as his rivals and opponents! This is not at all surprising in this day of words forgotten, principles lost, philosophies overthrown, and resolutions and solemn promises discarded.

N. I. Bukharin's paper has especially high scientific value because he examines the main facts of the world economy relating to imperialism as a whole, as a definite stage of development of the most highly developed capitalism. There was an epoch of relatively "peaceful" capitalism, when it had completely defeated feudalism in the leading European countries and was free to develop with the utmost—*relative*—tranquillity and smoothness, expanding "peacefully" over the vast expanses of the as yet unsettled lands and the countries not yet irrevocably drawn into the capitalist maelstrom. Of course, even in that period, roughly between 1871 and 1914, "peaceful" capitalism created conditions of life that were a very far cry from actual "peace", both in the military and the class sense. For nine-tenths of the population of the leading countries, for hundreds of millions in the colonies and backward countries, that epoch was not one of "peace" but of oppression, suffering and horror, which was the more terrible, possibly, for appearing to be a "horror without end". This epoch is gone for good, it has given way to an epoch which is relatively much more violent, spasmodic, disastrous and conflicting, an epoch which for the mass of the population is typified not so much by a "horror without end" as by a "horrible end".

In all this it is extremely important to bear in mind that this change has been brought about in no other way but the immediate development, expansion and continuation of the most profound and basic trends in capitalism and in commodity production in general. These main trends, which have been in evidence all over the world for centuries, are the growth of exchange and the growth of large-scale production. At a definite stage in the development of exchange, at a definite stage in the growth of large-scale production, namely, at the stage which was attained towards the turn of the century, exchange so internationalised economic relations and capital, and large-scale production assumed such proportions that monopoly began to replace free competition.

Monopoly associations of entrepreneurs, trusts, instead of enterprises, "freely" competing with each other—at home and *in relations between the countries*—became typical. Finance capital took over as the typical "lord" of the world; it is particularly mobile and flexible, particularly interknit at home and internationally, and particularly impersonal and divorced from production proper; it lends itself to concentration with particular ease, and has been concentrated to an unusual degree already, so that literally a few hundred multimillionaires and millionaires control the destiny of the world.

Abstract theoretical reasoning may lead to the conclusion at which Kautsky has arrived—in a somewhat different fashion but also by abandoning Marxism—namely, that the time is not too far off when these magnates of capital will unite on a world scale in a single world trust, substituting an internationally united finance capital for the competition and struggle between sums of finance capital nationally isolated. This conclusion is, however, just as abstract, simplified and incorrect as the similar conclusion drawn by our Struvists and Economists of the nineties, when they drew conclusions from the progressive nature of capitalism, its inevitability and its final victory in Russia that ranged from the apologetic (admiration for capitalism, reconciliation with it, and glorification instead of struggle), and the apolitical (that is, a denial of politics or a denial of the importance of politics, the probability of general political upheavals, etc., a mistake specifically Economist), to the outrightly "strike-ist" (the "general strike", as the apotheosis of the strike movement, brought up to a point where other forms of movement are forgotten or ignored and capitalism is overcome solely by a "leap" from it to a strike, pure and simple). There is evidence that even today the indisputable fact that capitalism is progressive, when compared with the semi-philistine "paradise" of free competition, and that imperialism and its final victory over "peaceful" capitalism in the leading countries of the world are inevitable—that this fact is still capable of producing an equally great and varied number of political and apolitical mistakes and misadventures.

With Kautsky, in particular, his clear break with Marxism has not taken the form of a denial or neglect of politics, or of a "leap" *over* the political conflicts, upheavals and

transformations, so numerous and varied in the imperialist
epoch; it has not taken the form of an apology of imperialism
but of a *dream of "peaceful" capitalism*. That "peaceful"
capitalism has given way to non-peaceful, aggressive, cata-
clysmic imperialism Kautsky is forced to admit, because that
is something he had admitted as far back as 1909 in the
paper [6] in which he last produced some integrated conclusions
as a Marxist. But if it is impossible to toy in rude, simple
fashion with the dream of a straightforward retreat from
imperialism to "peaceful" capitalism, why not let these dreams,
which are essentially petty-bourgeois, take the form of
innocent speculation on *"peaceful"* "ultra-imperialism"? If the
international integration of national (rather nationally isolated) imperialisms is to be called ultra-imperialism, which
"could" remove the conflicts, such as wars, political upheavals, etc., which the petty bourgeois finds especially unpal-
atable, disquieting, and alarming, why not, in that case,
make an escape from the present highly conflicting and cata-
clysmic epoch of imperialism, which is the here and now, by
means of innocent dreams of an "ultra-imperialism" which is
relatively peaceful, relatively lacking in conflict and relatively uncataclysmic? Why not try to escape the acute problems that have been and are being posed by the epoch of imperialism that has dawned for Europe by dreaming up the
possibility of it soon passing away and being followed by a
relatively "peaceful" epoch of "ultra-imperialism" that will
not require any "abrupt" tactics? Kautsky says precisely that
"such a [ultra-imperialist] new phase of capitalism is at
any rate imaginable", but that "there are not yet enough
prerequisites to decide whether or not it is feasible" (*Die
Neue Zeit*,[7] April 30, 1915, p. 144).

There is not a whit of Marxism in this urge to ignore the
imperialism which is here and to escape into the realm of an
"ultra-imperialism" which may or may not arrive. In this
formulation, Marxism is recognised in that "new phase
of capitalism" which its inventor himself does not warrant
can be realised, while in the present stage (which is already
here) the petty-bourgeois and profoundly reactionary desire
to blunt the contradictions is substituted for Marxism.
Kautsky *swore* to be a Marxist in this coming, acute and cata-
clysmic epoch, which he was forced to predict and recognise

very definitely in his 1909 paper on this coming epoch. Now that this epoch has most definitely arrived, Kautsky once again *swears* to be a Marxist in the coming epoch of ultra-imperialism, which may or may not arrive! In short, any number of promises to be a Marxist in *another* epoch, not now, not under present conditions, not in this epoch! Marxism on credit, Marxism in promises, Marxism tomorrow, a petty-bourgeois, opportunist theory—*and not only a theory* —of blunting contradictions today. This is something like the internationalism for export which is very popular today with ardent—oh, so ardent!—internationalists and Marxists who sympathise with every manifestation of internationalism—in the enemy camp, anywhere, but not at home, not among their allies; they sympathise with democracy—when it remains an "allied" promise; they sympathise with "the self-determination of nations", but only *not* of those dependent on the nation which has the honour of having the sympathiser among its citizens. In a word, it is one of the 1,001 varieties of hypocrisy.

Can it be denied, however, that a new phase of capitalism is "imaginable" in the abstract *after* imperialism, namely, ultra-imperialism? No, it cannot. Such a phase can be imagined. But in practice this means becoming an opportunist, turning away from the acute problems of the day to dream of the unacute problems of the future. In theory this means refusing to be guided by actual developments, *forsaking* them arbitrarily for such dreams. There is no doubt that the trend of development is *towards* a single world trust absorbing all enterprises without exception and all states without exception. But this development proceeds in such circumstances, at such a pace, through such contradictions, conflicts and upheavals—not only economic but political, national, etc.— that inevitably imperialism will burst and capitalism will be transformed into its opposite *long before* one world trust materialises, before the "ultra-imperialist", world-wide amalgamation of national finance capitals takes place.

V. Ilyin

December 1915

First published in *Pravda* No. 17, January 21, 1927

Published according to the manuscript

OPPORTUNISM AND THE COLLAPSE
OF THE SECOND INTERNATIONAL [8]

I

Has the Second International really ceased to exist? This is being stubbornly denied by its most authoritative representatives, like Kautsky and Vandervelde. Their point of view is that, save for the rupture of relations, nothing has really happened; all is quite well.

To get at the truth of the matter, let us turn to the *Manifesto of the Basle Congress* of 1912, which applies particularly to the present imperialist world war and which was accepted by all the socialist parties of the world. No socialist, be it noted, will dare in theory deny the necessity of making a concrete, historical appraisal of every war.

Now that war has broken out, neither the avowed opportunists nor the Kautskyites dare repudiate the Basle Manifesto or compare its demands with the conduct of the socialist parties during the war. Why? Because the Manifesto completely exposes both.

There is not a single word in the Basle Manifesto about the defence of the fatherland, or about the difference between a war of aggression and a war of defence; there is nothing in it at all about what the opportunists and Kautskyites* of Germany and of the Quadruple Alliance [9] at all crossroads are now dinning into the ears of the world. Nor could it have said anything of the sort, because what it does say absolutely rules out the use of such concepts. It makes a highly concrete reference to the series of political

---

* This does not refer to the personalities of Kautsky's followers in Germany, but to the international type of pseudo-Marxist who vacillates between opportunism and radicalism, but is in reality only a fig-leaf for opportunism.

and economic conflicts which had for decades been preparing the ground for the present war, and which had become quite apparent in 1912, and which brought about the war in 1914. The Manifesto recalls the Russo-Austrian conflict for "hegemony in the Balkans"; the conflicts between Britain, France and Germany (between *all* these countries!) over their "policy of conquest in Asia Minor"; the Austro-Italian conflict over the "striving for domination" in Albania, etc. In short, the Manifesto defines all these as conflicts emanating from "capitalist imperialism". Thus, the Manifesto very clearly recognises the predatory, imperialist, reactionary, slave-driving character of the present war, i.e., a character which makes the idea of defending the fatherland theoretical nonsense and a practical absurdity. The big sharks are fighting each other to gobble up other peoples' "fatherlands". The Manifesto draws the inevitable conclusions from undisputed historical facts: the war "cannot be justified on the slightest pretext of its being in the interest of the people"; it is being prepared "for the sake of the capitalists' profits and the ambitions of dynasties". It would be a "crime" for the workers to "shoot each other down". That is what the Manifesto says.

The epoch of capitalist imperialism is one of ripe and rotten-ripe capitalism, which is about to collapse, and which is mature enough to make way for socialism. The period between 1789 and 1871 was one of progressive capitalism, when the overthrow of feudalism and absolutism, and liberation from the foreign yoke were on history's agenda. "Defence of the fatherland", i.e., defence against oppression, was permissible on these grounds, and on these *alone*. The term would be applicable even now in a war *against* the imperialist Great Powers, but it would be absurd to apply it to a war *between* the imperialist Great Powers, a war to decide who gets the biggest piece of the Balkan countries, Asia Minor, etc. It is not surprising, therefore, that the "socialists" who advocate "defence of the fatherland" in the present war shun the Basle Manifesto as a thief shuns the scene of his crime. For the Manifesto proves them to be social-chauvinists, i.e., socialists in words, but chauvinists in deeds, who are helping "their own" bourgeoisie to rob other countries and enslave other nations. That is the very substance of chauvinism—to defend one's "own" fatherland even when its acts are aimed at enslaving other peoples' fatherlands.

Recognition that a war is being fought for national liberation implies one set of tactics; its recognition as an imperialist war, another. The Manifesto clearly points to the latter. The war, it says, "will bring on an economic and political crisis", which must be "utilised", not to lessen the crisis, not to defend the fatherland, but, on the contrary, to "*rouse*" the masses and "hasten the downfall of capitalist rule". It is impossible to hasten something for which historical conditions are not yet mature. The Manifesto declares that social revolution is *possible*, that the conditions for it *have matured*, and that it will break out precisely *in connection* with war. Referring to the examples of the *Paris Commune and the Revolution of 1905* in Russia, i.e., examples of mass strikes and of civil war, the Manifesto declares that "the ruling classes" fear "a proletarian revolution". It is sheer falsehood to claim, as Kautsky does, that the socialist attitude to the *present* war has not been defined. This question was not merely discussed, but decided in Basle, where the tactics of revolutionary proletarian mass struggle were recognised.

It is downright hypocrisy to ignore the Basle Manifesto altogether, or in its most essential parts, and to quote instead the speeches of leaders, or the resolutions of various parties, which, in the first place, *antedate* the Basle Congress, secondly, were not decisions adopted by the parties of the whole world, and thirdly, applied to various *possible* wars, but never to the present war. The point is that the epoch of national wars between the big European powers has been superseded by an epoch of imperialist wars between them, and that the Basle Manifesto had to recognise this fact officially for the first time.

It would be a mistake to regard the Basle Manifesto as an empty threat, a collection of platitudes, as so much hot air. Those whom the Manifesto exposes would like to have it that way. But it is not true. The Manifesto is but the fruit of the great propaganda work carried on throughout the entire epoch of the Second International; it is but the summary of all that the socialists had disseminated among the masses in the hundreds of thousands of speeches, articles and manifestos in all languages. It merely reiterates what *Jules Guesde*, for example, wrote in 1899, when he castigated socialist ministerialism in the event of war: he wrote of war provoked by the "capitalist pirates" (*En Garde!*, p. 175); it merely repeats what *Kautsky* wrote in 1909 in his *Road to Power*, where he admitted that the "peaceful" epoch was over and that the epoch of wars and revolutions was on. To represent the Basle Manifesto as so much talk, or as a mistake, is to regard as mere talk, or as a mistake, everything the socialists have done in the last twenty-five years. The opportunists and the Kautskyites find the contradiction between the Manifesto and its non-application so intolerable because it lays bare the profound contradictions in the work of the Second International. The relatively "peaceful" character of the period between 1871 and 1914 served to foster opportunism first as a *mood*, then as a *trend*, until finally it formed a *group or stratum* among the labour bureaucracy and petty-bourgeois fellow-travellers. These elements were able to gain control of the labour movement only by paying lip-service to revolutionary aims and revolutionary tactics. They were able to win the confidence of the masses only by their protestations that all this "peaceful" work served to *prepare* the proletarian revolution. This contradiction was a boil which just had to burst, and burst it has. Here is the question: is it worth trying, as Kautsky and Co. are doing, to force the pus back into the body for the sake of "unity" (with the pus), or should the pus be removed as quickly and as thoroughly as possible, regardless of the pang of pain caused by the process, to help bring about the complete recovery of the body of the labour movement.

Those who voted for war credits, entered cabinets and advocated defence of the fatherland in 1914-15 have patently betrayed socialism. Only hypocrites will deny it. This betrayal must be explained.

II

It would be absurd to regard the whole question as one of personalities. What has opportunism to do with it when men like *Plekhanov* and *Guesde*, etc.?—asks *Kautsky* (*Die Neue Zeit*, May 28, 1915). What has opportunism to do with it when *Kautsky*, etc.?—replies *Axelrod* on behalf of the opportunists of the Quadruple Alliance (*Die Krise der Sozialdemokratie*, Zurich, 1915, p. 21). This is a complete farce. *If the crisis of the whole movement is to be explained, an examination must be made, firstly, of the economic significance of the present policy; secondly, its underlying ideas; and thirdly, its connection with the history of the various trends in the socialist movement.*

What is the economic substance of defencism in the war of 1914-15? The bourgeoisie of *all* the big powers are waging the war to divide and exploit the world, and oppress other nations. A few crumbs of the bourgeoisie's huge profits may come the way of the small group of labour bureaucrats, labour aristocrats, and petty-bourgeois fellow-travellers. Social-chauvinism and opportunism have the same class basis, namely, the alliance of a small section of privileged workers with "their" national bourgeoisie *against* the working-class masses; the alliance between the lackeys of the bourgeoisie and the bourgeoisie *against* the class the latter is exploiting.

Opportunism and social-chauvinism have the same political content, namely, class collaboration, repudiation of the dictatorship of the proletariat, repudiation of revolutionary action, unconditional acceptance of bourgeois legality, confidence in the bourgeoisie and lack of confidence in the proletariat. *Social chauvinism is the direct continuation and consummation of British liberal-labour politics, of Millerandism and Bernsteinism.*[10]

The struggle between the two main trends in the labour movement—revolutionary socialism and opportunist socialism—fills the entire period from 1889 to 1914. Even today there are two main trends on the attitude to war in every country. Let us drop the bourgeois and opportunist habit of referring to personalities. Let us take the *trends* in a number of countries. Let us take ten European countries: Germany, Britain, Russia, Italy, Holland, Sweden, Bulgaria, Switzerland, Belgium and France. In the first eight the division into opportunist and revolutionary trends corresponds to the division into social-chauvinists and internationalists. In Germany the strongholds of social-chauvinism are *Sozialistische Monatshefte*[11] and Legien and Co.; in

Britain the Fabians[12] and the Labour Party [13] (the I.L.P. [14] has always been allied with them and has supported their organ, and in this bloc it has always been weaker than the social-chauvinists, whereas three-sevenths of the B.S.P. [15] are internationalists); in Russia this trend is represented by *Nasha Zarya*[16] (now *Nashe Dyelo*), by the Organising Committee, [17] and by the Duma group led by Chkheidze; in Italy it is represented by the reformists with Bissolati at their head; in Holland, by Troelstra's party; in Sweden, by the majority of the Party led by Branting; in Bulgaria, by the so-called "Shiroki" [18] socialists; in Switzerland by Greulich and Co. In *all* these countries it is the revolutionary Social-Democrats who have voiced a more or less vigorous protest against social-chauvinism. France and Belgium are the two exceptions; there internationalism also exists, but is very weak.

Social-chauvinism is opportunism in its finished form. It is quite ripe for an open, frequently vulgar, alliance with the bourgeoisie and the general staffs. It is this alliance that gives it great power and a monopoly of the legal press and of deceiving the masses. *It is absurd to go on regarding opportunism as an inner-party phenomenon.* It is ridiculous to think of carrying out the Basle resolution together with David, Legien, Hyndman, Plekhanov and Webb. Unity with the social-chauvinists means unity with one's "own" national bourgeoisie, which exploits other nations; it means splitting the international proletariat. This does not mean that an immediate break with the opportunists is possible everywhere; it means only that historically this break is imminent; that it is necessary and inevitable for the revolutionary struggle of the proletariat; that history, which has led us from "peaceful" capitalism to imperialist capitalism, has paved the way for this break. *Volentem ducunt fata, nolentem trahunt.**

III

This is very well understood by the shrewd representatives of the bourgeoisie. That is why they are so lavish in their praise of the present socialist parties, headed by the "de-

---

* The fates lead the willing, drag the unwilling.—*Ed.*

fenders of the fatherland", i.e., the defenders of imperialist plunder. That is why the social-chauvinist leaders are rewarded by their governments either with ministerial posts (in France and Britain), or with a monopoly of unhindered legal existence (in Germany and Russia). That is why in Germany, where the Social-Democratic Party was strongest and where its transformation into a national-liberal *counter-revolutionary* labour party has been most obvious, things have got to the stage where the public prosecutor qualifies the struggle between the "minority" and the "majority" as "incitement to class hatred"! That is why the greatest concern of the clever opportunists is to retain the former "unity" of the old parties, which did the bourgeoisie so many good turns in 1914 and 1915. The views held by these opportunists in all countries of the world were expounded with commendable frankness by a German Social-Democrat in an article signed "Monitor" which appeared in April 1915, in the reactionary magazine *Preussische Jahrbücher*. [19] Monitor thinks that it would be very dangerous for the bourgeoisie if the Social-Democrats were to move *still further to the right*. "It must preserve its character as a labour party with socialist ideals; for the day it gives this up a new party will arise and adopt the programme the old party had disavowed, giving it a still more radical formulation" (*Preussische Jahrbücher*, 1915, No. 4, pp. 50-51).

Monitor hit the nail on the head. That is just what the British Liberals and the French Radicals have always wanted—phrases with a revolutionary ring to deceive the masses and induce them to place their trust in the Lloyd Georges, the Sembats, the Renaudels, the Legiens, and the Kautskys, in the men capable of preaching "defence of the fatherland" in a predatory war.

But Monitor represents only one variety of opportunism, the frank, crude, cynical variety. Others act with stealth, subtlety, and "honesty". Engels once said that for the working class "honest" opportunists were the greatest danger. [20] Here is one example.

Kautsky wrote in *Die Neue Zeit* (November 26, 1915) as follows: "The opposition against the majority is growing; the masses are in an opposition mood.... After the war [only *after* the war? —*N. L.*] class antagonisms will become so sharp that radicalism will gain the upper hand among the masses.... After the war [only *after* the war? —*N. L.*] we shall be menaced with the desertion of the radical elements from the Party and their influx into the party of anti-parliamentary [?? meaning extra-parliamentary] mass action.... Thus, our Party is splitting up into two extreme camps which have nothing in common." To preserve unity, Kautsky tries to persuade the majority in the Reichstag to allow the minority to make a few radical parliamentary speeches. That means Kautsky wants to use a few radical parliamentary speeches to reconcile the revolutionary masses with the opportunists, who have "nothing in common" with revolution, who have long had the leadership of the trade unions, and now, relying on their close alliance with the bourgeoisie and the government, have also captured the leadership of the Party. What essential difference is there between this and Monitor's "programme"? There is none, save for the sugary phrases which prostitute Marxism.

At a meeting of the Reichstag group on March 18, 1915, *Wurm*, a Kautskyite, "warned" against "pulling the strings too taut. There is growing opposition among the workers' masses to the majority of the group, we must keep to the Marxist [?! probably a misprint: this should read "the Monitor"] Centre" (*Klassenkampf gegen den Krieg! Material zum Fall Liebknecht.* Als Manuskript gedruckt,* p. 67). Thus we find that the revolutionary sentiment of the *masses* was admitted as a *fact* on behalf of *all* the Kautskyites (the so-called Centre) *as early as March, 1915*!! But eight and a half months later, Kautsky again comes forward with the proposal to "reconcile" the militant masses with the opportunist, counter-revolutionary party —and he wants to do this with a few revolutionary-sounding phrases!!

War is often useful in exposing what is rotten and discarding the conventionalities.

Let us compare the British Fabians with the German Kautskyites. Here is what a *real* Marxist, Frederick Engels, wrote about the former on January 18, 1893: "...a band of careerists who have understanding enough to realise the inevi-

---

* *The Class Struggle Against the War. Material on the Liebknecht Case.* Printed for private circulation only.—*Ed.*

5*

tability of the social revolution, but who could not possibly
entrust this gigantic task to the raw proletariat alone....
Fear of the revolution is their fundamental principle"
(Letters to Sorge, p. 390). [21]

And on November 11, 1893, he wrote: "...these haughty
bourgeois who kindly condescend to emancipate the proletariat from above if only it would have sense enough to
realise that such a raw, uneducated mass cannot liberate
itself and can achieve nothing without the kindness of these
clever lawyers, writers and sentimental old women" (ibid.,
p. 401). [22]

In theory Kautsky looks down upon the Fabians with the
contempt of a Pharisee for a poor sinner, for he swears by
"Marxism". But what actual difference is there between the
two. Both signed the Basle Manifesto, and both treated it
as Wilhelm II treated Belgian neutrality. But Marx all his
life castigated those who strove to quench the revolutionary
spirit of the workers.

Kautsky has put forward his new theory of "ultra-imperialism" in opposition to the revolutionary Marxists. By
this he means that the "rivalries of national finance capitals" are to be superseded by the "joint exploitation of the
world by international finance capital" (Die Neue Zeit,
April 30, 1915). But he adds: "We do not as yet have sufficient data to decide whether this new phase of capitalism
is possible." On the grounds of the mere assumption of a
"new phase", which he does not even dare declare definitely
"possible", the inventor of this "phase" rejects his own revolutionary declarations as well as the revolutionary tasks
and revolutionary tactics of the proletariat—rejects them
now, in the "phase" of a crisis, which has already broken out,
the phase of war and the unprecedented aggravation of class
antagonisms! Is this not Fabianism at its most abominable?

Axelrod, the leader of the Russian Kautskyites, says,
"The centre of gravity of the problem of internationalising
the proletarian movement for emancipation is the internationalisation of everyday practice"; for example, "labour
protection and insurance legislation must become the object
of the workers' international organisation and action"
(Axelrod, The Crisis of Social-Democracy, Zurich, 1915,
pp. 39-40). Not only Legien, David and the Webbs, but even

Lloyd George himself, and Naumann, Briand and Milyukov would quite obviously subscribe to such "internationalism". As in 1912, Axelrod is quite prepared to utter the most revolutionary phrases for the very distant future, if the future International "comes out [against the governments in the event of war] and raises a revolutionary storm". How brave we are! But when it comes to supporting and developing the incipient revolutionary ferment among the masses *now*, Axelrod says that these tactics of revolutionary mass action "would be justified to some extent if we were on the very eve of the social revolution, as was the case in Russia, for example, where the student demonstrations of 1901 heralded the approaching decisive battles against absolutism". At the present moment, however, all that is "utopia", "Bakuninism", etc. This is fully in the spirit of Kolb, David, Südekum and Legien.

What dear old Axelrod forgets is that in 1901 nobody in Russia knew, or could have known, that the first "decisive battle" would take place four years later—please note, *four* years later—and that it would be "*in*decisive". Nevertheless, we revolutionary Marxists alone were right at that time: we ridiculed the Krichevskys and Martynovs, who called for an immediate assault. We merely advised the workers to kick out the opportunists everywhere and to exert every effort to support, sharpen and extend the demonstrations and other mass revolutionary action. The present situation in Europe is absolutely similar. It would be absurd to call for an "immediate" assault; but it would be a shame to call oneself a Social-Democrat and not to advise the workers to break with the opportunists and exert all their efforts to strengthen, deepen, extend and sharpen the incipient revolutionary movement and demonstrations. Revolution never falls ready-made from the skies, and when revolutionary ferment starts no one can say whether and when it will lead to a "real", "genuine" revolution. Kautsky and Axelrod are giving the workers old, shop-worn, counter-revolutionary advice. Kautsky and Axelrod are feeding the masses with hopes that the *future* International will surely be revolutionary, but they are doing this for the sole purpose of protecting, camouflaging and prettifying the *present* domination of the counter-revolutionary elements—the

Legiens, Davids, Vanderveldes and Hyndmans. Is it not
obvious that "unity" with Legien and Co. is the best means
of preparing the "future" revolutionary International?

"It would be folly to strive to convert the world war into
civil war," declares *David*, the leader of the German opportunists (*Die Sozialdemokratie und der Weltkrieg*, 1915,
p. 172), in reply to the manifesto of the Central Committee
of our Party, November 1, 1914. This manifesto says,
inter alia:

> "However difficult such a transformation may seem at any given
> moment, socialists will never relinquish systematic, persistent and
> undeviating preparatory work in this direction now that war has
> become a fact." *

(This passage is also quoted by David, p. 171.) A month
before David's book appeared our Party published its
resolutions defining "systematic preparation" as follows:
(1) refusal to vote for credits; (2) disruption of the class
truce; (3) formation of illegal organisations; (4) support
for solidarity manifestations in the trenches; (5) support
for all revolutionary mass action.**

David is almost as brave as Axelrod. In 1912, he did not
think that reference to the Paris Commune in anticipation
of the war was "folly".

Plekhanov, a typical representative of the Entente social-
chauvinists, takes the same view of revolutionary tactics
as David. He calls them a "farcical dream". But listen to
Kolb, an avowed opportunist, who wrote: "The consequence
of the tactics of Liebknecht's followers would be that the
struggle within the German nation would be brought up to
boiling point" (*Die Sozialdemokratie am Scheidewege*, p. 50).

But what is a struggle brought up to boiling point if
not civil war?

If our Central Committee's tactics, which broadly coin-
cide with those of the Zimmerwald Left, [23] were "folly",
"dreams", "adventurism", "Bakuninism" —as David, Plekhanov, Axelrod, Kautsky and others have asserted —they

---

* See present edition, Vol, 21, "The War and Russian Social-
Democracy". —*Ed.*
** Ibid., Vol. 21, "The Conference of the R.S.D.L.P. Groups
Abroad". —*Ed.*

could never lead to a "struggle within a nation", let alone to a struggle brought up to boiling point. Nowhere in the world have anarchist phrases brought about a struggle within a nation. But the facts indicate that precisely in 1915, as a result of the crisis produced by the war, revolutionary ferment among the masses is on the increase, and there is a spread of strikes and political demonstrations in Russia, strikes in Italy and in Britain, and hunger demonstrations and political demonstrations in Germany. Are these not the beginnings of revolutionary mass struggles?

The sum and substance of Social-Democracy's practical programme in this war is to support, develop, extend and sharpen mass revolutionary action, and to set up illegal organisations, for without them there is no way of telling the truth to the masses of people even in the "free" countries. The rest is either lies or mere verbiage, whatever its trappings of opportunist or pacifist theory.*

When we are told that these "Russian tactics" (David's expression) are not suitable for Europe, we usually reply by pointing to the facts. On October 30, a delegation of Berlin women comrades called on the Party's Presidium in Berlin, and stated that "now that we have a large organising apparatus it is much easier to distribute illegal pamphlets and leaflets and to organise 'banned meetings' than it was under the Anti-Socialist Law.... Ways and means are not lacking, but the will evidently is " (*Berner Tagwacht*, [25] 1915, No. 271).

Had these bad comrades been led astray by the Russian "sectarians", etc.? Is it these comrades who represent the real *masses*, or is it Legien and Kautsky? Legien, who in his report on January 27, 1915, fumed against the "anarchistic" idea of forming underground organisations; or Kautsky,

---

* At the International Women's Congress held in Berne in March 1915, the representatives of the Central Committee of our Party urged that it was absolutely necessary to set up illegal organisations. This was rejected. The British women laughed at this proposal and praised British "liberty". But a few months later British newspapers, like the *Labour Leader*, [24] reached us with blank spaces, and then came the news of police raids, confiscation of pamphlets, arrests, and Draconian sentences imposed on comrades who had spoken in Britain about peace, nothing but peace!

who has become such a counter-revolutionary that on November 26, *four* days before the 10,000-strong demonstration in Berlin, he denounced street demonstrations as "adventurism"!!

We've had enough of empty talk, and of prostituted "Marxism" *à la* Kautsky! After twenty-five years of the Second International, after the Basle Manifesto, the workers will no longer believe fine words. Opportunism is rotten-ripe; it has been transformed into social-chauvinism and has definitely deserted to the bourgeois camp. It has severed its spiritual and political ties with Social-Democracy. It will also break off its organisational ties. The workers are already demanding "illegal" pamphlets and "banned" meetings, i.e., underground organisations to support the revolutionary mass movement. Only when "war against war" is conducted on these lines does it cease to be empty talk and becomes Social-Democratic work. In spite of all difficulties, set-backs, mistakes, delusions and interruptions, this work will lead humanity to the victorious proletarian revolution.

Published in January 1916
in *Vorbote* No. 1
Signed: *N. Lenin*

First published in Russian
in 1929 in the second and
third editions of Lenin's
Collected Works, Vol. XIX

Published according to
the text in *Vorbote*
Translated from the German

DRAFT RESOLUTION ON THE CONVOCATION OF THE SECOND SOCIALIST CONFERENCE [26]

The Bureau (I.S.C.[27]), having conferred with a number of representatives of several countries, resolves:

to convene the second *conference* of socialists supporting the Zimmerwald decisions.

Agenda:

(1) struggle against war;

(2) international unification of socialists opposing war and nationalism;

(3) practical measures of organisation, propaganda and struggle against governments;

(4) development of Zimmerwald decisions.

To set the date of its convocation for April 15, 1916.

To publish the present decision (altering the date to March 15 in the notice).

To call on all socialist organisations supporting the Zimmerwald decisions to discuss all the items on the agenda and the draft resolutions. [28] The drafts (signed by 2-3 delegates) to be published in *Berner Tagwacht*.

Written between January 23 and 26 (February 5 and 8), 1916

Published for the first time

Published according to the manuscript

FOR THE CONFERENCE TO BE HELD
ON APRIL 24, 1916
PROPOSAL OF THE DELEGATION [29]

1. Only representatives of political or trade union organisations or individuals supporting the decisions of the Zimmerwald Conference shall be allowed to attend.

2. From countries where official parties or trade union organisations are affiliated with the I.S.C., only representatives appointed by these organisations shall be allowed to attend.

3. From countries where official parties or trade union organisations are not affiliated with the I.S.C., representatives shall be allowed to attend only from organisations and groups which:

(a) in the given country campaign orally or in writing in the spirit of the Zimmerwald decisions;

(b) support the I.S.C. by their activities.

4. Individuals shall be admitted only as an exception and only with voice but no vote.

5. Final decisions in disputes over the validity of credentials shall be made, after hearing the motives and taking account of the circumstances, by a 9-man commission elected by the conference, which shall include 4 members of the I.S.C.

6. The conference shall establish the voting procedure. [Amendment, not to be published; entered in the minutes:

Comrades who were present at Zimmerwald have *the right* ("le droit"—in the French text) to participate in the second conference with a voice but no vote.]

Written in German between January 23
and 26 (February 5 and 8), 1916

Published on February 29, 1916
in *Bulletin. Internationale
Sozialistische Kommission zu Bern* No. 3

Published in Russian for the first time
in the 4th Russian edition
of Lenin's *Collected Works*

Published according to
the manuscript
Translated from the German

SPEECH DELIVERED
AT AN INTERNATIONAL MEETING IN BERNE, FEBRUARY 8, 1916 [30]

Comrades! The European war has been raging for more than eighteen months. With every passing day, and month, it becomes clearer and clearer to the mass of the workers that the Zimmerwald Manifesto [31] expressed the truth when it declared that talk about "defence of the fatherland" and suchlike phrases are nothing but a capitalist fraud. It is becoming more evident every day that this is *a war between capitalists*, *between big robbers*, who are quarrelling over who is to get the largest slice, who is to plunder the greatest number of countries, and to suppress and enslave the greatest number of nations.

It may sound incredible, especially to Swiss comrades, but it is true, nevertheless, that *in Russia*, too, it is not only murderous tsarism, or the capitalists, but also a section of the so-called, or former, socialists who are saying that Russia is fighting a "defensive war", that she is only fighting against the German invasion. But the whole world knows that for decades tsarism has been oppressing more than a hundred million people belonging to other nationalities in Russia, and that for decades Russia has been pursuing a predatory policy towards China, Persia, Armenia and Galicia. *Neither Russia, nor Germany, nor any other Great Power for that matter has any right to claim that it is waging a "defensive war"*: all the Great Powers are waging a capitalist imperialist war, a predatory war, a war for the oppression of small and foreign nations, a war for the profits of the capitalists, who have been converting proletarian blood and the horrible sufferings of the masses into the pure gold of their immense fortunes.

Four years ago, in November 1912, when it had become quite clear that war was in the offing, representatives of the socialist parties of the world met at the International Socialist Congress in Basle. Even at that time there was no room for doubt that the impending war would be a war between the Great Powers, between these great plunderers and that the responsibility would fall upon the governments and the capitalist class of *all* the Great Powers. This truth was openly stated in the Basle Manifesto, which was adopted *unanimously* by the socialist parties of the world. *The Basle Manifesto says nothing at all about a "defensive war" or "defence of the fatherland".* It castigates the governments and the bourgeoisie of *all* the Great Powers, without exception. It says openly that war would be the greatest of crimes, that the workers consider it a crime to shoot at each other, and that the horrors of war and the indignation these would rouse among the workers would inevitably lead to a *proletarian revolution*.

When the war actually broke out it became evident that its character had been correctly defined at Basle. But the socialist and labour organisations were not unanimous in carrying out the Basle decisions; they split. We find that the socialist and labour organisations are now split into two big camps in all countries of the world. The smaller section, the leaders, functionaries and officials, have betrayed socialism and have sided with their governments. The other section, to which the mass of class-conscious workers belong, continues to gather its forces and to fight against the war and for the proletarian revolution.

The views of this latter section were expressed in the Zimmerwald Manifesto, to mention one document.

In Russia, from the very beginning of the war, the *workers' deputies* in the Duma waged a determined revolutionary struggle against the war and the tsarist monarchy. Five workers' deputies—Petrovsky, Badayev, Muranov, Shagov and Samoilov—distributed revolutionary leaflets against the war and carried on persistent revolutionary agitation. The tsarist government ordered the arrest of these five deputies; they were tried and sentenced to exile in Siberia for life. The leaders of the working class of Russia have languished in Siberia for months, but their cause has not been defeated; their work is being continued along the same lines by the class-conscious workers of all Russia.

Comrades! You have heard speakers from various countries who have told you about the workers' revolutionary struggle against the war. I merely want to add another example, that of the United States of America, the biggest and richest country. Its capitalists are now making enormous profits out of the European war. And they are also campaigning for war. They are saying that America, too, must prepare to enter the war, and that hundreds of millions of the people's dollars must be siphoned off into new armaments, into armaments without end. A section of the socialists in America have also responded to this false, criminal call. Let me read a statement by Comrade *Eugene Debs*, a most popular leader of the American socialists, and the presidential candidate of the American Socialist Party.

In the September 11, 1915, issue of the American weekly, *Appeal to Reason*,[32] he says: "*I am not a capitalist soldier; I am a proletarian revolutionist. I do not belong to the regular army of the plutocracy, but to the irregular army of the people. I refuse to obey any command to fight from the ruling class.... I am opposed to every war but one; I am for that war with heart and soul, and that is the world-wide war of the social revolution. In that war I am prepared to fight in any way the ruling class may make necessary....*"

This is what *Eugene Debs*, the American Bebel, the beloved leader of the American workers, is telling them.

This goes to show once again, comrades, that *the rallying of the working class forces is truly under way in all countries of the world*. War inflicts horrible sufferings on the people, but we must not, and we have no reason at all, to despair of the future.

The millions of victims who will fall in the war, and as a consequence of the war, will not have died in vain. The millions who are starving, the millions who are sacrificing their lives in the trenches, are not only suffering, they are also gathering strength; they are pondering over the real causes of the war; they are becoming more determined and are acquiring a clearer revolutionary understanding. In *all* countries of the world there is growing discontent among the masses and greater ferment; there are strikes, demonstrations and protests against the war. *This is an earnest of the proletarian revolution against capitalism that is bound to follow the European war.*

Berner Tagwacht No. 33,
February 9, 1916

First published in Russian in 1929
in the second and third editions
of Lenin's *Collected Works*, Vol. XIX

Published according to
the text in *Berner Tagwacht*

Translated from the German

THE TASKS OF THE OPPOSITION IN FRANCE
LETTER TO COMRADE SAFAROV

February 10, 1916

Dear Comrade,

I was forcefully reminded of the burning question of the situation and the tasks of the opposition in France by your deportation from that country, reported, by the way, with a protest even by the chauvinist paper, *La Bataille*,[33] which, however, did not care to tell the truth, namely, that you were deported for sympathising with the opposition.

I saw Bourderon and Merrheim in Zimmerwald. I heard their reports and read about their work in the newspapers. I cannot in the least doubt their sincerity and devotion to the cause of the proletariat. Nevertheless, it is obvious that their tactics are mistaken. Both fear a split more than anything else. The slogan of both Bourderon and Merrheim is not a step, not a word that might lead to a split in the Socialist Party or in the trade unions in France, that might lead to a split in the Second International, to the creation of the Third International.

Nevertheless, the split in the labour and socialist movements throughout the world is a fact. We have two irreconcilable working-class tactics and policies in respect of the war. It is ridiculous to close your eyes to this fact. Any attempt to reconcile the irreconcilable will make all our work futile. In Germany, even Deputy Otto Rühle, a comrade of Liebknecht's, has openly admitted that a split in the party is inevitable, because its present majority, the official "leaders" of the German party, have gone over to the bourgeoisie. The arguments advanced against Rühle and against a split by the so-called representatives of the "Centre" or "marsh" (*le marais*), by Kautsky and *Vorwärts*,[34] are nothing but lies and hypocrisy, however "well-intentioned" such hypocrisy may be. Kautsky and *Vorwärts* cannot deny, and do not even attempt to deny, that the majority of the German party is in fact carrying out the policy of the *bourgeoisie*. Unity with such a majority is doing harm to the working class. It means subordinating the working class to the bourgeoisie of its "own" nation; it means a split in the international working class. Actually Rühle is quite right; there are *two parties* in Germany. One, the official party, is carrying out the policy of the bourgeoisie. The other, the minority, is publishing illegal leaflets, organising demonstrations, etc. We see the same thing all over the world, and the impotent diplomats, or the "marsh", such as Kautsky in Germany, Longuet in France, and Martov and Trotsky in Russia, are doing the labour movement great harm by their insistence upon a *fictitious* unity, thereby *hindering* the now imminent unification of the *opposition* in all countries and the creation of the Third International. In Britain even a moderate paper like the *Labour Leader* publishes Russell Williams' letters urging the necessity for a *split* with the trade union "leaders" and with the Labour Party, which, he says, has sold out the interests of the working class. A number of members of the Independent Labour Party have declared in the press that they sympathise with Russell Williams. In Russia, even Trotsky, the "conciliator", is now compelled to admit that a split is inevitable with the "patriots", i.e., the party of the Organising Committee, the O.C., who approve of workers' participating in the war industries committees.[35] It is only false pride that compels Trotsky to continue to defend "unity" with Chkheidze's Duma group, which is the best friend, shield and protector of the "patriots" and the O.C.

Even in the United States of America there is actually a complete split. Some socialists in that country want an army, and "preparedness", and war. Others, including Eugene Debs, the most popular leader of the workers and the Socialist Party's presidential candidate, want civil war against the war of nations!

Look at what Bourderon and Merrheim are doing! They say they are opposed to a split. But read the resolution which Bourderon moved at the Congress of the French Socialist Party.[36] It demands the withdrawal of the socialists from the Cabinet!! The resolution bluntly "disapproves" of the C.A.P. and the G.P. (C.A.P.=Com. Adm. Perm., G.P.=Groupe Parlem.*)!!! It is as clear as daylight that the adoption of such a resolution would cause a split in both the Socialist Party *and* the trade unions, because Messrs. Renaudel, Sembat, Jouhaux and Co. would never accept that.

Bourderon and Merrheim share the error, the weakness and the timidity of the *majority* of the Zimmerwald Conference. On the one hand, this majority *indirectly* calls for *revolutionary* struggle in its Manifesto, but is afraid to do so openly. On the one hand, it declares that the capitalists of *all* countries are *lying* when they talk about "defence of the fatherland" in the present war. On the other hand, the majority was afraid to add the obvious truth which, in any case, every thinking worker will add for himself, that not only are the capitalists *lying*, but so also are Renaudel, Sembat, Longuet, Hyndman, Kautsky, Plekhanov and Co.! Once again the majority of the Zimmerwald Conference *wants* to make peace with Vandervelde, Huysmans, Renaudel and Co. This is *harmful* to the working class, and the Zimmerwald Left did the right thing in *openly* telling the workers the truth.

Look at the hypocrisy of *les socialistes-chauvins*: in France they praise the *German minorité*, in Germany, the *French*!!

What enormous significance there would be in the action of the French opposition if it straightforwardly, fearlessly, openly told the world: We are in agreement *only* with the *German* opposition, *only with Rühle* and his associates!! Only with those who fearlessly sever all connections with overt and covert social-chauvinism, *socialisme chauvin*, i.e., with all the "defenders of the fatherland" in the present war!! We ourselves *are not afraid* to break with the French "patriots" who call the defence of colonies "defence of the fatherland", and we urge socialists and syndicalists in all countries *to do the same*!! We extend our hand to Otto Rühle and Liebknecht, *only* to them and their associates; and we denounce the French and the German *majorité* and *le marais*. We proclaim a great international unification

---

* The French abbreviations for Permanent Administrative Commission and parliamentary group.—*Ed.*

of socialists all over the world who in this war repudiate
"defence of the fatherland" as a fraud, and who are engaged
in campaigning and preparing for the world proletarian
revolution!

Such an appeal would be of tremendous importance. It
would disperse the hypocrites, expose and unmask the
international fraud, and would give a great impetus to the
rallying of workers all over the world who have *really*
remained loyal to internationalism.

Anarchist phrase-mongering has always done a lot of
harm in France. But now the anarchist-patriots, the anarch-
ist-*chauvins*, like Kropotkin, Grave, Cornelissen and the
other knights of *La Bataille Chauviniste* will help to cure
very many workers of anarchist phrase-mongering. Down
with the socialist-patriots and socialist-*chauvins* and down
also with anarchist-patriots and anarchist-*chauvins*! This
call *will* be echoed in the hearts of the workers of France. Not
anarchist phrase-mongering about revolution, but sustained,
earnest, tenacious, persistent, systematic work of *everywhere* creating illegal organisations among the *workers*, of
spreading *uncensored*, i.e., illegal, literature, of preparing
the movement of the *masses* against their governments. This
is what the working class of all countries needs!

It is not true to say that "the French are incapable" of
carrying on illegal work regularly. It is *not* true! The French
quickly learned to hide in the trenches; they will soon learn
to do illegal work in the *new* conditions and systematically
to build up a *revolutionary mass* movement. I have faith
in the French revolutionary proletariat. It will also stimulate the French opposition.

> With best wishes,
>   Yours,
>   *Lenin*

P.S. I suggest that the French comrades publish a translation of this letter (in full) *as a separate leaflet.*[37]

Published in French as
a separate leaflet in 1916

First published in Russian
in 1924 in *Proletarskaya
Revolutsia* No. 4 (27)

Published according to
the manuscript

HAVE THE ORGANISING COMMITTEE
AND THE CHKHEIDZE GROUP
A POLICY OF THEIR OWN?

In their magazine,[38] and more definitely in their report to the International Socialist Committee (No. 2 of the *Bulletin* which appeared in German on November 27, 1915[39]), the adherents of the Organising Committee (O.C.) assure the public that the Chkheidze group[40] and the O.C. have a policy of their own, which is completely internationalist and differs from the policy of *Nashe Dyelo*. This is flagrantly untrue. First of all, since the formation of the O.C. (August 1912), we have witnessed for *many years* the most complete political agreement on all fundamental points, and the closest political co-operation, between the Chkheidze group and the O.C., and the *Nasha Zarya* group; and *only* this group has carried on any systematic work among the masses (the liquidators' daily papers). If there are any real differences between such close "friends", they must be proved, not by words but by weighty facts. *Not a single fact of this kind can be produced*. Secondly, for a *number of years*, from 1912 to 1914, the Chkheidze group and the O.C. have been *Nasha Zarya*'s pawns and have systematically defended its policy (a fact very well known to workers in St. Petersburg and elsewhere) but *never* have they used their influence in any way to change the policy of *Nasha Zarya*, *Luch*,[41] etc.

Nasha Zarya was the only group to act independently on policies concerning the *masses*—for example, the struggle against the "strike fever", the election of leaders of the biggest trade unions (metalworkers and others) and of the most important insurance organisations (the All-Russia Insurance Council); the O.C. and the Chkheidze group merely assisted it, and served it most loyally. Thirdly, there is *not a single fact* in the last eighteen months of the war to testify to any change in the long established relationship between the Chkheidze group and the O.C., and *Nasha Zarya*. On the contrary, the opposite is proved by facts, even of the kind that may be given publicity (most facts of this kind may not). It is a fact that in Russia there is *not a single instance* of either the O.C. or the Chkheidze group opposing the policy of *Nashe Dyelo*; and it would take more than one protest, in fact, a prolonged and victorious struggle, to effect a real change of policy; for *Nashe Dyelo* is a political magnitude fostered by liberal connections, whereas the O.C. and the Chkheidze group are merely political décor. It is a fact that *Utro* and *Rabocheye Utro*, [42] which follow the *Nashe Dyelo* line most faithfully, demonstrate their political proximity to the Chkheidze group even outwardly and speak in the name of the entire August bloc. It is a fact that the Chkheidze group has been collecting funds for *Rabocheye Utro*. It is a fact that the whole of the Chkheidze group has become a contributor to the Samara social-chauvinist paper *Nash Golos* (see No. 17). It is a fact that Chkhenkeli, a most prominent member of the Chkheidze group, has come out in the press, in the "defencist" or social-chauvinist magazine *Sovremenny Mir*, [43] the magazine published by Plekhanov and Alexinsky, with a declaration of principles quite in the spirit of Plekhanov, *Nashe Dyelo*, Kautsky and Axelrod. We quoted Chkhenkeli's declaration a long time ago, and yet neither the adherents of the O.C. in their magazine, nor Trotsky in his *Nashe Slovo* [44] have dared to defend this declaration, although they have defended and advertised the Chkheidze group. Fourthly, our points are proved by the direct political statements made on behalf of the whole of the Chkheidze group and of the whole of the O.C. Take the most important pronouncements, which have been reprinted in the O.C.'s magazine: the declaration of Chkheidze and Co. and the manifesto of the O.C. Their approach is *identical*, their attitude is the same. Since the O.C. is the supreme governing body of the "August bloc" against our Party, and since the O.C.'s manifesto was printed illegally, which means that it could speak more freely and directly than Chkheidze could in the Duma, let us examine the O.C.'s manifesto.

It is interesting to note, by the way, that this manifesto has already been the subject of a controversy in the German Social-Democratic press, in the Berne Social-Democratic paper. A contributor described the manifesto as "patriotic". This aroused the indignation of the Secretariat of the O.C. Abroad, which published a refutation, declaring that "we, the Secretariat Abroad, are guilty of such patriotism" too, and invited the editors of the paper to act as arbiter, as it were; for this purpose it submitted to them a full German translation of the manifesto. Let us note that the paper's editors are notoriously partial to the O.C. to the point of giving it publicity. What then did these sympathising editors say?

"We have read a manifesto issued by the O.C.," they said (No. 250), "and we must admit that the text may undoubtedly give rise to a misunderstanding and impart to the whole a meaning which was perhaps alien to the authors of the manifesto."

Why have the adherents of the O.C. not reprinted in their magazine this opinion of the editors, whom they had themselves invited to act as arbiters? Because it is the opinion of their friends who have publicly refused to defend them! The opinion was couched in terms of exquisite diplomatic courtesy, which makes it particularly evident that the editors desired to say something "pleasant" to Axelrod and Martov. It turned out that the "pleasantest" thing they could say is: "Perhaps [*only* "perhaps"!] the O.C. did not say what it meant to say; but what it did say 'may undoubtedly give rise to a misunderstanding'"!!

We strongly urge our readers to read the O.C.'s manifesto, which is reproduced in the *Bund's Bulletin* (No. 9). The careful reader will note the following clear and simple facts: (1) the manifesto does not contain a single statement repudiating national defence in the present war as a matter of principle; (2) there is absolutely nothing in the manifesto which "defencists" or social-chauvinists would find unacceptable in principle; (3) there are a number of statements in the manifesto which are completely identical with "defencism", such as, "The proletariat cannot remain indifferent to the impending defeat" (repeating almost word for word what *Rabocheye Utro* said in No. 2: "not indifferent" to "saving the country from defeat"); "the proletariat is vitally interested in national self-preservation"; "a popular revolution" must save the country "from external defeat", etc. Anyone really hostile to social-chauvinism would have said *instead*: The landowners, the tsar and the bourgeoisie are lying; by national self-preservation they mean preserving the Great-Russian oppression of Poland and retaining her by force; they are lying, their talk about saving the "country" from defeat being designed to conceal their desire to "save" their Great-Power privileges and divert the proletariat from the tasks of fighting the *international* bourgeoisie. To admit in one breath the need for the international solidarity of the proletariat of the belligerent countries in this predatory imperialist war and the permissibility of phrases about "saving" *one* of these countries from "defeat" is sheer hypocrisy and signifies that one's declarations are nothing more than idle talk and false oratory. The implication there is that the tactics of the proletariat depend on the military situation of a given country at a given time; if that is the case the French social-chauvinists would also be right in helping to "save" Austria or Turkey from "defeat".

The O.C. Secretariat Abroad writing in the *German* Social-Democratic press (the Berne paper) has put forward yet another sophism which is so shameless, so crude, and so deliberately "set" to catch the Germans in particular, that the adherents of the O.C. wisely refrained from repeating it before the Russian public.

"If it is patriotism," they write *for the benefit of the Germans* in a tone of noble indignation, "to tell the proletariat that revolution is the only means of saving the country from disaster", then we, too, are "patriots", and "we wish the International had many more 'patriots' like this in every Socialist Party; we are sure that Liebknecht, Rosa Luxemburg and Merrheim would be very glad to have many more 'patriots' like these around them to appeal to the German and French workers with manifestos of *this* kind".

This is deliberate misrepresentation; the five secretaries know perfectly well that there is not a hint of any *bourgeois* revolutionary mood or any *bourgeois* social movement striving for revolution for the sake of *victory over the enemy* either in France or Germany, both of which are headed for socialist revolution; in Russia, however, just because she is headed for a *bourgeois*-democratic revolution, *such* a movement does exist, as everybody knows. The five secretaries are trying to deceive the Germans by an amusing sophism: the O.C. and Chkheidze and Co. cannot be *revolutionary chauvinists* in Russia, they argue, because in Europe a combination of revolutionism with chauvinism is an absurdity!

Indeed, it would be an absurdity in Europe. But in Russia, it is a fact. You may reproach the *Prizyv* [45] crowd for being bad bourgeois revolutionaries, but you cannot deny that in their own way they combine chauvinism with revolutionism. The July Conference of the Narodniks in Russia, [46] *Nashe Dyelo* and *Rabocheye Utro* most faithfully take the *Prizyv* attitude in this respect; they, too, combine chauvinism with revolutionism.

The *same* stand is taken by the Chkheidze group in its declaration (pp. 141-43 of the O.C.'s magazine). Chkheidze uses the same chauvinist phrases about the "danger of defeat"; he admits the imperialist character of the war, stands for "peace without annexations", "the general tasks of the entire international proletariat", "the struggle for peace", etc., etc., but so does *Rabocheye Utro*; and so do the petty-bourgeois Russian Narodniks. We read on page 146 of this very magazine of the O.C. that the petty-bourgeois Narodniks have admitted the imperialist character of the war, have adopted the demand for "peace without annexations" and have admitted that socialists (the Narodniks, as well as the *Rabocheye Utro* group wish to be known as socialists) "must strive for an early restoration of the international solidarity of socialist organisations in order to stop the war", etc. The petty-bourgeois Narodniks use all these phrases to camouflage the slogan of "national defence", which they have openly advanced, whereas Chkheidze, the O.C., and *Rabocheye Utro* spell out the same slogan as "save the country from defeat"!

The net result is that Chkheidze and the O.C. have poured out a string of revolutionary phrases, which commit them to nothing at all and which in no way hinder the practical policies of *Prizyv* and *Nashe Dyelo*, but have *hushed up these policies*. In one way or another they support participation in the war industries committees.

What is needed, gentlemen, is less talk about revolution and more clarity, straightforwardness and honesty in the practical policies of today. You *promise* to be revolutionaries, but for the time being you are helping the chauvinists, the bourgeoisie and tsarism: either you openly advocate workers' participation in the war industries committees, or you tacitly defend those who do participate by not fighting them.

Martov may wriggle as much as he likes. Trotsky may shout against our factionalism to cover up his own "expectations" (an old trick of Turgenev's hero! [47]), which are surely non-factional, that someone in Chkheidze's group is "in agreement" with him and swears that he is a Leftist, an internationalist, etc. But facts are facts. There is *not* a hint of any serious political difference not only between the O. C. and the Chkheidze group; there is none even between them and *Rabocheye Utro* or *Prizyv*.

That is why they are all together in opposing our Party *in practice*; that is why they all stand *for* the bourgeois policy of workers' participating in the war industries committees, and are together in siding with the non-party workers and the Narodniks. The verbal reservations and the avowals of "disagreement" made by the "secretaries abroad" is idle talk, which does not affect the real policy of the masses in much the same way as the vows of Südekum, Legien and David that they are "for peace" and "against war" do not absolve them of chauvinism.

Sotsial-Demokrat No. 50,
February 18, 1916

Published according to
the *Sotsial-Demokrat* text

PEACE WITHOUT ANNEXATIONS
AND THE INDEPENDENCE OF POLAND
AS SLOGANS OF THE DAY IN RUSSIA

The Berne resolution of our Party declared: "Pacifism, the preaching of peace in the abstract is one of the means of duping the working class.... At the present time, the propaganda of peace unaccompanied by a call for revolutionary mass action can only sow illusions and demoralise the proletariat, for it makes the proletariat believe that the bourgeoisie is humane and turns it into a plaything in the hands of the secret diplomacy of the belligerent countries" (see *Sotsial-Demokrat* [48] No. 40, and "Socialism and War").*

The opponents of our point of view on the question of peace, who are numerous among Russian political émigrés, but not among the Russian workers, have never taken the trouble to analyse these propositions. Theoretically irrefutable, these propositions have now received striking and practical confirmation from the turn of events in our country.

Rabocheye Utro, the organ of the Petersburg legalist-liquidators, which is ideologically supported by the Organising Committee, is known to have adopted a social-chauvinist, "defencist" position from its very first issue. It published the "defencist" manifestos of the Petersburg and Moscow social-chauvinists. Both manifestos express, *inter alia*, the idea of "peace without annexations", and *Rabocheye Utro* No. 2, which particularly stresses that slogan, prints it in italics and calls it "a line which provides the country with a way out of the impasse". It is calumny to call us chauvinists, the paper seems to say; we fully accept the most "democratic", even "truly socialist" slogan of "peace without annexations".

---

* See present edition, Vol.21, "The Conference of the R.S.D.L.P. Groups Abroad".—*Ed.*

No doubt Nicholas the Bloody finds it to his advantage to have his loyal subjects put forward such a slogan at the present time. Tsarism, supported by the landowners and the bourgeoisie, led its armies to rob and enslave Galicia (not to mention the treaty to carve up Turkey, etc.). The armies of the no less predatory German imperialists repulsed the Russian robbers and expelled them, not only from Galicia, but also from "Russian Poland". (In this struggle for the interests of both these cliques, hundreds of thousands of Russian and German workers and peasants fell on the field of battle.) The peace-without-annexations slogan thus turned out to be an excellent "plaything in the hands of the secret diplomacy" of tsarism; the latter can now say: Look, we are the aggrieved; we have been robbed, deprived of Poland; we are opposed to annexations!

How much the *Rabocheye Utro* social-chauvinists "relish" the part of lackeys to tsarism is particularly evident from an article in the first issue of that paper, entitled "Polish Emigration". "The months of the war," we read, "have engendered in the minds of broad sections of the Polish people a strong urge to independence." The implication is that there was no such thing before the war. "The mass [this seems to be a misprint and ought to read "the idea, the thought", etc.] of Poland's national independence has triumphed in the social consciousness of broad sections of Polish democrats.... The Polish question looms relentlessly in all its magnitude before Russian democrats...." "The Russian liberals" refuse to give straightforward answers to the vexed questions "of Poland's independence".

Nicholas the Bloody, Khvostov, Chelnokov, Milyukov and Co. are, of course, entirely in favour of Poland's independence—they are heart and soul in favour of it *now*, when this slogan, *put into practice*, means *victory* over Germany, the country which has deprived Russia of Poland. Let us not forget that *before the war*, the creators of "the Stolypin labour party" [49] were wholly and unreservedly opposed to the slogan of the self-determination of nations and Poland's right to secede, putting up the opportunist Semkovsky for the noble purpose of defending the tsarist oppression of Poland. Now that Poland has been taken from Russia they are *in favour* of the "independence" of Poland (from Germany; but on this point they maintain a discreet silence).

You social-chauvinist gentlemen will not deceive the class-conscious workers of Russia! Your *1915* "Octobrist" [50] slogan on independence for Poland and peace without annexations is in practice servility to tsarism, which at the present time, in February 1916 to be precise, is sorely in need of camouflaging *its* war with fine words about "peace without annexations" (driving Hindenburg out of Poland) and independence for Poland (independence from Wilhelm, but dependence upon Nicholas II).

The Russian Social-Democrat who has not forgotten his Programme argues differently. Russian democracy, he will say, having Great-Russian democracy in mind first of all and most of all, for it alone in Russia has always enjoyed freedom of language—this democracy has undoubtedly *gained* from the fact that *at present* Russia does not oppress Poland and hold it by force. The Russian proletariat has undoubtedly gained from the fact that it no longer oppresses a people it had helped to oppress yesterday. German democracy has undoubtedly lost, for as long as the German proletariat tolerates Germany's oppression of Poland it will remain in a position which is worse than that of a slave; it is the position of a flunkey helping to keep others enslaved. Only the German Junkers and the bourgeoisie have really gained.

Hence, Russian Social-Democrats must expose the *deception* of the people by tsarism, *now that* the slogans of "peace without annexations" and "independence for Poland" are being played up in Russia, for in the present situation both these slogans express and justify the desire to continue the war. We must say, No war over Poland! The Russian people do not want to become Poland's oppressor again!

But how can we help liberate Poland from Germany? Isn't it our duty to do so? Of course it is, though never by supporting the imperialist war waged by Russia, be it tsarist, or bourgeois, or even bourgeois-republican, but by *supporting* the revolutionary proletariat of Germany, by supporting those elements in the Social-Democratic Party of Germany who are fighting against the *counter-revolutionary* labour party of the Südekums, and Kautsky and Co. Kautsky very recently demonstrated his counter-revolutionary nature in a most flagrant manner; on November 26, 1915, he described street demonstrations as *"adventurism"* (just as Struve said on the eve of January 9, 1905, that there were no revolutionary people in Russia), and yet, on November 30, 1915, ten thousand working women demonstrated in Berlin!

All those who do not want to back the freedom of nations, the right of nations to self-determination, *hypocritically*, in the Südekum, Plekhanov, Kautsky fashion, but want to do this *sincerely*, must *oppose* the war over the oppression of Poland; they must stand *for* the right of the nations Russia is *now* oppressing, namely, the Ukraine, Finland, etc., to secede from Russia. Those who do not wish to be social-chauvinists *in deed* must support only those elements in the socialist parties of all countries which are working, directly, immediately, right now, for the proletarian revolution in their own countries.

Not "peace without annexations", but peace to the cottages, war on the palaces; peace to the proletariat and the working people, war on the bourgeoisie!

Sotsial-Demokrat No. 51,   Published according to the
    February 29, 1916   *Sotsial-Demokrat* text

WILHELM KOLB AND GEORGY PLEKHANOV

The pamphlet by the avowed German opportunist, Wilhelm Kolb, entitled *Social-Democracy at the Crossroads* (Karlsrühe, 1915), appeared opportunely after the publication of Plekhanov's symposium, *War*. The Kautskyite Rudolf Hilferding wrote a very feeble reply to Kolb in *Die Neue Zeit*, in which he evaded the main issue and snivelled over Kolb's correct assertion that the unity of the German Social-Democrats was "purely formal".

Whoever wishes to give serious thought to the significance of the collapse of the Second International would do well to compare Kolb's *ideological* position with Plekhanov's. Like Kautsky, both agree on the *fundamental issue*; both reject and ridicule the idea of revolutionary action in connection with the present war; both accuse the revolutionary Social-Democrats of "defeatism", to use the pet expression of Plekhanov's followers. Plekhanov, who describes the idea of a revolution in connection with the present war as a "farcical dream", rails against "revolutionary phraseology". Kolb at every step curses "revolutionary phrases", the "revolutionary fantasies", the "petty radical (*Radikalinski*) hystericals", "sectarianism", etc. Kolb and Plekhanov agree on the main issue; both are opposed to revolution. The fact that Kolb is generally opposed to revolution, whereas Plekhanov and Kautsky are "generally in favour", is only a difference in shade, in words; in reality, Plekhanov and Kautsky are Kolb's underlings.

Kolb is more honest, not in a personal, but in a political sense, that is, being consistent in his stand, he is not a hypocrite. Hence, he is not afraid to admit the truth that, from his point of view, the entire International had been imbued with "the spirit of revolutionary fantasy", that it had uttered "threats" (threats of revolution, Messrs. Plekhanov and Kolb!) in connection with the war. Kolb is right when he says that it is ridiculous to "repudiate" capitalist society "in principle" after the Social-Democratic parties of Europe had risen in its defence at the very moment when the capitalist state was cracking from top to bottom, when "its very existence was in question". This admission of the objective revolutionary situation is the truth.

"The consequence" (of the tactics of Liebknecht's followers), writes Kolb, "would be that the *internal* struggle within the German nation would be brought up to boiling point and this would weaken its military and political power" ...*to the advantage and victory* "of the imperialism of the Triple Entente"!! Here you have the crux of the opportunist railing against "defeatism"!!

This is really the crux of the whole question. "Internal struggle which has been brought up to boiling point" is civil war. Kolb is right when he says that the tactics of the Left *lead* to this; he is right when he says that they mean the "military weakening" of Germany, i.e., desiring and aiding its defeat, defeatism. Kolb is wrong only—only!—in that he refuses to see the international character of these tactics of the Left. For it is *possible* "to bring the internal struggle up to boiling point", "weaken the military power" of the imperialist bourgeoisie and (by virtue of this, in connection with it, by means of it) transform the imperialist war into civil war in all the belligerent countries. This is the crux of the whole matter. We thank Kolb for his good wishes, admissions and illustrations; since all this comes from a most consistent, honest and avowed enemy of the revolution, it is particularly useful as a means of exposing to the workers the hideous hypocrisy and the shameful spinelessness of the Plekhanovs and Kautskys.

Sotsial-Demokrat No. 51,
February 29, 1916

Published according to the
Sotsial-Demokrat text

THE SOCIALIST REVOLUTION AND THE RIGHT OF NATIONS TO SELF-DETERMINATION

THESES

1. IMPERIALISM, SOCIALISM AND THE LIBERATION OF OPPRESSED NATIONS

Imperialism is the highest stage in the development of capitalism. In the foremost countries capital has outgrown the bounds of national states, has replaced competition by monopoly and has created all the objective conditions for the achievement of socialism. In Western Europe and in the United States, therefore, the revolutionary struggle of the proletariat for the overthrow of capitalist governments and the expropriation of the bourgeoisie is on the order of the day. Imperialism forces the masses into this struggle by sharpening class contradictions on a tremendous scale, by worsening the conditions of the masses both economically —trusts, high cost of living—and politically—the growth of militarism, more frequent wars, more powerful reaction, the intensification and expansion of national oppression and colonial plunder. Victorious socialism must necessarily establish a full democracy and, consequently, not only introduce full equality of nations but also realise the right of the oppressed nations to self-determination, i. e., the right to free political separation. Socialist parties which did not show by all their activity, both now, during the revolution, and after its victory, that they would liberate the enslaved nations and build up relations with them on the basis of a free union—and free union is a false phrase without the right to secede—these parties would be betraying social-ism.

Democracy, of course, is also a form of state which must disappear when the state disappears, but that will only take place in the transition from conclusively victorious and consolidated socialism to full communism.

2. THE SOCIALIST REVOLUTION AND THE STRUGGLE FOR DEMOCRACY

The socialist revolution is not a single act, it is not one battle on one front, but a whole epoch of acute class conflicts, a long series of battles on all fronts, i.e., on all questions of economics and politics, battles that can only end in the expropriation of the bourgeoisie. It would be a radical mistake to think that the struggle for democracy was capable of diverting the proletariat from the socialist revolution or of hiding, overshadowing it, etc. On the contrary, in the same way as there can be no victorious socialism that does not practise full democracy, so the proletariat cannot prepare for its victory over the bourgeoisie without an all-round, consistent and revolutionary struggle for democracy.

It would be no less a mistake to remove one of the points of the democratic programme, for example, the point on the self-determination of nations, on the grounds of it being "impracticable" or "illusory" under imperialism. The contention that the right of nations to self-determination is impracticable within the bounds of capitalism can be understood either in the absolute, economic sense, or in the conditional, political sense.

In the first case it is radically incorrect from the standpoint of theory. First, in that sense, such things as, for example, labour money, or the abolition of crises, etc., are impracticable under capitalism. It is absolutely untrue that the self-determination of nations is *equally* impracticable. Secondly, even the one example of the secession of Norway from Sweden in 1905 is sufficient to refute "impracticability" in that sense. Thirdly, it would be absurd to deny that some slight change in the political and strategic relations of, say, Germany and Britain, might today or tomorrow make the formation of a new Polish, Indian and other similar state fully "practicable". Fourthly, finance capital, in its drive to expand, can "freely" buy or bribe the freest democratic or republican government and the elective officials of any, even an "independent", country. The domination of finance capital and of capital in general is not to be abolished by *any* reforms in the sphere of political democracy; and self-determination belongs wholly and exclusively to this sphere. This domination of finance capital, however, does not in the least nullify the significance of political democracy as a freer, wider and clearer *form* of class oppression and class struggle. Therefore all arguments about the "impracticability", in the economic sense, of one of the demands of political democracy under capitalism are reduced to a theoretically incorrect definition of the general and basic relationships of capitalism and of political democracy as a whole.

In the second case the assertion is incomplete and inaccurate. This is because not only the right of nations to self-determination, but *all* the fundamental demands of political democracy are only partially "practicable" under imperialism, and then in a distorted form and by way of exception (for example, the secession of Norway from Sweden in 1905). The demand for the immediate liberation of the colonies that is put forward by all revolutionary Social-Democrats is also "impracticable" under capitalism without a series of revolutions. But from this it does not by any means follow that Social-Democracy should reject the immediate and most determined struggle for *all* these demands—such a rejection would only play into the hands of the bourgeoisie and reaction—but, on the contrary, it follows that these demands must be formulated and put through in a revolutionary and not a reformist manner, going beyond the bounds of bourgeois legality, breaking them down, going beyond speeches in parliament and verbal protests, and drawing the masses into decisive action, extending and intensifying the struggle for every fundamental democratic demand up to a direct proletarian onslaught on the bourgeoisie, i.e., up to the socialist revolution that expropriates the bourgeoisie. The socialist revolution may flare up not only through some big strike, street demonstration or hunger riot or a military insurrection or colonial revolt, but also as a result of a political crisis such as the Dreyfus case[51] or the Zabern incident,[52] or in connection with a referendum on the secession of an oppressed nation, etc.

Increased national oppression under imperialism does not mean that Social-Democracy should reject what the bourgeoisie call the "utopian" struggle for the freedom of nations to secede but, on the contrary, it should make greater use of the conflicts that arise in this sphere, *too*, as grounds for mass action and for revolutionary attacks on the bourgeoisie.

3. THE SIGNIFICANCE OF THE RIGHT TO SELF-DETERMINATION AND ITS RELATION TO FEDERATION

The right of nations to self-determination implies exclusively the right to independence in the political sense, the right to free political separation from the oppressor nation. Specifically, this demand for political democracy implies complete freedom to agitate for secession and for a referendum on secession by the seceding nation. This demand, therefore, is not the equivalent of a demand for separation, fragmentation and the formation of small states. It implies only a consistent expression of struggle against all national oppression. The closer a democratic state system is to complete freedom to secede the less frequent and less ardent will the desire for separation be in practice, because big states afford indisputable advantages, both from the standpoint of economic progress and from that of the interests of the masses and, furthermore, these advantages increase with the growth of capitalism. Recognition of self-determination is not synonymous with recognition of federation as a principle. One may be a determined opponent of that principle and a champion of democratic centralism but still prefer federation to national inequality as the only way to full democratic centralism. It was from this standpoint that Marx, who was a centralist, preferred even the federation of Ireland and England to the forcible subordination of Ireland to the English. [53]

The aim of socialism is not only to end the division of mankind into tiny states and the isolation of nations in any form, it is not only to bring the nations closer together but to integrate them. And it is precisely in order to achieve this aim that we must, on the one hand, explain to the masses the reactionary nature of Renner and Otto Bauer's idea of so-called "cultural and national autonomy" [54] and, on the other, demand the liberation of oppressed nations in a clearly and precisely formulated political programme that takes special account of the hypocrisy and cowardice of socialists in the oppressor nations, and not in general nebulous phrases, not in empty declamations and not by way of "relegating" the question until socialism has been achieved. In the same way as mankind can arrive at the abolition of classes only through a transition period of the dictatorship of the oppressed class, it can arrive at the inevitable integration of nations only through a transition period of the complete emancipation of all oppressed nations, i.e., their freedom to secede.

4. THE PROLETARIAN-REVOLUTIONARY PRESENTATION OF THE QUESTION OF THE SELF-DETERMINATION OF NATIONS

The petty bourgeoisie had put forward not only the demand for the self-determination of nations but *all* the points of our democratic minimum programme long *before*, as far back as the seventeenth and eighteenth centuries. They are still putting them *all* forward in a utopian manner because they fail to see the class struggle and its increased intensity under democracy, and because they believe in "peaceful" capitalism. That is the exact nature of the utopia of a peaceful union of equal nations under imperialism which deceives the people and which is defended by Kautsky's followers. The programme of Social-Democracy, as a counter-balance to this petty-bourgeois, opportunist utopia, must postulate the division of nations into oppressor and oppressed as basic, significant and inevitable under imperialism.

The proletariat of the oppressor nations must not confine themselves to general, stereotyped phrases against annexation and in favour of the equality of nations in general, such as any pacifist bourgeois will repeat. The proletariat cannot remain silent on the question of the *frontiers* of a state founded on national oppression, a question so "unpleasant" for the imperialist bourgeoisie. The proletariat must struggle against the enforced retention of oppressed nations within the bounds of the given state, which means that they must fight for the right to self-determination. The proletariat must demand freedom of political separation for the colonies and nations oppressed by "their own" nation. Otherwise, the internationalism of the proletariat would be nothing but empty words; neither confidence nor class solidarity would be possible between the workers of the oppressed and the oppressor nations; the hypocrisy of the reformists and Kautskyites, who defend self-determination but remain silent about the nations oppressed by "their own" nation and kept in "their own" state by force, would remain unexposed.

On the other hand, the socialists of the oppressed nations must, in particular, defend and implement the full and unconditional unity, including organisational unity, of the workers of the oppressed nation and those of the oppressor nation. Without this it is impossible to defend the independent policy of the proletariat and their class solidarity with the proletariat of other countries in face of all manner of intrigues, treachery and trickery on the part of the bourgeoisie. The bourgeoisie of the oppressed nations persistently utilise the slogans of national liberation to deceive the workers; in their internal policy they use these slogans for reactionary agreements with the bourgeoisie of the dominant nation (for example, the Poles in Austria and Russia who come to terms with reactionaries for the oppression of the Jews and Ukrainians); in their foreign policy they strive to come to terms with one of the rival imperialist powers for the sake of implementing their predatory plans (the policy of the small Balkan states, etc.).

The fact that the struggle for national liberation against one imperialist power may, under certain conditions, be utilised by another "great" power for its own, equally imperialist, aims, is just as unlikely to make the Social-Democrats refuse to recognise the right of nations to self-determination as the numerous cases of bourgeois utilisation of republican slogans for the purpose of political deception and financial plunder (as in the Romance countries, for example) are unlikely to make the Social-Democrats reject their republicanism.*

---

* It would, needless to say, be quite ridiculous to reject the right to self-determination on the grounds that it implies "defence of the fatherland". With equal right, i.e., with equal lack of seriousness, the social-chauvinists of 1914-16 refer to any of the demands of de-

5. MARXISM AND PROUDHONISM
ON THE NATIONAL QUESTION

In contrast to the petty-bourgeois democrats, Marx regarded every democratic demand without exception not as an absolute, but as an historical expression of the struggle of the masses of the people, led by the bourgeoisie, against feudalism. There is not one of these demands which could not serve and has not served, under certain circumstances, as an instrument in the hands of the bourgeoisie for deceiving the workers. To single out, in this respect, one of the demands of political democracy, specifically, the self-determination of nations, and to oppose it to the rest, is fundamentally wrong in theory. In practice, the proletariat can retain its independence only by subordinating its struggle for all democratic demands, not excluding the demand for a republic, to its revolutionary struggle for the overthrow of the bourgeoisie.

On the other hand, in contrast to the Proudhonists who "denied" the national problem "in the name of social revolution", Marx, mindful in the first place of the interests of the proletarian class struggle in the advanced countries, put the fundamental principle of internationalism and socialism in the foreground—namely, that no nation can be free if it oppresses other nations. [55] It was from the standpoint of the interests of the German workers' revolutionary movement that Marx in 1848 demanded that victorious democracy in Germany should proclaim and grant freedom to the nations oppressed by the Germans. [56] It was from the standpoint of the revolutionary struggle of the English workers that Marx, in 1869, demanded the separation of Ireland from England, and added: "...even if federation should follow upon separation." [57] Only by putting forward this demand was Marx really educating the English workers in the spirit

---

mocracy (to its republicanism, for example) and to any formulation of the struggle against national oppression in order to justify "defence of the fatherland". Marxism deduces the defence of the fatherland in wars, for example, in the great French Revolution or the wars of Garibaldi, in Europe, and the renunciation of defence of the fatherland in the imperialist war of 1914-16, from an analysis of the concrete historical peculiarities of each individual war and never from any "general principle", or any one point of a programme.

of internationalism. Only in this way could he counterpose the opportunists and bourgeois reformism —which even to this day, half a century later, has not carried out the Irish "reform" —with a revolutionary solution of the given historical task. Only in this way could Marx maintain —in contradiction to the apologists of capital who shout that the freedom of small nations to secede is utopian and impracticable and that not only economic but also political concentration is progressive —that this concentration is progressive when it is *non*-imperialist, and that nations should not be brought together by force, but by a free union of the proletarians of all countries. Only in this way could Marx, in opposition to the merely verbal, and often hypocritical, recognition of the equality and self-determination of nations, advocate the revolutionary action of the masses in the settlement of national questions *as well*. The imperialist war of 1914-16, and the Augean stables of hypocrisy on the part of the opportunists and Kautskyites that it has exposed, have strikingly confirmed the correctness of Marx's policy, which should serve as a model for all advanced countries, for all of them are now oppressing other nations. *

6. THREE TYPES OF COUNTRIES WITH RESPECT TO THE SELF-DETERMINATION OF NATIONS

In this respect, countries must be divided into three main types.

First, the advanced capitalist countries of Western Europe and the United States. In these countries progressive bourgeois national movements came to an end long ago. Every

---

* Reference is often made—e.g., recently by the German chauvinist Lensch in *Die Glocke* [53] Nos. 8 and 9—to the fact that Marx's objection to the national movement of certain peoples, to that of the Czechs in 1848, for example, refutes the necessity of recognising the self-determination of nations from the Marxist standpoint. But this is incorrect, for in 1848 there were historical and political grounds for drawing a distinction between "reactionary" and revolutionary-democratic nations. Marx was right to condemn the former and defend the latter. [59] The right to self-determination is one of the demands of democracy which must naturally be subordinated to its general interests. In 1848 and the following years these general interests consisted primarily in combating tsarism.

one of these "great" nations oppresses other nations both in the colonies and at home. The tasks of the proletariat of these ruling nations are the same as those of the proletariat in England in the nineteenth century in relation to Ireland.*

Secondly, Eastern Europe: Austria, the Balkans and particularly Russia. Here it was the twentieth century that particularly developed the bourgeois-democratic national movements and intensified the national struggle. The tasks of the proletariat in these countries, both in completing their bourgeois-democratic reforms, and rendering assistance to the socialist revolution in other countries, cannot be carried out without championing the right of nations to self-determination. The most difficult and most important task in this is to unite the class struggle of the workers of the oppressor nations with that of the workers of the oppressed nations.

Thirdly, the semi-colonial countries, such as China, Persia and Turkey, and all the colonies, which have a combined population of 1,000 million. In these countries the bourgeois-democratic movements either have hardly begun, or have still a long way to go. Socialists must not only demand the unconditional and immediate liberation of the colonies without compensation—and this demand in its political expression signifies nothing else than the recognition of the right to self-determination; they must also render determined support to the more revolutionary elements in the bourgeois-democratic movements for national liberation

---

* In some small states which have kept out of the war of 1914-16—Holland and Switzerland, for example—the bourgeoisie makes extensive use of the "self-determination of nations" slogan to justify participation in the imperialist war. This is a motive inducing the Social-Democrats in such countries to repudiate self-determination. Wrong arguments are being used to defend a correct proletarian policy, the repudiation of "defence of the fatherland" in an *imperialist* war. This results in a distortion of Marxism in theory, and in practice leads to a peculiar small-nation narrow-mindedness, neglect of the *hundreds of millions* of people in nations that are enslaved by the "dominant" nations. Comrade Gorter, in his excellent pamphlet *Imperialism, War and Social-Democracy* wrongly rejects the principle of self-determination of nations, but correctly *applies* it, when he demands the *immediate* granting of "political and *national* independence" to the Dutch Indies and exposes the Dutch opportunists who refuse to put forward this demand and to fight for it.

in these countries and assist their uprising —or revolutionary
war, in the event of one —*against* the imperialist powers that
oppress them.

7. SOCIAL-CHAUVINISM AND THE SELF-DETERMINATION OF NATIONS

The imperialist epoch and the war of 1914-16 has laid
special emphasis on the struggle against chauvinism and
nationalism in the leading countries. There are two main
trends on the self-determination of nations among the social-
chauvinists, that is, among the opportunists and Kautskyites,
who hide the imperialist, reactionary nature of the war by
applying to it the "defence of the fatherland" concept.

On the one hand, we see quite undisguised servants of
the bourgeoisie who defend annexation on the plea that imperialism and political concentration are progressive, and
who deny what they call the utopian, illusory, petty-bourgeois, etc., right to self-determination. This includes Cunow,
Parvus and the extreme opportunists in Germany, some of
the Fabians and trade union leaders in England, and the
opportunists in Russia: Semkovsky, Liebman, Yurkevich,
etc.

On the other hand, we see the Kautskyites, among whom
are Vandervelde, Renaudel, many pacifists in Britain and
France, and others. They favour unity with the former and
in practice are completely identified with them; they defend
the right to self-determination hypocritically and by words
alone: they consider "excessive" ("*zu viel verlangt*": Kautsky
in *Die Neue Zeit*, May 21, 1915) the demand for free political
separation, they do not defend the necessity for revolutionary
tactics on the part of the socialists of the oppressor nations
in particular but, on the contrary, obscure their revolutionary obligations, justify their opportunism, make easy
for them their deception of the people, and avoid the very
question of the *frontiers* of a state forcefully retaining under-
privileged nations within its bounds, etc.

Both are equally opportunist, they prostitute Marxism,
having lost all ability to understand the theoretical significance and practical urgency of the tactics which Marx explained with Ireland as an example.

As for annexations, the question has become particularly urgent in connection with the war. But what is annexation? It is quite easy to see that a protest against annexations either boils down to recognition of the self-determination of nations or is based on the pacifist phrase that defends the *status quo* and is hostile to *any*, even revolutionary, violence. Such a phrase is fundamentally false and incompatible with Marxism.

8. THE CONCRETE TASKS OF THE PROLETARIAT IN THE IMMEDIATE FUTURE

The socialist revolution may begin in the very near future. In this case the proletariat will be faced with the immediate task of winning power, expropriating the banks and effecting other dictatorial measures. The bourgeoisie—and especially the intellectuals of the Fabian and Kautskyite type—will, at such a moment, strive to split and check the revolution by foisting limited, democratic aims on it. Whereas *any* purely democratic demands are in a certain sense liable to act as a hindrance to the revolution, provided the proletarian attack on the pillars of bourgeois power has begun, the necessity to proclaim and grant liberty to *all* oppressed peoples (i.e., their right to self-determination) will be as urgent in the socialist revolution as it was for the victory of the bourgeois-democratic revolution in, say, Germany in 1848, or Russia in 1905.

It is possible, however, that five, ten or more years will elapse before the socialist revolution begins. This will be the time for the revolutionary education of the masses in a spirit that will make it impossible for socialist-chauvinists and opportunists to belong to the working-class party and gain a victory, as was the case in 1914-16. The socialists must explain to the masses that British socialists who do not demand freedom to separate for the colonies and Ireland, German socialists who do not demand freedom to separate for the colonies, the Alsatians, Danes and Poles, and who do not extend their revolutionary propaganda and revolutionary mass activity directly to the sphere of struggle against national oppression, or who do not make use of such incidents as that at Zabern for the broadest illegal propaganda among the proletariat of the oppressor nation, for street demonstrations and revolutionary mass action—Russian socialists who do not demand freedom to separate for Finland, Poland, the Ukraine, etc., etc.—that such socialists act as chauvinists and lackeys of bloodstained and filthy imperialist monarchies and the imperialist bourgeoisie.

9. THE ATTITUDE OF RUSSIAN AND POLISH SOCIAL-DEMOCRATS AND OF THE SECOND INTERNATIONAL TO SELF-DETERMINATION

The differences between the revolutionary Social-Democrats of Russia and the Polish Social-Democrats on the question of self-determination came out into the open as early as 1903, at the Congress which adopted the Programme of the R.S.D.L. Party, and which, despite the protest by the Polish Social-Democrat delegation, inserted Clause 9, recognising the right of nations to self-determination. Since then the Polish Social-Democrats have on no occasion repeated, in the name of their party, the proposal to remove Clause 9 from our Party's Programme, or to replace it by some other formula.

In Russia, where the oppressed nations account for no less than 57 per cent of the population, or over 100 million, where they occupy mostly the border regions, where some of them are more highly cultured than the Great Russians, where the political system is especially barbarous and medieval, where the bourgeois-democratic revolution has not been consummated—there, in Russia, recognition of the right of nations oppressed by tsarism to free secession from Russia is absolutely obligatory for Social-Democrats, for the furtherance of their democratic and socialist aims. Our Party, re-established in January 1912, adopted a resolution in 1913[60] reaffirming the right to self-determination and explaining it in precisely the above concrete sense. The rampage of Great-Russian chauvinism in 1914-16 both among the bourgeoisie and among the opportunist socialists (Rubanovich, Plekhanov, *Nashe Dyelo*, etc.) has given us even more reason to insist on this demand and to regard those who deny it as actual supporters of Great-Russian chauvinism and tsarism. Our Party declares that it most emphatically declines to accept any responsibility for such actions against the right to self-determination.

The latest formulation of the position of the Polish Social-Democrats on the national question (the declaration of the Polish Social-Democrats at the Zimmerwald Conference) contains the following ideas:

The declaration condemns the German and other governments that regard the "Polish regions" as a pawn in the forthcoming compensation game, *"depriving the Polish people of the opportunity of deciding their own fate themselves"*. "Polish Social-Democrats resolutely and solemnly protest against the *carving up and parcelling out of a whole country"* ....They flay the socialists who left it to the Hohenzollerns *"to liberate the oppressed peoples"*. They express the conviction that only participation in the approaching struggle of the international revolutionary proletariat, the struggle for socialism, *"will break the fetters of national oppression* and destroy *all forms of foreign* rule, will ensure for *the Polish people* the possibility of free all-round development as an *equal* member of a concord of nations". The declaration recognises that *"for the Poles"* the war is *"doubly* fratricidal". (*Bulletin of the International Socialist Committee* No. 2, September 27, 1915, p. 15. Russian translation in the symposium *The International and the War*, p. 97.)

These propositions do not differ in substance from recognition of the right of nations to self-determination, although their political formulations are even vaguer and more indeterminate than those of most programmes and resolutions of the Second International. Any attempt to express these ideas as precise political formulations and to define their applicability to the capitalist system or only to the socialist system will show even more clearly the mistake the Polish Social-Democrats make in denying the self-determination of nations.

The decision of the London International Socialist Congress of 1896, which recognised the self-determination of nations, should be supplemented on the basis of the above theses by specifying: (1) the particular urgency of this demand under imperialism, (2) the political conventionalism and class content of all the demands of political democracy, the one under discussion included, (3) the necessity to distinguish the concrete tasks of the Social-Democrats of the oppressor nations from those of the Social-Democrats of the oppressed nations, (4) the inconsistent, purely verbal recognition of self-determination by the opportunists and the Kautskyites, which is, therefore, hypocritical in its political significance, (5) the actual identity of the chauvinists and those Social-Democrats, especially those of the Great Powers (Great Russians, Anglo-Americans, Germans, French, Italians, Japanese, etc.), who do not uphold the freedom to secede for colonies and nations oppressed by "their own" nations, (6) the necessity to subordinate the struggle for the demand under discussion and for all the basic demands of political democracy directly to the revolutionary mass struggle for the overthrow of the bourgeois governments and for the achievement of socialism.

The introduction into the International of the viewpoint of certain small nations, especially that of the Polish Social-Democrats, who have been led by their struggle against the Polish bourgeoisie, which deceives the people with its nationalist slogans, to the incorrect denial of self-determination, would be a theoretical mistake, a substitution of Proudhonism for Marxism implying in practice involuntary support for the most dangerous chauvinism and opportunism of the Great-Power nations.

> *Editorial Board of* Sotsial-Demokrat,
> *Central Organ of R.S.D.L.P.*

Postscript. In *Die Neue Zeit* for March 3, 1916, which has just appeared, Kautsky openly holds out the hand of Christian reconciliation to Austerlitz, a representative of the foulest German chauvinism, rejecting freedom of separation for the oppressed nations of Hapsburg Austria but recognising it for *Russian* Poland, as a menial service to Hindenburg and Wilhelm II. One could not have wished for a better self-exposure of Kautskyism!

Written January-February 1916

Printed in April 1916 in
the magazine *Vorbote* No. 2

Printed in Russian in October 1916
in *Sbornik Sotsial-Demokrata* No. 1

Published according to
the *Sbornik* text

LETTER
FROM THE COMMITTEE
OF ORGANISATIONS ABROAD
TO THE SECTIONS OF THE R.S.D.L.P.

Dear Comrades,

The recent No. 25 issue (the *second* to come out during the war) of *Gazeta Robotnicza*,[61] the organ of the *opposition* of the Polish Social-Democratic Party, carries the resolutions of their conference (a conference of the Editorial Board) adopted back in *June* 1915.

These resolutions clearly show that *as a body* (we say nothing of its members as individuals, some of whom are doing extremely useful work in the German Social-Democratic press), the Polish Social-Democrats are *once again* vacillating in a *most* spineless manner.

There's not a word against *Kautskyism*, not a word about any determined and resolute struggle against *opportunism*, as the *source* and *buttress* of social-chauvinism!! This can be read in one way only: they are prepared once again (as in Brussels, July 3-16, 1914[62]) "to play ball" with the Kautskyites.

We quote the main (IV) resolution in full. Here it is:

Gazeta Robotnicza P.S.D. (of the opposition) No. 25 (January 1916). "Resolutions of the Editorial Board conference held on June 1-2, 1915."

IV. *The Attitude of the Social-Democrats of Poland and Lithuania to the R.S.D.L.P.**

"The Polish revolutionary Social-Democrats regard the Central Committee of the R.S.D.L.P. as a body consisting

---

* The *Gazeta Robotnicza* resolution was translated by N. K. Krupskaya. The words in bold-face type here are Lenin's additions and corrections to the translation from the Polish.—*Ed.*

of the most resolute revolutionary internationalist elements
in Russia, and, while leaving it to the regional organisation
to settle its organisational relations with it in the future,
will give it political support and co-ordinate their activity
with it.

"The common revolutionary stand of the Polish Social-
Democrats and the Central Committee on the main essential
[*wytycznych* (**definite?**)] points of their policy makes it in-
cumbent on the Social-Democrats of Poland and Lithuania to
continue taking a critical attitude to its obvious tactical
exaggerations [*wybujałości* ("**wild**" **growth of corn, etc.**)].

"While justly desiring to emphasise the proletariat's
unquestionably hostile attitude to tsarism's **plunderous**
policy, the Central Committee puts forward the slogan of
Russia's defeat, basing it on the especially reactionary part
tsarism has to play in Europe and the specific significance
of a Russian revolution; however, this brings the Central
Committee into contradiction with the method of internationalism, which does not allow proletarian hopes and tasks
to be pinned on any definite outcome of the war, and even
provides the German social-patriots with arguments.

"While justly noting the need for revolutionary action
to build a new International, while justly opposing every
attempt to **gloss over** the conflict, and piece together the
broken old International, the C.C., however, overrate the
importance of automatically fencing themselves off from all
less resolute elements which do not accept their standpoint
a priori, and **forget** [*przeocza*] that the task of the revolutionary **camp** [*obozu*] must not be to repulse these elements
but to draw them into the struggle against the **fraud** [*szal-
bierstwem*] of social-patriotism, and to promote their radi-
calisation by sharply criticising their ideological insta-
bility.

"As for the O.C. (R.S.D.L.P), the **conference** [*narada*]
reaffirms that its main **group**, which is in Russia, and also
its **literary representative** [*ekspozytura literacka*] take the
social-patriotic standpoint, and that its weak internationalist wing has neither the strength nor the courage to break
with the social-patriots, and that the O.C. Centre takes the
pacifist standpoint; the **conference** considers that the attitude of the Social-Democrats of Poland and Lithuania to

the O.C. can consist exclusively of criticism of its position, promoting its disintegration [*rozkładu*] and separating from the O.C. **its** internationalist **elements** grouped around *Nashe Slovo*, an organ which has done a great deal to elaborate [crystallise] internationalist-revolutionary views in the ranks of the R.S.D.L.P.

"The same applies, in particular, also to the Bund, which is a part of the O.C., for its attitude is an even greater chaotic mixture of social-patriotic and pacifist, Russophile and Germanophile elements."

The Polish Social-Democrats say here that they wish to "co-ordinate" their activity with the Central Committee.

We believe it to be our unquestionable duty to tell the Central Committee this: the Central Committee must not and *cannot* "co-ordinate" their activity with the P.S.D.

Why not?

Because the P.S.D. is *vacillating* again and again, for the nth time (or playing a game, which is objectively the same thing) on our Party's *cardinal* question. There is no doubt that the key issue in the Russian Social-Democratic movement today is that of the *split*.

On this point we are adamant, because the *entire* experience of the Social-Democratic movement in Russia, especially in the 1903-09 period, and even more between 1910 and 1914, and most of all in the years 1915 and 1916, *has served to convince* us that unity with the O.C. (or with the Chkheidze group, which is the same thing) is *harmful* to the working-class movement, and *ensures* its subjugation to the bourgeoisie.

The war and Gvozdyovism [63] have provided the final proof.

But it is on this chief, basic and fundamental issue that the Polish Social-Democrats are again *equivocating*.

They say *not a word* about the war having convinced them of the need for a split and of the *erroneousness* of their tactics at Brussels (July 3-16, 1914).

On the contrary, they have inserted in the resolution a *phrase* which looks as if it had been deliberately worded to justify and do another "Brussels" desertion to the O.C. or Chkheidze. Here it is:

"The Central Committee overrate the importance of automatically fencing themselves off...."

That is the whole point. The rest is just rhetoric. If the Central Committee "overrate" the need for a split, it is clear that the P.S.D. are entitled today or tomorrow to vote *again* for another Brussels-Kautskyite "unity" resolution.

It is the same old Tyszka trick,[64] the old game between the C.C. and the O.C., the old eclectical (to put it mildly) use of the pendulum position.

We have no objection at all to *working with* the P.S.D., either in general, or in the Zimmerwald Left in particular; nor do we defend every *letter* of our resolutions; but *we are adamant* on (1) the split in Russia and (2) that there be no reconciliation with Kautskyism in Europe. We consider it to be our duty to warn all comrades that the Polish Social-Democrats are *unreliable*, and to insist that the C.C. must not let itself be drawn once again into a repetition of "Brussels" experiments, or trust the authors of these experiments or participants in them.

With comradely greetings, *C.O.A.*

Written   February-March 1916
  First published in 1937   Published according
  in *Lenin Miscellany XXX*   to the manuscript

THE PEACE PROGRAMME

The question of the Social-Democratic peace programme is one of the most important on the agenda of the Second International Conference of the Zimmerwald group.[65] In order to bring home to the reader its *essentials* let us quote a pertinent declaration by Kautsky, a most authoritative representative of the Second International and a most authoritative champion of the social-chauvinists in all countries.

"The International is not a fit war-time instrument; it is, essentially, an instrument of peace.... The fight for peace, class struggle in peace time...." (*Die Neue Zeit*, November 27, 1914). "All peace programmes formulated by the International, the programmes of the Copenhagen, London and Vienna congresses, all demand, and quite rightly, recognition of the independence of nations. This demand must also serve as our compass in the present war" (ibid., May 21, 1915).

These few words excellently express the "programme" of international social-chauvinist unity and conciliation. Everybody knows that Südekum's friends and adherents met in Vienna and acted entirely in his spirit, championing the cause of German imperialism under the cloak of "defence of the fatherland". The French, English and Russian Südekums met in London and championed the cause of "their" national imperialisms under the same cloak. The real policy of the London and Vienna heroes of social-chauvinism is to justify participation in the imperialist war, to justify the killing of German workers by French workers, and vice versa, over which national bourgeoisie shall have the advantage in robbing other countries. And to conceal their real policy, to deceive the workers, both the London and

the Vienna heroes resort to the *phrase*, we "recognise" the
"independence of nations" or in other words, recognise the
self-determination of nations, repudiate annexations, etc.,
etc.

It is as clear as daylight that this "recognition" is a flagrant lie and foul hypocrisy, for it justifies participation in
a war waged by *both* sides to enslave nations, not to make
them independent. Instead of exposing, unmasking and condemning this hypocrisy, Kautsky, the great authority,
sanctifies it. To Kautsky, the unanimous desire of the chauvinists who have betrayed socialism to deceive the workers,
is proof of the "unanimity" and viability of the International
on the question of peace!!! Kautsky converts crude, patent,
flagrant, nationalist hypocrisy, which is so obvious to the
workers, into subtle, disguised, internationalist hypocrisy,
designed to blind the workers. Kautsky's policy is a hundred
times more harmful and dangerous to the labour movement
than Südekum's policy; Kautsky's hypocrisy is a hundred
times more repulsive.

This does not apply to Kautsky alone. The policy pursued
by Axelrod, Martov and Chkheidze in Russia, by Longuet
and Pressemane in France, Treves in Italy, etc., is essentially the same. Objectively, this policy means fostering
bourgeois lies among the working class; it means inculcat-
ing bourgeois ideas upon the proletariat. That both Südekum and Plekhanov merely repeat the bourgeois lies of the
capitalists of "their" respective nations is obvious; but it
is not so obvious that Kautsky sanctifies *these* lies and ranks
them as the "supreme truth" of a "unanimous" International.
That the workers should regard the Südekums and Plekhanovs authoritative and unanimous "socialists" who have
temporarily fallen out is exactly what the bourgeoisie wants.
That's the very thing the bourgeoisie wants; it wants the
workers *diverted* from the revolutionary struggle in war-time
by means of hypocritical, idle and non-committal phrases
about peace; it wants them lulled and soothed by hopes
of "peace without annexations", a democratic peace, etc.,
etc.

Huysmans has merely popularised Kautsky's peace
programme, adding courts of arbitration, democratisation of
foreign policies, etc., whereas the first and fundamental

point of a socialist peace programme must be *to unmask the hypocrisy* of the Kautskyist peace programme, which *strengthens* bourgeois influence on the proletariat.

Let us recall the fundamental postulates of socialist doctrine distorted by the Kautskyites. War is the continuation, by violent means, of the politics pursued by the ruling classes of the belligerent powers long before the outbreak of war. Peace is a continuation of the *very same* politics, with a *record* of the changes brought about in the relation of the rival forces by the military operations. War does not alter the direction of pre-war policies, but only *accelerates* their development.

The war of 1870-71 was a continuation of the progressive bourgeois policy (which had been pursued for decades) of liberating and uniting Germany. The debacle and overthrow of Napoleon III hastened that liberation. The peace programme of the socialists of that epoch took this progressive bourgeois result into account and advocated support for the democratic bourgeoisie, urging no plunder of France and an honourable peace with the republic.

What a clownish attempt to ape this example in the atmosphere of the imperialist war of 1914-16! This war is a continuation of the politics of a rotten-ripe reactionary bourgeoisie, which has plundered the world, seized colonies, etc. Owing to the objective situation, the present war *cannot*, on the basis of bourgeois relations, lead to any democratic "progress"; whatever its outcome, this war can do nothing but intensify and extend oppression in general, and national oppression in particular.

That war accelerated development in a democratic bourgeois-progressive direction; it resulted in the overthrow of Napoleon III and in the unification of Germany. *This* war is accelerating development *only* in the direction of the socialist revolution. *At that time*, the programme of a democratic (bourgeois) peace had an *objective* historical basis. *Now*, there is *no* such basis, and all phrases about a democratic peace are a bourgeois lie, the objective purpose of which is to divert the workers from the revolutionary struggle for socialism! *At that time*, the socialists, with their programme of a democratic peace, supported a deep-going bourgeois-democratic movement of the *masses* (for the overthrow of Napoleon III and the unification of Germany), which had been in evidence for decades. *Now*, with their programme of a democratic peace on the basis of bourgeois relations, the socialists are helping the bourgeoisie to *deceive* the people so as to divert the proletariat from the *socialist* revolution.

Just as phrases about "defence of the fatherland" fraudulently inculcate upon the masses the ideology of a national liberation war, so phrases about a democratic peace *smuggle in* that very same bourgeois lie.

"That means that you have no peace programme, that you are opposed to democratic demands," the Kautskyites argue, hoping that inattentive people will not notice that this objection substitutes non-existent bourgeois-democratic tasks for the existing socialist tasks.

Oh no, gentlemen, we reply to the Kautskyites. We are *in favour* of democratic demands, we *alone* are fighting for them *sincerely*, for because of the objective historical situation they cannot be advanced except in connection with the socialist revolution. Take, for example, the "compass" used by Kautsky and Co. for the bourgeois deception of the workers.

Südekum and Plekhanov are "unanimous" in their "peace programme". Down with annexations! Support the independence of nations! And note this. The Südekums are *right* when they say that Russia's attitude towards Poland, Finland, etc., is annexationist. Plekhanov is right, too, when he says that Germany's attitude towards Alsace-Lorraine, Serbia, Belgium, etc., is also annexationist. Both are right, are they not? And in this way Kautsky "reconciles" the German Südekums with the Russian Südekums!!!

But every alert worker will see at once that Kautsky and *both types* of Südekum are hypocrites. This is obvious. The duty of a socialist is not to make peace with hypocritical democracy, but to *unmask* it. How can it be unmasked? Very simply. "Recognition" of the independence of nations can be regarded as sincere *only* where the representative of the oppressor nation has demanded, both before and during the war, freedom of secession for the nation which is oppressed by *his own* "fatherland".

This demand alone is in accord with Marxism. Marx advanced it in the interests of the British proletariat when he demanded freedom for Ireland, although he assumed the probability of a federation following upon secession. In other words, he did not demand the right of secession for the sake of splitting and isolating countries, but to create more durable and democratic ties. In all cases where there are oppressed and oppressing nations, where no special circumstances distinguish revolutionary-democratic nations from reactionary nations (as was the case in the forties of the nineteenth century), Marx's policy in relation to Ireland must serve as a model for proletarian policy. But imperialism is the epoch in which the division of nations into oppressors and oppressed is essential and typical, and it is quite impossible to draw any distinction between reactionary and revolutionary nations in Europe.

As early as 1913, our Party, in a resolution on the national question, made it the duty of Social-Democrats to apply the concept of self-determination in the sense here indicated. We have been fully vindicated by the war of 1914-16.

Take Kautsky's latest article in *Die Neue Zeit* of March 3, 1916. He makes no bones about being *in agreement* with Austerlitz, the notorious, German ultra-chauvinist in Austria, the editor of the chauvinist Vienna *Arbeiter Zeitung*,[66] when he says that "a nation's independence must not be confused with its sovereignty". In other words, national autonomy within a "state of nationalities" is good enough for the oppressed nations, and it is not necessary to demand for them an equal right to political independence. In this very article, however, Kautsky asserts that it is impossible to prove that "it is essential for the Poles to belong to the Russian state"!!!

What does he mean? He means that to please Hindenburg, Südekum, Austerlitz and Co., he recognises Poland's *right to secede* from Russia, although Russia is a "state of nationalities" but not a word does he say about freedom for the Poles to secede from Germany!!! In this very same article Kautsky declares that the French socialists had departed from internationalism by wanting to achieve the freedom of Alsace-Lorraine *by means of war*. But he says nothing about the German Südekums and Co. having deviated from internationalism by refusing to demand freedom for Alsace-Lorraine to secede *from Germany*!

Kautsky employs "state of nationalities"—a catchword that can be applied both to Britain in relation to Ireland, and to Germany in relation to Poland, Alsace-Lorraine, etc. — for the obvious purpose of defending social-chauvinism. He has converted the "fight-against-annexations" slogan into a "programme of *peace*"... with the chauvinists, and a glaring hypocrisy. In this same article, mealy-mouthed Kautsky reiterates, "The International has never ceased to demand the consent of the population concerned, when state frontiers are moved." Is it not clear that Südekum and Co. demand the "consent" of the Alsatians and Belgians to be annexed to Germany, and that Austerlitz and Co. demand the "consent" of the Poles and Serbs to be annexed to Austria?

And what about the Russian Kautskyite, Martov? He wrote to the Gvozdyovist journal, *Nash Golos*[67] (Samara), to prove the indisputable truth that the self-determination of nations does not necessarily imply defence of the fatherland in an imperialist war. But Martov says nothing about the fact that a Russian Social-Democrat betrays the principle of self-determination if he does not demand the *right of secession* for the nations oppressed by the Great Russians, and in this way Martov extends the hand of peace to the Alexinskys, the Gvozdyovs, the Potresovs, and the Plekhanovs! Nor has Martov said anything on this point in the illegal press! He argues against the Dutchman Gorter, although Gorter, while wrongly repudiating the principle of self-determination of nations, *applies* it correctly by demanding *political independence* for the Dutch Indies and by unmasking the betrayal of socialism by the Dutch opportunists who disagree with this demand. Martov, however, does not argue against his co-secretary, Semkovsky, who from 1912 to 1915 was the *only* writer in the liquidationist press who dealt with this issue and *repudiated* the right of secession and self-determination in general!

Is it not plain that Martov "advocates" self-determination just as hypocritically as Kautsky does, that he, too, covers up his desire *to make peace* with the chauvinists?

What about Trotsky? He is body and soul *for* self-determination, but in his case, too, it is an empty phrase, for he does not demand freedom of secession for nations oppressed by the "fatherland" of the socialist of the *given* nationality; he is *silent* about the hypocrisy of Kautsky and his followers!

This kind of "struggle against annexations" serves to deceive the workers and not *to explain* the programme of the Social-Democrats; it is an *evasion* of the problem and not a concrete indication of the duty of internationalists; it is not a struggle against nationalism but a concession to nationalist prejudices and to the selfish interests of nationalism ("we" all, bourgeois and social-chauvinists alike, derive "benefits" from "our" fatherland's oppression of other nations!).

The "peace programme" of Social-Democracy must, in the first place, unmask the hypocrisy of the bourgeois, social-chauvinist and Kautskyite talk about peace. This is the first and fundamental thing. Unless we do that we shall be, willy-nilly, helping to *deceive* the masses. Our "peace programme" demands that the principal democratic point of this question—the repudiation of annexations—should be applied in practice and not in words, that it should serve to promote the propaganda of internationalism and not of national hypocrisy. To do this, we must explain to the masses that the repudiation of annexations, *i.e.*, the recognition of self-determination, is sincere only when the socialists of *every* nation demand the right of secession for nations oppressed by their own nations. As a positive slogan, drawing the masses into the revolutionary struggle and explaining the necessity for revolutionary measures to attain a "democratic" peace, we must advance this slogan: repudiation of debts contracted by states.

Finally, our "peace programme" must explain that the imperialist powers and the imperialist bourgeoisie *cannot* grant a democratic peace. Such a peace *must* be sought for and fought for, not in the *past*, *not* in a reactionary utopia of a *non*-imperialist capitalism, not in a league of equal nations *under* capitalism, but *in the future*, in the socialist revolution of the proletariat. Not a single fundamental democratic demand can be achieved to any considerable extent, or with any degree of permanency, in the advanced imperialist states, except through revolutionary battles under the banner of socialism.

Whoever promises the nations a "democratic" peace, without at the same time preaching the socialist revolution, or while repudiating the struggle for it—a struggle now, during the war—is deceiving the proletariat.

Sotsial-Demokrat No. 52,   Published according to the
      March 25, 1916   *Sotsial-Demokrat* text

PROPOSALS SUBMITTED
BY THE CENTRAL COMMITTEE OF THE R.S.D.L.P
TO THE SECOND SOCIALIST CONFERENCE

(*Theses* on points 5, 6, 7a, 7b, and 8 of the agenda: the struggle to end the war; the attitude towards the problems of peace, parliamentary action and mass struggles, and the convocation of the International Socialist Bureau. [68])

(The International Socialist Committee, in its notice convening the Second Conference, invited the affiliated organisations to discuss the above questions, and to send in their proposals. In reply to this invitation our Party submits the following theses.)

---

1. Just as all war is but a continuation by violent means of the politics which the belligerent states and their ruling classes had been conducting for many years, sometimes for decades, before the outbreak of war, so the peace that ends any war can be nothing but a consideration and a record of the actual changes brought about in the relation of forces in the course of and as a result of the war.

2. As long as the foundations of present, i.e., bourgeois, social relations remain intact, an imperialist war can lead only to an imperialist peace, i.e., to greater, more extensive and more intense oppression of weak nations and countries by finance capital, which grew to gigantic proportions not only in the period prior to the war, but also during the war. The objective content of the policies pursued by the bourgeoisie and the governments of *both* groups of Great Powers before and during the war leads to intensified economic oppression, national enslavement and political reaction. Therefore, provided the bourgeois social system remains,

the peace that follows upon the war, whatever its outcome, must perpetuate this worsening of the economic and political condition of the masses.

To assume that a democratic peace may emerge from an imperialist war is, in theory, to substitute vulgar phrases for an historical study of the policies conducted before and during that war. In practice, it is to deceive the masses of the people by beclouding their political consciousness, by covering up and prettifying the real policies pursued by the ruling classes to prepare the ground for the coming peace, by concealing from the masses the main thing, namely, that a democratic peace is impossible without a whole series of revolutions.

3. Socialists do not refuse to fight for reform. Even now, for example, they must vote in parliament for improvements, however slight, in the condition of the masses, for increased relief to the inhabitants of the devastated areas, for the lessening of national oppression, etc. But it is sheer bourgeois deception to preach reforms as a solution for problems for which history and the actual political situation demand revolutionary solutions. That is precisely the kind of problems the present war has brought to the fore. These are the fundamental questions of imperialism, i.e., the very existence of capitalist society, the questions of postponing the collapse of capitalism by a redivision of the world to correspond to the new relation of forces among the "Great" Powers, which in the last few decades have developed, not only at fantastic speed, but—and this is particularly important—also with extreme unevenness. Real political activity working a change in the relation of social forces, and not merely deceiving the masses with words, is now possible only in one of two forms—either helping "one's own" national bourgeoisie to rob other countries (and calling this "defence of the fatherland" or "saving the country"), or assisting the proletarian socialist revolution, fostering and stirring up the ferment which is beginning among the masses in all the belligerent countries, aiding the incipient strikes and demonstrations, etc., extending and sharpening these as yet feeble expressions of revolutionary mass struggle into a general proletarian assault to overthrow the bourgeoisie.

Just as all the social-chauvinists are at present deceiving the people by covering up the real, i.e., imperialist, policy of the capitalists, which is being continued in the present war with hypocritical phrases about the "dishonest" attack and "honest" defence on the part of this or that group of predatory capitalists, so phrases about a "democratic peace" serve only to deceive the people, as if the coming peace, which is already being prepared by the capitalists and diplomats, could "simply" abolish "dishonest" attacks and restore "honest" relations, and as if it would not be a continuation, a development, and a perpetuation of this very imperialist policy, i.e., a policy of financial looting, colonial robbery, national oppression, political reaction and intensified capitalist exploitation in every form. What the capitalists and their diplomats now need is "socialist" servants of the bourgeoisie to deafen, dupe and drug the people with talk about a "democratic peace" so as to cover up the real policy of the bourgeoisie, making it difficult for the masses to realise the real nature of this policy and diverting them from the revolutionary struggle.

4. The "democratic" peace programme, in drafting which prominent representatives of the Second International are now engaged, is precisely such a piece of bourgeois deception and hypocrisy. For example, Huysmans at the Arnhem Congress[69] and Kautsky in *Die Neue Zeit*, the most authoritative, official, and "theoretical" spokesmen of this International, formulated this programme as suspension of the revolutionary struggle until the imperialist governments have concluded peace; in the meantime, there are verbal repudiation of annexations and indemnities, verbal recognition of the self-determination of nations, democratisation of foreign politics, courts of arbitration to examine international conflicts between states, disarmament, a United States of Europe,[70] etc., etc. The real political significance of this "peace programme" was revealed with particular force by Kautsky, when, to prove the "unanimity of the International" on this question, he cited the unanimous adoption by the London Conference (February 1915) and the Vienna Conference (April 1915) of the main point of this programme, namely, the "independence of nations". Kautsky, before the whole world, thus openly gave his sanction to the

deliberate deception of the people perpetrated by the social-chauvinists, who combine verbal, hypocritical recognition of "independence" or self-determination of nations, recognition that binds no one and leads nowhere, with support for "their own" governments in the imperialist war, notwithstanding the fact that on *both* sides the war is *accompanied by* systematic violations of the "independence" of weak nations and is being waged *for the purpose* of consolidating and extending their oppression.

Objectively, this cheap "peace programme" reinforces the subjection of the working class to the bourgeoisie by "reconciling" the workers, who are beginning to develop a revolutionary struggle, with their chauvinist leaders, by underplaying the gravity of the crisis in the socialist movement to bring back the pre-war state of affairs in the socialist parties which led the majority of the leaders to desert to the bourgeoisie. The fact that this "Kautskyite" policy is clothed in plausible phrases and that it is being conducted not only in Germany but in all countries, makes it all the more dangerous for the proletariat. In Britain, for instance, this policy is being pursued by the majority of the leaders; in France, by Longuet, Pressemane and others; in Russia, by Axelrod, Martov, Chkheidze and others; Chkheidze is screening the chauvinist idea of "defence of the country" in the present war with the "save the country" phrase, paying lip-service to Zimmerwald, on the one hand, and on the other, praising Huysmans's notorious Arnhem speech in an official declaration by his group; but neither from the floor of the Duma nor in the press has he actually opposed the participation of the workers in the war industries committees, and remains on the staff of newspapers advocating such participation. In Italy, a similar policy is being pursued by Treves: see the threat made by *Avanti!*,[71] the Central Organ of the Italian Socialist Party, of March 5, 1916, to expose Treves and other "reformist-possibilists", to expose those "who resorted to every means to prevent the Party Executive and Oddino Morgari from taking action to secure unity at Zimmerwald and to create a new International", etc., etc.

5. The chief of the "peace questions" at the present time is that of annexations. It most strikingly reveals the now

prevailing socialist hypocrisy and the tasks of real socialist propaganda and agitation.

It is necessary to explain the meaning of annexations, and why and how socialists must fight against them. Not *every* appropriation of "foreign" territory can be described as an annexation, for, generally speaking, socialists favour the abolition of frontiers between nations and the formation of larger states; nor can every disturbance of the *status quo* be described as an annexation, for this would be extremely reactionary and a mockery of the fundamental concepts of the science of history; nor can every military seizure of territory be called annexation, for socialists cannot repudiate violence and wars in the interests of the majority of the population. Annexation must apply only to the appropriation of territory *against the will* of the population of that territory; in other words, the concept of annexation is inseparably bound up with the concept of self-determination of nations.

The present war, however—precisely because it is an imperialist war insofar as *both* groups of belligerent powers are concerned—inevitably had to and did give rise to the phenomenon of the bourgeoisie and the social-chauvinists "fighting" violently against annexations when this is done by an enemy state. This kind of "struggle against annexations" and this kind of "unanimity" on the question of annexation is plainly sheer hypocrisy. Obviously, the French socialists who defend war over Alsace-Lorraine, and the German socialists who do not demand freedom for Alsace-Lorraine, for German Poland, etc., to separate from Germany, and the Russian socialists who describe the war being waged to return Poland to tsarist bondage as a war to "save the country", and who demand that Polish territory be annexed to Russia in the name of "peace without annexations", etc., etc., are *in fact annexationists*.

To prevent the struggle against annexations from being mere hypocrisy, or an empty phrase, to make it really educate the masses in the spirit of internationalism, the question must be presented in such a way as to open the eyes of the masses to the fraud in this matter of annexations, instead of covering it up. It is not enough for the socialists of each country to pay lip-service to the equality of nations or to orate, swear and invoke the name of God to witness their opposition to annexations. The socialists of every country must demand immediate and unconditional *freedom to secede* for the colonies and nations oppressed by *their own* "fatherland".

Without this condition, recognition of the self-determination of nations and principles of internationalism would, even in the Zimmerwald Manifesto, remain a dead letter, at best.

6. The socialists' "peace programme", and their programme of "struggle to end the war", must proceed from the exposure of the lie of the "democratic peace", the pacific intentions of the belligerents, etc., now being spread among the people by demagogic ministers, pacifist bourgeois, social-chauvinists, and Kautskyites in all countries. Any "peace programme" will deceive the people and be a piece of hypocrisy, unless its principal object is to explain to the masses the need for a revolution, and to support, aid, and develop the mass revolutionary struggles breaking out everywhere (ferment among the masses, protests, fraternisation in the trenches, strikes, demonstrations, letters from the front to relatives—for example, in France—urging them not to subscribe to war loans, etc., etc.).

It is the duty of socialists to support, extend and intensify every popular movement to end the war. But it is actually being fulfilled only by those socialists who, like Liebknecht, in their parliamentary speeches, call upon the soldiers to lay down their arms, and preach revolution and transformation of the imperialist war into a civil war for socialism.

The positive slogan we must put forward to draw the masses into revolutionary struggle and to explain the necessity for revolutionary measures to make a "democratic" peace possible, is that of repudiation of debts incurred by states.

It is not enough to hint at revolution, as the Zimmerwald Manifesto does, by saying that the workers must make sacrifices for their own and not for someone else's cause. The masses must be shown their road clearly and definitely. They must know where to go and why. That mass revolutionary actions during the war, if successfully developed, can lead only to the transformation of the imperialist war into a civil war for socialism is obvious, and it is harmful to conceal this from the masses. On the contrary, this aim must be indicated clearly, no matter how difficult its attainment may appear now, while we are still at the beginning of the road. It is not enough to say, as the Zimmerwald Manifesto does, that "the capitalists lie when they speak about defence of the fatherland" in the present war, and that the workers in their revolutionary struggle must ignore their country's military situation; it is necessary to state clearly what is merely hinted at here, namely, that not only the capitalists, but also the social-chauvinists and the Kautsky-ites lie when they allow the term "defence of the father-land" to be applied in the present, imperialist war and that revolutionary action during the war is impossible unless "one's own" government is threatened with defeat; it must be stated clearly that every defeat of the government in a reactionary war facilitates revolution, which alone is capable of bringing about a lasting and democratic peace. Finally, the masses must be told that unless they themselves create illegal organisations and a press that is free from military censorship, i.e., an illegal press, it will be quite impossible to render serious support to the incipient revolutionary struggle, to develop it, to criticise some of its steps, to correct its errors and systematically to extend and sharpen it.

7. On the question of socialist parliamentary action, it must be borne in mind that the Zimmerwald resolution not only expresses sympathy for the five Social-Democratic deputies in the State Duma, who belong to our Party, and who have been sentenced to exile to Siberia, but also expresses its solidarity with their tactics. It is impossible to recognise the revolutionary struggle of the masses while resting content with exclusively legal socialist activity in parliament. This can only arouse legitimate dissatisfaction among the workers, cause them to desert Social-Democracy for anti-parliamentary anarchism or syndicalism. It must be stated clearly and publicly that Social-Democratic members of parliament must use their position not only to make speeches in parliament, but also to render all possible aid outside parliament to the underground organisation and the

revolutionary struggle of the workers, and that the masses
themselves, through their illegal organisation, must supervise these activities of their leaders.

8. The question of the convocation of the International
Socialist Bureau boils down to a fundamental question of
principle, i.e., whether the old parties and the Second
International can be united. Every step forward taken by the
international labour movement along the road mapped out
by Zimmerwald shows more and more clearly the inconsistency of the position adopted by the Zimmerwald majority;
for, on the one hand, it identifies the policy of the old
parties and of the Second International with *bourgeois* policy
in the labour movement, with a policy which does not
pursue the interests of the proletariat, but of the bourgeoisie
(for example, the statement in the Zimmerwald Manifesto
that the "capitalists" lie when they speak of "defence of
the fatherland" in the present war; also the still more
definite statements contained in the circular of the International Socialist Committee of February 10, 1916[72]); on
the other hand, the International Socialist Committee is
afraid of a break with the International Socialist Bureau
and has promised officially to dissolve when the Bureau
reconvenes.[73]

We state that not only was such a promise never voted
on, but it was never even discussed in Zimmerwald.

The six months since Zimmerwald have proved that
actual work in the spirit of Zimmerwald—not empty phrases
but work—is bound up throughout the world with the split
that is becoming deeper and wider. In Germany, illegal
anti-war leaflets are being printed despite the Party's decisions, i.e., schismatically. When Deputy Otto Rühle, Karl
Liebknecht's closest friend, said openly that there were
actually two parties in existence, one helping the bourgeoisie, and the other fighting against it, many, including the
Kautskyites, reviled him, but no one refuted him. In France,
Bourderon, a member of the Socialist Party, is a determined opponent of a split, but at the same time he submits
a resolution to his Party disapproving of the Party's Central
Committee and of the parliamentary group (*désapprouver
Comm. Adm. Perm. et Gr. Parl.*), which, if adopted, would
certainly have caused an immediate split. In Britain, T. Rus-

sell Williams, a member of the I.L.P., writing in the moderate *Labour Leader*, openly admits that a split is inevitable and finds support in letters written by local functionaries. The example of America is perhaps still more instructive, because even there, in a neutral country, two irreconcilably hostile trends in the Socialist Party have become revealed: on the one hand, the adherents of so-called "preparedness",* i.e., war, militarism, and navalism, and on the other, socialists like Eugene Debs, former presidential candidate from the Socialist Party, who openly preaches civil war for socialism, precisely in connection with the coming war.

Actually, there is already a split throughout the world; two entirely irreconcilable working-class policies in relation to the war have crystallised. We must not close our eyes to this fact; to do so would only result in confusing the masses of the workers, in befogging their minds, in hindering the revolutionary mass struggle with which all Zimmerwaldists officially sympathise, and in strengthening the influence over the masses of those leaders whom the International Socialist Committee, in its circular of February 10, 1916, openly accuses of "misleading" the masses and of hatching a "plot" (*Pakt*) *against* socialism.

It is the social-chauvinists and Kautskyites of all countries who will undertake the task of restoring the bankrupt International Socialist Bureau. The task of the socialists is to explain to the masses the inevitability of a split with those who pursue a bourgeois policy under the flag of socialism.

Written February-March 1916

Published on April 22, 1916
in *Bulletin. Internationale Sozialistische Kommission zu Bern* No. 4

Published in Russian on June 10, 1916 in *Sotsial-Demokrat* No. 54-55

Published according to the manuscript

---

* The word is in English in the original.—*Ed.*

7*

SPLIT OR DECAY?

That was how *Sotsial-Demokrat* posed the alternative with regard to the German Social-Democratic Party, back in its issue No. 35,* when it elaborated the fundamental ideas of the Manifesto on war issued by our Party's Central Committee.** Notice how *the facts* bear out this conclusion.

The German Social-Democratic Party is clearly disintegrating. *Otto Rühle*, Karl Liebknecht's closest associate, quite apart from the I.S.D. group (International Socialists of Germany),[74] which has been *consistently* fighting the hypocritical Kautskyites, has *openly* come out for a split. *Vorwärts* had no serious, honest answer. There are actually *two* workers' parties in Germany.

Even in Britain, a statement was made by T. Russell Williams in the moderate, pacifist *Labour Leader* (the Central Organ of the Independent Labour Party), and he was supported by many local functionaries. Comrade *Ornatsky*,[75] who has done very good internationalist work in Britain, came out in the conciliatory *Nashe Slovo* in Paris for an immediate split there. We are naturally in full agreement with *Ornatsky* in his polemic with T. Rothstein, a correspondent of *Kommunist*,[76] who takes a Kautskyite attitude.

In France, Bourderon is a fervent opponent of any split *but*—has proposed to the Party Congress a resolution calling for outright disapproval both of the Party's Central Committee and the parliamentary group! Adoption of such a resolution would mean an immediate split in the Party.

---

* See present edition, Vol. 21, "The War and Russian Social-Democracy".—*Ed.*
** Ibid., "Dead Chauvinism and Living Socialism".—*Ed.*

In America, the Socialist Party appears to be united. Actually, some of its members, like Russell and others, preach "preparedness", stand for war, and want an army and navy. Others, like Eugene Debs, the Party's presidential candidate, openly preach *civil war* "in the event" of an imperialist war, rather, in connection with one.

There are now actually two parties all over the world. There are in fact already two Internationals. And if the Zimmerwald majority are afraid to recognise this, if they dream of unity with the social-chauvinists, and declare their readiness to have such unity, these "pious hopes" in practice remain nothing but hopes, expressive of inconsistency and timidity of thought. Consciousness lags behind reality.

Written February-April 1916

First published in 1931
in *Lenin Miscellany XVII*

Published according
to the manuscript

GERMAN AND NON-GERMAN CHAUVINISM [77]

The German chauvinists, as we know, have succeeded in imposing their influence upon the overwhelming majority of the leaders and officers of the so-called Social-Democratic —now, in fact, National-Liberal—Labour Party. We shall see presently how far this applies also to the non-German chauvinists like Potresov, Levitsky and Co. At the moment we must deal with the German chauvinists, among whom, in fairness, Kautsky must also be included, notwithstanding the fact that P. B. Axelrod, in his German pamphlet, for example, very assiduously and very incorrectly defends Kautsky and calls him an "internationalist".

One of the characteristics of German chauvinism is that "socialists"—socialists in quotation marks—talk about the independence of nations, except those which are oppressed by their own nation. It does not make very much difference whether they say so directly, or whether they defend, justify and shield those who say it.

The German chauvinists (who include Parvus, the publisher of a little magazine, called *Die Glocke*, among whose contributors are Lensch, Haenisch, Grünwald and all the rest of the crew of "socialist" lackeys of the German imperialist bourgeoisie) speak at great length and very eagerly, for example, about independence for the peoples oppressed by Britain. It is not only the social-chauvinists of Germany, i.e., socialists in words, and chauvinists in deeds, but the whole bourgeois press of Germany that is trumpeting with all its might about the shameful, brutal and reactionary, etc., fashion in which Britain rules her colonies. The German newspapers write about the liberation movement in India with great gusto, malicious glee, delight and rapture.

It is easy to see why the German bourgeoisie is full of malicious joy: it hopes to improve its military position by fanning the discontent and the anti-British movement in India. These hopes are silly, of course, because it is simply impossible seriously to entertain the idea of influencing the life of a multi-million people, and a very peculiar people at that, from outside, from afar, in a foreign language, particularly when the influence is not systematic, but casual, only for the duration of the war. Rather than the desire to influence India the efforts of the German imperialist bourgeoisie are more of an attempt at self-consolation, more of a desire to fool the German people and to divert their attention from home to foreign parts.

But this general, theoretical question automatically arises: What is at the root of the falsehood of such arguments; how can the hypocrisy of the German imperialists be exposed with unerring certainty? The correct theoretical answer pointing to the root of falsehood always serves as a means of exposing the hypocrites who, for reasons all too obvious, are inclined to cover up their falsehood, to obscure it, to clothe it in flowery phrases, all sorts of phrases, phrases about everything in the world, even about internationalism. Even the Lensches, Südekums and Scheidemanns, all these agents of the German bourgeoisie, who, unfortunately, belong to the so-called "Social-Democratic" Party of Germany, insist that they are internationalists. Men must not be judged by their words, however, but by their deeds. This is a home truth. Will anyone in Russia judge Potresov, Levitsky, Bulkin and Co. by their words? Of course, not.

The falsehood of the German chauvinists has its roots in their shouting their sympathy for the independence of the peoples oppressed by Britain, their enemy in the war, and modestly, sometimes much too modestly, keeping silent about the independence of the peoples oppressed by *their own* nation.

Take the Danes. When Prussia annexed Schleswig she also seized, as all "Great" Powers are wont to do, a part inhabited by Danes. The violation of the rights of this population was so patent that when Austria ceded to Prussia her "rights" to Schleswig under the Peace of Prague, August 23-30, 1866, the treaty stipulated that the population of the northern part of the province was to be asked in a plebiscite whether they wished to join Denmark and were to be joined to Denmark in the event of a vote to that effect. This condition, however, was not fulfilled by Prussia who, in 1878, had this "unpleasant" clause deleted.

Frederick Engels, who was never indifferent to the chauvinism of Great-Power nations, specifically pointed to this violation of the rights of a small nation by Prussia.[78] But the present-day German social-chauvinists, while recognising the right to self-determination of nations in words, as Kautsky also does, have never carried on any consistently-democratic and resolutely-democratic agitation in favour of liberating an oppressed nation when that oppression was exercised by "their own" nation. That is the whole secret, the kernel of the question of chauvinism and of its exposure.

A once popular pun in Russia was that *Russkoye Znamya*[79] frequently behaved like *Prusskoye Znamya*.* But this does not apply to *Russkoye Znamya* alone; for Potresov, Levitsky and Co. reason in Russia in the very same way as Lensch, Kautsky and Co. reason in Germany. Take a look in the liquidationist *Rabocheye Utro*, for example, and you will find similar "Prussian", or rather, international-chauvinist arguments and methods of reasoning. Chauvinism remains true to itself, whatever its national brand, whatever its pacifist cover-up phrase.

Published on May 31, 1916
in *Voprosy Strakhovania* No 5 (54)

Published according
to the manuscript

---

* *Russkoye Znamya*—Russian Banner; *Prusskoye Znamya*—Prussian Banner.—*Ed.*

IMPERIALISM,
THE HIGHEST STAGE OF CAPITALISM[80]

A POPULAR OUTLINE

Written January-June 1916
First published in mid-1917
in pamphlet form,
Petrograd

Published according to the
manuscript and verified with
the text of the pamphlet

Н. ЛЕНИНЪ (ВЛ. ИЛЬИНЪ).

ИМПЕРІАЛИЗМЪ,

КАКЪ НОВЕЙШІЙ ЭТАПЪ

КАПИТАЛИЗМА.

(Популярный очеркъ).

СКЛАДЪ ИЗДАНІЯ:
Книжный складъ и магазинъ „Жизнь и Знаніе"
Петроградъ, Поварской пер., 2, кв. 9 и 10. Тел. 227—42.
1917 г.

Cover of *Imperialism, the Highest Stage
of Capitalism*. 1917
Reduced

PREFACE

The pamphlet here presented to the reader was written in the spring of 1916, in Zurich. In the conditions in which I was obliged to work there I naturally suffered somewhat from a shortage of French and English literature and from a serious dearth of Russian literature. However, I made use of the principal English work on imperialism, the book by J. A. Hobson, with all the care that, in my opinion, that work deserves.

This pamphlet was written with an eye to the tsarist censorship. Hence, I was not only forced to confine myself strictly to an exclusively theoretical, specifically economic analysis of facts, but to formulate the few necessary observations on politics with extreme caution, by hints, in an allegorical language—in that accursed Aesopian language — to which tsarism compelled all revolutionaries to have recourse whenever they took up the pen to write a "legal" work.

It is painful, in these days of liberty, to re-read the passages of the pamphlet which have been distorted, cramped, compressed in an iron vice on account of the censor. That the period of imperialism is the eve of the socialist revolution; that social-chauvinism (socialism in words, chauvinism in deeds) is the utter betrayal of socialism, complete desertion to the side of the bourgeoisie; that this split in the working-class movement is bound up with the objective conditions of imperialism, etc.—on these matters I had to speak in a "slavish" tongue, and I must refer the reader who is interested in the subject to the articles I wrote abroad in 1914-17, a new edition of which is soon to appear. Special attention should be drawn to a passage on pages 119-20.*
In order to show the reader, in a guise acceptable to the

censors, how shamelessly untruthful the capitalists and the social-chauvinists who have deserted to their side (and whom Kautsky opposes so inconsistently) are on the question of annexations; in order to show how shamelessly they *screen* the annexations of *their* capitalists, I was forced to quote as an example—Japan! The careful reader will easily substitute Russia for Japan, and Finland, Poland, Courland, the Ukraine, Khiva, Bokhara, Estonia or other regions peopled by non-Great Russians, for Korea.

I trust that this pamphlet will help the reader to understand the fundamental economic question, that of the economic essence of imperialism, for unless this is studied, it will be impossible to understand and appraise modern war and modern politics.

Author

Petrograd, April 26, 1917

* See pp. 297-98 of this volume.—*Ed.*

PREFACE
TO THE FRENCH AND GERMAN EDITIONS [81]

I

As was indicated in the preface to the Russian edition, this pamphlet was written in 1916, with an eye to the tsarist censorship. I am unable to revise the whole text at the present time, nor, perhaps, would this be advisable, since the main purpose of the book was, and remains, to present, on the basis of the summarised returns of irrefutable bourgeois statistics, and the admissions of bourgeois scholars of all countries, a *composite picture* of the world capitalist system in its international relationships at the beginning of the twentieth century—on the eve of the first world imperialist war.

To a certain extent it will even be useful for many Communists in advanced capitalist countries to convince themselves by the example of this pamphlet, *legal from the standpoint of the tsarist censor*, of the possibility, and necessity, of making use of even the slight remnants of legality which still remain at the disposal of the Communists, say, in contemporary America or France, after the recent almost wholesale arrests of Communists, in order to explain the utter falsity of social-pacifist views and hopes for "world democracy". The most essential of what should be added to this censored pamphlet I shall try to present in this preface.

II

It is proved in the pamphlet that the war of 1914-18 was imperialist (that is, an annexationist, predatory, war of plunder) on the part of both sides; it was a war for the division of the world, for the partition and repartition of colonies and spheres of influence of finance capital, etc.

Proof of what was the true social, or rather, the true class character of the war is naturally to be found, not in the diplomatic history of the war, but in an analysis of the *objective* position of the ruling *classes* in *all* the belligerent countries. In order to depict this objective position one must not take examples or isolated data (in view of the extreme complexity of the phenomena of social life it is always possible to select any number of examples or separate data to prove any proposition), but *all* the data on the *basis* of economic life in *all* the belligerent countries and the *whole* world.

It is precisely irrefutable summarised data of this kind that I quoted in describing the *partition of the world* in 1876 and 1914 (in Chapter VI) and the division of the world's *railways* in 1890 and 1913 (in Chapter VII). Railways are a summation of the basic capitalist industries, coal, iron and steel; a summation and the most striking index of the development of world trade and bourgeois-democratic civilisation. How the railways are linked up with large-scale industry, with monopolies, syndicates, cartels, trusts, banks and the financial oligarchy is shown in the preceding chapters of the book. The uneven distribution of the railways, their uneven development—sums up, as it were, modern monopolist capitalism on a world-wide scale. And this summary proves that imperialist wars are absolutely inevitable under *such* an economic system, *as long as* private property in the means of production exists.

The building of railways seems to be a simple, natural, democratic, cultural and civilising enterprise; that is what it is in the opinion of the bourgeois professors who are paid to depict capitalist slavery in bright colours, and in the opinion of petty-bourgeois philistines. But as a matter of fact the capitalist threads, which in thousands of different intercrossings bind these enterprises with private property in the means of production in general, have converted this railway construction into an instrument for oppressing *a thousand million* people (in the colonies and semi-colonies), that is, more than half the population of the globe that inhabits the dependent countries, as well as the wage-slaves of capital in the "civilised" countries.

Private property based on the labour of the small pro-prietor, free competition, democracy, all the catchwords with which the capitalists and their press deceive the workers and the peasants—are things of the distant past. Capitalism has grown into a world system of colonial oppression and of the financial strangulation of the overwhelming majority of the population of the world by a handful of "advanced" countries. And this "booty" is shared between two or three powerful world plunderers armed to the teeth (America, Great Britain, Japan), who are drawing the whole world into *their* war over the division of *their* booty.

III

The Treaty of Brest-Litovsk dictated by monarchist Germany, and the subsequent much more brutal and despicable Treaty of Versailles dictated by the "democratic" republics of America and France and also by "free" Britain, have rendered a most useful service to humanity by exposing both imperialism's hired coolies of the pen and petty-bourgeois reactionaries who, although they call themselves pacifists and socialists, sang praises to "Wilsonism", and insisted that peace and reforms were possible under imperialism.

The tens of millions of dead and maimed left by the war —a war to decide whether the British or German group of financial plunderers is to receive the most booty—and those two "peace treaties", are with unprecedented rapidity opening the eyes of the millions and tens of millions of people who are downtrodden, oppressed, deceived and duped by the bourgeoisie. Thus, out of the universal ruin caused by the war a world-wide revolutionary crisis is arising which, however prolonged and arduous its stages may be, cannot end otherwise than in a proletarian revolution and in its victory.

The Basle Manifesto of the Second International, which in 1912 gave an appraisal of the very war that broke out in 1914 and not of war in general (there are different kinds of wars, including revolutionary wars)—this Manifesto is now a monument exposing to the full the shameful bankruptcy and treachery of the heroes of the Second International.

That is why I reproduce this Manifesto as a supplement to the present edition, and again and again I urge the reader

to note that the heroes of the Second International are as
assiduously avoiding the passages of this Manifesto which
speak precisely, clearly and definitely of the connection
between that impending war and the proletarian revolution, as a thief avoids the scene of his crime.

IV

Special attention has been devoted in this pamphlet to
a criticism of Kautskyism, the international ideological
trend represented in all countries of the world by the "most
prominent theoreticians", the leaders of the Second International (Otto Bauer and Co. in Austria, Ramsay MacDonald
and others in Britain, Albert Thomas in France, etc., etc.)
and a multitude of socialists, reformists, pacifists, bourgeois-
democrats and parsons.

This ideological trend is, on the one hand, a product of
the disintegration and decay of the Second International,
and, on the other hand, the inevitable fruit of the ideology
of the petty bourgeoisie, whose entire way of life holds
them captive to bourgeois and democratic prejudices.

The views held by Kautsky and his like are a complete
renunciation of those same revolutionary principles of Marxism that writer has championed for decades, especially,
by the way, in his struggle against socialist opportunism
(of Bernstein, Millerand, Hyndman, Gompers, etc.). It is
not a mere accident, therefore, that Kautsky's followers all
over the world have now united in practical politics with
the extreme opportunists (through the Second, or Yellow
International) and with the bourgeois governments (through
bourgeois coalition governments in which socialists take
part).

The growing world proletarian revolutionary movement
in general, and the communist movement in particular,
cannot dispense with an analysis and exposure of the theoretical errors of Kautskyism. The more so since pacifism
and "democracy" in general, which lay no claim to Marxism
whatever, but which, like Kautsky and Co., are obscuring
the profundity of the contradictions of imperialism and the
inevitable revolutionary crisis to which it gives rise, are

still very widespread all over the world. To combat these tendencies is the bounden duty of the party of the proletariat, which must win away from the bourgeoisie the small proprietors who are duped by them, and the millions of working people who enjoy more or less petty-bourgeois conditions of life.

V

A few words must be said about Chapter VIII, "Parasitism and Decay of Capitalism". As already pointed out in the text, Hilferding, ex-"Marxist", and now a comrade-in-arms of Kautsky and one of the chief exponents of bourgeois, reformist policy in the Independent Social-Democratic Party of Germany,[82] has taken a step backward on this question compared with the *frankly* pacifist and reformist Englishman, Hobson. The international split of the entire working-class movement is now quite evident (the Second and the Third Internationals). The fact that armed struggle and civil war is now raging between the two trends is also evident—the support given to Kolchak and Denikin in Russia by the Mensheviks and Socialist-Revolutionaries against the Bolsheviks; the fight the Scheidemanns and Noskes have conducted in conjunction with the bourgeoisie against the Spartacists[83] in Germany; the same thing in Finland, Poland, Hungary, etc. What is the economic basis of this world-historical phenomenon?

It is precisely the parasitism and decay of capitalism, characteristic of its highest historical stage of development, i.e., imperialism. As this pamphlet shows, capitalism has now singled out a *handful* (less than one-tenth of the inhabitants of the globe; less than one-fifth at a most "generous" and liberal calculation) of exceptionally rich and powerful states which plunder the whole world simply by "clipping coupons". Capital exports yield an income of eight to ten thousand million francs per annum, at pre-war prices and according to pre-war bourgeois statistics. Now, of course, they yield much more.

Obviously, out of such enormous *superprofits* (since they are obtained over and above the profits which capitalists squeeze out of the workers of their "own" country) it is *possible to bribe* the labour leaders and the upper stratum of the labour aristocracy. And that is just what the capitalists of the "advanced" countries are doing: they are bribing them in a thousand different ways, direct and indirect, overt and covert.

This stratum of workers-turned-bourgeois, or the labour aristocracy, who are quite philistine in their mode of life, in the size of their earnings and in their entire outlook, is the principal prop of the Second International, and in our days, the principal *social* (not military) *prop of the bourgeoisie.* For they are the real *agents of the bourgeoisie in the working-class* movement, the labour lieutenants of the capitalist class, real vehicles of reformism and chauvinism. In the civil war between the proletariat and the bourgeoisie they inevitably, and in no small numbers, take the side of the bourgeoisie, the "Versaillais" against the "Communards".

Unless the economic roots of this phenomenon are understood and its political and social significance is appreciated, not a step can be taken toward the solution of the practical problems of the communist movement and of the impending social revolution.

Imperialism is the eve of the social revolution of the proletariat. This has been confirmed since 1917 on a world-wide scale.

N. Lenin

July 6, 1920

Имперіализмъ, какъ высшая стадія капитализма.

(Популярный очеркъ).

За послѣднія 15-20 лѣтъ, особенно послѣ испано-американской (1898) и англо-бурской (1899-1902) войны, экономическая, а также политическая, литература стараго и новаго свѣта все чаще и чаще останавливается на понятіи „имперіализмъ" для характеристики переживаемой нами эпохи. Въ 1902 году в Лондонѣ и Нью-Іоркѣ вышло всвѣтъ сочиненіе англійскаго экономиста Дж. А. Гобсона: „Имперіализмъ". Авторъ, стоящій на точкѣ зрѣнія буржуазнаго соціалъ-реформизма и пацифизма — однородной, в сущности, съ теперешней позиціей бывшаго марксиста К. Каутскаго, — далъ очень хорошее и обстоятельное описаніе основныхъ экономическихъ и политическихъ особенностей имперіализма. Въ 1910 году в Вѣнѣ вышло в свѣтъ сочиненіе австрійскаго марксиста Рудольфа Гильфердинга: „Финансовый капиталъ" (рус

First page of manuscript,
*Imperialism, the Highest Stage
of Capitalism.*
January-June 1916
Reduced

During the last fifteen to twenty years, especially since the Spanish-American War (1898) and the Anglo-Boer War (1899-1902), the economic and also the political literature of the two hemispheres has more and more often adopted the term "imperialism" in order to describe the present era. In 1902, a book by the English economist J. A. Hobson, *Imperialism*, was published in London and New York. This author, whose point of view is that of bourgeois social-reformism and pacifism which, in essence, is identical with the present point of view of the ex-Marxist, Karl Kautsky, gives a very good and comprehensive description of the principal specific economic and political features of imperialism. In 1910, there appeared in Vienna the work of the Austrian Marxist, Rudolf Hilferding, *Finance Capital* (Russian edition, Moscow, 1912). In spite of the mistake the author makes on the theory of money, and in spite of a certain inclination on his part to reconcile Marxism with opportunism, this work gives a very valuable theoretical analysis of "the latest phase of capitalist development", as the subtitle runs. Indeed, what has been said of imperialism during the last few years, especially in an enormous number of magazine and newspaper articles, and also in the resolutions, for example, of the Chemnitz and Basle congresses which took place in the autumn of 1912, has scarcely gone beyond the ideas expounded, or more exactly, summed up by the two writers mentioned above....

Later on, I shall try to show briefly, and as simply as possible, the connection and relationships between the *principal* economic features of imperialism. I shall not be able to deal with the non-economic aspects of the question, however much they deserve to be dealt with. References to literature and other notes which, perhaps, would not interest all readers, are to be found at the end of this pamphlet.[84]

I. CONCENTRATION OF PRODUCTION AND MONOPOLIES

The enormous growth of industry and the remarkably rapid concentration of production in ever-larger enterprises are one of the most characteristic features of capitalism. Modern production censuses give most complete and most exact data on this process.

In Germany, for example, out of every 1,000 industrial enterprises, large enterprises, i.e., those employing more than 50 workers, numbered three in 1882, six in 1895 and nine in 1907; and out of every 100 workers employed, this group of enterprises employed 22, 30 and 37, respectively. Concentration of production, however, is much more intense than the concentration of workers, since labour in the large enterprises is much more productive. This is shown by the figures on steam-engines and electric motors. If we take what in Germany is called industry in the broad sense of the term, that is, including commerce, transport, etc., we get the following picture. Large-scale enterprises, 30,588 out of a total of 3,265,623, that is to say, 0.9 per cent. These enterprises employ 5,700,000 workers out of a total of 14,400,000, i.e., 39.4 per cent; they use 6,600,000 steam horse power out of a total of 8,800,000, i.e., 75.3 per cent, and 1,200,000 kilowatts of electricity out of a total of 1,500,000, i.e., 77.2 per cent.

Less than one-hundredth of the total number of enterprises utilise *more than three-fourths* of the total amount of steam and electric power! Two million nine hundred and seventy thousand small enterprises (employing up to five workers), constituting 91 per cent of the total, utilise only 7 per cent of the total amount of steam and electric power! Tens of thousands of huge enterprises are everything; millions of small ones are nothing.

In 1907, there were in Germany 586 establishments employing one thousand and more workers, nearly *one-tenth*

(1,380,000) of the total number of workers employed in industry, and they consumed *almost one-third* (32 per cent) of the total amount of steam and electric power.* As we shall see, money capital and the banks make this superiority of a handful of the largest enterprises still more overwhelming, in the most literal sense of the word, i.e., millions of small, medium and even some big "proprietors" are in fact in complete subjection to some hundreds of millionaire financiers.

In another advanced country of modern capitalism, the United States of America, the growth of the concentration of production is still greater. Here statistics single out industry in the narrow sense of the word and classify enterprises according to the value of their annual output. In 1904 large-scale enterprises with an output valued at one million dollars and over numbered 1,900 (out of 216,180, i.e., 0.9 per cent). These employed 1,400,000 workers (out of 5,500,000, i.e., 25.6 per cent) and the value of their output amounted to $5,600,000,000 (out of $14,800,000,000, i.e., 38 per cent). Five years later, in 1909, the corresponding figures were: 3,060 enterprises (out of 268,491, i.e., 1.1 per cent) employing 2,000,000 workers (out of 6,600,000, i.e., 30.5 per cent) with an output valued at $9,000,000,000 (out of $20,700,000,000, i.e., 43.8 per cent).**

Almost half the total production of all the enterprises of the country was carried on by *one-hundredth part* of these enterprises! These 3,000 giant enterprises embrace 258 branches of industry. From this it can be seen that, at a certain stage of its development concentration itself, as it were, leads straight to monopoly, for a score or so of giant enterprises can easily arrive at an agreement, and on the other hand, the hindrance to competition, the tendency towards monopoly, arises from the huge size of the enterprises. This transformation of competition into monopoly is one of the most important—if not the most important—phenomena of modern capitalist economy, and we must deal with it in greater detail. But first we must clear up one possible misunderstanding.

---

* Figures taken from *Annalen des deutschen Reichs*, 1911, Zahn.
** *Statistical Abstract of the United States 1912*, p. 202.

American statistics speak of 3,000 giant enterprises in
250 branches of industry, as if there were only a dozen
enterprises of the largest scale for each branch of industry.

But this is not the case. Not in every branch of industry
are there large-scale enterprises; and moreover, a very
important feature of capitalism in its highest stage of development is so-called *combination* of production, that is to say,
the grouping in a single enterprise of different branches of
industry, which either represent the consecutive stages in
the processing of raw materials (for example, the smelting
of iron ore into pig-iron, the conversion of pig-iron into
steel, and then, perhaps, the manufacture of steel goods)—
or are auxiliary to one another (for example, the utilisation
of scrap, or of by-products, the manufacture of packing
materials, etc.).

"Combination," writes Hilferding, "levels out the fluctuations of trade and therefore assures to the combined
enterprises a more stable rate of profit. Secondly, combination
has the effect of eliminating trade. Thirdly, it has the effect
of rendering possible technical improvements, and, consequently, the acquisition of superprofits over and above
those obtained by the 'pure' [i.e., non-combined] enterprises.
Fourthly, it strengthens the position of the combined
enterprises relative to the 'pure' enterprises, strengthens
them in the competitive struggle in periods of serious
depression, when the fall in prices of raw materials does not
keep pace with the fall in prices of manufactured goods."*

The German bourgeois economist, Heymann, who has
written a book especially on "mixed", that is, combined,
enterprises in the German iron industry, says: "Pure enterprises perish, they are crushed between the high price of raw
material and the low price of the finished product." Thus
we get the following picture: "There remain, on the one hand,
the big coal companies, producing millions of tons yearly,
strongly organised in their coal syndicate, and on the other,
the big steel plants, closely allied to the coal mines, having
their own steel syndicate. These giant enterprises, producing
400,000 tons of steel per annum, with a tremendous output
of ore and coal and producing finished steel goods, employing

---

* *Finance Capital*, Russ. ed., pp. 286-87.

10,000 workers quartered in company houses, and sometimes owning their own railways and ports, are the typical representatives of the German iron and steel industry. And concentration goes on further and further. Individual enterprises are becoming larger and larger. An ever-increasing number of enterprises in one, or in several different industries, join together in giant enterprises, backed up and directed by half a dozen big Berlin banks. In relation to the German mining industry, the truth of the teachings of Karl Marx on concentration is definitely proved; true, this applies to a country where industry is protected by tariffs and freight rates. The German mining industry is ripe for expropriation."*

Such is the conclusion which a bourgeois economist who, by way of exception is conscientious, had to arrive at. It must be noted that he seems to place Germany in a special category because her industries are protected by high tariffs. But this is a circumstance which only accelerates concentration and the formation of monopolist manufacturers' associations, cartels, syndicates, etc. It is extremely important to note that in free-trade Britain, concentration *also* leads to monopoly, although somewhat later and perhaps in another form. Professor Hermann Levy, in his special work of research entitled *Monopolies, Cartels and Trusts*, based on data on British economic development, writes as follows:

"In Great Britain it is the size of the enterprise and its high technical level which harbour a monopolist tendency. This, for one thing, is due to the great investment of capital per enterprise, which gives rise to increasing demands for new capital for the new enterprises and thereby renders their launching more difficult. Moreover (and this seems to us to be the more important point), every new enterprise that wants to keep pace with the gigantic enterprises that have been formed by concentration would here produce such an enormous quantity of surplus goods that it could dispose of them only by being able to sell them profitably as a result of an enormous increase in demand; otherwise, this surplus

* Hans Gideon Heymann, *Die gemischten Werke im deutschen Grosseisengewerbe*, Stuttgart, 1904 (S. 256, 278).

would force prices down to a level that would be unprofitable both for the new enterprise and for the monopoly combines." Britain differs from other countries where protective tariffs facilitate the formation of cartels in that monopolist manufacturers' associations, cartels and trusts arise in the majority of cases only when the number of the chief competing enterprises has been reduced to "a couple of dozen or so". "Here the influence of concentration on the formation of large industrial monopolies in a whole sphere of industry stands out with crystal clarity."*

Half a century ago, when Marx was writing *Capital*, free competition appeared to the overwhelming majority of economists to be a "natural law". Official science tried, by a conspiracy of silence, to kill the works of Marx, who by a theoretical and historical analysis of capitalism had proved that free competition gives rise to the concentration of production, which, in turn, at a certain stage of development, leads to monopoly. Today, monopoly has become a fact. Economists are writing mountains of books in which they describe the diverse manifestations of monopoly, and continue to declare in chorus that "Marxism is refuted". But facts are stubborn things, as the English proverb says, and they have to be reckoned with, whether we like it or not. The facts show that differences between capitalist countries, e.g., in the matter of protection or free trade, only give rise to insignificant variations in the form of monopolies or in the moment of their appearance; and that the rise of monopolies, as the result of the concentration of production, is a general and fundamental law of the present stage of development of capitalism.

For Europe, the time when the new capitalism *definitely* superseded the old can be established with fair precision; it was the beginning of the twentieth century. In one of the latest compilations on the history of the "formation of monopolies", we read:

"Isolated examples of capitalist monopoly could be cited from the period preceding 1860; in these could be discerned the embryo of the forms that are so common today; but

---

* Hermann Levy, *Monopole, Kartelle und Trusts*, Jena, 1909, S. 286, 290, 298.

all this undoubtedly represents the prehistory of the cartels. The real beginning of modern monopoly goes back, at
the earliest, to the sixties. The first important period of
development of monopoly commenced with the international
industrial depression of the seventies and lasted until the
beginning of the nineties." "If we examine the question on
a European scale, we will find that the development of free
competition reached its apex in the sixties and seventies.
It was then that Britain completed the construction of her
old-style capitalist organisation. In Germany, this organisation had entered into a fierce struggle with handicraft
and domestic industry, and had begun to create for itself
its own forms of existence."

"The great revolution, commenced with the crash of 1873,
or rather, the depression which followed it and which, with
hardly discernible interruptions in the early eighties, and
the unusually violent, but short-lived boom round about
1889, marks twenty-two years of European economic history." "During the short boom of 1889-90, the system of
cartels was widely resorted to in order to take advantage of
favourable business conditions. An ill-considered policy
drove prices up still more rapidly and still higher than would
have been the case if there had been no cartels, and nearly
all these cartels perished ingloriously in the smash. Another
five-year period of bad trade and low prices followed, but a
new spirit reigned in industry; the depression was no longer
regarded as something to be taken for granted; it was
regarded as nothing more than a pause before another boom.

"The cartel movement entered its second epoch: instead
of being a transitory phenomenon, the cartels have become
one of the foundations of economic life. They are winning
one field of industry after another, primarily, the raw materials industry. At the beginning of the nineties the cartel
system had already acquired—in the organisation of the coke
syndicate on the model of which the coal syndicate was later
formed—a cartel technique which has hardly been improved
on. For the first time the great boom at the close of the
nineteenth century and the crisis of 1900-03 occurred
entirely—in the mining and iron industries at least—under
the aegis of the cartels. And while at that time it appeared
to be something novel, now the general public takes it for

granted that large spheres of economic life have been, as a general rule, removed from the realm of free competition."*

Thus, the principal stages in the history of monopolies are the following: (1) 1860-70, the highest stage, the apex of development of free competition; monopoly is in the barely discernible, embryonic stage. (2) After the crisis of 1873, a lengthy period of development of cartels; but they are still the exception. They are not yet durable. They are still a transitory phenomenon. (3) The boom at the end of the nineteenth century and the crisis of 1900-03. Cartels become one of the foundations of the whole of economic life. Capitalism has been transformed into imperialism.

Cartels come to an agreement on the terms of sale, dates of payment, etc. They divide the markets among themselves. They fix the quantity of goods to be produced. They fix prices. They divide the profits among the various enterprises, etc.

The number of cartels in Germany was estimated at about 250 in 1896 and at 385 in 1905, with about 12,000 firms participating.** But it is generally recognised that these figures are underestimations. From the statistics of German industry for 1907 we quoted above, it is evident that even these 12,000 very big enterprises probably consume more than half the steam and electric power used in the country. In the United States of America, the number of trusts in 1900 was estimated at 185 and in 1907, 250. American statistics divide all industrial enterprises into those belonging to individuals, to private firms or to corporations. The latter in 1904 comprised 23.6 per cent, and in 1909, 25.9 per cent, i.e., more than one-fourth of the total industrial enterprises in the country. These employed in 1904, 70.6 per cent, and in 1909, 75.6 per cent, i.e., more than three-

---

* Th. Vogelstein, "Die finanzielle Organisation der kapitalistischen Industrie und die Monopolbildungen" in *Grundriss der Sozialökonomik*, VI. Abt., Tübingen, 1914. Cf., also by the same author: *Organisationsformen der Eisenindustrie und Textilindustrie in England und Amerika*, Bd. I, Lpz., 1910.

** Dr. Riesser, *Die deutschen Grossbanken und ihre Konzentration im Zusammenhange mit der Entwicklung der Gesamtwirtschaft in Deutschland*, 4. Aufl., 1912, S. 149; Robert Liefmann, *Kartelle und Trusts und die Weiterbildung der volkswirtschaftlichen Organisation*, 2. Aufl., 1910, S. 25.

fourths of the total wage-earners. Their output at these two dates was valued at $10,900,000,000, and $16,300,000,000, i. e., 73.7 per cent and 79.0 per cent of the total, respectively.

At times cartels and trusts concentrate in their hands seven- or eight-tenths of the total output of a given branch of industry. The Rhine-Westphalian Coal Syndicate, at its foundation in 1893, concentrated 86.7 per cent of the total coal output of the area, and in 1910 it already concentrated 95.4 per cent.* The monopoly so created assures enormous profits, and leads to the formation of technical production units of formidable magnitude. The famous Standard Oil Company in the United States was founded in 1900: "It has an authorised capital of $150,000,000. It issued $100,000,000 common and $106,000,000 preferred stock. From 1900 to 1907 the following dividends were paid on the latter: 48, 48, 45, 44, 36, 40, 40, 40 per cent in the respective years, i.e., in all, $367,000,000. From 1882 to 1907, out of total net profits amounting to $889,000,000, $606,000,000 were distributed in dividends, and the rest went to reserve capital."** "In 1907 the various works of the United States Steel Corporation employed no less than 210,180 people. The largest enterprise in the German mining industry, Gelsenkirchener Bergwerksgesellschaft, in 1908 had a staff of 46,048 workers and office employees."*** In 1902, the United States Steel Corporation already produced 9,000,000 tons of steel.**** Its output constituted in 1901, 66.3 per cent, and in 1908, 56.1 per cent of the total output of steel in the United States.***** The output of ore was 43.9 per cent and 46.3 per cent, respectively.

The report of the American Government Commission on Trusts states: "Their superiority over competitors is due

---

* Dr. Fritz Kestner, *Der Organisationszwang. Eine Untersuchung über die Kämpfe zwischen Kartellen und Aussenseitern*, Berlin, 1912, S. 11.

** R. Liefmann, *Beteiligungs- und Finanzierungsgesellschaften. Eine Studie über den modernen Kapitalismus und das Effektenwesen*, 1. Aufl., Jena, 1909, S. 212.

*** Ibid., S. 218.

**** Dr. S. Tschierschky, *Kartell und Trust*, Göttingen, 1903, S. 13.

***** Th. Vogelstein, *Organisationsformen*, S. 275.

to the magnitude of their enterprises and their excellent technical equipment. Since its inception, the Tobacco Trust has devoted all its efforts to the universal substitution of mechanical for manual labour. With this end in view it has bought up all patents that have anything to do with the manufacture of tobacco and has spent enormous sums for this purpose. Many of these patents at first proved to be of no use, and had to be modified by the engineers employed by the trust. At the end of 1906, two subsidiary companies were formed solely to acquire patents. With the same object in view, the trust has built its own foundries, machine shops and repair shops. One of these establishments, that in Brooklyn, employs on the average 300 workers; here experiments are carried out on inventions concerning the manufacture of cigarettes, cheroots, snuff, tinfoil for packing, boxes, etc. Here, also, inventions are perfected."* "Other trusts also employ what are called development engineers whose business it is to devise new methods of production and to test technical improvements. The United States Steel Corporation grants big bonuses to its workers and engineers for all inventions that raise technical efficiency, or reduce cost of production."**

In German large-scale industry, e.g., in the chemical industry, which has developed so enormously during these last few decades, the promotion of technical improvement is organised in the same way. By 1908 the process of concentration of production had already given rise to two main "groups" which, in their way, were also in the nature of monopolies. At first these groups constituted "dual alliances" of two pairs of big factories, each having a capital of from twenty to twenty-one million marks—on the one hand, the former Meister Factory in Höchst and the Casella Factory in Frankfurt am Main; and on the other hand, the aniline and soda factory at Ludwigshafen and the former Bayer Factory at Elberfeld. Then, in 1905, one of these groups, and in 1908 the other group, each concluded an

---

* *Report of the Commissioner of Corporations on the Tobacco Industry*, Washington, 1909, p. 266, cited according to Dr. Paul Tafel, *Die nordamerikanischen Trusts und ihre Wirkungen auf den Fortschritt der Technik*, Stuttgart, 1913, S. 48.

** Dr. P. Tafel, ibid., S. 49.

agreement with yet another big factory. The result was the formation of two "triple alliances", each with a capital of from forty to fifty million marks. And these "alliances" have already begun to "approach" each other, to reach "an understanding" about prices, etc.*

Competition becomes transformed into monopoly. The result is immense progress in the socialisation of production. In particular, the process of technical invention and improvement becomes socialised.

This is something quite different from the old free competition between manufacturers, scattered and out of touch with one another, and producing for an unknown market. Concentration has reached the point at which it is possible to make an approximate estimate of all sources of raw materials (for example, the iron ore deposits) of a country and even, as we shall see, of several countries, or of the whole world. Not only are such estimates made, but these sources are captured by gigantic monopolist associations. An approximate estimate of the capacity of markets is also made, and the associations "divide" them up amongst themselves by agreement. Skilled labour is monopolised, the best engineers are engaged; the means of transport are captured—railways in America, shipping companies in Europe and America. Capitalism in its imperialist stage leads directly to the most comprehensive socialisation of production; it, so to speak, drags the capitalists, against their will and consciousness, into some sort of a new social order, a transitional one from complete free competition to complete socialisation.

Production becomes social, but appropriation remains private. The social means of production remain the private property of a few. The general framework of formally recognised free competition remains, and the yoke of a few monopolists on the rest of the population becomes a hundred times heavier, more burdensome and intolerable.

The German economist, Kestner, has written a book especially devoted to "the struggle between the cartels and outsiders", i.e., the capitalists outside the cartels. He

---

* Riesser, op. cit., third edition, p. 547 et seq. The newspapers (June 1916) report the formation of a new gigantic trust which combines the chemical industry of Germany.

entitled his work *Compulsory Organisation*, although, in order to present capitalism in its true light, he should, of course, have written about compulsory submission to monopolist associations. It is instructive to glance at least at the list of the methods the monopolist associations resort to in the present-day, the latest, the civilised struggle for "organisation": (1) stopping supplies of raw materials (…"one of the most important methods of compelling adherence to the cartel"); (2) stopping the supply of labour by means of "alliances" (i.e., of agreements between the capitalists and the trade unions by which the latter permit their members to work only in cartelised enterprises); (3) stopping deliveries; (4) closing trade outlets; (5) agreements with the buyers, by which the latter undertake to trade only with the cartels; (6) systematic price cutting (to ruin "outside" firms, i.e., those which refuse to submit to the monopolists. Millions are spent in order to sell goods for a certain time below their cost price; there were instances when the price of petrol was thus reduced from 40 to 22 marks, i.e., almost by half!); (7) stopping credits; (8) boycott.

Here we no longer have competition between small and large, between technically developed and backward enterprises. We see here the monopolists throttling those who do not submit to them, to their yoke, to their dictation. This is how this process is reflected in the mind of a bourgeois economist:

"Even in the purely economic sphere," writes Kestner, "a certain change is taking place from commercial activity in the old sense of the word towards organisational-speculative activity. The greatest success no longer goes to the merchant whose technical and commercial experience enables him best of all to estimate the needs of the buyer, and who is able to discover and, so to speak, 'awaken' a latent demand; it goes to the speculative genius [?!] who knows how to estimate, or even only to sense in advance, the organisational development and the possibilities of certain connections between individual enterprises and the banks…."

Translated into ordinary human language this means that the development of capitalism has arrived at a stage when, although commodity production still "reigns" and continues to be regarded as the basis of economic life, it has in reality been undermined and the bulk of the profits go to the "geniuses" of financial manipulation. At the basis of these manipulations and swindles lies socialised production; but the immense progress of mankind, which achieved this socialisation, goes to benefit ... the speculators. We shall see later how "on these grounds" reactionary, petty-bourgeois critics of capitalist imperialism dream of going *back* to "free", "peaceful", and "honest" competition.

"The prolonged raising of prices which results from the formation of cartels," says Kestner, "has hitherto been observed only in respect of the most important means of production, particularly coal, iron and potassium, but never in respect of manufactured goods. Similarly, the increase in profits resulting from this raising of prices has been limited only to the industries which produce means of production. To this observation we must add that the industries which process raw materials (and not semi-manufactures) not only secure advantages from the cartel formation in the shape of high profits, to the detriment of the finished goods industry, but have also secured a *dominating position* over the latter, which did not exist under free competition."*

The words which I have italicised reveal the essence of the case which the bourgeois economists admit so reluctantly and so rarely, and which the present-day defenders of opportunism, led by Kautsky, so zealously try to evade and brush aside. Domination, and the violence that is associated with it, such are the relationships that are typical of the "latest phase of capitalist development"; this is what inevitably had to result, and has resulted, from the formation of all-powerful economic monopolies.

I shall give one more example of the methods employed by the cartels. Where it is possible to capture all or the chief sources of raw materials, the rise of cartels and formation of monopolies is particularly easy. It would be wrong, however, to assume that monopolies do not arise in other industries in which it is impossible to corner the sources of raw materials. The cement industry, for instance, can find its raw materials everywhere. Yet in Germany this industry too is strongly cartelised. The cement manufac-

* Kestner, op. cit., S. 254.

turers have formed regional syndicates: South German, Rhine-Westphalian, etc. The prices fixed are monopoly prices: 230 to 280 marks a car-load, when the cost price is 180 marks! The enterprises pay a dividend of from 12 to 16 per cent—and it must not be forgotten that the "geniuses" of modern speculation know how to pocket big profits besides what they draw in dividends. In order to prevent competition in such a profitable industry, the monopolists even resort to various stratagems: they spread false rumours about the bad situation in their industry; anonymous warnings are published in the newspapers, like the following: "Capitalists, don't invest your capital in the cement industry!"; lastly, they buy up "outsiders" (those outside the syndicates) and pay them compensation of 60,000, 80,000 and even 150,000 marks.* Monopoly hews a path for itself everywhere without scruple as to the means, from paying a "modest" sum to buy off competitors, to the American device of employing dynamite against them.

The statement that cartels can abolish crises is a fable spread by bourgeois economists who at all costs desire to place capitalism in a favourable light. On the contrary, the monopoly created in *certain* branches of industry increases and intensifies the anarchy inherent in capitalist production *as a whole*. The disparity between the development of agriculture and that of industry, which is characteristic of capitalism in general, is increased. The privileged position of the most highly cartelised, so-called *heavy* industry, especially coal and iron, causes "a still greater lack of co-ordination" in other branches of industry—as Jeidels, the author of one of the best works on "the relationship of the German big banks to industry", admits.**

"The more developed an economic system is," writes Liefmann, an unblushing apologist of capitalism, "the more it resorts to risky enterprises, or enterprises in other countries, to those which need a great deal of time to develop, or finally, to those which are only of local importance."*** The

---

* L. Eschwege, "Zement" in *Die Bank*, 1909, 1, S. 115 et seq.
** Jeidels, *Das Verhältnis der deutschen Grossbanken zur Industrie mit besonderer Berücksichtigung der Eisenindustrie*, Leipzig, 1905, S. 271.
*** Liefmann, *Beteiligungs- und Finanzierungsgesellschaften*, S. 434.

increased risk is connected in the long run with a prodigious increase of capital, which, as it were, overflows the brim, flows abroad, etc. At the same time the extremely rapid rate of technical progress gives rise to increasing elements of disparity between the various spheres of national economy, to anarchy and crises. Liefmann is obliged to admit that: "In all probability mankind will see further important technical revolutions in the near future which will also affect the organisation of the economic system"... electricity and aviation.... "As a general rule, in such periods of radical economic change, speculation develops on a large scale."...*

Crises of every kind —economic crises most frequently, but not only these—in their turn increase very considerably the tendency towards concentration and towards monopoly. In this connection, the following reflections of Jeidels on the significance of the crisis of 1900, which, as we have already seen, marked the turning-point in the history of modern monopoly, are exceedingly instructive:

"Side by side with the gigantic plants in the basic industries, the crisis of 1900 still found many plants organised on lines that today would be considered obsolete, the 'pure' (non-combined) plants, which were brought into being at the height of the industrial boom. The fall in prices and the falling off in demand put these 'pure' enterprises in a precarious position, which did not affect the gigantic combined enterprises at all or only affected them for a very short time. As a consequence of this the crisis of 1900 resulted in a far greater concentration of industry than the crisis of 1873: the latter crisis also produced a sort of selection of the best-equipped enterprises, but owing to the level of technical development at that time, this selection could not place the firms which successfully emerged from the crisis in a position of monopoly. Such a durable monopoly exists to a high degree in the gigantic enterprises in the modern iron and steel and electrical industries owing to their very complicated technique, far-reaching organisation and magnitude of capital, and, to a lesser degree, in the engineering industry, certain branches of the metallurgical industry, transport, etc."**

* Ibid., S. 465-66.
** Jeidels, op. cit., S. 108.

Monopoly! This is the last word in the "latest phase of capitalist development". But we shall only have a very insufficient, incomplete, and poor notion of the real power and the significance of modern monopolies if we do not take into consideration the part played by the banks.

II. BANKS AND THEIR NEW ROLE

The principal and primary function of banks is to serve as middlemen in the making of payments. In so doing they transform inactive money capital into active, that is, into capital yielding a profit; they collect all kinds of money revenues and place them at the disposal of the capitalist class.

As banking develops and becomes concentrated in a small number of establishments, the banks grow from modest middlemen into powerful monopolies having at their command almost the whole of the money capital of all the capitalists and small businessmen and also the larger part of the means of production and sources of raw materials in any one country and in a number of countries. This transformation of numerous modest middlemen into a handful of monopolists is one of the fundamental processes in the growth of capitalism into capitalist imperialism; for this reason we must first of all examine the concentration of banking.

In 1907-08, the combined deposits of the German joint-stock banks, each having a capital of more than a million marks, amounted to 7,000 million marks; in 1912-13, these deposits already amounted to 9,800 million marks, an increase of 40 per cent in five years; and of the 2,800 million increase, 2,750 million was divided among 57 banks, each having a capital of more than 10 million marks. The distribution of the deposits between big and small banks was as follows:*

---

* Alfred Lansburgh, "Fünf Jahre deutsches Bankwesen" in *Die Bank*, 1913, No. 8, S. 728.

Percentage of Total Deposits

	In 9 big Berlin banks	In the other 48 banks with a capital of more than 10 million marks	In 115 banks with a capital of 1-10 million marks	In small banks (with a capital of less than million marks)
1907-08	47	32.5	16.5	4
1912-13	49	36	12	3

The small banks are being squeezed out by the big banks, of which only nine concentrate in their hands almost half the total deposits. But we have left out of account many important details, for instance, the transformation of numerous small banks into actual branches of the big banks, etc. Of this I shall speak later on.

At the end of 1913, Schulze-Gaevernitz estimated the deposits in the nine big Berlin banks at 5,100 million marks, out of a total of about 10,000 million marks. Taking into account not only the deposits, but the total bank capital, this author wrote: "At the end of 1909, the nine big Berlin banks, *together with their affiliated banks*, controlled 11,300 million marks, that is, about 83 per cent of the total German bank capital. The Deutsche Bank, which *together with its affiliated banks* controls nearly 3,000 million marks, represents, parallel to the Prussian State Railway Administration, the biggest and also the most decentralised accumulation of capital in the Old World."*

I have emphasised the reference to the "affiliated" banks because it is one of the most important distinguishing features of modern capitalist concentration. The big enterprises, and the banks in particular, not only completely absorb the small ones, but also "annex" them, subordinate them, bring them into their "own" group or "concern" (to use the technical term) by acquiring "holdings" in their capital, by purchasing or exchanging shares, by a system of credits, etc., etc. Professor Liefmann has written a voluminous "work" of about 500 pages describing modern "holding

---

* Schulze-Gaevernitz, "Die deutsche Kreditbank" in *Grundriss der Sozialökonomik*, Tübingen, 1915, S. 12, 137.

and finance companies",* unfortunately adding very dubious "theoretical" reflections to what is frequently undigested raw material. To what results this "holding" system leads in respect of concentration is best illustrated in the book written on the big German banks by Riesser, himself a banker. But before examining his data, let us quote a concrete example of the "holding" system.

The Deutsche Bank "group" is one of the biggest, if not the biggest, of the big banking groups. In order to trace the main threads which connect all the banks in this group, a distinction must be made between holdings of the first and second and third degree, or what amounts to the same thing, between dependence (of the lesser banks on the Deutsche Bank) in the first, second and third degree. We then obtain the following picture**:

	Direct or 1st degree dependence	2nd degree dependence	3rd degree dependence
The Deutsche Bank has holdings Permanently	in 17 other banks	9 of the 17 have holdings in 34 other banks	4 of the 9 have holdings in 7 other banks
For an indefinite period	in 5 other banks	—	—
Occasionally	in 8 other banks	5 of the 8 have holdings in 14 other banks	2 of the 5 have holdings in 2 other banks
Totals	in 30 other banks	14 of the 30 have holdings in 48 other banks	6 of the 14 have holdings in 9 other banks

Included in the eight banks "occasionally" dependent on the Deutsche Bank in the "first degree", are three foreign banks: one Austrian (the Wiener Bankverein) and two Russian (the Siberian Commercial Bank and the Russian Bank for Foreign Trade). Altogether, the Deutsche Bank group

---

* R. Liefmann, *Beteiligungs- und Finanzierungsgesellschaften. Eine Studie über den modernen Kapitalismus und das Effektenwesen,* 1 Aufl., Jena, 1909, S. 212.

** Alfred Lansburgh, "Das Beteiligungssystem im deutschen Bankwesen" in *Die Bank*, 1910, 1, S. 500.

comprises, directly and indirectly, partially and totally, 87 banks; and the total capital —its own and that of others which it controls —is estimated at between two and three thousand million marks.

It is obvious that a bank which stands at the head of such a group, and which enters into agreement with half a dozen other banks only slightly smaller than itself for the purpose of conducting exceptionally big and profitable financial operations like floating state loans, has already outgrown the part of "middleman" and has become an association of a handful of monopolists.

The rapidity with which the concentration of banking proceeded in Germany at the turn of the twentieth century is shown by the following data which we quote in an abbreviated form from Riesser:

Six Big Berlin Banks

Year	Branches in Germany	Deposit banks and exchange offices	Constant holdings in German joint-stock banks	Total establishments
1895	16	14	1	42
1900	21	40	8	80
1911	104	276	63	450

We see the rapid expansion of a close network of channels which cover the whole country, centralising all capital and all revenues, transforming thousands and thousands of scattered economic enterprises into a single national capitalist, and then into a world capitalist economy. The "decentralisation" that Schulze-Gaevernitz, as an exponent of present-day bourgeois political economy, speaks of in the passage previously quoted, really means the subordination to a single centre of an increasing number of formerly relatively "independent", or rather, strictly local economic units. In reality it is *centralisation*, the enhancement of the role, importance and power of monopolist giants.

In the older capitalist countries this "banking network" is still more close. In Great Britain and Ireland, in 1910, there were in all 7,151 branches of banks. Four big banks had more than 400 branches each (from 447 to 689); four had more than 200 branches each, and eleven more than 100 each.

In France, *three* very big banks, Crédit Lyonnais, the
Comptoir National and the Société Générale, extended their
operations and their network of branches in the following
manner.*

	Number of branches and offices			Capital (000,000 francs)	
	In the provinces	In Paris	Total	Own capital	Deposits used as capital
1870	47	17	64	200	427
1890	192	66	258	265	1,245
1909	1,033	196	1,229	887	4,363

In order to show the "connections" of a big modern bank,
Riesser gives the following figures of the number of letters dispatched and received by the Disconto-Gesellschaft,
one of the biggest banks in Germany and in the world (its
capital in 1914 amounted to 300 million marks):

	Letters received	Letters dispatched
1852	6,135	6,292
1870	85,800	87,513
1900	533,102	626,043

The number of accounts of the big Paris bank, the Crédit
Lyonnais, increased from 28,535 in 1875 to 633,539 in
1912.**

These simple figures show perhaps better than lengthy
disquisitions how the concentration of capital and the
growth of bank turnover are radically changing the significance of the banks. Scattered capitalists are transformed
into a single collective capitalist. When carrying the current accounts of a few capitalists, a bank, as it were,
transacts a purely technical and exclusively auxiliary operation. When, however, this operation grows to enormous
dimensions we find that a handful of monopolists subordinate to their will all the operations, both commercial and
industrial, of the whole of capitalist society; for they are
enabled—by means of their banking connections, their
current accounts and other financial operations—first, to

---

* Eugen Kaufmann, *Das französische Bankwesen*, Tübingen,
1911, S. 356 und 362.
** Jean Lescure, *L'épargne en France*, Paris, 1914, p. 52.

ascertain exactly the financial position of the various capitalists, then to *control* them, to influence them by restricting or enlarging, facilitating or hindering credits, and finally to *entirely determine* their fate, determine their income, deprive them of capital, or permit them to increase their capital rapidly and to enormous dimensions, etc.

We have just mentioned the 300 million marks capital of the Disconto-Gesellschaft of Berlin. This increase of the capital of the bank was one of the incidents in the struggle for hegemony between two of the biggest Berlin banks—the Deutsche Bank and the Disconto. In 1870, the first was still a novice and had a capital of only 15 million marks, while the second had a capital of 30 million marks. In 1908, the first had a capital of 200 million, while the second had 170 million. In 1914, the first increased its capital to 250 million and the second, by merging with another first-class big bank, the Schaaffhausenscher Bankverein, increased its capital to 300 million. And, of course, this struggle for hegemony went hand in hand with the more and more frequent conclusion of "agreements" of an increasingly durable character between the two banks. The following are the conclusions that this development forces upon banking specialists who regard economic questions from a standpoint which does not in the least exceed the bounds of the most moderate and cautious bourgeois reformism.

Commenting on the increase of the capital of the Disconto-Gesellschaft to 300 million marks, the German review, *Die Bank*, wrote: "Other banks will follow this same path and in time the three hundred men, who today govern Germany economically, will gradually be reduced to fifty, twenty-five or still fewer. It cannot be expected that this latest move towards concentration will be confined to banking. The close relations that exist between individual banks naturally lead to the bringing together of the industrial syndicates which these banks favour.... One fine morning we shall wake up in surprise to see nothing but trusts before our eyes, and to find ourselves faced with the necessity of substituting state monopolies for private monopolies. However, we have nothing to reproach ourselves with, except that we have allowed things to follow their own course, slightly accelerated by the manipulation of stocks."*

This is an example of the impotence of bourgeois journalism which differs from bourgeois science only in that the latter is less sincere and strives to obscure the essence of the matter, to hide the forest behind the trees. To be "surprised" at the results of concentration, to "reproach" the government of capitalist Germany, or capitalist "society" ("ourselves"), to fear that the introduction of stocks and shares might "accelerate" concentration in the same way as the German "cartel" specialist Tschierschky fears the American trusts and "prefers" the German cartels on the grounds that they "may not, like the trusts, excessively accelerate technical and economic progress"**—is not all this a sign of impotence?

But facts remain facts. There are no trusts in Germany; there are "only" cartels—but Germany is *governed* by not more than three hundred magnates of capital, and the number of these is constantly diminishing. At all events, banks greatly intensify and accelerate the process of concentration of capital and the formation of monopolies in all capitalist countries, notwithstanding all the differences in their banking laws.

The banking system "possesses, indeed, the form of universal book-keeping and distribution of means of production on a social scale, but solely the form", wrote Marx in *Capital* half a century ago (Russ. trans., Vol. III, part II, p. 144[85]). The figures we have quoted on the growth of bank capital, on the increase in the number of the branches and offices of the biggest banks, the increase in the number of their accounts, etc., present a concrete picture of this "universal book-keeping" of the *whole* capitalist class; and not only of the capitalists, for the banks collect, even though temporarily, all kinds of money revenues—of small businessmen, office clerks, and of a tiny upper stratum of the working class. "Universal distribution of means of production"—that, from the formal aspect, is what *grows* out of the modern banks, which, numbering some three to six of the biggest

* A. Lansburgh, "Die Bank mit den 300 Millionen" in *Die Bank*, 1914, 1, S. 426.
** S. Tschierschky, op. cit., S. 128.

in France, and six to eight in Germany, control millions and millions. In *substance*, however, the distribution of means of production is not at all "universal", but private, i.e., it conforms to the interests of big capital, and primarily, of huge, monopoly capital, which operates under conditions in which the masses live in want, in which the whole development of agriculture hopelessly lags behind the development of industry, while within industry itself the "heavy industries" exact tribute from all other branches of industry.

In the matter of socialising capitalist economy the savings-banks and post-offices are beginning to compete with the banks; they are more "decentralised", i.e., their influence extends to a greater number of localities, to more remote places, to wider sections of the population. Here is the data collected by an American commission on the comparative growth of deposits in banks and savings-banks*:

Deposits (000,000,000 marks)

	Britain		France		Germany		
	Banks	Savings-banks	Banks	Savings-banks	Banks	Credit societies	Savings-banks
1880	8.4	1.6	?	0.9	0.5	0.4	2.6
1888	12.4	2.0	1.5	2.1	1.1	0.4	4.5
1908	23.2	4.2	3.7	4.2	7.1	2.2	13.9

As they pay interest at the rate of 4 per cent and $4^1/_4$ per cent on deposits, the savings-banks must seek "profitable" investments for their capital, they must deal in bills, mortgages, etc. The boundaries between the banks and the savings-banks "become more and more obliterated". The Chambers of Commerce of Bochum and Erfurt, for example, demand that savings-banks be "prohibited" from engaging in "purely" banking business, such as discounting bills; they demand the limitation of the "banking" operations of the post-office.** The banking magnates seem to be afraid that state monopoly will steal upon them from an unexpected quarter. It goes without saying, however, that this fear is

---

* *Statistics of the National Monetary Commission*, quoted in *Die Bank*, 1910, 1, S. 1200.
** *Die Bank*, 1913, S. 811, 1022; 1914, S. 713.

no more than an expression of the rivalry, so to speak, between two department managers in the same office; for, on the one hand, the millions entrusted to the savings-banks are in the final analysis actually controlled by *these very same* bank capital magnates, while, on the other hand, state monopoly in capitalist society is merely a means of increasing and guaranteeing the income of millionaires in some branch of industry who are on the verge of bankruptcy.

The change from the old type of capitalism, in which free competition predominated, to the new capitalism, in which monopoly reigns, is expressed, among other things, by a decline in the importance of the Stock Exchange. The review, *Die Bank*, writes: "The Stock Exchange has long ceased to be the indispensable medium of circulation that it formerly was when the banks were not yet able to place the bulk of new issues with their clients."*

"'Every bank is a Stock Exchange', and the bigger the bank, and the more successful the concentration of banking, the truer does this modern aphorism ring."** "While formerly, in the seventies, the Stock Exchange, flushed with the exuberance of youth" (a "subtle" allusion to the Stock Exchange crash of 1873, the company promotion scandals,[86] etc.), "opened the era of the industrialisation of Germany, nowadays the banks and industry are able to 'manage it alone'. The domination of our big banks over the Stock Exchange ... is nothing else than the expression of the completely organised German industrial state. If the domain of the automatically functioning economic laws is thus restricted, and if the domain of conscious regulation by the banks is considerably enlarged, the national economic responsibility of a few guiding heads is immensely increased," so writes the German Professor Schulze-Gaevernitz,*** an apologist of German imperialism, who is regarded as an authority by the imperialists of all countries, and who tries to gloss over the "mere detail" that the "conscious regulation" of economic life by the banks consists in the fleecing of the public by a handful of "completely organised" monop-

---

* *Die Bank*, 1914, 1, S. 316.
** Dr. Oscar Stillich, *Geld- und Bankwesen*, Berlin, 1907, S. 169.
*** Schulze-Gaevernitz, "Die deutsche Kreditbank" in *Grundriss der Sozialökonomik*, Tübingen, 1915, S. 101.

olists. The task of a bourgeois professor is not to lay bare the entire mechanism, or to expose all the machinations of the bank monopolists, but rather to present them in a favourable light.

In the same way, Riesser, a still more authoritative economist and himself a banker, makes shift with meaningless phrases in order to explain away undeniable facts: "... the Stock Exchange is steadily losing the feature which is absolutely essential for national economy as a whole and for the circulation of securities in particular—that of being not only a most exact measuring-rod, but also an almost automatic regulator of the economic movements which converge on it."*

In other words, the old capitalism, the capitalism of free competition with its indispensable regulator, the Stock Exchange, is passing away. A new capitalism has come to take its place, bearing obvious features of something transient, a mixture of free competition and monopoly. The question naturally arises: *into what* is this new capitalism "developing"? But the bourgeois scholars are afraid to raise this question.

"Thirty years ago, businessmen, freely competing against one another, performed nine-tenths of the work connected with their business other than manual labour. At the present time, nine-tenths of this 'brain work' is performed by *employees*. Banking is in the forefront of this evolution."** This admission by Schulze-Gaevernitz brings us once again to the question: into what is this new capitalism, capitalism in its imperialist stage, developing?

Among the few banks which remain at the head of all capitalist economy as a result of the process of concentration, there is naturally to be observed an increasingly marked tendency towards monopolist agreements, towards a *bank trust*. In America, not nine, but *two* very big banks, those of the multimillionaires Rockefeller and Morgan, control a capital of eleven thousand million marks.*** In Germany the absorption of the Schaaffhausenscher Bankverein by

---

* Riesser, op. cit., 4th ed., S. 629.
** Schulze-Gaevernitz, "Die deutsche Kreditbank" in *Grundriss der Sozialökonomik*, Tübingen, 1915, S. 151.
*** *Die Bank*, 1912, 1, S. 435.

the Disconto-Gesellschaft to which I referred above, was commented on in the following terms by the *Frankfurter Zeitung*,[87] an organ of Stock Exchange interests:

"The concentration movement of the banks is narrowing the circle of establishments from which it is possible to obtain credits, and is consequently increasing the dependence of big industry upon a small number of banking groups. In view of the close connection between industry and the financial world, the freedom of movement of industrial companies which need banking capital is restricted. For this reason, big industry is watching the growing trustification of the banks with mixed feelings. Indeed, we have repeatedly seen the beginnings of certain agreements between the individual big banking concerns, which aim at restricting competition."*

Again and again, the final word in the development of banking is monopoly.

As regards the close connection between the banks and industry, it is precisely in this sphere that the new role of the banks is, perhaps, most strikingly felt. When a bank discounts a bill for a firm, opens a current account for it, etc., these operations, taken separately, do not in the least diminish its independence, and the bank plays no other part than that of a modest middleman. But when such operations are multiplied and become an established practice, when the bank "collects" in its own hands enormous amounts of capital, when the running of a current account for a given firm enables the bank—and this is what happens—to obtain fuller and more detailed information about the economic position of its client, the result is that the industrial capitalist becomes more completely dependent on the bank.

At the same time a personal link-up, so to speak, is established between the banks and the biggest industrial and commercial enterprises, the merging of one with another through the acquisition of shares, through the appointment of bank directors to the Supervisory Boards (or Boards of Directors) of industrial and commercial enterprises, and vice versa. The German economist, Jeidels, has compiled most detailed data on this form of concentration of capital

---

* Quoted by Schulze-Gaevernitz, op. cit., S. 155.

and of enterprises. Six of the biggest Berlin banks were represented by their directors in *344* industrial companies; and by their board members in *407* others, making a total of *751* companies. In *289* of these companies they either had two of their representatives on each of the respective Supervisory Boards, or held the posts of chairmen. We find these industrial and commercial companies in the most diverse branches of industry: insurance, transport, restaurants, theatres, art industry, etc. On the other hand, on the Supervisory Boards of these six banks (in 1910) were fifty-one of the biggest industrialists, including the director of Krupp, of the powerful "Hapag" (Hamburg-Amerika Line), etc., etc. From 1895 to 1910, each of these six banks participated in the share and bond issues of many hundreds of industrial companies (the number ranging from 281 to 419).*

The "personal link-up" between the banks and industry is supplemented by the "personal link-up" between both of them and the government. "Seats on Supervisory Boards," writes Jeidels, "are freely offered to persons of title, also to ex-civil servants, who are able to do a great deal to facilitate [!!] relations with the authorities." ... "Usually, on the Supervisory Board of a big bank, there is a member of parliament or a Berlin city councillor."

The building and development, so to speak, of the big capitalist monopolies is therefore going on full steam ahead in all "natural" and "supernatural" ways. A sort of division of labour is being systematically developed amongst the several hundred kings of finance who reign over modern capitalist society:

"Simultaneously with this widening of the sphere of activity of certain big industrialists [joining the boards of banks, etc.] and with the assignment of provincial bank managers to definite industrial regions, there is a growth of specialisation among the directors of the big banks. Generally speaking, this specialisation is only conceivable when banking is conducted on a large scale, and particularly when it has widespread connections with industry. This division of labour proceeds along two lines: on the one hand, relations with industry as a whole are entrusted to one director,

* Jeidels, op. cit.; Riesser, op. cit.

as his special function; on the other, each director
assumes the supervision of several separate enterprises, or
of a group of enterprises in the same branch of industry or
having similar interests.... [Capitalism has already reached
the stage of organised *supervision* of individual enterprises.]
One specialises in German industry, sometimes even in
West German industry alone [the West is the most industrialised part of Germany], others specialise in relations with
foreign states and foreign industry, in information on the
characters of industrialists and others, in Stock Exchange
questions, etc. Besides, each bank director is often assigned
a special locality or a special branch of industry; one works
chiefly on Supervisory Boards of electric companies, another,
on chemical, brewing, or beet sugar plants, a third, in a few
isolated industrial enterprises, but at the same time works
on the Supervisory Boards of insurance companies.... In
short, there can be no doubt that the growth in the dimensions and diversity of the big banks' operations is accompanied
by an increase in the division of labour among their directors with the object (and result) of, so to speak, lifting
them somewhat out of pure banking and making them better
experts, better judges of the general problems of industry
and the special problems of each branch of industry, thus
making them more capable of acting within the respective
bank's industrial sphere of influence. This system is supplemented by the banks' endeavours to elect to their Supervisory Boards men who are experts in industrial affairs, such
as industrialists, former officials, especially those formerly
in the railway service or in mining," etc.*

We find the same system only in a slightly different form
in French banking. For instance, one of the three biggest
French banks, the Crédit Lyonnais, has organised a financial research service (*service des études financières*), which
permanently employs over fifty engineers, statisticians,
economists, lawyers, etc. This costs from six to seven hundred thousand francs annually. The service is in turn divided
into eight departments: one specialises in collecting information on industrial establishments, another studies

---

* Jeidels, op. cit., S. 157.

general statistics, a third, railway and steamship companies, a fourth, securities, a fifth, financial reports, etc.*

The result is, on the one hand, the ever-growing merger, or, as N. I. Bukharin aptly calls it, coalescence, of bank and industrial capital and, on the other hand, the growth of the banks into institutions of a truly "universal character". On this question I find it necessary to quote the exact terms used by Jeidels, who has best studied the subject:

"An examination of the sum total of industrial relationships reveals the universal *character* of the financial establishments working on behalf of industry. Unlike other kinds of banks, and contrary to the demand sometimes expressed in the literature that banks should specialise in one kind of business or in one branch of industry in order to prevent the ground from slipping from under their feet — the big banks are striving to make their connections with industrial enterprises as varied as possible in respect of the locality or branches of industry and are striving to eliminate the unevenness in the distribution of capital among localities and branches of industry resulting from the historical development of individual enterprises." "One tendency is to make the connections with industry general; another tendency is to make them durable and close. In the six big banks both these tendencies are realised, not in full, but to a considerable extent and to an equal degree."

Quite often industrial and commercial circles complain of the "terrorism" of the banks. And it is not surprising that such complaints are heard, for the big banks "command", as will be seen from the following example. On November 19, 1901, one of the big, so-called Berlin "D" banks (the names of the four biggest banks begin with letter D) wrote to the Board of Directors of the German Central Northwest Cement Syndicate in the following terms: "As we learn from the notice you published in a certain newspaper of the 18th inst., we must reckon with the possibility that the next general meeting of your syndicate, to be held on the 30th of this month, may decide on measures which are likely

---

* An article by Eug. Kaufmann on French banks in *Die Bank*, 1909, 2, S. 851 et seq.

to effect changes in your enterprise which are unacceptable
to us. We deeply regret that, for these reasons, we are obliged henceforth to withdraw the credit which had hitherto
been allowed you.... But if the said next general meeting
does not decide upon measures which are unacceptable to us,
and if we receive suitable guarantees on this matter for the
future, we shall be quite willing to open negotiations with
you on the grant of a new credit."*

As a matter of fact, this is small capital's old complaint
about being oppressed by big capital, but in this case it
was a whole syndicate that fell into the category of "small"
capital! The old struggle between small and big capital is
being resumed at a new and immeasurably higher stage of
development. It stands to reason that the big banks' enterprises, worth many millions, can accelerate technical
progress with means that cannot possibly be compared with
those of the past. The banks, for example, set up special
technical research societies, and, of course, only "friendly"
industrial enterprises benefit from their work. To this
category belong the Electric Railway Research Association,
the Central Bureau of Scientific and Technical Research,
etc.

The directors of the big banks themselves cannot fail
to see that new conditions of national economy are being
created; but they are powerless in the face of these phenomena.

"Anyone who has watched, in recent years," writes Jeidels, "the changes of incumbents of directorships and seats
on the Supervisory Boards of the big banks, cannot fail to
have noticed that power is gradually passing into the hands
of men who consider the active intervention of the big
banks in the general development of industry to be necessary and of increasing importance. Between these new men
and the old bank directors, disagreements on this subject
of a business and often of a personal nature are growing.
The issue is whether or not the banks, as credit institutions,
will suffer from this intervention in industry, whether they
are sacrificing tried principles and an assured profit to
engage in a field of activity which has nothing in common

---

* Dr. Oscar Stillich, *Geld- und Bankwesen*, Berlin, 1907, S. 148.

with their role as middlemen in providing credit, and which
is leading the banks into a field where they are more than
ever before exposed to the blind forces of trade fluctuations.
This is the opinion of many of the older bank directors,
while most of the young men consider active intervention
in industry to be a necessity as great as that which gave
rise, simultaneously with big modern industry, to the big
banks and modern industrial banking. The two parties are
agreed only on one point: that there are neither firm principles nor a concrete aim in the new activities of the big
banks."*

The old capitalism has had its day. The new capitalism
represents a transition towards something. It is hopeless,
of course, to seek for "firm principles and a concrete aim"
for the purpose of "reconciling" monopoly with free competition. The admission of the practical men has quite a different ring from the official praises of the charms of "organised"
capitalism sung by its apologists, Schulze-Gaevernitz,
Liefmann and similar "theoreticians".

At precisely what period were the "new activities" of the
big banks finally established? Jeidels gives us a fairly exact
answer to this important question:

"The connections between the banks and industrial enterprises, with their new content, their new forms and their
new organs, namely, the big banks which are organised
on both a centralised and a decentralised basis, were scarcely
a characteristic economic phenomenon before the nineties;
in one sense, indeed, this initial date may be advanced to
the year 1897, when the important 'mergers' took place and
when, for the first time, the new form of decentralised organisation was introduced to suit the industrial policy of
the banks. This starting-point could perhaps be placed at
an even later date, for it was the crisis of 1900 that enormously accelerated and intensified the process of concentration of industry and of banking, consolidated that process,
for the first time transformed the connection with industry
into the actual monopoly of the big banks, and made this
connection much closer and more active."**

---

* Jeidels, op. cit., S. 183-84.
** Ibid., S. 181.

Thus, the twentieth century marks the turning-point from the old capitalism to the new, from the domination of capital in general to the domination of finance capital.

III. FINANCE CAPITAL AND THE FINANCIAL OLIGARCHY

"A steadily increasing proportion of capital in industry," writes Hilferding, "ceases to belong to the industrialists who employ it. They obtain the use of it only through the medium of the banks which, in relation to them, represent the owners of the capital. On the other hand, the bank is forced to sink an increasing share of its funds in industry. Thus, to an ever greater degree the banker is being transformed into an industrial capitalist. This bank capital, i.e., capital in money form, which is thus actually transformed into industrial capital, I call 'finance capital'." "Finance capital is capital controlled by banks and employed by industrialists."*

This definition is incomplete insofar as it is silent on one extremely important fact—on the increase of concentration of production and of capital to such an extent that concentration is leading, and has led, to monopoly. But throughout the whole of his work, and particularly in the two chapters preceding the one from which this definition is taken, Hilferding stresses the part played by *capitalist monopolies.*

The concentration of production; the monopolies arising therefrom; the merging or coalescence of the banks with industry—such is the history of the rise of finance capital and such is the content of that concept.

We now have to describe how, under the general conditions of commodity production and private property, the "business operations" of capitalist monopolies inevitably lead to the domination of a financial oligarchy. It should be noted that German—and not only German—bourgeois scholars, like Riesser, Schulze-Gaevernitz, Liefmann and others, are all apologists of imperialism and of finance capital.

---

* R. Hilferding, *Finance Capital*, Moscow, 1912 (in Russian), pp. 338-39.

Instead of revealing the "mechanics" of the formation of an oligarchy, its methods, the size of its revenues "impeccable and peccable", its connections with parliaments, etc., etc., they obscure or gloss over them. They evade these "vexed questions" by pompous and vague phrases, appeals to the "sense of responsibility" of bank directors, by praising "the sense of duty" of Prussian officials, giving serious study to the petty details of absolutely ridiculous parliamentary bills for the "supervision" and "regulation" of monopolies, playing spillikins with theories, like, for example, the following "scholarly" definition, arrived at by Professor Liefmann: *"Commerce is an occupation having for its object the collection, storage and supply of goods."** (The Professor's bold-face italics.) ...From this it would follow that commerce existed in the time of primitive man, who knew nothing about exchange, and that it will exist under socialism!

But the monstrous facts concerning the monstrous rule of the financial oligarchy are so glaring that in all capitalist countries, in America, France and Germany, a whole literature has sprung up, written from the *bourgeois* point of view, but which, nevertheless, gives a fairly truthful picture and criticism—petty-bourgeois, naturally—of this oligarchy.

Paramount importance attaches to the "holding system", already briefly referred to above. The German economist, Heymann, probably the first to call attention to this matter, describes the essence of it in this way:

"The head of the concern controls the principal company [literally: the "mother company"]; the latter reigns over the subsidiary companies ["daughter companies"] which in their turn control still other subsidiaries ["grandchild companies"], etc. In this way, it is possible with a comparatively small capital to dominate immense spheres of production. Indeed, if holding 50 per cent of the capital is always sufficient to control a company, the head of the concern needs only one million to control eight million in the second subsidiaries. And if this 'interlocking' is extended,

* R. Liefmann, op. cit., S. 476.

it is possible with one million to control sixteen million, thirty-two million, etc."*

As a matter of fact, experience shows that it is sufficient to own 40 per cent of the shares of a company in order to direct its affairs,** since in practice a certain number of small, scattered shareholders find it impossible to attend general meetings, etc. The "democratisation" of the ownership of shares, from which the bourgeois sophists and opportunist so-called "Social-Democrats" expect (or say that they expect) the "democratisation of capital", the strengthening of the role and significance of small-scale production, etc., is, in fact, one of the ways of increasing the power of the financial oligarchy. Incidentally, this is why, in the more advanced, or in the older and more "experienced" capitalist countries, the law allows the issue of shares of smaller denomination. In Germany, the law does not permit the issue of shares of less than one thousand marks denomination, and the magnates of German finance look with an envious eye at Britain, where the issue of one-pound shares (=20 marks, about 10 rubles) is permitted. Siemens, one of the biggest industrialists and "financial kings" in Germany, told the Reichstag on June 7, 1900, that "the one-pound share is the basis of British imperialism".*** This merchant has a much deeper and more "Marxist" understanding of imperialism than a certain disreputable writer who is held to be one of the founders of Russian Marxism[88] and believes that imperialism is a bad habit of a certain nation....

But the "holding system" not only serves enormously to increase the power of the monopolists; it also enables them to resort with impunity to all sorts of shady and dirty tricks to cheat the public, because formally the directors of the "mother company" are not legally responsible for the "daughter company", which is supposed to be "independent", and *through the medium* of which they can "pull off" *any-*

---

* Hans Gideon Heymann, *Die gemischten Werke im deutschen Grosseisengewerbe*, Stuttgart, 1904, S. 268-69.
** Liefmann, *Beteiligungsgesellschaften*, etc., S. 258 of the first edition.
*** Schulze-Gaevernitz in *Grundriss der Sozialökonomie*, V, 2, S. 110.

thing. Here is an example taken from the German review, *Die Bank*, for May 1914:

"The Spring Steel Company of Kassel was regarded some years ago as being one of the most profitable enterprises in Germany. Through bad management its dividends fell from 15 per cent to nil. It appears that the Board, without consulting the shareholders, had loaned *six million marks* to one of its 'daughter companies', the Hassia Company, which had a nominal capital of only some hundreds of thousands of marks. This commitment, amounting to nearly treble the capital of the 'mother company' was never mentioned in its balance-sheets. This omission was quite legal and could be hushed up for two whole years because it did not violate any point of company law. The chairman of the Supervisory Board, who as the responsible head had signed the false balance-sheets, was, and still is, the president of the Kassel Chamber of Commerce. The shareholders only heard of the loan to the Hassia Company, long afterwards, when it had been proved to be a mistake "... (the writer should put this word in inverted commas) ... "and when Spring Steel shares dropped nearly 100 per cent, because those in the know were getting rid of them....

"*This typical example of balance-sheet jugglery, quite common* in joint-stock companies, explains why their Boards of Directors are willing to undertake risky transactions with a far lighter heart than individual businessmen. Modern methods of drawing up balance-sheets not only make it possible to conceal doubtful undertakings from the ordinary shareholder, but also allow the people most concerned to escape the consequence of unsuccessful speculation by selling their shares in time when the individual businessman risks his own skin in everything he does....

"The balance-sheets of many joint-stock companies put us in mind of the palimpsests of the Middle Ages from which the visible inscription had first to be erased in order to discover beneath it another inscription giving the real meaning of the document. [Palimpsests are parchment documents from which the original inscription has been erased and another inscription imposed.]

"The simplest and, therefore, most common procedure for making balance-sheets indecipherable is to divide a single

business into several parts by setting up 'daughter companies'—or by annexing them. The advantages of this system
for various purposes—legal and illegal—are so evident
that big companies which do not employ it are quite the
exception."*

As an example of a huge monopolist company that extensively employs this system, the author quotes the famous
General Electric Company (the A.E.G., to which I shall
refer again later on). In 1912, it was calculated that this
company held shares in *175* to *200* other companies, dominating them, of course, and thus controlling a total capital
of about *1,500 million marks.***

None of the rules of control, the publication of balance-
sheets, the drawing up of balance-sheets according to a
definite form, the public auditing of accounts, etc., the
things about which well-intentioned professors and officials—that is, those imbued with the good intention of
defending and prettyfying capitalism—discourse to the
public, are of any avail; for private property is sacred, and
no one can be prohibited from buying, selling, exchanging
or hypothecating shares, etc.

The extent to which this "holding system" has developed
in the big Russian banks may be judged by the figures given
by E. Agahd, who for fifteen years was an official of the
Russo-Chinese Bank and who, in May 1914, published a
book, not altogether correctly entitled *Big Banks and the
World Market.**** The author divides the big Russian banks
into two main groups: (*a*) banks that come under the
"holding system", and (*b*) "independent" banks—"independence", however, being arbitrarily taken to mean independence of *foreign* banks. The author divides the first group
into three subgroups: (1) German holdings, (2) British
holdings, and (3) French holdings, having in view the

---

* L. Eschwege, "Tochtergesellschaften" in *Die Bank*, 1914, 1,
S. 545.

** Kurt Heinig, "Der Weg des Elektrotrusts" in *Die Neue Zeit*,
1912, 30. Jahrg., 2, S. 484.

*** E. Agahd, *Grossbanken und Weltmarkt. Die wirtschaftliche und
politische Bedeutung der Grossbanken im Weltmarkt unter Berücksichtigung ihres Einflusses auf Russlands Volkswirtschaft und die deutsche-
russischen Beziehungen*, Berlin, 1914.

"holdings" and domination of the big foreign banks of the particular country mentioned. The author divides the capital of the banks into "productively" invested capital (industrial and commercial undertakings), and "speculatively" invested capital (in Stock Exchange and financial operations), assuming, from his petty-bourgeois reformist point of view, that it is possible, under capitalism, to separate the first form of investment from the second and to abolish the second form.

Here are the figures he supplies:

Bank Assets

(*According to Reports for October-November 1913*)
000,000 rubles

Groups of Russian banks	Capital invested		
	Produc-tively	Specula-tively	Total
a 1) Four banks: Siberian Commercial, Russian, International, and Discount Bank	413.7	859.1	1,272.8
a 2) Two banks: Commercial and Industrial, and Russo-British	239.3	169.1	408.4
a 3) Five banks: Russian-Asiatic, St. Petersburg Private, Azov-Don, Union Moscow, Russo-French Commercial	711.8	661.2	1,373.0
(11 banks) *Total*: . . . . . a) ===	1,364.8	1,689.4	3,054.2
b) Eight banks: Moscow Merchants, Volga-Kama, Junker and Co., St. Petersburg Commercial (formerly Wawelberg), Bank of Moscow (formerly Ryabushinsky), Moscow Discount, Moscow Commercial, Moscow Private	504.2	391.1	895.3
(19 banks) *Total*	1,869.0	2,080.5	3,949.5

According to these figures, of the approximately 4,000 million rubles making up the "working" capital of the big banks, *more than three-fourths*, more than 3,000 million, belonged to banks which in reality were only "daughter companies" of foreign banks, and chiefly of Paris banks (the famous trio: Union Parisienne, Paris et Pays-Bas

and Société Générale), and of Berlin banks (particularly
the Deutsche Bank and Disconto-Gesellschaft). Two of the
biggest Russian banks, the Russian (Russian Bank for
Foreign Trade) and the International (St. Petersburg International Commercial Bank), between 1906 and 1912 increased
their capital from 44 to 98 million rubles, and their
reserves from 15 million to 39 million "employing three-
fourths German capital". The first bank belongs to the
Berlin Deutsche Bank "concern" and the second to the
Berlin Disconto-Gesellschaft. The worthy Agahd is deeply
indignant at the majority of the shares being held by the
Berlin banks, so that the Russian shareholders are, therefore, powerless. Naturally, the country which exports capital skims the cream; for example, the Berlin Deutsche Bank,
before placing the shares of the Siberian Commercial Bank
on the Berlin market, kept them in its portfolio for a whole
year, and then sold them at the rate of 193 for 100, that is,
at nearly twice their nominal value, "earning" a profit of
nearly six million rubles, which Hilferding calls "promoter's
profits".

Our author puts the total "capacity" of the principal St.
Petersburg banks at 8,235 million rubles, well over 8,000
million, and the "holdings", or rather, the extent to which
foreign banks dominated them, he estimates as follows:
French banks, 55 per cent; British, 10 per cent; German,
35 per cent. The author calculates that of the total of 8,235
million rubles of functioning capital, 3,687 million rubles,
or over 40 per cent, fall to the share of the Produgol and
Prodamet syndicates[89] and the syndicates in the oil,
metallurgical and cement industries. Thus, owing to the
formation of capitalist monopolies, the merging of bank
and industrial capital has also made enormous strides in
Russia.

Finance capital, concentrated in a few hands and
exercising a virtual monopoly, exacts enormous and ever-
increasing profits from the floating of companies, issue of
stock, state loans, etc., strengthens the domination of the
financial oligarchy and levies tribute upon the whole of
society for the benefit of monopolists. Here is an example,
taken from a multitude of others, of the "business" methods
of the American trusts, quoted by Hilferding. In 1887,

Havemeyer founded the Sugar Trust by amalgamating fifteen small firms, whose total capital amounted to 6,500,000 dollars. Suitably "watered", as the Americans say, the capital of the trust was declared to be 50 million dollars. This "over-capitalisation" anticipated the monopoly profits, in the same way as the United States Steel Corporation anticipates its monopoly profits in buying up as many iron ore fields as possible. In fact, the Sugar Trust set up monopoly prices, which secured it such profits that it could pay 10 per cent dividend on capital "watered" *sevenfold, or about 70 per cent on the capital actually invested at the time the trust was formed*! In 1909, the capital of the Sugar Trust amounted to 90 million dollars. In twenty-two years, it had increased its capital more than tenfold.

In France the domination of the "financial oligarchy" (*Against the Financial Oligarchy in France*, the title of the well-known book by Lysis, the fifth edition of which was published in 1908) assumed a form that was only slightly different. Four of the most powerful banks enjoy, not a relative, but an "absolute monopoly" in the issue of bonds. In reality, this is a "trust of big banks". And monopoly ensures monopoly profits from bond issues. Usually a borrowing country does not get more than 90 per cent of the sum of the loan, the remaining 10 per cent goes to the banks and other middlemen. The profit made by the banks out of the Russo-Chinese loan of 400 million francs amounted to 8 per cent; out of the Russian (1904) loan of 800 million francs the profit amounted to 10 per cent; and out of the Moroccan (1904) loan of 62,500,000 francs it amounted to 18.75 per cent. Capitalism, which began its development with petty usury capital, is ending its development with gigantic usury capital. "The French," says Lysis, "are the usurers of Europe." All the conditions of economic life are being profoundly modified by this transformation of capitalism. With a stationary population, and stagnant industry, commerce and shipping, the "country" can grow rich by usury. "Fifty persons, representing a capital of eight million francs, can control *2,000 million* francs deposited in four banks." The "holding system", with which we are already familiar, leads to the same result. One of the biggest banks, the Société Générale, for instance, issues 64,000

bonds for its "daughter company", the Egyptian Sugar
Refineries. The bonds are issued at 150 per cent, i.e., the bank
gains 50 centimes on the franc. The dividends of the new
company were found to be fictitious, the "public" lost from
90 to 100 million francs. "One of the directors of the Société
Générale was a member of the board of directors of the
Sugar Refineries." It is not surprising that the author is
driven to the conclusion that "the French Republic is a
financial monarchy"; "it is the complete domination of the
financial oligarchy; the latter dominates over the press and
the goverment."*

The extraordinarily high rate of profit obtained from
the issue of bonds, which is one of the principal functions
of finance capital, plays a very important part in the
development and consolidation of the financial oligarchy.
"There is not a single business of this type within the
country that brings in profits even approximately equal to
those obtained from the flotation of foreign loans," says
*Die Bank.***

"No banking operation brings in profits comparable with
those obtained from the issue of securities!" According to
the *German Economist*, the average annual profits made on
the issue of industrial stock were as follows:

		Per cent
1895	. . . .	38.6
1896	. . . .	36.1
1897	. . . .	66.7
1898	. . . .	67.7
1899	. . . .	66.9
1900	. . . .	55.2

"In the ten years from 1891 to 1900, *more than a thousand
million* marks were 'earned' by issuing German industrial
stock."***

During periods of industrial boom, the profits of finance
capital are immense, but during periods of depression,

---

* Lysis, *Contre l'oligarchie financière en France*, 5 éd. Paris, 1908,
pp. 11, 12, 26, 39, 40, 48.
** *Die Bank*, 1913, No. 7, S. 630.
*** Stillich, op. cit., S. 143, also W. Sombart, *Die deutsche Volkswirtschaft im 19. Jahrhundert*, 2. Aufl., 1909, S. 526, Anlage 8.

small and unsound businesses go out of existence, and the big banks acquire "holdings" in them by buying them up for a mere song, or participate in profitable schemes for their "reconstruction" and "reorganisation". In the "reconstruction" of undertakings which have been running at a loss, "the share capital is written down, that is, profits are distributed on a smaller capital and continue to be calculated on this smaller basis. Or, if the income has fallen to zero, new capital is called in, which, combined with the old and less remunerative capital, will bring in an adequate return. "Incidentally," adds Hilferding, "all these reorganisations and reconstructions have a twofold significance for the banks: first, as profitable transactions; and secondly, as opportunities for securing control of the companies in difficulties."*

Here is an instance. The Union Mining Company of Dortmund was founded in 1872. Share capital was issued to the amount of nearly 40 million marks and the market price of the shares rose to 170 after it had paid a 12 per cent dividend for its first year. Finance capital skimmed the cream and earned a trifle of something like 28 million marks. The principal sponsor of this company was that very big German Disconto-Gesellschaft which so successfully attained a capital of 300 million marks. Later, the dividends of the Union declined to nil; the shareholders had to consent to a "writing down" of capital, that is, to losing some of it in order not to lose it all. By a series of "reconstructions", more than 73 million marks were written off the books of the Union in the course of thirty years. "At the present time, the original shareholders of the company possess only 5 per cent of the nominal value of their shares"** but the banks "earned something" out of every "reconstruction".

Speculation in land situated in the suburbs of rapidly growing big towns is a particularly profitable operation for finance capital. The monopoly of the banks merges here with the monopoly of ground-rent and with monopoly of the means of communication, since the rise in the price of land and the possibility of selling it profitably in lots, etc., is mainly

---

* *Finance Capital*, p. 172.
** Stillich, op. cit., S. 138 and Liefmann, S. 51.

dependent on good means of communication with the centre
of the town; and these means of communication are in the
hands of large companies which are connected with these
same banks through the holding system and the distribution of seats on the boards. As a result we get
what the German writer, L. Eschwege, a contributor to
Die Bank who has made a special study of real estate business and mortgages, etc., calls a "bog". Frantic speculation
in suburban building lots; collapse of building enterprises
like the Berlin firm of Boswau and Knauer, which acquired
as much as 100 million marks with the help of the "sound
and solid" Deutsche Bank—the latter, of course, acting
through the holding system, i.e., secretly, behind the scenes
—and got out of it with a loss of "only" 12 million marks,
then the ruin of small proprietors and of workers who get
nothing from the fictitious building firms, fraudulent deals
with the "honest" Berlin police and administration for the
purpose of gaining control of the issue of cadastral certifi-
cates, building licences, etc., etc.*

"American ethics", which the European professors and
well-meaning bourgeois so hypocritically deplore, have, in
the age of finance capital, become the ethics of literally
every large city in any country.

At the beginning of 1914, there was talk in Berlin of
the formation of a "transport trust", i.e., of establishing
"community of interests" between the three Berlin transport
undertakings: the city electric railway, the tramway company and the omnibus company. "We have been aware," wrote
Die Bank, "that this plan was contemplated ever since it became
known that the majority of the shares in the bus company
had been acquired by the other two transport companies....
We may fully believe those who are pursuing this aim when
they say that by uniting the transport services, they will
secure economies, part of which will in time benefit the
public. But the question is complicated by the fact that
behind the transport trust that is being formed are the
banks, which, if they desire, can subordinate the means of

_____

* In *Die Bank*, 1913, S. 952, L. Eschwege, *Der Sumpf*; ibid.,
1912, 1, S. 223 et seq.

transportation, which they have monopolised, to the interests of their real estate business. To be convinced of the reasonableness of such a conjecture, we need only recall that the interests of the big bank that encouraged the formation of the Electric Railway Company were already involved in it at the time the company was formed. That is to say: the interests of this transport undertaking were interlocked with the real estate interests. The point is that the eastern line of this railway was to run across land which this bank sold at an enormous profit for itself and for several partners in the transactions when it became certain the line was to be laid down."*

A monopoly, once it is formed and controls thousands of millions, inevitably penetrates into *every* sphere of public life, regardless of the form of government and all other "details". In German economic literature one usually comes across obsequious praise of the integrity of the Prussian bureaucracy, and allusions to the French Panama scandal[90] and to political corruption in America. But the fact is that *even* bourgeois literature devoted to German banking matters constantly has to go far beyond the field of purely banking operations; it speaks, for instance, about "the attraction of the banks" in reference to the increasing frequency with which public officials take employment with the banks, as follows: "How about the integrity of a state official who in his innermost heart is aspiring to a soft job in the Behrenstrasse?"** (The Berlin street where the head office of the Deutsche Bank is situated.) In 1909, the publisher of *Die Bank*, Alfred Lansburgh, wrote an article entitled "The Economic Significance of Byzantinism", in which he incidentally referred to Wilhelm II's tour of Palestine, and to "the immediate result of this journey, the construction of the Baghdad railway, that fatal 'great product of German enterprise', which is more responsible for the 'encirclement' than all our political blunders put together".*** (By encirclement is meant the policy of Edward VII

---

* "Verkehrstrust" in *Die Bank*, 1914, 1, S. 89.
** "Der Zug zur Bank" in *Die Bank*, 1909, 1, S. 79.
*** Ibid., S. 301.

to isolate Germany and surround her with an imperialist anti-German alliance.) In 1911, Eschwege, the contributor to this same magazine to whom I have already referred, wrote an article entitled "Plutocracy and Bureaucracy", in which he exposed, for example, the case of a German official named Völker, who was a zealous member of the Cartel Committee and who, it turned out some time later, obtained a lucrative post in the biggest cartel, the Steel Syndicate. Similar cases, by no means casual, forced this bourgeois author to admit that "the economic liberty guaranteed by the German Constitution has become in many departments of economic life, a meaningless phrase" and that under the existing rule of the plutocracy, "even the widest political liberty cannot save us from being converted into a nation of unfree people".*

As for Russia, I shall confine myself to one example. Some years ago, all the newspapers announced that Davydov, the director of the Credit Department of the Treasury, had resigned his post to take employment with a certain big bank at a salary which, according to the contract, would total over one million rubles in the course of several years. The Credit Department is an institution, the function of which is to "co-ordinate the activities of all the credit institutions of the country" and which grants subsidies to banks in St. Petersburg and Moscow amounting to between 800 and 1,000 million rubles.**

It is characteristic of capitalism in general that the ownership of capital is separated from the application of capital to production, that money capital is separated from industrial or productive capital, and that the rentier who lives entirely on income obtained from money capital, is separated from the entrepreneur and from all who are directly concerned in the management of capital. Imperialism, or the domination of finance capital, is that highest stage of capitalism in which this separation reaches vast proportions. The supremacy of finance capital over all other forms of capital means the predominance of the rentier and

---

* Ibid., 1911, 2, S. 825; 1913, 2, S. 962.
** E. Agahd, op. cit., S. 202.

of the financial oligarchy; it means that a small number of financially "powerful" states stand out among all the rest. The extent to which this process is going on may be judged from the statistics on emissions, i.e., the issue of all kinds of securities.

In the *Bulletin of the International Statistical Institute*, A. Neymarck* has published very comprehensive, complete and comparative figures covering the issue of securities all over the world, which have been repeatedly quoted in part in economic literature. The following are the totals he gives for four decades:

Total Issues in Francs per Decade
(000,000,000)

1871- 80	76.1
1881- 90	64.5
1891-1900	100.4
1901- 10	197.8

In the 1870s the total amount of issues for the whole world was high, owing particularly to the loans floated in connection with the Franco-Prussian War, and the company-promotion boom which set in in Germany after the war. On the whole, the increase was relatively not very rapid during the three last decades of the nineteenth century, and only in the first ten years of the twentieth century is an enormous increase of almost 100 per cent to be observed. Thus the beginning of the twentieth century marks the turning-point, not only in the growth of monopolies (cartels, syndicates, trusts), of which we have already spoken, but also in the growth of finance capital.

Neymarck estimates the total amount of issued securities current in the world in 1910 at about 815,000 million francs. Deducting from this sum amounts which might have been duplicated, he reduces the total to 575,000-600,000 million,

---

* *Bulletin de l'institut international de statistique*, t. XIX, livr. II, La Haye, 1912. Data concerning small states, second column, are estimated by adding 20 per cent to the 1902 figures.

which is distributed among the various countries as follows
(I take 600,000 million):

Financial Securities Current in 1910
(000,000,000 francs)

Great Britain	142		Holland	12.5
United States	132	479	Belgium	7.5
France	110		Spain	7.5
Germany	95		Switzerland	6.25
Russia	31		Denmark	3.75
Austria-Hungary . .	24		Sweden, Norway,	
Italy	14		Rumania, etc.	2.5
Japan	12			

Total 600

From these figures we at once see standing out in sharp
relief four of the richest capitalist countries, each of which
holds securities to amounts ranging approximately from
100,000 to 150,000 million francs. Of these four countries,
two, Britain and France, are the oldest capitalist countries,
and, as we shall see, possess the most colonies; the other
two, the United States and Germany, are capitalist countries leading in the rapidity of development and the
degree of extension of capitalist monopolies in industry. Together, these four countries own 479,000 million francs, that is,
nearly 80 per cent of the world's finance capital. In one
way or another, nearly the whole of the rest of the world is
more or less the debtor to and tributary of these international banker countries, these four "pillars" of world finance
capital.

It is particularly important to examine the part which
the export of capital plays in creating the international
network of dependence on and connections of finance capital.

IV. EXPORT OF CAPITAL

Typical of the old capitalism, when free competition held
undivided sway, was the export of *goods*. Typical of the
latest stage of capitalism, when monopolies rule, is the export
of *capital*.

Capitalism is commodity production at its highest stage
of development, when labour-power itself becomes a commodity. The growth of internal exchange, and, particularly,

of international exchange, is a characteristic feature of capitalism. The uneven and spasmodic development of individual enterprises, individual branches of industry and individual countries is inevitable under the capitalist system. England became a capitalist country before any other, and by the middle of the nineteenth century, having adopted free trade, claimed to be the "workshop of the world", the supplier of manufactured goods to all countries, which in exchange were to keep her provided with raw materials. But in the last quarter of the nineteenth century, *this* monopoly was already undermined; for other countries, sheltering themselves with "protective" tariffs, developed into independent capitalist states. On the threshold of the twentieth century we see the formation of a new type of monopoly: firstly, monopolist associations of capitalists in all capitalistically developed countries; secondly, the monopolist position of a few very rich countries, in which the accumulation of capital has reached gigantic proportions. An enormous "surplus of capital" has arisen in the advanced countries.

It goes without saying that if capitalism could develop agriculture, which today is everywhere lagging terribly behind industry, if it could raise the living standards of the masses, who in spite of the amazing technical progress are everywhere still half-starved and poverty-stricken, there could be no question of a surplus of capital. This "argument" is very often advanced by the petty-bourgeois critics of capitalism. But if capitalism did these things it would not be capitalism; for both uneven development and a semi-starvation level of existence of the masses are fundamental and inevitable conditions and constitute premises of this mode of production. As long as capitalism remains what it is, surplus capital will be utilised not for the purpose of raising the standard of living of the masses in a given country, for this would mean a decline in profits for the capitalists, but for the purpose of increasing profits by exporting capital abroad to the backward countries. In these backward countries profits are usually high, for capital is scarce, the price of land is relatively low, wages are low, raw materials are cheap. The export of capital is made possible by a number of backward countries having already been drawn into

world capitalist intercourse; main railways have either
been or are being built in those countries, elementary conditions for industrial development have been created, etc.
The need to export capital arises from the fact that in a
few countries capitalism has become "overripe" and (owing
to the backward state of agriculture and the poverty of the
masses) capital cannot find a field for "profitable" investment.

Here are approximate figures showing the amount of
capital invested abroad by the three principal countries*:

Capital Invested Abroad
(000,000,000 francs)

Year	Great Britain	France	Germany
1862	3.6	—	—
1872	15.0	10 (1869)	—
1882	22.0	15 (1880)	?
1893	42.0	20 (1890)	?
1902	62.0	27-37	12.5
1914	75-100.0	60	44.0

This table shows that the export of capital reached enormous dimensions only at the beginning of the twentieth
century. Before the war the capital invested abroad by
the three principal countries amounted to between 175,000
million and 200,000 million francs. At the modest rate of
5 per cent, the income from this sum should reach from
8,000 to 10,000 million francs a year—a sound basis for
the imperialist oppression and exploitation of most of the
countries and nations of the world, for the capitalist parasitism of a handful of wealthy states!

* Hobson, *Imperialism*, London, 1902, p. 58; Riesser, op. cit.,
S. 395 und 404; P. Arndt in *Weltwirtschaftliches Archiv*, Bd. 7, 1916,
S. 35; Neymarck in *Bulletin*; Hilferding, *Finance Capital*, p. 492;
Lloyd George, Speech in the House of Commons, May 4, 1915, report-
ed in the *Daily Telegraph*, May 5, 1915; B. Harms, *Probleme der
Weltwirtschaft*, Jena, 1912, S. 235 et seq.; Dr. Siegmund Schilder,
Entwicklungstendenzen der Weltwirtschaft, Berlin, 1912, Band I,
S. 150; George Paish, "Great Britain's Capital Investments, etc.",
in *Journal of the Royal Statistical Society*, Vol. LXXIV, 1910-11,
p. 167 et seq.; Georges Diouritch, *L'Expansion des banques allemandes
à l'étranger, ses rapports avec le développement économique de l'Alle-
magne*, Paris, 1909, p. 84.

How is this capital invested abroad distributed among the various countries? *Where* is it invested? Only an approximate answer can be given to these questions, but it is one sufficient to throw light on certain general relations and connections of modern imperialism.

Distribution (Approximate) of Foreign Capital in Different Parts of the Globe (circa 1910)

	Great Britain	France	Germany	Total
	(000,000,000 marks)			
Europe	4	23	18	45
America	37	4	10	51
Asia, Africa and Australia . . .	29	8	7	44
Total . . .	70	35	35	140

The principal spheres of investment of British capital are the British colonies, which are very large also in America (for example, Canada), not to mention Asia, etc. In this case, enormous exports of capital are bound up most closely with vast colonies, of the importance of which for imperialism I shall speak later. In the case of France the situation is different. French capital exports are invested mainly in Europe, primarily in Russia (at least ten thousand million francs). This is mainly *loan* capital, government loans, and not capital invested in industrial undertakings. Unlike British colonial imperialism, French imperialism might be termed usury imperialism. In the case of Germany, we have a third type; colonies are inconsiderable, and German capital invested abroad is divided most evenly between Europe and America.

The export of capital influences and greatly accelerates the development of capitalism in those countries to which it is exported. While, therefore, the export of capital may tend to a certain extent to arrest development in the capital-exporting countries, it can only do so by expanding and deepening the further development of capitalism throughout the world.

The capital-exporting countries are nearly always able to obtain certain "advantages", the character of which throws light on the peculiarity of the epoch of finance capital and monopoly. The following passage, for instance, appeared in the Berlin review, *Die Bank*, for October 1913:

"A comedy worthy of the pen of Aristophanes is lately being played on the international capital market. Numerous foreign countries, from Spain to the Balkan states, from Russia to Argentina, Brazil and China, are openly or secretly coming into the big money market with demands, sometimes very persistent, for loans. The money markets are not very bright at the moment and the political outlook is not promising. But not a single money market dares to refuse a loan for fear that its neighbour may forestall it, consent to grant a loan and so secure some reciprocal service. In these international transactions the creditor nearly always manages to secure some extra benefit: a favourable clause in a commercial treaty, a coaling station, a contract to construct a harbour, a fat concession, or an order for guns."*

Finance capital has created the epoch of monopolies, and monopolies introduce everywhere monopolist principles: the utilisation of "connections" for profitable transactions takes the place of competition on the open market. The most usual thing is to stipulate that part of the loan granted shall be spent on purchases in the creditor country, particularly on orders for war materials, or for ships, etc. In the course of the last two decades (1890-1910), France has very often resorted to this method. The export of capital thus becomes a means of encouraging the export of commodities. In this connection, transactions between particularly big firms assume a form which, as Schilder ** "mildly" puts it, "borders on corruption". Krupp in Germany, Schneider in France, Armstrong in Britain are instances of firms which have close connections with powerful banks and governments and which cannot easily be "ignored" when a loan is being arranged.

France, when granting loans to Russia, "squeezed" her in the commercial treaty of September 16, 1905, stipulating for certain concessions to run till 1917. She did the same in the commercial treaty with Japan of August 19, 1911. The tariff war between Austria and Serbia, which lasted,

---

* *Die Bank*, 1913, 2, S. 1024.
** Schilder, op. cit., S. 346, 350, 371.

with a seven months' interval, from 1906 to 1911, was partly caused by Austria and France competing to supply Serbia with war materials. In January 1912, Paul Deschanel stated in the Chamber of Deputies that from 1908 to 1911 French firms had supplied war materials to Serbia to the value of 45 million francs.

A report from the Austro-Hungarian Consul at Sao-Paulo (Brazil) states: "The Brazilian railways are being built chiefly by French, Belgian, British and German capital. In the financial operations connected with the construction of these railways the countries involved stipulate for orders for the necessary railway materials."

Thus finance capital, literally, one might say, spreads its net over all countries of the world. An important role in this is played by banks founded in the colonies and by their branches. German imperialists look with envy at the "old" colonial countries which have been particularly "successful" in providing for themselves in this respect. In 1904, Great Britain had 50 colonial banks with 2,279 branches (in 1910 there were 72 banks with 5,449 branches); France had 20 with 136 branches; Holland, 16 with 68 branches; and Germany had "only" 13 with 70 branches.* The American capitalists, in their turn, are jealous of the English and German: "In South America," they complained in 1915, "five German banks have forty branches and five British banks have seventy branches.... Britain and Germany have invested in Argentina, Brazil, and Uruguay in the last twenty-five years approximately four thousand million dollars, and as a result together enjoy 46 per cent of the total trade of these three countries."**

The capital-exporting countries have divided the world among themselves in the figurative sense of the term. But finance capital has led to the *actual* division of the world.

---

* Riesser, op. cit., 4th ed., S. 375; Diouritch, p. 283.
** *The Annals of the American Academy of Political and Social Science*, Vol. LIX, May 1915, p. 301. In the same volume on p. 331, we read that the well-known statistician Paish, in the last issue of the financial magazine *The Statist*, estimated the amount of capital exported by Britain, Germany, France, Belgium and Holland at $40,000 million, i.e. 200,000 million francs,

V. DIVISION OF THE WORLD
AMONG CAPITALIST ASSOCIATIONS

Monopolist capitalist associations, cartels, syndicates and trusts first divided the home market among themselves and obtained more or less complete possession of the industry of their own country. But under capitalism the home market is inevitably bound up with the foreign market. Capitalism long ago created a world market. As the export of capital increased, and as the foreign and colonial connections and "spheres of influence" of the big monopolist associations expanded in all ways, things "naturally" gravitated towards an international agreement among these associations, and towards the formation of international cartels.

This is a new stage of world concentration of capital and production, incomparably higher than the preceding stages. Let us see how this supermonopoly develops.

The electrical industry is highly typical of the latest technical achievements and is most typical of capitalism at the *end* of the nineteenth and the beginning of the twentieth centuries. This industry has developed most in the two leaders of the new capitalist countries, the United States and Germany. In Germany, the crisis of 1900 gave a particularly strong impetus to its concentration. During the crisis, the banks, which by that time had become fairly well merged with industry, enormously accelerated and intensified the ruin of relatively small firms and their absorption by the large ones. "The banks," writes Jeidels, "refused a helping hand to the very firms in greatest need of capital, and brought on first a frenzied boom and then the hopeless failure of the companies which have not been connected with them closely enough." *

As a result, after 1900, concentration in Germany progressed with giant strides. Up to 1900 there had been seven or eight "groups" in the electrical industry. Each consisted of several companies (altogether there were 28) and each was backed by from 2 to 11 banks. Between 1908 and 1912 all these groups were merged into two, or one. The following diagram shows the process:

---

* Jeidels, op. cit., S. 232.

Groups in the Electrical Industry

Prior to 1900	Felten & Guillaume	Lahmeyer	Union A.E.G.	Siemens & Halske	Schuckert & Co.	Berg-mann	Kum-mer
	Felten & Lahmeyer		A.E.G. (G.E.C.)	Siemens & Halske-Schuckert		Berg-mann	Failed in 1900
By 1912;	A.E.G. (G.E.C.) Siemens & Halske-Schuckert						

(In close "co-operation" since 1908)

The famous A.E.G. (General Electric Company), which grew up in this way, controls 175 to 200 companies (through the "holding" system), and a total capital of approximately *1,500 million* marks. Of direct agencies abroad alone, it has thirty-four, of which twelve are joint-stock companies, in more than ten countries. As early as 1904 the amount of capital invested abroad by the German electrical industry was estimated at 233 million marks. Of this sum, 62 million were invested in Russia. Needless to say, the A.E.G. is a huge "combine"—its manufacturing companies alone number no less than sixteen—producing the most diverse articles, from cables and insulators to motor-cars and flying machines.

But concentration in Europe was also a component part of the process of concentration in America, which developed in the following way:

General Electric Company

United States:	Thomson-Houston Co. establishes a firm in Europe	Edison Co. establishes in Europe the French Edison Co. which transfers its patents to the German firm
Germany:	Union Electric Co.	General Electric Co. (A.E.G.)

General Electric Co. (A.E.G.)

Thus, *two* electrical "great powers" were formed: "there are no other electrical companies in the world *completely* independent of them," wrote Heinig in his article "The Path of the Electric Trust". An idea, although far from complete, of the turnover and the size of the enterprises of the two "trusts" can be obtained from the following figures:

		Turnover (000,000 marks)	Number of employees	Net profits (000,000 marks)
America: General Electric Co. (G.E.C.)	1907	252	28,000	35.4
	1910	298	32,000	45.6
Germany: General Electric Co. (A.E.G.)	1907	216	30,700	14.5
	1911	362	60,800	21.7

And then, in 1907, the German and American trusts concluded an agreement by which they divided the world between them. Competition between them ceased. The American General Electric Company (G.E.C.) "got" the United States and Canada. The German General Electric Company (A.E.G.) "got" Germany, Austria, Russia, Holland, Denmark, Switzerland, Turkey and the Balkans. Special agreements, naturally secret, were concluded regarding the penetration of "daughter companies" into new branches of industry, into "new" countries formally not yet allotted. The two trusts were to exchange inventions and experiments.[*]

The difficulty of competing against this trust, actually a single world-wide trust controlling a capital of several thousand million, with "branches", agencies, representatives, connections, etc., in every corner of the world, is self-evident. But the division of the world between two powerful trusts does not preclude *redivision* if the relation of forces changes as a result of uneven development, war, bankruptcy, etc.

An instructive example of an attempt at such a redivision, of the struggle for redivision, is provided by the oil industry.

"The world oil market," wrote Jeidels in 1905, "is even today still divided between two great financial groups — Rockefeller's American Standard Oil Co., and Rothschild and Nobel, the controlling interests of the Russian oilfields in Baku. The two groups are closely connected. But for several years five enemies have been threatening their monopoly"[**]: (1) the exhaustion of the American oilfields;

---

[*] Riesser. op. cit.; Diouritch, op. cit., p. 239; Kurt Heining, op. cit.

[**] Jeidels, op. cit., S. 193.

(2) the competition of the firm of Mantashev of Baku; (3) the Austrian oilfields; (4) the Rumanian oilfields; (5) the overseas oilfields, particularly in the Dutch colonies (the extremely rich firms, Samuel, and Shell, also connected with British capital). The three last groups are connected with the big German banks, headed by the huge Deutsche Bank. These banks independently and systematically developed the oil industry in Rumania, for example, in order to have a foothold of their "own". In 1907, the foreign capital invested in the Rumanian oil industry was estimated at 185 million francs, of which 74 million was German capital.*

A struggle began for the "division of the world", as, in fact, it is called in economic literature. On the one hand, the Rockefeller "oil trust" wanted to lay its hands on *everything*; it formed a "daughter company" *right in* Holland, and bought up oilfields in the Dutch Indies, in order to strike at its principal enemy, the Anglo-Dutch Shell trust. On the other hand, the Deutsche Bank and the other German banks aimed at "retaining" Rumania "for themselves" and at uniting her with Russia against Rockefeller. The latter possessed far more capital and an excellent system of oil transportation and distribution. The struggle had to end, and did end in 1907, with the utter defeat of the Deutsche Bank, which was confronted with the alternative: either to liquidate its "oil interests" and lose millions, or submit. It chose to submit, and concluded a very disadvantageous agreement with the "oil trust". The Deutsche Bank agreed "not to attempt anything which might injure American interests". Provision was made, however, for the annulment of the agreement in the event of Germany establishing a state oil monopoly.

Then the "comedy of oil" began. One of the German finance kings, von Gwinner, a director of the Deutsche Bank, through his private secretary, Stauss, launched a campaign *for* a state oil monopoly. The gigantic machine of the huge German bank and all its wide "connections" were set in motion. The press bubbled over with "patriotic" indignation against the "yoke" of the American trust, and, on March 15, 1911, the Reichstag, by an almost unanimous vote, adopted

* Diouritch, op. cit., p. 245.

a motion asking the government to introduce a bill for the
establishment of an oil monopoly. The government seized
upon this "popular" idea, and the game of the Deutsche
Bank, which hoped to cheat its American counterpart and
improve its business by a state monopoly, appeared to have
been won. The German oil magnates already saw visions of
enormous profits, which would not be less than those of the
Russian sugar refiners.... But, firstly, the big German banks
quarrelled among themselves over the division of the spoils.
The Disconto-Gesellschaft exposed the covetous aims of the
Deutsche Bank; secondly, the government took fright at the
prospect of a struggle with Rockefeller, for it was very doubtful whether Germany could be sure of obtaining oil from
other sources (the Rumanian output was small); thirdly,
just at that time the 1913 credits of a thousand million
marks were voted for Germany's war preparations. The oil
monopoly project was postponed. The Rockefeller "oil trust"
came out of the struggle, for the time being, victorious.

The Berlin review, *Die Bank*, wrote in this connection
that Germany could fight the oil trust only by establishing
an electricity monopoly and by converting water-power into
cheap electricity. "But," the author added, "the electricity
monopoly will come when the producers need it, that is
to say, when the next great crash in the electrical industry
is imminent, and when the gigantic, expensive power stations now being put up at great cost everywhere by private
electrical concerns, which are already obtaining certain
franchises from towns, from states, etc., can no longer work
at a profit. Water-power will then have to be used. But it
will be impossible to convert it into cheap electricity at
state expense; it will also have to be handed over to a
'private monopoly controlled by the state', because private
industry has already concluded a number of contracts and has
stipulated for heavy compensation.... So it was with the
nitrate monopoly, so it is with the oil monopoly, so it will
be with the electric power monopoly. It is time our state
socialists, who allow themselves to be blinded by a beauti-
ful principle, understood, at last, that in Germany the
monopolies have never pursued the aim, nor have they had the
result, of benefiting the consumer, or even of handing over
to the state part of the promoter's profits; they have served

only to facilitate, at the expense of the state, the recovery of private industries which were on the verge of bankruptcy."*

Such are the valuable admissions which the German bourgeois economists are forced to make. We see plainly here how private and state monopolies are interwoven in the epoch of finance capital; how both are but separate links in the imperialist struggle between the big monopolists for the division of the world.

In merchant shipping, the tremendous development of concentration has ended also in the division of the world. In Germany two powerful companies have come to the fore: the Hamburg-Amerika and the Norddeutscher Lloyd, each having a capital of 200 million marks (in stocks and bonds) and possessing shipping tonnage to the value of 185 to 189 million marks. On the other hand, in America, on January 1, 1903, the International Mercantile Marine Co., known as the Morgan trust was formed; it united nine American and British steamship companies, and possessed a capital of 120 million dollars (480 million marks). As early as 1903, the German giants and this American-British trust concluded an agreement to divide the world with a consequent division of profits. The German companies undertook not to compete in the Anglo-American traffic. Which ports were to be "allotted" to each was precisely stipulated; a joint committee of control was set up, etc. This agreement was concluded for twenty years, with the prudent provision for its annulment in the event of war.**

Extremely instructive also is the story of the formation of the International Rail Cartel. The first attempt of the British, Belgian and German rail manufacturers to form such a cartel was made as early as 1884, during a severe industrial depression. The manufacturers agreed not to compete with one another in the home markets of the countries involved, and they divided the foreign markets in the following quotas: Great Britain, 66 per cent; Germany, 27 per cent; Belgium, 7 per cent. India was reserved entirely for Great Britain. Joint war was declared against a British firm which remained outside the cartel, the cost of which

* *Die Bank*, 1912, 1, S. 1036; 1912, 2, S. 629; 1913, 1, S. 388.
** Riesser, op. cit., S. 125.

was met by a percentage levy on all sales. But in 1886 the cartel collapsed when two British firms retired from it. It is characteristic that agreement could not be achieved during subsequent boom periods.

At the beginning of 1904, the German steel syndicate was formed. In November 1904, the International Rail Cartel was revived, with the following quotas: Britain, 53.5 per cent; Germany, 28.83 per cent; Belgium, 17.67 per cent. France came in later and received 4.8 per cent, 5. 8 per cent and 6.4 per cent in the first, second and third year respectively, over and above the 100 per cent limit, i.e., out of a total of 104.8 per cent, etc. In 1905, the United States Steel Corporation entered the cartel; then Austria and Spain. "At the present time," wrote Vogelstein in 1910, "the division of the world is complete, and the big consumers, primarily the state railways—since the world has been parcelled out without consideration for their interests—can now dwell like the poet in the heavens of Jupiter."*

Let me also mention the International Zinc Syndicate which was established in 1909 and which precisely apportioned output among five groups of factories: German, Belgian, French, Spanish and British; and also the International Dynamite Trust, which, Liefmann says, is "quite a modern, close alliance of all the German explosives manufacturers who, with the French and American dynamite manufacturers, organised in a similar manner, have divided the whole world among themselves, so to speak". *

Liefmann calculated that in 1897 there were altogether about forty international cartels in which Germany had a share, while in 1910 there were about a hundred.

Certain bourgeois writers (now joined by Karl Kautsky, who has completely abandoned the Marxist position he had held, for example, in 1909) have expressed the opinion that international cartels, being one of the most striking expressions of the internationalisation of capital, give the hope of peace among nations under capitalism. Theoretically, this opinion is absolutely absurd, while in practice it is sophistry and a dishonest defence of the worst opportunism.

---

* Vogelstein, *Organisationsformen*, S. 100.
** Liefmann, *Kartelle und Trusts*, 2. A., S. 161.

International cartels show to what point capitalist monopolies have developed, and *the object* of the struggle between the various capitalist associations. This last circumstance is the most important; it alone shows us the historico-economic meaning of what is taking place; for the *forms* of the struggle may and do constantly change in accordance with varying, relatively specific and temporary causes, but the *substance* of the struggle, its class *content*, positively *cannot* change while classes exist. Naturally, it is in the interests of, for example, the German bourgeoisie, to whose side Kautsky has in effect gone over in his theoretical arguments (I shall deal with this later), to obscure the *substance* of the present economic struggle (the division of the world) and to emphasise now this and now another *form* of the struggle. Kautsky makes the same mistake. Of course, we have in mind not only the German bourgeoisie, but the bourgeoisie all over the world. The capitalists divide the world, not out of any particular malice, but because the degree of concentration which has been reached forces them to adopt this method in order to obtain profits. And they divide it "in proportion to capital", "in proportion to strength", because there cannot be any other method of division under commodity production and capitalism. But strength varies with the degree of economic and political development. In order to understand what is taking place, it is necessary to know what questions are settled by the changes in strength. The question as to whether these changes are "purely" economic or *non*-economic (e.g., military) is a secondary one, which cannot in the least affect fundamental views on the latest epoch of capitalism. To substitute the question of the form of the struggle and agreements (today peaceful, tomorrow warlike, the next day warlike again) for the question of the *substance* of the struggle and agreements between capitalist associations is to sink to the role of a sophist.

The epoch of the latest stage of capitalism shows us that certain relations between capitalist associations grow up, *based* on the economic division of the world; while parallel to and in connection with it, certain relations grow up between political alliances, between states, on the basis of the territorial division of the world, of the struggle for colonies, of the "struggle for spheres of influence".

VI. DIVISION OF THE WORLD
AMONG THE GREAT POWERS

In his book, on "the territorial development of the European colonies", A. Supan,* the geographer, gives the following brief summary of this development at the end of the nineteenth century:

Percentage of Territory Belonging to the European Colonial Powers (Including the United States)

	1876	1900	Increase or decrease
Africa	10.8	90.4	+79.6
Polynesia	56.8	98.9	+42.1
Asia	51.5	56.6	+ 5.1
Australia	100.0	100.0	—
America	27.5	27.2	— 0.3

"The characteristic feature of this period," he concludes, "is, therefore, the division of Africa and Polynesia." As there are no unoccupied territories—that is, territories that do not belong to any state—in Asia and America, it is necessary to amplify Supan's conclusion and say that the characteristic feature of the period under review is the final partitioning of the globe—final, not in the sense that *repartition* is impossible; on the contrary, repartitions are possible and inevitable—but in the sense that the colonial policy of the capitalist countries has *completed* the seizure of the unoccupied territories on our planet. For the first time the world is completely divided up, so that in the future *only* redivision is possible, i.e., territories can only pass from one "owner" to another, instead of passing as ownerless territory to an "owner".

Hence, we are living in a peculiar epoch of world colonial policy, which is most closely connected with the "latest stage in the development of capitalism", with finance capital. For this reason, it is essential first of all to deal in greater detail with the facts, in order to ascertain as exactly as possible what distinguishes this epoch from those preceding it, and what the present situation is. In the first

* A. Supan, *Die territoriale Entwicklung der europäischen Kolonien*, 1906, S. 254.

place, two questions of fact arise here: is an intensification of colonial policy, a sharpening of the struggle for colonies, observed precisely in the epoch of finance capital? And how, in this respect, is the world divided at the present time?

The American writer, Morris, in his book on the history of colonisation,* made an attempt to sum up the data on the colonial possessions of Great Britain, France and Germany during different periods of the nineteenth century. The following is a brief summary of the results he has obtained:

Colonial Possessions

	Great Britain		France		Germany	
Year	Area (000,000 sq. m.)	Pop. (000,000)	Area (000,000 sq. m.)	Pop. (000,000)	Area (000,000 sq. m.)	Pop. (000,000)
1815-30	?	126.4	0.02	0.5	—	—
1860	2.5	145.1	0.2	3.4	—	—
1880	7.7	267.9	0.7	7.5	—	—
1899	9.3	309.0	3.7	56.4	1.0	14.7

For Great Britain, the period of the enormous expansion of colonial conquests was that between 1860 and 1880, and it was also very considerable in the last twenty years of the nineteenth century. For France and Germany this period falls precisely in these twenty years. We saw above that the development of pre-monopoly capitalism, of capitalism in which free competition was predominant, reached its limit in the 1860s and 1870s. We now see that it is *precisely after that period* that the tremendous "boom" in colonial conquests begins, and that the struggle for the territorial division of the world becomes extraordinarily sharp. It is beyond doubt, therefore, that capitalism's transition to the stage of monopoly capitalism, to finance capital, *is connected* with the intensification of the struggle for the partitioning of the world.

Hobson, in his work on imperialism, marks the years 1884-1900 as the epoch of intensified "expansion" of the chief European states. According to his estimate, Great Britain during these years acquired 3,700,000 square miles

---

* Henry C. Morris, *The History of Colonization*, New York, 1900, Vol. II, p. 88; Vol. I, p. 419; Vol. II, p. 304.

of territory with 57,000,000 inhabitants; France, 3,600,000 square miles with 36,500,000; Germany, 1,000,000 square miles with 14,700,000; Belgium, 900,000 square miles with 30,000,000; Portugal, 800,000 square miles with 9,000,000 inhabitants. The scramble for colonies by all the capitalist states at the end of the nineteenth century and particularly since the 1880s is a commonly known fact in the history of diplomacy and of foreign policy.

In the most flourishing period of free competition in Great Britain, i.e., between 1840 and 1860, the leading British bourgeois politicians were *opposed* to colonial policy and were of the opinion that the liberation of the colonies, their complete separation from Britain, was inevitable and desirable. M. Beer, in an article, "Modern British Imperialism", * published in 1898, shows that in 1852, Disraeli, a statesman who was generally inclined towards imperialism, declared: "The colonies are millstones round our necks." But at the end of the nineteenth century the British heroes of the hour were Cecil Rhodes and Joseph Chamberlain, who openly advocated imperialism and applied the imperialist policy in the most cynical manner!

It is not without interest to observe that even then these leading British bourgeois politicians saw the connection between what might be called the purely economic and the socio-political roots of modern imperialism. Chamberlain advocated imperialism as a "true, wise and economical policy", and pointed particularly to the German, American and Belgian competition which Great Britain was encountering in the world market. Salvation lies in monopoly, said the capitalists as they formed cartels, syndicates and trusts. Salvation lies in monopoly, echoed the political leaders of the bourgeoisie, hastening to appropriate the parts of the world not yet shared out. And Cecil Rhodes, we are informed by his intimate friend, the journalist Stead, expressed his imperialist views to him in 1895 in the following terms: "I was in the East End of London [a working-class quarter] yesterday and attended a meeting of the unemployed. I listened to the wild speeches, which

---

* *Die Neue Zeit*, XVI, I, 1898, S. 302.

were just a cry for 'bread! bread!'and on my way home I pondered over the scene and I became more than ever convinced of the importance of imperialism.... My cherished idea is a solution for the social problem, i.e., in order to save the 40,000,000 inhabitants of the United Kingdom from a bloody civil war, we colonial statesmen must acquire new lands to settle the surplus population, to provide new markets for the goods produced in the factories and mines. The Empire, as I have always said, is a bread and butter question. If you want to avoid civil war, you must become imperialists." *

That was said in 1895 by Cecil Rhodes, millionaire, a king of finance, the man who was mainly responsible for the Anglo-Boer War. True, his defence of imperialism is crude and cynical, but in substance it does not differ from the "theory" advocated by Messrs. Maslov, Südekum, Potresov, David, the founder of Russian Marxism and others. Cecil Rhodes was a somewhat more honest social-chauvinist....

To present as precise a picture as possible of the territorial division of the world and of the changes which have occurred during the last decades in this respect, I shall utilise the data furnished by Supan in the work already quoted on the colonial possessions of all the powers of the world. Supan takes the years 1876 and 1900; I shall take the year 1876—a year very aptly selected, for it is precisely by that time that the pre-monopolist stage of development of West-European capitalism can be said to have been, in the main, completed—and the year 1914, and instead of Supan's figures I shall quote the more recent statistics of Hübner's *Geographical and Statistical Tables.* Supan gives figures only for colonies; I think it useful, in order to present a complete picture of the division of the world, to add brief data on non-colonial and semi-colonial countries, in which category I place Persia, China and Turkey: the first of these countries is already almost completely a colony, the second and third are becoming such.

We thus get the following result:

---

* Ibid., S. 304,

Colonial Possessions of the Great Powers
(000,000 square kilometres and 000,000 inhabitants)

	Colonies				Metropolitan countries		Total	
	1876		1914		1914		1914	
	Area	Pop.	Area	Pop.	Area	Pop.	Area	Pop.
Great Britain	22.5	251.9	33.5	393.5	0.3	46.5	33.8	440.0
Russia . .	17.0	15.9	17.4	33.2	5.4	136.2	22.8	169.4
France . .	0.9	6.0	10.6	55.5	0.5	39.6	11.1	95.1
Germany	—	—	2.9	12.3	0.5	64.9	3.4	77.2
United States .	—	—	0.3	9.7	9.4	97.0	9.7	106.7
Japan . .	—	—	0.3	19.2	0.4	53.0	0.7	72.2
Total for 6 Great Powers	40.4	273.8	65.0	523.4	16.5	437.2	81.5	960.6

Colonies of other powers (Belgium, Holland, etc.) . .	9.9	45.3
Semi-colonial countries (Persia, China, Turkey) . . .	14.5	361.2
Other countries	28.0	289.9
Total for the world	133.9	1,657.0

We clearly see from these figures how "complete" was the partition of the world at the turn of the twentieth century. After 1876 colonial possessions increased to enormous dimensions, by more than fifty per cent, from 40,000,000 to 65,000,000 square kilometres for the six biggest powers; the increase amounts to 25,000,000 square kilometres, fifty per cent more than the area of the metropolitan countries (16,500,000 square kilometres). In 1876 three powers had no colonies, and a fourth, France, had scarcely any. By 1914 these four powers had acquired colonies with an area of 14,100,000 square kilometres, i.e., about half as much again as the area of Europe, with a population of nearly 100,000,000. The unevenness in the rate of expansion of colonial possessions is very great. If, for instance, we compare France, Germany and Japan, which do not differ very much in area and population, we see that the first has acquired almost three times as much colonial territory as the other two combined. In regard to finance capital, France, at the beginning of the period we are considering, was also, perhaps, several times richer than Germany and Japan put together. In addition to, and on the basis of, purely economic conditions, geographical and other conditions also affect the dimensions of colonial possessions. However strong the process of levelling the world, of levelling the economic and living conditions in different countries, may have been in the past decades as a result of the pressure of large-scale industry, exchange and finance capital, considerable differences still remain; and among the six countries mentioned we see, firstly, young capitalist countries (America, Germany, Japan) whose progress has been extraordinarily rapid; secondly, countries with an old capitalist development (France and Great Britain), whose progress lately has been much slower than that of the previously mentioned countries, and thirdly, a country most backward economically (Russia), where modern capitalist imperialism is enmeshed, so to speak, in a particularly close network of pre-capitalist relations.

Alongside the colonial possessions of the Great Powers, we have placed the small colonies of the small states, which are, so to speak, the next objects of a possible and probable "redivision" of colonies. These small states mostly retain their colonies only because the big powers are torn by conflicting interests, friction, etc., which prevent them from coming to an agreement on the division of the spoils. As to the "semi-colonial" states, they provide an example of the transitional forms which are to be found in all spheres of nature and society. Finance capital is such a great, such a decisive, you might say, force in all economic and in all international relations, that it is capable of subjecting, and actually does subject, to itself even states enjoying the fullest political independence; we shall shortly see examples of this. Of course, finance capital finds most "convenient", and derives the greatest profit from, a *form* of subjection which involves the loss of the political independence of the subjected countries and peoples. In this respect, the semi-colonial countries provide a typical example of the "middle stage". It is natural that the struggle for these semi-dependent countries should have become particularly bitter in the epoch of finance capital, when the rest of the world has already been divided up.

Colonial policy and imperialism existed before the latest stage of capitalism, and even before capitalism. Rome, founded on slavery, pursued a colonial policy and practised imperialism. But "general" disquisitions on imperialism, which ignore, or put into the background, the fundamental difference between socio-economic formations, inevitably turn into the most vapid banality or bragging, like the comparison: "Greater Rome and Greater Britain." * Even the capitalist colonial policy of *previous* stages of capitalism is essentially different from the colonial policy of finance capital.

The principal feature of the latest stage of capitalism is the domination of monopolist associations of big employers. These monopolies are most firmly established when *all* the sources of raw materials are captured by one group, and we have seen with what zeal the international capitalist associations exert every effort to deprive their rivals of all opportunity of competing, to buy up, for example, ironfields, oilfields, etc. Colonial possession alone gives the monopolies complete guarantee against all contingencies in the struggle against competitors, including the case of the adversary wanting to be protected by a law establishing a state monopoly. The more capitalism is developed, the more strongly the shortage of raw materials is felt, the more intense the competition and the hunt for sources of raw materials throughout the whole world, the more desperate the struggle for the acquisition of colonies.

"It may be asserted," writes Schilder, "although it may sound paradoxical to some, that in the more or less foreseeable future the growth of the urban and industrial population is more likely to be hindered by a shortage of raw materials for industry than by a shortage of food." For example, there is a growing shortage of timber—the price of

---

* C. P. Lucas, *Greater Rome and Greater Britain*, Oxford, 1912, or the Earl of Cromer's *Ancient and Modern Imperialism*, London, 1910.

which is steadily rising—of leather, and of raw materials for the textile industry. "Associations of manufacturers are making efforts to create an equilibrium between agriculture and industry in the whole of world economy; as an example of this we might mention the International Federation of Cotton Spinners' Associations in several of the most important industrial countries, founded in 1904, and the European Federation of Flax Spinners' Associations, founded on the same model in 1910." *

Of course, the bourgeois reformists, and among them particularly the present-day adherents of Kautsky, try to belittle the importance of facts of this kind by arguing that raw materials "could be" obtained in the open market without a "costly and dangerous" colonial policy; and that the supply of raw materials "could be" increased enormously by "simply" improving conditions in agriculture in general. But such arguments become an apology for imperialism, an attempt to paint it in bright colours, because they ignore the principal feature of the latest stage of capitalism: monopolies. The free market is becoming more and more a thing of the past; monopolist syndicates and trusts are restricting it with every passing day, and "simply" improving conditions in agriculture means improving the conditions of the masses, raising wages and reducing profits. Where, except in the imagination of sentimental reformists, are there any trusts capable of concerning themselves with the condition of the masses instead of the conquest of colonies?

Finance capital is interested not only in the already discovered sources of raw materials but also in potential sources, because present-day technical development is extremely rapid, and land which is useless today may be improved tomorrow if new methods are devised (to this end a big bank can equip a special expedition of engineers, agricultural experts, etc.), and if large amounts of capital are invested. This also applies to prospecting for minerals, to new methods of processing up and utilising raw materials, etc., etc. Hence, the inevitable striving of finance capital to enlarge its spheres of influence and even its actual territory.

---

* Schilder, op. cit., S. 38-42.

In the same way that the trusts capitalise their property at two or three times its value, taking into account its "potential" (and not actual) profits and the further results of monopoly, so finance capital in general strives to seize the largest possible amount of land of all kinds in all places, and by every means, taking into account potential sources of raw materials and fearing to be left behind in the fierce struggle for the last remnants of independent territory, or for the repartition of those territories that have been already divided.

The British capitalists are exerting every effort to develop cotton growing in *their* colony, Egypt (in 1904, out of 2,300,000 hectares of land under cultivation, 600,000, or more than one-fourth were under cotton); the Russians are doing the same in *their* colony, Turkestan, because in this way they will be in a better position to defeat their foreign competitors, to monopolise the sources of raw materials and form a more economical and profitable textile trust in which *all* the processes of cotton production and manufacturing will be "combined" and concentrated in the hands of one set of owners.

The interests pursued in exporting capital also give an impetus to the conquest of colonies, for in the colonial market it is easier to employ monopoly methods (and sometimes they are the only methods that can be employed) to eliminate competition, to ensure supplies, to secure the necessary "connections", etc.

The non-economic superstructure which grows up on the basis of finance capital, its politics and its ideology, stimulates the striving for colonial conquest. "Finance capital does not want liberty, it wants domination," as Hilferding very truly says. And a French bourgeois writer, developing and supplementing, as it were, the ideas of Cecil Rhodes quoted above,* writes that social causes should be added to the economic causes of modern colonial policy: "owing to the growing complexities of life and the difficulties which weigh not only on the masses of the workers, but also on the middle classes, 'impatience, irritation and hatred are accumulating in all the countries of the old civilisation

---

* See pp. 256-57 of this volume.—*Ed.*

and are becoming a menace to public order; the energy which is being hurled out of the definite class channel must be given employment abroad in order to avert an explosion at home'." *

Since we are speaking of colonial policy in the epoch of capitalist imperialism, it must be observed that finance capital and its foreign policy, which is the struggle of the great powers for the economic and political division of the world, give rise to a number of *transitional* forms of state dependence. Not only are the two main groups of countries, those owning colonies, and the colonies themselves, but also the diverse forms of dependent countries which, politically, are formally independent, but in fact, are enmeshed in the net of financial and diplomatic dependence, are typical of this epoch. We have already referred to one form of dependence—the semi-colony. An example of another is provided by Argentina.

"South America, and especially Argentina," writes Schulze-Gaevernitz in his work on British imperialism, "is so dependent financially on London that it ought to be described as almost a British commercial colony." ** Basing himself on the reports of the Austro-Hungarian Consul at Buenos Aires for 1909, Schilder estimated the amount of British capital invested in Argentina at 8,750 million francs. It is not difficult to imagine what strong connections British finance capital (and its faithful "friend", diplomacy) thereby acquires with the Argentine bourgeoisie, with the circles that control the whole of that country's economic and political life.

A somewhat different form of financial and diplomatic dependence, accompanied by political independence, is presented by Portugal. Portugal is an independent sovereign state, but actually, for more than two hundred years, since the war of the Spanish Succession (1701-14), it has been a British protectorate. Great Britain has protected Portugal

---

* Wahl, *La France aux colonies* quoted by Henri Russier, *Le Partage de l'Océanie*, Paris, 1905, p. 165.
** Schulze-Gaevernitz, *Britischer Imperialismus und englischer Freihandel zu Beginn des 20-ten Jahrhunderts*, Leipzig, 1906, S. 318. Sartorius v. Waltershausen says the same in *Das volkswirtschaftliche System der Kapitalanlage im Auslande*, Berlin, 1907, S. 46.

and her colonies in order to fortify her own positions in the fight against her rivals, Spain and France. In return Great Britain has received commercial privileges, preferential conditions for importing goods and especially capital into Portugal and the Portuguese colonies, the right to use the ports and islands of Portugal, her telegraph cables, etc., etc. * Relations of this kind have always existed between big and little states, but in the epoch of capitalist imperialism they become a general system, they form part of the sum total of "divide the world" relations and become links in the chain of operations of world finance capital.

In order to finish with the question of the division of the world, I must make the following additional observation. This question was raised quite openly and definitely not only in American literature after the Spanish-American War, and in English literature after the Anglo-Boer War, at the very end of the nineteenth century and the beginning of the twentieth; not only has German literature, which has "most jealously" watched "British imperialism", systematically given its appraisal of this fact. This question has also been raised in French bourgeois literature as definitely and broadly as is thinkable from the bourgeois point of view. Let me quote Driault, the historian, who, in his book, *Political and Social Problems at the End of the Nineteenth Century*, in the chapter "The Great Powers and the Division of the World", wrote the following: "During the past few years, all the free territory of the globe, with the exception of China, has been occupied by the powers of Europe and North America. This has already brought about several conflicts and shifts of spheres of influence, and these foreshadow more terrible upheavals in the near future. For it is necessary to make haste. The nations which have not yet made provision for themselves run the risk of never receiving their share and never participating in the tremendous exploitation of the globe which will be one of the most essential features of the next century [i.e., the twentieth]. That is why all Europe and America have lately been afflicted with the fever of colonial expansion, of 'imperialism', that most noteworthy feature of the

---

* Schilder, op. cit., Vol. I, S. 160-61.

end of the nineteenth century." And the author added: "In this partition of the world, in this furious hunt for the treasures and the big markets of the globe, the relative strength of the empires founded in this nineteenth century is totally out of proportion to the place occupied in Europe by the nations which founded them. The dominant powers in Europe, the arbiters of her destiny, are *not* equally preponderant in the whole world. And, as colonial might, the hope of controlling as yet unassessed wealth, will evidently react upon the relative strength of the European powers, the colonial question—'imperialism', if you will—which has already modified the political conditions of Europe itself, will modify them more and more." *

VII. IMPERIALISM, AS A SPECIAL STAGE OF CAPITALISM

We must now try to sum up, to draw together the threads of what has been said above on the subject of imperialism. Imperialism emerged as the development and direct continuation of the fundamental characteristics of capitalism in general. But capitalism only became capitalist imperialism at a definite and very high stage of its development, when certain of its fundamental characteristics began to change into their opposites, when the features of the epoch of transition from capitalism to a higher social and economic system had taken shape and revealed themselves in all spheres. Economically, the main thing in this process is the displacement of capitalist free competition by capitalist monopoly. Free competition is the basic feature of capitalism, and of commodity production generally; monopoly is the exact opposite of free competition, but we have seen the latter being transformed into monopoly before our eyes, creating large-scale industry and forcing out small industry, replacing large-scale by still larger-scale industry, and carrying concentration of production and capital to the point where out of it has grown and is growing monopoly: cartels, syndicates and trusts, and merging with them, the capital

---

* J.-E. Driault, *Problèmes politiques et sociaux*, Paris, 1907, p. 299.

of a dozen or so banks, which manipulate thousands of millions. At the same time the monopolies, which have grown out of free competition, do not eliminate the latter, but exist above it and alongside it, and thereby give rise to a number of very acute, intense antagonisms, frictions and conflicts. Monopoly is the transition from capitalism to a higher system.

If it were necessary to give the briefest possible definition of imperialism we should have to say that imperialism is the monopoly stage of capitalism. Such a definition would include what is most important, for, on the one hand, finance capital is the bank capital of a few very big monopolist banks, merged with the capital of the monopolist associations of industrialists; and, on the other hand, the division of the world is the transition from a colonial policy which has extended without hindrance to territories unseized by any capitalist power, to a colonial policy of monopolist possession of the territory of the world, which has been completely divided up.

But very brief definitions, although convenient, for they sum up the main points, are nevertheless inadequate, since we have to deduce from them some especially important features of the phenomenon that has to be defined. And so, without forgetting the conditional and relative value of all definitions in general, which can never embrace all the concatenations of a phenomenon in its full development, we must give a definition of imperialism that will include the following five of its basic features:

(1) the concentration of production and capital has developed to such a high stage that it has created monopolies which play a decisive role in economic life; (2) the merging of bank capital with industrial capital, and the creation, on the basis of this "finance capital", of a financial oligarchy; (3) the export of capital as distinguished from the export of commodities acquires exceptional importance; (4) the formation of international monopolist capitalist associations which share the world among themselves, and (5) the territorial division of the whole world among the biggest capitalist powers is completed. Imperialism is capitalism at that stage of development at which the dominance of monopolies and finance capital is established; in

which the export of capital has acquired pronounced importance; in which the division of the world among the international trusts has begun, in which the division of all territories of the globe among the biggest capitalist powers has been completed.

We shall see later that imperialism can and must be defined differently if, we bear in mind not only the basic, purely economic concepts—to which the above definition is limited—but also the historical place of this stage of capitalism in relation to capitalism in general, or the relation between imperialism and the two main trends in the working-class movement. The thing to be noted at this point is that imperialism, as interpreted above, undoubtedly represents a special stage in the development of capitalism. To enable the reader to obtain the most well-grounded idea of imperialism, I deliberately tried to quote as extensively as possible *bourgeois* economists who have to admit the particularly incontrovertible facts concerning the latest stage of capitalist economy. With the same object in view, I have quoted detailed statistics which enable one to see to what degree bank capital, etc., has grown, in what precisely the transformation of quantity into quality, of developed capitalism into imperialism, was expressed. Needless to say, of course, all boundaries in nature and in society are conventional and changeable, and it would be absurd to argue, for example, about the particular year or decade in which imperialism "definitely" became established.

In the matter of defining imperialism, however, we have to enter into controversy, primarily, with Karl Kautsky, the principal Marxist theoretician of the epoch of the so-called Second International—that is, of the twenty-five years between 1889 and 1914. The fundamental ideas expressed in our definition of imperialism were very resolutely attacked by Kautsky in 1915, and even in November 1914, when he said that imperialism must not be regarded as a "phase" or stage of economy, but as a policy, a definite policy "preferred" by finance capital; that imperialism must not be "identified" with "present-day capitalism"; that if imperialism is to be understood to mean "all the phenomena of present-day capitalism"—cartels, protection, the domination of the financiers, and colonial policy—then the question as to whether imperialism is necessary to capitalism becomes reduced to the "flattest tautology", because, in that case, "imperialism is naturally a vital necessity for capitalism", and so on. The best way to present Kautsky's idea is to quote his own definition of imperialism, which is diametrically opposed to the substance of the ideas which I have set forth (for the objections coming from the camp of the German Marxists, who have been advocating similar ideas for many years already, have been long known to Kautsky as the objections of a definite trend in Marxism).

Kautsky's definition is as follows:

"Imperialism is a product of highly developed industrial capitalism. It consists in the striving of every industrial capitalist nation to bring under its control or to annex all large areas of *agrarian* [Kautsky's italics] territory, irrespective of what nations inhabit it." *

This definition is of no use at all because it one-sidedly, i.e., arbitrarily, singles out only the national question (although the latter is extremely important in itself as well as in its relation to imperialism), it arbitrarily and *inaccurately* connects this question *only* with industrial capital in the countries which annex other nations, and in an equally arbitrary and inaccurate manner pushes into the forefront the annexation of agrarian regions.

Imperialism is a striving for annexations—this is what the *political* part of Kautsky's definition amounts to. It is correct, but very incomplete, for politically, imperialism is, in general, a striving towards violence and reaction. For the moment, however, we are interested in the *economic* aspect of the question, which Kautsky *himself* introduced into *his* definition. The inaccuracies in Kautsky's definition are glaring. The characteristic feature of imperialism is *not* industrial *but* finance capital. It is not an accident that in France it was precisely the extraordinarily rapid development of *finance* capital, and the weakening of industrial capital, that from the eighties onwards, gave rise to the extreme intensification of annexationist (colonial) policy. The characteristic feature of imperialism is precisely

---

* *Die Neue Zeit*, 1914, 2 (B. 32), S. 909, Sept. 11, 1914; cf. 1915, 2, S. 107 et seq.

that it strives to annex *not only* agrarian territories, but even most highly industrialised regions (German appetite for Belgium; French appetite for Lorraine), because (1) the fact that the world is already partitioned obliges those contemplating a *redivision* to reach out for *every kind* of territory, and (2) an essential feature of imperialism is the rivalry between several great powers in the striving for hegemony, i.e., for the conquest of territory, not so much directly for themselves as to weaken the adversary and undermine *his* hegemony. (Belgium is particularly important for Germany as a base for operations against Britain; Britain needs Baghdad as a base for operations against Germany, etc.)

Kautsky refers especially—and repeatedly—to English writers who, he alleges, have given a purely political meaning to the word "imperialism" in the sense that he, Kautsky, understands it. We take up the work by the English writer Hobson, *Imperialism*, which appeared in 1902, and there we read:

"The new imperialism differs from the older, first, in substituting for the ambition of a single growing empire the theory and the practice of competing empires, each motivated by similar lusts of political aggrandisement and commercial gain; secondly, in the dominance of financial or investing over mercantile interests." *

We see that Kautsky is absolutely wrong in referring to English writers generally (unless he meant the vulgar English imperialists, or the avowed apologists for imperialism). We see that Kautsky, while claiming that he continues to advocate Marxism, as a matter of fact takes a step backward compared with the *social-liberal* Hobson, who *more correctly* takes into account two "historically concrete" (Kautsky's definition is a mockery of historical concreteness!) features of modern imperialism: (1) the competition between *several* imperialisms, and (2) the predominance of the financier over the merchant. If it is chiefly a question of the annexation of agrarian countries by industrial countries, then the role of the merchant is put in the forefront.

---

* Hobson, *Imperialism*, London, 1902, p. 324.

Kautsky's definition is not only wrong and un-Marxist. It serves as a basis for a whole system of views which signify a rupture with Marxist theory and Marxist practice all along the line. I shall refer to this later. The argument about words which Kautsky raises as to whether the latest stage of capitalism should be called imperialism or the stage of finance capital is not worth serious attention. Call it what you will, it makes no difference. The essence of the matter is that Kautsky detaches the politics of imperialism from its economics, speaks of annexations as being a policy "preferred" by finance capital, and opposes to it another bourgeois policy which, he alleges, is possible on this very same basis of finance capital. It follows, then, that monopolies in the economy are compatible with non-monopolistic, non-violent, non-annexationist methods in politics. It follows, then, that the territorial division of the world, which was completed during this very epoch of finance capital, and which constitutes the basis of the present peculiar forms of rivalry between the biggest capitalist states, is compatible with a non-imperialist policy. The result is a slurring-over and a blunting of the most profound contradictions of the latest stage of capitalism, instead of an exposure of their depth; the result is bourgeois reformism instead of Marxism.

Kautsky enters into controversy with the German apologist of imperialism and annexations, Cunow, who clumsily and cynically argues that imperialism is present-day capitalism; the development of capitalism is inevitable and progressive; therefore imperialism is progressive; therefore, we should grovel before it and glorify it! This is something like the caricature of the Russian Marxists which the Narodniks drew in 1894-95. They argued: if the Marxists believe that capitalism is inevitable in Russia, that it is progressive, then they ought to open a tavern and begin to implant capitalism! Kautsky's reply to Cunow is as follows: imperialism is not present-day capitalism; it is only one of the forms of the policy of present-day capitalism. This policy we can and should fight, fight imperialism, annexations, etc.

The reply seems quite plausible, but in effect it is a more subtle and more disguised (and therefore more dangerous) advocacy of conciliation with imperialism, because a "fight" against the policy of the trusts and banks that does not affect the economic basis of the trusts and banks is mere bourgeois reformism and pacifism, the benevolent and innocent expression of pious wishes. Evasion of existing contradictions, forgetting the most important of them, instead of revealing their full depth—such is Kautsky's theory, which has nothing in common with Marxism. Naturally, such a "theory" can only serve the purpose of advocating unity with the Cunows!

"From the purely economic point of view," writes Kautsky, "it is not impossible that capitalism will yet go through a new phase, that of the extension of the policy of the cartels to foreign policy, the phase of ultra-imperialism," * i.e., of a superimperialism, of a union of the imperialisms of the whole world and not struggles among them, a phase when wars shall cease under capitalism, a phase of "the joint exploitation of the world by internationally united finance capital". **

We shall have to deal with this "theory of ultra-imperialism" later on in order to show in detail how decisively and completely it breaks with Marxism. At present, in keeping with the general plan of the present work, we must examine the exact economic data on this question. "From the purely economic point of view", is "ultra-imperialism" possible, or is it ultra-nonsense?

If the purely economic point of view is meant to be a "pure" abstraction, then all that can be said reduces itself to the following proposition: development is proceeding towards monopolies, hence, towards a single world monopoly, towards a single world trust. This is indisputable, but it is also as completely meaningless as is the statement that "development is proceeding" towards the manufacture of foodstuffs in laboratories. In this sense the "theory" of ultra-imperialism is no less absurd than a "theory of ultra-agriculture" would be.

If, however, we are discussing the "purely economic" conditions of the epoch of finance capital as a historically concrete epoch which began at the turn of the twentieth

* *Die Neue Zeit*, 1914, 2 (B. 32), S. 921, Sept. 11, 1914. Cf. 1915, 2, S. 107 et seq.
** *Die Neue Zeit*, 1915, 1, S. 144, April 30, 1915.

century, then the best reply that one can make to the lifeless abstractions of "ultra-imperialism" (which serve exclusively a most reactionary aim: that of diverting attention from the depth of *existing* antagonisms) is to contrast them with the concrete economic realities of the present-day world economy. Kautsky's utterly meaningless talk about ultra-imperialism encourages, among other things, that profoundly mistaken idea which only brings grist to the mill of the apologists of imperialism, i.e., that the rule of finance capital *lessens* the unevenness and contradictions inherent in the world economy, whereas in reality it *increases* them.

R. Calwer, in his little book, *An Introduction to the World Economy*,* made an attempt to summarise the main, purely economic, data that enable one to obtain a concrete picture of the internal relations of the world economy at the turn of the twentieth century. He divides the world into five "main economic areas", as follows: (1) Central Europe (the whole of Europe with the exception of Russia and Great Britain; (2) Great Britain; (3) Russia; (4) Eastern Asia; (5) America; he includes the colonies in the "areas" of the states to which they belong and "leaves aside" a few countries not distributed according to areas, such as Persia, Afghanistan, and Arabia in Asia, Morocco and Abyssinia in Africa, etc.

Here is a brief summary of the economic data he quotes on these regions:

Principal economic areas	Area (000,000 sq. km.)	Population (000,000)	Transport		Trade	Industry		
			Railways (000 km.)	Mercantile fleet (000,000 tons)	Imports and exports (000,000,000 marks)	Output (000,000 tons)		Number of cotton spindles (000,000)
						Coal	Iron	
1) Central Europe	27.6 (23.6)**	388 (146)	204	8	41	251	15	26
2) Britain	28.9 (28.6)**	398 (355)	140	11	25	249	9	51
3) Russia	22	131	63	1	3	16	3	7
4) Eastern Asia	12	389	8	1	2	8	0.02	2
5) America	30	148	379	6	14	245	14	19

* R. Calwer, *Einführung in die Weltwirtschaft*, Berlin, 1906.
** The figures in parentheses show the area and population of the colonies.

We see three areas of highly developed capitalism (high development of means of transport, of trade and of industry): the Central European, the British and the American areas. Among these are three states which dominate the world: Germany, Great Britain, and the United States. Imperialist rivalry and the struggle between these countries have become extremely keen because Germany has only an insignificant area and few colonies; the creation of "Central Europe" is still a matter for the future, it is being born in the midst of a desperate struggle. For the moment the distinctive feature of the whole of Europe is political disunity. In the British and American areas, on the other hand, political concentration is very highly developed, but there is a vast disparity between the immense colonies of the one and the insignificant colonies of the other. In the colonies, however, capitalism is only beginning to develop. The struggle for South America is becoming more and more acute.

There are two areas where capitalism is little developed: Russia and Eastern Asia. In the former, the population is extremely sparse, in the latter it is extremely dense; in the former political concentration is high, in the latter it does not exist. The partitioning of China is only just beginning, and the struggle for it between Japan, the U.S., etc., is continually gaining in intensity.

Compare this reality—the vast diversity of economic and political conditions, the extreme disparity in the rate of development of the various countries, etc., and the violent struggles among the imperialist states—with Kautsky's silly little fable about "peaceful" ultra-imperialism. Is this not the reactionary attempt of a frightened philistine to hide from stern reality? Are not the international cartels which Kautsky imagines are the embryos of "ultra-imperialism" (in the same way as one "can" describe the manufacture of tablets in a laboratory as ultra-agriculture in embryo) an example of the division *and the redivision* of the world, the transition from peaceful division to non-peaceful division and vice versa? Is not American and other finance capital, which divided the whole world peacefully with Germany's participation in, for example, the international rail syndicate, or in the international mercantile shipping trust, now engaged in *redividing* the world on the basis of a new relation of forces that is being changed by methods *anything but* peaceful?

Finance capital and the trusts do not diminish but increase the differences in the rate of growth of the various parts of the world economy. Once the relation of forces is changed, what other solution of the contradictions can be found *under capitalism* than that of *force*? Railway statistics * provide remarkably exact data on the different rates of growth of capitalism and finance capital in world economy. In the last decades of imperialist development, the total length of railways has changed as follows:

	Railways (000 kilometres)		
	1890	1913	+
Europe	224	346	+122
U.S.	268	411	+143
All colonies	82 ⎫	210 ⎫	+128 ⎫
Independent and semi-independent states of Asia and America	43 ⎭ } 125	137 ⎭ } 347	+ 94 ⎭ } +222
Total	617	1,104	

Thus, the development of railways has been most rapid in the colonies and in the independent (and semi-independent) states of Asia and America. Here, as we know, the finance capital of the four or five biggest capitalist states holds undisputed sway. Two hundred thousand kilometres of new railways in the colonies and in the other countries of Asia and America represent a capital of more than 40,000 million marks newly invested on particularly advantageous terms, with special guarantees of a good return and with profitable orders for steel works, etc., etc.

Capitalism is growing with the greatest rapidity in the colonies and in overseas countries. Among the latter, *new* imperialist powers are emerging (e.g., Japan). The struggle

---

* *Statistisches Jahrbuch für das deutsche Reich, 1915*; *Archiv für Eisenbahnwesen, 1892*. Minor details for the distribution of railways among the colonies of the various countries in 1890 had to be estimated approximately.

among the world imperialisms is becoming more acute. The tribute levied by finance capital on the most profitable colonial and overseas enterprises is increasing. In the division of this "booty", an exceptionally large part goes to countries which do not always stand at the top of the list in the rapidity of the development of their productive forces. In the case of the biggest countries, together with their colonies, the total length of railways was as follows:

	(000 kilometres)		
	1890	*1913*	
U. S.	268	413	+145
British Empire	107	208	+101
Russia	32	78	+ 46
Germany	43	68	+ 25
France	41	63	+ 22
Total for 5 powers	491	830	+339

Thus, about 80 per cent of the total existing railways are concentrated in the hands of the five biggest powers. But the concentration of the *ownership* of these railways, the concentration of finance capital, is immeasurably greater since the French and British millionaires, for example, own an enormous amount of shares and bonds in American, Russian and other railways.

Thanks to her colonies, Great Britain has increased the length of "her" railways by 100,000 kilometres, four times as much as Germany. And yet, it is well known that the development of productive forces in Germany, and especially the development of the coal and iron industries, has been incomparably more rapid during this period than in Britain—not to speak of France and Russia. In 1892, Germany produced 4,900,000 tons of pig-iron and Great Britain produced 6,800,000 tons; in 1912, Germany produced 17,600,000 tons and Great Britain, 9,000,000 tons. Germany, therefore, had an overwhelming superiority over Britain in this respect.* The question is: what means other

---

* Cf. also Edgar Crammond, "The Economic Relations of the British and German Empires" in *The Journal of the Royal Statistical Society*, July 1914, p. 777 et seq.

than war could there be *under capitalism* to overcome the
disparity between the development of productive forces
and the accumulation of capital on the one side, and the
division of colonies and spheres of influence for finance
capital on the other?

VIII. PARASITISM AND DECAY OF CAPITALISM

We now have to examine yet another significant aspect
of imperialism to which most of the discussions on the
subject usually attach insufficient importance. One of the
shortcomings of the Marxist Hilferding is that on this
point he has taken a step backward compared with the non-
Marxist Hobson. I refer to parasitism, which is characteristic of imperialism.

As we have seen, the deepest economic foundation of
imperialism is monopoly. This is capitalist monopoly, i.e.,
monopoly which has grown out of capitalism and which
exists in the general environment of capitalism, commodity
production and competition, in permanent and insoluble
contradiction to this general environment. Nevertheless,
like all monopoly, it inevitably engenders a tendency to
stagnation and decay. Since monopoly prices are established,
even temporarily, the motive cause of technical and,
consequently, of all other progress disappears to a certain
extent and, further, the *economic* possibility arises of
deliberately retarding technical progress. For instance, in
America, a certain Owens invented a machine which
revolutionised the manufacture of bottles. The German bottle-
manufacturing cartel purchased Owens's patent, but pigeon-
holed it, refrained from utilising it. Certainly, monopoly
under capitalism can never completely, and for a very long
period of time, eliminate competition in the world market
(and this, by the by, is one of the reasons why the theory
of ultra-imperialism is so absurd). Certainly, the possibility
of reducing the cost of production and increasing profits by
introducing technical improvements operates in the direction of change. But the *tendency* to stagnation and decay,
which is characteristic of monopoly, continues to operate,
and in some branches of industry, in some countries, for
certain periods of time, it gains the upper hand.

The monopoly ownership of very extensive, rich or well-situated colonies, operates in the same direction.

Further, imperialism is an immense accumulation of money capital in a few countries, amounting, as we have seen, to 100,000-150,000 million francs in securities. Hence the extraordinary growth of a class, or rather, of a stratum of rentiers, i.e., people who live by "clipping coupons", who take no part in any enterprise whatever, whose profession is idleness. The export of capital, one of the most essential economic bases of imperialism, still more completely isolates the rentiers from production and sets the seal of parasitism on the whole country that lives by exploiting the labour of several overseas countries and colonies.

"In 1893," writes Hobson, "the British capital invested abroad represented about 15 per cent of the total wealth of the United Kingdom."* Let me remind the reader that by 1915 this capital had increased about two and a half times. "Aggressive imperialism," says Hobson further on, "which costs the tax-payer so dear, which is of so little value to the manufacturer and trader ... is a source of great gain to the investor.... The annual income Great Britain derives from commissions in her whole foreign and colonial trade, import and export, is estimated by Sir. R. Giffen at £18,000,000 [nearly 170 million rubles] for 1899, taken at $2\frac{1}{2}$ per cent, upon a turnover of £800,000,000." Great as this sum is, it cannot explain the aggressive imperialism of Great Britain, which is explained by the income of £90 million to £100 million from "invested" capital, the income of the rentiers.

The income of the rentiers is *five times greater* than the income obtained from the foreign trade of the biggest "trading" country in the world! This is the essence of imperialism and imperialist parasitism.

For that reason the term "rentier state" (Rentnerstaat), or usurer state, is coming into common use in the economic literature that deals with imperialism. The world has become divided into a handful of usurer states and a vast majority of debtor states. "At the top of the list of foreign investments," says Schulze-Gaevernitz, "are those placed

* Hobson, op. cit., pp. 59, 60.

in politically dependent or allied countries: Great Britain grants loans to Egypt, Japan, China and South America. Her navy plays here the part of bailiff in case of necessity. Great Britain's political power protects her from the indignation of her debtors."* Sartorius von Waltershausen in his book, *The National Economic System of Capital Investments Abroad*, cites Holland as the model "rentier state" and points out that Great Britain and France are now becoming such.** Schilder is of the opinion that five industrial states have become "definitely pronounced creditor countries": Great Britain, France, Germany, Belgium and Switzerland. He does not include Holland in this list simply because she is "industrially little developed".*** The United States is a creditor only of the American countries.

"Great Britain," says Schulze-Gaevernitz, "is gradually becoming transformed from an industrial into a creditor state. Notwithstanding the absolute increase in industrial output and the export of manufactured goods, there is an increase in the relative importance of income from interest and dividends, issues of securities, commissions and speculation in the whole of the national economy. In my opinion it is precisely this that forms the economic basis of imperialist ascendancy. The creditor is more firmly attached to the debtor than the seller is to the buyer."**** In regard to Germany, A. Lansburgh, the publisher of the Berlin *Die Bank*, in 1911, in an article entitled "Germany—a Rentier State", wrote the following: "People in Germany are ready to sneer at the yearning to become rentiers that is observed in France. But they forget that as far as the bourgeoisie is concerned the situation in Germany is becoming more and more like that in France." *****

The rentier state is a state of parasitic, decaying capitalism, and this circumstance cannot fail to influence all the socio-political conditions of the countries concerned, in general, and the two fundamental trends in the working-

---

* Schulze-Gaevernitz, *Britischer Imperialismus*, S. 320 et seq.
** Sartorius von Waltershausen, *Das volkswirtschaftliche System, etc.* Berlin, 1907, Buch IV.
*** Schilder, op. cit., S. 393.
**** Schulze-Gaevernitz, op. cit., S. 122.
***** *Die Bank*, 1911, 1, S. 10-11.

class movement, in particular. To demonstrate this in the clearest possible manner let me quote Hobson, who is a most reliable witness, since he cannot be suspected of leaning towards Marxist orthodoxy; on the other hand, he is an Englishman who is very well acquainted with the situation in the country which is richest in colonies, in finance capital, and in imperialist experience.

With the Anglo-Boer War fresh in his mind, Hobson describes the connection between imperialism and the interests of the "financiers", their growing profits from contracts, supplies, etc., and writes: "While the directors of this definitely parasitic policy are capitalists, the same motives appeal to special classes of the workers. In many towns most important trades are dependent upon government employment or contracts; the imperialism of the metal and shipbuilding centres is attributable in no small degree to this fact." Two sets of circumstances, in this writer's opinion, have weakened the old empires: (1) "economic parasitism", and (2) the formation of armies recruited from subject peoples. "There is first the habit of economic parasitism, by which the ruling state has used its provinces, colonies, and dependencies in order to enrich its ruling class and to bribe its lower classes into acquiescence." And I shall add that the economic possibility of such bribery, whatever its form may be, requires high monopolist profits.

As for the second circumstance, Hobson writes: "One of the strangest symptoms of the blindness of imperialism is the reckless indifference with which Great Britain, France and other imperial nations are embarking on this perilous dependence. Great Britain has gone farthest. Most of the fighting by which we have won our Indian Empire has been done by natives; in India, as more recently in Egypt, great standing armies are placed under British commanders; almost all the fighting associated with our African dominions, except in the southern part, has been done for us by natives."

Hobson gives the following economic appraisal of the prospect of the partitioning of China: "The greater part of Western Europe might then assume the appearance and character already exhibited by tracts of country in the

South of England, in the Riviera, and in the tourist-ridden
or residential parts of Italy and Switzerland, little clusters
of wealthy aristocrats drawing dividends and pensions from
the Far East, with a somewhat larger group of professional
retainers and tradesmen and a larger body of personal
servants and workers in the transport trade and in the final
stages of production of the more perishable goods; all the
main arterial industries would have disappeared, the staple
foods and manufactures flowing in as tribute from Asia
and Africa.... We have foreshadowed the possibility of even
a larger alliance of Western states, a European federation
of great powers which, so far from forwarding the cause of
world civilisation, might introduce the gigantic peril of a
Western parasitism, a group of advanced industrial
nations, whose upper classes drew vast tribute from Asia and
Africa, with which they supported great tame masses of
retainers, no longer engaged in the staple industries of
agriculture and manufacture, but kept in the performance
of personal or minor industrial services under the control
of a new financial aristocracy. Let those who would scout
such a theory [it would be better to say: prospect] as
undeserving of consideration examine the economic and social
condition of districts in Southern England today which
are already reduced to this condition, and reflect upon the
vast extension of such a system which might be rendered
feasible by the subjection of China to the economic control
of similar groups of financiers, investors, and political and
business officials, draining the greatest potential reservoir
of profit the world has ever known, in order to consume it
in Europe. The situation is far too complex, the play of
world forces far too incalculable, to render this or any other
single interpretation of the future very probable; but the
influences which govern the imperialism of Western Europe
today are moving in this direction, and, unless counteracted or diverted, make towards some such consummation."*

The author is quite right: *if* the forces of imperialism
had not been counteracted they would have led precisely
to what he has described. The significance of a "United
States of Europe" in the present imperialist situation is

---

* Hobson, op. cit., pp. 103, 205, 144, 335, 386.

correctly appraised. He should have added, however, that, also *within* the working-class movement, the opportunists, who are for the moment victorious in most countries, are "working" systematically and undeviatingly in this very direction. Imperialism, which means the partitioning of the world, and the exploitation of other countries besides China, which means high monopoly profits for a handful of very rich countries, makes it economically possible to bribe the upper strata of the proletariat, and thereby fosters, gives shape to, and strengthens opportunism. We must not, however, lose sight of the forces which counteract imperialism in general, and opportunism in particular, and which, naturally, the social-liberal Hobson is unable to perceive.

The German opportunist, Gerhard Hildebrand, who was once expelled from the Party for defending imperialism, and who could today be a leader of the so-called "Social-Democratic" Party of Germany, supplements Hobson well by his advocacy of a "United States of Western Europe" (without Russia) for the purpose of "joint" action . . against the African Negroes, against the "great Islamic movement", for the maintenance of a "powerful army and navy", against a "Sino-Japanese coalition",* etc.

The description of "British imperialism" in Schulze-Gaevernitz's book reveals the same parasitical traits. The national income of Great Britain approximately doubled from 1865 to 1898, while the income "from abroad" increased *ninefold* in the same period. While the "merit" of imperialism is that it "trains the Negro to habits of industry" (you cannot manage without coercion...), the "danger" of imperialism lies in that "Europe will shift the burden of physical toil—first agricultural and mining, then the rougher work in industry—on to the coloured races, and itself be content with the role of rentier, and in this way, perhaps, pave the way for the economic, and later, the political emancipation of the coloured races".

An increasing proportion of land in England is being taken out of cultivation and used for sport, for the diversion

---

* Gerhard Hildebrand, *Die Erschütterung der Industrieherrschaft und des Industriesozialismus*, 1910, S. 229 et seq.

of the rich. As far as Scotland —the most aristocratic place
for hunting and other sports —is concerned, it is said that
"it lives on its past and on Mr. Carnegie" (the American
multimillionaire). On horse racing and fox hunting alone
England annually spends £14,000,000 (nearly 130 million
rubles). The number of rentiers in England is about one
million. The percentage of the productively employed
population to the total population is declining:

	Population England and Wales (000,000)	Workers in basic industries (000,000)	Per cent of total population
1851	17.9	4.1	23
1901	32.5	4.9	15

And in speaking of the British working class the bourgeois student of "British imperialism at the beginning of
the twentieth century" is obliged to distinguish systematically between the *"upper stratum"* of the workers and the
"lower stratum of the proletariat proper". The upper stratum
furnishes the bulk of the membership of co-operatives,
of trade unions, of sporting clubs and of numerous religious
sects. To this level is adapted the electoral system, which
in Great Britain is still *"sufficiently restricted to exclude
the lower stratum of the proletariat proper"*! In order to
present the condition of the British working class in a rosy
light, only this upper stratum —which constitutes a *minority*
of the proletariat —is usually spoken of. For instance,
"the problem of unemployment is mainly a London problem and that of the lower proletarian stratum, *to which
the politicians attach little importance....*"* He should have
said: to which the bourgeois politicians and the "socialist"
opportunists attach little importance.

One of the special features of imperialism connected
with the facts I am describing, is the decline in emigration from imperialist countries and the increase in immigration into these countries from the more backward countries where lower wages are paid. As Hobson observes,
emigration from Great Britain has been declining since
1884. In that year the number of emigrants was 242,000,

---

* Schulze-Gaevernitz, *Britischer Imperialismus*, S. 301.

while in 1900, the number was 169,000. Emigration from Germany reached the highest point between 1881 and 1890, with a total of 1,453,000 emigrants. In the course of the following two decades, it fell to 544,000 and to 341,000. On the other hand, there was an increase in the number of workers entering Germany from Austria, Italy, Russia and other countries. According to the 1907 census, there were 1,342,294 foreigners in Germany, of whom 440,800 were industrial workers and 257,329 agricultural workers.* In France, the workers employed in the mining industry are, "in great part", foreigners: Poles, Italians and Spaniards.** In the United States, immigrants from Eastern and Southern Europe are engaged in the most poorly paid jobs, while American workers provide the highest percentage of overseers or of the better-paid workers.*** Imperialism has the tendency to create privileged sections also among the workers, and to detach them from the broad masses of the proletariat.

It must be observed that in Great Britain the tendency of imperialism to split the workers, to strengthen opportunism among them and to cause temporary decay in the working-class movement, revealed itself much earlier than the end of the nineteenth and the beginning of the twentieth centuries; for two important distinguishing features of imperialism were already observed in Great Britain in the middle of the nineteenth century —vast colonial possessions and a monopolist position in the world market. Marx and Engels traced this connection between opportunism in the working-class movement and the imperialist features of British capitalism systematically, during the course of several decades. For example, on October 7, 1858, Engels wrote to Marx: "The English proletariat is actually becoming more and more bourgeois, so that this most bourgeois of all nations is apparently aiming ultimately at the possession of a bourgeois aristocracy and a bourgeois proletariat *alongside* the bourgeoisie. For a nation which exploits the whole world this is of course to a certain extent justifiable."[91] Almost a quarter of a century later, in

---

* *Statistik des Deutschen Reichs*, Bd. 211.
** Henger, *Die Kapitalsanlage der Franzosen*, Stuttgart, 1913.
*** Hourwich, *Immigration and Labour*, New York, 1913.

a letter dated August 11, 1881, Engels speaks of the "worst English trade unions which allow themselves to be led by men sold to, or at least paid by, the middle class". In a letter to Kautsky, dated September 12, 1882, Engels wrote: "You ask me what the English workers think about colonial policy. Well, exactly the same as they think about politics in general. There is no workers' party here, there are only Conservatives and Liberal-Radicals, and the workers gaily share the feast of England's monopoly of the world market and the colonies."* (Engels expressed similar ideas in the press in his preface to the second edition of *The Condition of the Working Class in England*, which appeared in 1892.)

This clearly shows the causes and effects. The causes are: (1) exploitation of the whole world by this country; (2) its monopolist position in the world market; (3) its colonial monopoly. The effects are: (1) a section of the British proletariat becomes bourgeois; (2) a section of the proletariat allows itself to be led by men bought by, or at least paid by, the bourgeoisie. The imperialism of the beginning of the twentieth century completed the division of the world among a handful of states, each of which today exploits (in the sense of drawing superprofits from) a part of the "whole world" only a little smaller than that which England exploited in 1858; each of them occupies a monopolist position in the world market thanks to trusts, cartels, finance capital and creditor and debtor relations; each of them enjoys to some degree a colonial monopoly (we have seen that out of the total of 75,000,000 sq. km., which comprise the *whole* colonial world, *65,000,000* sq. km., or 86 per cent, belong to six powers; *61,000,000* sq. km., or 81 per cent, belong to three powers).

The distinctive feature of the present situation is the prevalence of such economic and political conditions that are bound to increase the irreconcilability between opportunism and the general and vital interests of the working-class movement: imperialism has grown from an embryo into the predominant system; capitalist monopolies occupy

---

* Briefwechsel von Marx und Engels, Bd. II, S. 290; IV, 433.— Karl Kautsky, *Sozialismus und Kolonialpolitik*, Berlin, 1907, S. 79; this pamphlet was written by Kautsky in those infinitely distant days when he was still a Marxist.

first place in economics and politics; the division of the world has been completed; on the other hand, instead of the undivided monopoly of Great Britain, we see a few imperialist powers contending for the right to share in this monopoly, and this struggle is characteristic of the whole period of the early twentieth century. Opportunism cannot now be completely triumphant in the working-class movement of one country for decades as it was in Britain in the second half of the nineteenth century; but in a number of countries it has grown ripe, overripe, and rotten, and has become completely merged with bourgeois policy in the form of "social-chauvinism".*

IX. CRITIQUE OF IMPERIALISM

By the critique of imperialism, in the broad sense of the term, we mean the attitude of the different classes of society towards imperialist policy in connection with their general ideology.

The enormous dimensions of finance capital concentrated in a few hands and creating an extraordinarily dense and widespread network of relationships and connections which subordinates not only the small and medium, but also the very small capitalists and small masters, on the one hand, and the increasingly intense struggle waged against other national state groups of financiers for the division of the world and domination over other countries, on the other hand, cause the propertied classes to go over entirely to the side of imperialism. "General" enthusiasm over the prospects of imperialism, furious defence of it and painting it in the brightest colours—such are the signs of the times. Imperialist ideology also penetrates the working class. No Chinese Wall separates it from the other classes. The leaders of the present-day, so-called, "Social-Democratic" Party of Germany are justly called "social-imperialists", that is, socialists in words and imperialists in deeds; but

---

* Russian social-chauvinism in its overt form, represented by the Potresovs, Chkhenkelis, Maslovs, etc., and in its covert form (Chkheidze, Skobelev, Axelrod, Martov, etc.), also emerged from the Russian variety of opportunism, namely, liquidationism.

as early as 1902, Hobson noted the existence in Britain
of "Fabian imperialists" who belonged to the opportunist
Fabian Society.

Bourgeois scholars and publicists usually come out in
defence of imperialism in a somewhat veiled form; they
obscure its complete domination and its deep-going roots,
strive to push specific and secondary details into the forefront and do their very best to distract attention from
essentials by means of absolutely ridiculous schemes for
"reform", such as police supervision of the trusts or banks,
etc. Cynical and frank imperialists who are bold enough
to admit the absurdity of the idea of reforming the fundamental characteristics of imperialism are a rarer phenomenon.

Here is an example. The German imperialists attempt, in the magazine *Archives of World Economy*, to
follow the national emancipation movements in the colonies, particularly, of course, in colonies other than those
belonging to Germany. They note the unrest and the protest movements in India, the movement in Natal (South
Africa), in the Dutch East Indies, etc. One of them, commenting on an English report of a conference held on June 28-30,
1910, of representatives of various subject nations and
races, of peoples of Asia, Africa and Europe who are under
foreign rule, writes as follows in appraising the speeches
delivered at this conference: "We are told that we must
fight imperialism; that the ruling states should recognise
the right of subject peoples to independence; that an
international tribunal should supervise the fulfilment of
treaties concluded between the great powers and weak
peoples. Further than the expression of these pious wishes
they do not go. We see no trace of understanding of the fact
that imperialism is inseparably bound up with capitalism
in its present form and that, therefore [!!], an open struggle
against imperialism would be hopeless, unless, perhaps,
the fight were to be confined to protests against certain of its
especially abhorrent excesses."* Since the reform of the basis
of imperialism is a deception, a "pious wish", since the
bourgeois representatives of the oppressed nations go no

---

* *Weltwirtschaftliches Archiv*, Bd. II, S. 193.

"further" forward, the bourgeois representative of an oppressing nation goes "further" *backward*, to servility towards imperialism under cover of the claim to be "scientific". That is also "logic"!

The questions as to whether it is possible to reform the basis of imperialism, whether to go forward to the further intensification and deepening of the antagonisms which it engenders, or backward, towards allaying these antagonisms, are fundamental questions in the critique of imperialism. Since the specific political features of imperialism are reaction everywhere and increased national oppression due to the oppression of the financial oligarchy and the elimination of free competition, a petty-bourgeois-democratic opposition to imperialism arose at the beginning of the twentieth century in nearly all imperialist countries. Kautsky not only did not trouble to oppose, was not only unable to oppose this petty-bourgeois reformist opposition, which is really reactionary in its economic basis, but became merged with it in practice, and this is precisely where Kautsky and the broad international Kautskian trend deserted Marxism.

In the United States, the imperialist war waged against Spain in 1898 stirred up the opposition of the "anti-imperialists", the last of the Mohicans of bourgeois democracy, who declared this war to be "criminal", regarded the annexation of foreign territories as a violation of the Constitution, declared that the treatment of Aguinaldo, leader of the Filipinos (the Americans promised him the independence of his country, but later landed troops and annexed it), was "Jingo treachery", and quoted the words of Lincoln: "When the white man governs himself, that is self-government; but when he governs himself and also governs others, it is no longer self-government; it is despotism."* But as long as all this criticism shrank from recognising the inseverable bond between imperialism and the trusts, and, therefore, between imperialism and the foundations of capitalism, while it shrank from joining the forces engendered by large-scale capitalism and its development—it remained a "pious wish".

---

* J. Patouillet, *L'impérialisme américain*, Dijon, 1904, p. 272.

This is also the main attitude taken by Hobson in his critique of imperialism. Hobson anticipated Kautsky in protesting against the "inevitability of imperialism" argument, and in urging the necessity of "increasing the consuming capacity" of the people (under capitalism!). The petty-bourgeois point of view in the critique of imperialism, the omnipotence of the banks, the financial oligarchy, etc., is adopted by the authors I have often quoted, such as Agahd, A. Lansburgh, L. Eschwege, and among the French writers Victor Berard, author of a superficial book entitled *England and Imperialism* which appeared in 1900. All these authors, who make no claim to be Marxists, contrast imperialism with free competition and democracy, condemn the Baghdad railway scheme, which is leading to conflicts and war, utter "pious wishes" for peace, etc. This applies also to the compiler of international stock and share issue statistics, A. Neymarck, who, after calculating the thousands of millions of francs representing "international" securities, exclaimed in 1912: "Is it possible to believe that peace may be disturbed ... that, in the face of these enormous figures, anyone would risk starting a war?"*

Such simple-mindedness on the part of the bourgeois economists is not surprising; moreover, *it is in their interest* to pretend to be so naïve and to talk "seriously" about peace under imperialism. But what remains of Kautsky's Marxism, when, in 1914, 1915 and 1916, he takes up the same bourgeois-reformist point of view and affirms that "everybody is agreed" (imperialists, pseudo-socialists and social-pacifists) on the matter of peace? Instead of an analysis of imperialism and an exposure of the depths of its contradictions, we have nothing but a reformist "pious wish" to wave them aside, to evade them.

Here is a sample of Kautsky's economic criticism of imperialism. He takes the statistics of the British export and import trade with Egypt for 1872 and 1912; it seems that this export and import trade has grown more slowly than British foreign trade as a whole. From this Kautsky concludes that "we have no reason to suppose that without

* *Bulletin de l'Institut International de Statistique*, T. XIX, livr. II, p. 225.

military occupation the growth of British trade with Egypt would have been less, simply as a result of the mere operation of economic factors". "The urge of capital to expand ... can be best promoted, not by the violent methods of imperialism, but by peaceful democracy."*

This argument of Kautsky's, which is repeated in every key by his Russian armour-bearer (and Russian shielder of the social-chauvinists), Mr. Spectator,[92] constitutes the basis of Kautskian critique of imperialism, and that is why we must deal with it in greater detail. We will begin with a quotation from Hilferding, whose conclusions Kautsky on many occasions, and notably in April 1915, has declared to have been "unanimously adopted by all socialist theoreticians".

"It is not the business of the proletariat," writes Hilferding, "to contrast the more progressive capitalist policy with that of the now bygone era of free trade and of hostility towards the state. The reply of the proletariat to the economic policy of finance capital, to imperialism, cannot be free trade, but socialism. The aim of proletarian policy cannot today be the ideal of restoring free competition — which has now become a reactionary ideal—but the complete elimination of competition by the abolition of capitalism."**

Kautsky broke with Marxism by advocating in the epoch of finance capital a "reactionary ideal", "peaceful democracy", "the mere operation of economic factors", for *objectively* this ideal drags us back from monopoly to non-monopoly capitalism, and is a reformist swindle.

Trade with Egypt (or with any other colony or semi-colony) "would have grown more" *without* military occupation, without imperialism, and without finance capital. What does this mean? That capitalism would have developed more rapidly if free competition had not been restricted by monopolies in general, or by the "connections", yoke (i.e., also the monopoly) of finance capital, or by the monopolist possession of colonies by certain countries?

Kautsky's argument can have no other meaning; and

---

* Kautsky, *Nationalstaat, imperialistischer Staat und Staatenbund*, Nürnberg, 1915, S. 72, 70.
** *Finance Capital*, p. 567.

this "meaning" is meaningless. Let us assume that free competition, without any sort of monopoly, *would* have developed capitalism and trade more rapidly. But the more rapidly trade and capitalism develop, the greater is the concentration of production and capital which *gives rise* to monopoly. And monopolies have *already* arisen—precisely *out of* free competition! Even if monopolies have now begun to retard progress, it is not an argument in favour of free competition, which has become impossible after it has given rise to monopoly.

Whichever way one turns Kautsky's argument, one will find nothing in it except reaction and bourgeois reformism.

Even if we correct this argument and say, as Spectator says, that the trade of the colonies with Britain is now developing more slowly than their trade with other countries, it does not save Kautsky; for it is *also* monopoly, *also* imperialism that is beating Great Britain, only it is the monopoly and imperialism of another country (America, Germany). It is known that the cartels have given rise to a new and peculiar form of protective tariffs, i.e., goods suitable for export are protected (Engels noted this in Vol. III of *Capital*⁹²). It is known, too, that the cartels and finance capital have a system peculiar to themselves, that of "exporting goods at cut-rate prices", or "dumping", as the English call it: within a given country the cartel sells its goods at high monopoly prices, but sells them abroad at a much lower price to undercut the competitor, to enlarge its own production to the utmost, etc. If Germany's trade with the British colonies is developing more rapidly than Great Britain's, it only proves that German imperialism is younger, stronger and better organised than British imperialism, is superior to it; but it by no means proves the "superiority" of free trade, for it is not a fight between free trade and protection and colonial dependence, but between two rival imperialisms, two monopolies, two groups of finance capital. The superiority of German imperialism over British imperialism is more potent than the wall of colonial frontiers or of protective tariffs: to use this as an "argument" *in favour* of free trade and "peaceful democracy" is banal, it means forgetting the essential features and characteristics of imperialism, substituting petty-bourgeois reformism for Marxism.

It is interesting to note that even the bourgeois economist, A. Lansburgh, whose criticism of imperialism is as petty-bourgeois as Kautsky's, nevertheless got closer to a more scientific study of trade statistics. He did not compare one single country, chosen at random, and one single colony with the other countries; he examined the export trade of an imperialist country: (1) with countries which are financially dependent upon it, and borrow money from it; and (2) with countries which are financially independent. He obtained the following results:

Export Trade of Germany (000,000 marks)

		1889	1908	Per cent increase
To countries financially dependent on Germany	Rumania	48.2	70.8	47
	Portugal	19.0	32.8	73
	Argentina	60.7	147.0	143
	Brazil	48.7	84.5	73
	Chile	28.3	52.4	85
	Turkey	29.9	64.0	114
	Total	*234.8*	*451.5*	*92*
To countries financially independent of Germany	Great Britain	651.8	997.4	53
	France	210.2	437.9	108
	Belgium	137.2	322.8	135
	Switzerland	177.4	401.1	127
	Australia	21.2	64.5	205
	Dutch East Indies	8.8	40.7	363
	Total	*1,206.6*	*2,264.4*	*87*

Lansburgh did not draw *conclusions* and therefore, strangely enough, failed to observe that *if* the figures prove anything at all, they prove that *he is wrong*, for the exports to countries financially dependent on Germany have grown *more rapidly*, if only slightly, than exports to the countries which are financially independent. (I emphasise the "if", for Lansburgh's figures are far from complete.)

Tracing the connection between exports and loans, Lansburgh writes:

"In 1890-91, a Rumanian loan was floated through the German banks, which had already in previous years made advances on this loan. It was used chiefly to purchase railway materials in Germany. In 1891, German exports to Rumania amounted to 55 million marks. The following year they dropped to 39.4 million marks and, with fluctuations, to 25.4 million in 1900. Only in very recent years have they regained the level of 1891, thanks to two new loans.

"German exports to Portugal rose, following the loans of 1888-89, to 21,100,000 (1890); then, in the two following years, they dropped to 16,200,000 and 7,400,000, and regained their former level only in 1903.

"The figures of German trade with Argentina are still more striking. Loans were floated in 1888 and 1890; German exports to Argentina reached 60,700,000 marks (1889). Two years later they amounted to only 18,600,000 marks, less than one-third of the previous figure. It was not until 1901 that they regained and surpassed the level of 1889, and then only as a result of new loans floated by the state and by municipalities, with advances to build power stations, and with other credit operations.

"Exports to Chile, as a consequence of the loan of 1889, rose to 45,200,000 marks (in 1892), and a year later dropped to 22,500,000 marks. A new Chilean loan floated by the German banks in 1906 was followed by a rise of exports to 84,700,000 marks in 1907, only to fall again to 52,400,000 marks in 1908."*

From these facts Lansburgh draws the amusing petty-bourgeois moral of how unstable and irregular export trade is when it is bound up with loans, how bad it is to invest capital abroad instead of "naturally" and "harmoniously" developing home industry, how "costly" are the millions in bakhshish that Krupp has to pay in floating foreign loans, etc. But the facts tell us clearly: the increase in exports is connected with *just these* swindling tricks of finance capital, which is not concerned with bourgeois morality, but with skinning the ox twice—first, it pockets the profits from the loan; then it pockets other profits from the *same* loan which the borrower uses to make purchases from Krupp, or to purchase railway material from the Steel Syndicate, etc.

---

* *Die Bank*, 1909, 2, S. 819 et seq.

I repeat that I do not by any means consider Lansburgh's figures to be perfect; but I had to quote them because they are more scientific than Kautsky's and Spectator's and because Lansburgh showed the correct way to approach the question. In discussing the significance of finance capital in regard to exports, etc., one must be able to single out the connection of exports especially and solely with the tricks of the financiers, especially and solely with the sale of goods by cartels, etc. Simply to compare colonies with non-colonies, one imperialism with another imperialism, one semi-colony or colony (Egypt) with all other countries, is to evade and to obscure the very *essence* of the question.

Kautsky's theoretical critique of imperialism has nothing in common with Marxism and serves only as a preamble to propaganda for peace and unity with the opportunists and the social-chauvinists, precisely for the reason that it evades and obscures the very profound and fundamental contradictions of imperialism: the contradictions between monopoly and free competition which exists side by side with it, between the gigantic "operations" (and gigantic profits) of finance capital and "honest" trade in the free market, the contradiction between cartels and trusts, on the one hand, and non-cartelised industry, on the other, etc.

The notorious theory of "ultra-imperialism", invented by Kautsky, is just as reactionary. Compare his arguments on this subject in 1915, with Hobson's arguments in 1902.

Kautsky: "... Cannot the present imperialist policy be supplanted by a new, ultra-imperialist policy, which will introduce the joint exploitation of the world by internationally united finance capital in place of the mutual rivalries of national finance capitals? Such a new phase of capitalism is at any rate conceivable. Can it be achieved? Sufficient premises are still lacking to enable us to answer this question."*

Hobson: "Christendom thus laid out in a few great federal empires, each with a retinue of uncivilised dependencies, seems to many the most legitimate development of present

---

* *Die Neue Zeit*, April 30, 1915, S. 144.

tendencies, and one which would offer the best hope of permanent peace on an assured basis of inter-Imperialism."

Kautsky called ultra-imperialism or super-imperialism what Hobson, thirteen years earlier, described as inter-imperialism. Except for coining a new and clever catchword, replacing one Latin prefix by another, the only progress Kautsky has made in the sphere of "scientific" thought is that he gave out as Marxism what Hobson, in effect, described as the cant of English parsons. After the Anglo-Boer War it was quite natural for this highly honourable caste to exert their main efforts to *console* the British middle class and the workers who had lost many of their relatives on the battlefields of South Africa and who were obliged to pay higher taxes in order to guarantee still higher profits for the British financiers. And what better consolation could there be than the theory that imperialism is not so bad; that it stands close to inter- (or ultra-) imperialism, which can ensure permanent peace? No matter what the good intentions of the English parsons, or of sentimental Kautsky, may have been, the only objective, i. e., real, social significance of Kautsky's "theory" is this: it is a most reactionary method of consoling the masses with hopes of permanent peace being possible under capitalism, by distracting their attention from the sharp antagonisms and acute problems of the present times, and directing it towards illusory prospects of an imaginary "ultra-imperialism" of the future. Deception of the masses—that is all there is in Kautsky's "Marxist" theory.

Indeed, it is enough to compare well-known and indisputable facts to become convinced of the utter falsity of the prospects which Kautsky tries to conjure up before the German workers (and the workers of all lands). Let us consider India, Indo-China and China. It is known that these three colonial and semi-colonial countries, with a population of six to seven hundred million, are subjected to the exploitation of the finance capital of several imperialist powers: Great Britain, France, Japan, the U.S.A., etc. Let us assume that these imperialist countries form alliances against one another in order to protect or enlarge their possessions, their interests and their spheres of influence in these Asiatic states; these alliances will be "inter-imperialist", or "ultra-imperialist" alliances. Let us assume that *all* the imperialist countries conclude an alliance for the "peaceful" division of these parts of Asia; this alliance would be an alliance of "internationally united finance capital". There are actual examples of alliances of this kind in the history of the twentieth century—the attitude of the powers to China, for instance. We ask, is it "conceivable", assuming that the capitalist system remains intact—and this is precisely the assumption that Kautsky does make—that such alliances would be more than temporary, that they would eliminate friction, conflicts and struggle in every possible form?

The question has only to be presented clearly for any other than a negative answer to be impossible. This is because the only conceivable basis under capitalism for the division of spheres of influence, interests, colonies, etc., is a calculation of the *strength* of those participating, their general economic, financial, military strength, etc. And the strength of these participants in the division does not change to an equal degree, for the *even* development of different undertakings, trusts, branches of industry, or countries is impossible under capitalism. Half a century ago Germany was a miserable, insignificant country, if her capitalist strength is compared with that of the Britain of that time; Japan compared with Russia in the same way. Is it "conceivable" that in ten or twenty years' time the relative strength of the imperialist powers will have remained *un*changed? It is out of the question.

Therefore, in the realities of the capitalist system, and not in the banal philistine fantasies of English parsons, or of the German "Marxist", Kautsky, "inter-imperialist" or "ultra-imperialist" alliances, no matter what form they may assume, whether of one imperialist coalition against another, or of a general alliance embracing *all* the imperialist powers, are *inevitably* nothing more than a "truce" in periods between wars. Peaceful alliances prepare the ground for wars, and in their turn grow out of wars; the one conditions the other, producing alternating forms of peaceful and non-peaceful struggle on *one and the same* basis of imperialist connections and relations within world economics and world politics. But in order to pacify the workers and reconcile them with the social-chauvinists who have deserted to the side of the bourgeoisie, over-wise Kautsky *separates* one link of a single chain from another, separates the present peaceful (and ultra-imperialist, nay, ultra-ultra-imperialist) alliance of *all* the powers for the "pacification" of China (remember the suppression of the Boxer Rebellion[94]) from the non-peaceful conflict of tomorrow, which will prepare the ground for another "peaceful" general alliance for the partition, say, of Turkey, on the day after tomorrow, *etc.*, *etc.* Instead of showing the living connection between periods of imperialist peace and periods of imperialist war, Kautsky presents the workers with a lifeless abstraction in order to reconcile them to their lifeless leaders.

An American writer, Hill, in his *A History of the Diplomacy in the International Development of Europe* refers in his preface to the following periods in the recent history of diplomacy: (1) the era of revolution; (2) the constitutional movement; (3) the present era of "commercial imperialism" * Another writer divides the history of Great Britain's "world policy" since 1870 into four periods: (1) the first Asiatic period (that of the struggle against Russia's advance in Central Asia towards India); (2) the African period (approximately 1885-1902): that of the struggle against France for the partition of Africa (the "Fashoda incident" of 1898 which brought her within a hair's breadth of war with France); (3) the second Asiatic period (alliance with Japan against Russia); and (4) the "European" period, chiefly anti-German.** "The political patrol clashes take place on the financial field," wrote the banker, Riesser, in 1905, in showing how French finance capital operating in Italy was preparing the way for a political alliance of these countries, and how a conflict was developing between Germany and Great Britain over Persia, between all the European capitalists over Chinese loans, etc. Behold, the living reality of peaceful "ultra-imperialist" alliances in their inseverable connection with ordinary imperialist conflicts!

Kautsky's obscuring of the deepest contradictions of

---

  * David Jayne Hill, *A History of the Diplomacy in the International Development of Europe*, Vol. I, p. x.
  ** Schilder, op. cit., S. 178.

imperialism, which inevitably boils down to painting imperialism in bright colours, leaves its traces in this writer's criticism of the political features of imperialism. Imperialism is the epoch of finance capital and of monopolies, which introduce everywhere the striving for domination, not for freedom. Whatever the political system the result of these tendencies is everywhere reaction and an extreme intensification of antagonisms in this field. Particularly intensified become the yoke of national oppression and the striving for annexations, i.e., the violation of national independence (for annexation is nothing but the violation of the right of nations to self-determination). Hilferding rightly notes the connection between imperialism and the intensification of national oppression. "In the newly opened-up countries," he writes, "the capital imported into them intensifies antagonisms and excites against the intruders the constantly growing resistance of the peoples who are awakening to national consciousness; this resistance can easily develop into dangerous measures against foreign capital. The old social relations become completely revolutionised, the age-long agrarian isolation of 'nations without history' is destroyed and they are drawn into the capitalist whirlpool. Capitalism itself gradually provides the subjugated with the means and resources for their emancipation and they set out to achieve the goal which once seemed highest to the European nations: the creation of a united national state as a means to economic and cultural freedom. This movement for national independence threatens European capital in its most valuable and most promising fields of exploitation, and European capital can maintain its domination only by continually increasing its military forces."*

To this must be added that it is not only in newly opened-up countries, but also in the old, that imperialism is leading to annexation, to increased national oppression, and, consequently, also to increasing resistance. While objecting to the intensification of political reaction by imperialism, Kautsky leaves in the shade a question that has become particularly urgent, viz., the impossibility of unity with the opportunists in the epoch of imperialism. While object-

---

* *Finance Capital*, p. 487.

ing to annexations, he presents his objections in a form that is most acceptable and least offensive to the opportunists. He addresses himself to a German audience, yet he obscures the most topical and important point, for instance, the annexation of Alsace-Lorraine by Germany. In order to appraise this "mental aberration" of Kautsky's I shall take the following example. Let us suppose that a Japanese condemns the annexation of the Philippines by the Americans. The question is: will many believe that he does so because he has a horror of annexations as such, and not because he himself has a desire to annex the Philippines? And shall we not be constrained to admit that the "fight" the Japanese is waging against annexations can be regarded as being sincere and politically honest only if he fights against the annexation of Korea by Japan, and urges freedom for Korea to secede from Japan?

Kautsky's theoretical analysis of imperialism, as well as his economic and political critique of imperialism, are permeated *through and through* with a spirit, absolutely irreconcilable with Marxism, of obscuring and glossing over the fundamental contradictions of imperialism and with a striving to preserve at all costs the crumbling unity with opportunism in the European working-class movement.

X. THE PLACE OF IMPERIALISM IN HISTORY

We have seen that in its economic essence imperialism is monopoly capitalism. This in itself determines its place in history, for monopoly that grows out of the soil of free competition, and precisely out of free competition, is the transition from the capitalist system to a higher socio-economic order. We must take special note of the four principal types of monopoly, or principal manifestations of monopoly capitalism, which are characteristic of the epoch we are examining.

Firstly, monopoly arose out of the concentration of production at a very high stage. This refers to the monopolist capitalist associations, cartels, syndicates and trusts. We have seen the important part these play in present-day economic life. At the beginning of the twentieth century, monopolies had acquired complete supremacy in the advanced countries, and although the first steps towards the formation of the cartels were taken by countries enjoying the protection of high tariffs (Germany, America), Great Britain, with her system of free trade, revealed the same basic phenomenon, only a little later, namely, the birth of monopoly out of the concentration of production.

Secondly, monopolies have stimulated the seizure of the most important sources of raw materials, especially for the basic and most highly cartelised industries in capitalist society: the coal and iron industries. The monopoly of the most important sources of raw materials has enormously increased the power of big capital, and has sharpened the antagonism between cartelised and non-cartelised industry.

Thirdly, monopoly has sprung from the banks. The banks have developed from modest middleman enterprises into the monopolists of finance capital. Some three to five of the biggest banks in each of the foremost capitalist countries have achieved the "personal link-up" between industrial and bank capital, and have concentrated in their hands the control of thousands upon thousands of millions which form the greater part of the capital and income of entire countries. A financial oligarchy, which throws a close network of dependence relationships over all the economic and political institutions of present-day bourgeois society without exception—such is the most striking manifestation of this monopoly.

Fourthly, monopoly has grown out of colonial policy. To the numerous "old" motives of colonial policy, finance capital has added the struggle for the sources of raw materials, for the export of capital, for spheres of influence, i.e., for spheres for profitable deals, concessions, monopoly profits and so on, economic territory in general. When the colonies of the European powers, for instance, comprised only one-tenth of the territory of Africa (as was the case in 1876), colonial policy was able to develop by methods other than those of monopoly—by the "free grabbing" of territories, so to speak. But when nine-tenths of Africa had been seized (by 1900), when the whole world had been divided up, there was inevitably ushered in the era of monopoly possession of colonies and, consequently, of particularly intense struggle for the division and the redivision of the world.

The extent to which monopolist capital has intensified all the contradictions of capitalism is generally known. It is sufficient to mention the high cost of living and the tyranny of the cartels. This intensification of contradictions constitutes the most powerful driving force of the transitional period of history, which began from the time of the final victory of world finance capital.

Monopolies, oligarchy, the striving for domination and not for freedom, the exploitation of an increasing number of small or weak nations by a handful of the richest or most powerful nations—all these have given birth to those distinctive characteristics of imperialism which compel us to define it as parasitic or decaying capitalism. More and more prominently there emerges, as one of the tendencies of imperialism, the creation of the "rentier state", the usurer state, in which the bourgeoisie to an ever-increasing degree lives on the proceeds of capital exports and by "clipping coupons". It would be a mistake to believe that this tendency to decay precludes the rapid growth of capitalism. It does not. In the epoch of imperialism, certain branches of industry, certain strata of the bourgeoisie and certain countries betray, to a greater or lesser degree, now one and now another of these tendencies. On the whole, capitalism is growing far more rapidly than before; but this growth is not only becoming more and more uneven in general, its unevenness also manifests itself, in particular, in the decay of the countries which are richest in capital (Britain).

In regard to the rapidity of Germany's economic development, Riesser, the author of the book on the big German banks, states: "The progress of the preceding period (1848-70), which had not been exactly slow, compares with the rapidity with which the whole of Germany's national economy, and with it German banking, progressed during this period (1870-1905) in about the same way as the speed of the mail coach in the good old days compares with the speed of the present-day automobile ... which is whizzing past so fast that it endangers not only innocent pedestrians in its path, but also the occupants of the car." In its turn, this finance capital which has grown with such extraordinary rapidity is not unwilling, precisely because it has grown so quickly, to pass on to a more "tranquil" possession of colonies which have to be seized —and not only by peaceful methods —from richer nations. In the United States, economic development in the last decades has been even more rapid than in Germany, *and for this very reason*, the parasitic features of modern American capitalism have stood out with particular prominence. On the other hand, a comparison of, say, the republican American bourgeoisie with the monarchist Japanese or German bourgeoisie shows that the most pronounced political distinction diminishes to an extreme degree in the epoch of imperialism —not because it is unimportant in general, but because in all these cases we are talking about a bourgeoisie which has definite features of parasitism.

The receipt of high monopoly profits by the capitalists in one of the numerous branches of industry, in one of the numerous countries, etc., makes it economically possible for them to bribe certain sections of the workers, and for a time a fairly considerable minority of them, and win them to the side of the bourgeoisie of a given industry or given nation against all the others. The intensification of antagonisms between imperialist nations for the division of the world increases this urge. And so there is created that bond between imperialism and opportunism, which revealed itself first and most clearly in Great Britain, owing to the fact that certain features of imperialist development were observable there much earlier than in other countries. Some writers, L. Martov, for example, are prone to wave aside the connection between imperialism and opportunism in the working-class movement—a particularly glaring fact at the present time—by resorting to "official optimism" (*à la* Kautsky and Huysmans) like the following: the cause of the opponents of capitalism would be hopeless if it were progressive capitalism that led to the increase of opportunism, or, if it were the best-paid workers who were inclined towards opportunism, etc. We must have no illusions about "optimism" of this kind. It is optimism in respect of opportunism; it is optimism which serves to conceal opportunism. As a matter of fact the extraordinary rapidity and the particularly revolting character of the development of opportunism is by no means a guarantee that its victory will be durable: the rapid growth of a painful abscess on a healthy body can only cause it to burst more quickly and thus relieve the body of it. The most dangerous of all in this respect are those who do not wish to understand that the fight against imperialism is a sham and humbug unless it is inseparably bound up with the fight against opportunism.

From all that has been said in this book on the economic essence of imperialism, it follows that we must define it as capitalism in transition, or, more precisely, as moribund capitalism. It is very instructive in this respect to note that bourgeois economists, in describing modern capitalism, frequently employ catchwords and phrases like "interlocking", "absence of isolation", etc.; "in conformity with their functions and course of development", banks are "not purely private business enterprises; they are more and more outgrowing the sphere of purely private business regulation". And this very Riesser, whose words I have just quoted, declares with all seriousness that the "prophecy" of the Marxists concerning "socialisation" has "not come true"!

What then does this catchword "interlocking" express? It merely expresses the most striking feature of the process going on before our eyes. It shows that the observer counts the separate trees, but cannot see the wood. It slavishly copies the superficial, the fortuitous, the chaotic. It reveals the observer as one who is overwhelmed by the mass of raw material and is utterly incapable of appreciating its meaning and importance. Ownership of shares, the relations between owners of private property "interlock in a haphazard way". But underlying this interlocking, its very base, are the changing social relations of production. When a big enterprise assumes gigantic proportions, and, on the basis of an exact computation of mass data, organises according to plan the supply of primary raw materials to the extent of two-thirds, or three-fourths, of all that is necessary for tens of millions of people; when the raw materials are transported in a systematic and organised manner to the most suitable places of production, sometimes situated hundreds or thousands of miles from each other;

when a single centre directs all the consecutive stages of processing the material right up to the manufacture of numerous varieties of finished articles; when these products are distributed according to a single plan among tens and hundreds of millions of consumers (the marketing of oil in America and Germany by the American oil trust)—then it becomes evident that we have socialisation of production, and not mere "interlocking"; that private economic and private property relations constitute a shell which no longer fits its contents, a shell which must inevitably decay if its removal is artificially delayed, a shell which may remain in a state of decay for a fairly long period (if, at the worst, the cure of the opportunist abscess is protracted), but which will inevitably be removed.

The enthusiastic admirer of German imperialism, Schulze-Gaevernitz, exclaims:

"Once the supreme management of the German banks has been entrusted to the hands of a dozen persons, their activity is even today more significant for the public good than that of the majority of the Ministers of State.... [The "interlocking" of bankers, ministers, magnates of industry and rentiers is here conveniently forgotten.] If we imagine the development of those tendencies we have noted carried to their logical conclusion we will have: the money capital of the nation united in the banks; the banks themselves combined into cartels; the investment capital of the nation cast in the shape of securities. Then the forecast of that genius Saint-Simon will be fulfilled: 'The present anarchy of production, which corresponds to the fact that economic relations are developing without uniform regulation, must make way for organisation in production. Production will no longer be directed by isolated manufacturers, independent of each other and ignorant of man's economic needs; that will be done by a certain public institution. A central committee of management, being able to survey the large field of social economy from a more elevated point of view, will regulate it for the benefit of the whole of society, will put the means of production into suitable hands, and above all will take care that there be constant harmony between production and consumption. Institutions already exist which have assumed as part of their functions a certain organisation of economic labour, the banks.' We are still a long way from the fulfilment of Saint-Simon's forecast, but we are on the way towards it: Marxism, different from what Marx imagined, but different only in form."*

A crushing "refutation" of Marx, indeed, which retreats a step from Marx's precise, scientific analysis to Saint-Simon's guess-work, the guess-work of a genius, but guess-work all the same.

---

* *Grundriss der Sozialökonomik*, S. 146.

THE JUNIUS PAMPHLET

At last there has appeared in Germany, illegally, without any adaptation to the despicable Junker censorship, a Social-Democratic pamphlet dealing with questions of the war! The author, who evidently belongs to the "Left-radical" wing of the Party, takes the name of Junius[95] (which in Latin means junior) and gives his pamphlet the title: *The Crisis of Social-Democracy*. Appended are the "Theses on the Tasks of International Social-Democracy", which have already been submitted to the Berne I.S.C. (International Socialist Committee) and published in No. 3 of its *Bulletin*; the theses were drafted by the *Internationale* group, which in the spring of 1915 published one issue of a magazine under that title (with articles by Zetkin, Mehring, R. Luxemburg, Thalheimer, Duncker, Ströbel and others), and which in the winter of 1915-16 convened a conference of Social-Democrats from all parts of Germany[96] where these theses were adopted.

The pamphlet, the author says in the introduction dated January 2, 1916, was written in April 1915, and published "without any alteration". "Outside circumstances" had prevented its earlier publication. The pamphlet is devoted not so much to the "crisis of Social-Democracy" as to an analysis of the war, to refuting the legend of it being a war for national liberation, to proving that it is an imperialist war on the part of Germany as well as on the part of the other Great Powers, and to a revolutionary criticism of the behaviour of the official party. Written in a very lively style, Junius's pamphlet has undoubtedly played and will continue to play an important role in the struggle against the ex-Social-Democratic Party of Germany, which has deserted to the bourgeoisie and the Junkers, and we extend our hearty greetings to the author.

To the Russian reader who is familiar with the Social-Democratic literature in Russian published abroad in 1914-16, the Junius pamphlet does not offer anything new in principle. In reading this pamphlet and comparing the arguments of this German revolutionary Marxist with what has been stated, for example, in the Manifesto of the Central Committee of our Party (September-November 1914),* in the Berne resolutions (March 1915)** and in the numerous commentaries on them, it only becomes clear that Junius's arguments are very incomplete and that he makes two mistakes. Before proceeding with a criticism of Junius's faults and errors we must strongly emphasise that this is done for the sake of self-criticism, which is so necessary to Marxists, and of submitting to an all-round test the views which must serve as the ideological basis of the Third International. On the whole, the Junius pamphlet is a splendid Marxist work, and its defects are, in all probability, to a certain extent accidental.

The chief defect in Junius's pamphlet, and what marks a definite step backward compared with the legal (although immediately suppressed) magazine, *Internationale*, is its silence regarding the connection between social-chauvinism (the author uses neither this nor the less precise term social-patriotism) and opportunism. The author rightly speaks of the "capitulation" and collapse of the German Social-Democratic Party and of the "treachery" of its "official leaders", but he goes no further. The *Internationale*, however, did criticise the "Centre", i.e., Kautskyism, and quite properly poured ridicule on it for its spinelessness, its prostitution of Marxism and its servility to the opportunists. This same magazine *began* to expose the true role of the opportunists by revealing, for example, the very important fact that on August 4, 1914, the opportunists came out with an ultimatum, a ready-made decision to vote *for* war credits in *any* case. Neither the Junius pamphlet nor the theses say *anything* about opportunism or about Kautskyism! This is wrong from the standpoint of theory, for it

---

* See present edition, Vol. 21, "The War and Russian Social-Democracy".—*Ed.*

** Ibid., "The Conference of the R.S.D.L.P. Groups Abroad".— *Ed.*

is impossible to *account for* the "betrayal" without linking it up with opportunism as a *trend* with a long history behind it, the history of the whole Second International. It is a mistake from the practical political standpoint, for it is impossible either to understand the "crisis of Social-Democracy", or overcome it, without clarifying the meaning and the role of *two trends*—the openly opportunist trend (Legien, David, etc.) and the tacitly opportunist trend (Kautsky and Co.). This is a step backward compared with the historic article by Otto Rühle in *Vorwärts* of January 12, 1916, in which he directly and openly pointed out that a split in the Social-Democratic Party of Germany was *inevitable* (the editors of *Vorwärts* replied by repeating honeyed and hypocritical Kautskyite phrases, for they were unable to advance a single material argument to disprove the assertion that there were *already* two parties in existence, and that these two parties could not be reconciled). It is astonishingly inconsistent, because the *Internationale*'s thesis No. 12 *directly* states that it is necessary to create a "new" International, owing to the "treachery" of the "official representatives of the socialist parties of the leading countries" and their "adoption of the principles of bourgeois imperialist policies". It is clearly quite absurd to suggest that the old Social-Democratic Party of Germany, or the party which tolerates Legien, David and Co., would participate in a "new" International.

We do not know why the *Internationale* group took this step backward. A very great defect in revolutionary Marxism in Germany as a whole is its lack of a compact illegal organisation that would systematically pursue its own line and educate the masses in the spirit of the new tasks; such an organisation would also have to take a definite stand on opportunism and Kautskyism. This is all the more necessary now, since the German revolutionary Social-Democrats have been deprived of their last two daily papers; the one in Bremen (*Bremer Bürger-Zeitung*),[97] and the one in Brunswick (*Volksfreund*),[98] both of which have gone over to the Kautskyites. The International Socialists of Germany (I.S.D.) group *alone* clearly and definitely remains at its post.

Some members of the *Internationale* group have evidently once again slid down into the morass of unprincipled

Kautskyism. Ströbel, for instance, went so far as to drop a curtsey in *Die Neue Zeit* to Bernstein and Kautsky! And only the other day, on July 15, 1916, he had an article in the papers entitled "Pacifism and Social-Democracy", in which he defends the most vulgar type of Kautskyite pacifism. As for Junius, he strongly opposes Kautsky's fantastic schemes like "disarmament", "abolition of secret diplomacy", etc. There may be two trends within the *Internationale* group: a revolutionary trend and a trend inclining to Kautskyism.

The first of Junius's erroneous propositions is embodied in the fifth thesis of the *Internationale* group. "National wars are no longer possible in the epoch (era) of this unbridled imperialism. National interests serve only as an instrument of deception, in order to place the working masses at the service of their mortal enemy, imperialism." The beginning of the fifth thesis, which concludes with the above statement, discusses the nature of the *present* war as an imperialist war. It may be that this negation of national wars generally is either an oversight, or an accidental overstatement in emphasising the perfectly correct idea that the *present* war is an imperialist war, not a national war. This is a mistake that must be examined, for various Social-Democrats, in view of the false assertions that the *present* war is a national war, have likewise mistakenly denied the possibility of *any* national war.

Junius is perfectly right in emphasising the decisive influence of the "imperialist atmosphere" of the *present* war, in maintaining that behind Serbia stands Russia, "behind Serbian nationalism stands Russian imperialism", and that the participation of, say, Holland in the war would *likewise* be imperialist, for, first, Holland would be defending her colonies and, second, would be allied with one of the *imperialist* coalitions. That is irrefutable in respect to the *present* war. And when Junius stresses what for him is most important, namely, the struggle against the "phantom of national war", "which at present holds sway over Social-Democratic policies" (p. 81), then it must be admitted that his views are both correct and fully to the point.

The only mistake, however, would be to exaggerate this truth, to depart from the Marxist requirement of concreteness, to apply the appraisal of this war to all wars possible under imperialism, to ignore the national movements *against* imperialism. The sole argument in defence of the thesis, "national wars are no longer possible", is that the world has been divided among a small group of "great" imperialist powers and for that reason any war, even if it starts as a national war, is *transformed* into an imperialist war involving the interest of one of the imperialist powers or coalitions (Junius, p. 81).

The fallacy of this argument is obvious. That all dividing lines, both in nature and society, are conventional and dynamic, and that *every* phenomenon might, under certain conditions, be transformed into its opposite, is, of course, a basic proposition of Marxist dialectics. A national war *might* be transformed into an imperialist war *and vice versa.* Here is an example: the wars of the Great French Revolution began as national wars and indeed were such. They were revolutionary wars—the defence of the great revolution against a coalition of counter-revolutionary monarchies. But when Napoleon founded the French Empire and subjugated a number of big, viable and long-established national European states, these national wars of the French became imperialist wars and *in turn* led to wars of national liberation *against* Napoleonic imperialism.

Only a sophist can disregard the difference between an imperialist and a national war on the grounds that one *might* develop into the other. Not infrequently have dialectics served—and the history of Greek philosophy is an example—as a bridge to sophistry. But we remain dialecticians and we combat sophistry not by denying the possibility of all transformations in general, but by analysing the *given* phenomenon in its concrete setting and development.

Transformation of the present imperialist war of 1914-16 into a national war is highly improbable, for the class that represents *progressive* development is the proletariat which is objectively striving to transform it into a civil war against the bourgeoisie. Also this: there is no very considerable difference between the forces of the two coalitions, and international finance capital has created a reactionary bourgeoisie everywhere. But such a transformation should *not*

be proclaimed *impossible*: *if* the *European* proletariat
remains impotent, say, for twenty years; *if* the present war
ends in victories like Napoleon's and in the subjugation of
a number of viable national states; *if* the transition to socialism of non-European imperialism (primarily Japanese
and American) is also held up for twenty years by a war
between these two countries, for example, then a great
national war in Europe would be possible. It would hurl
Europe *back* several decades. That is improbable. But *not*
impossible, for it is undialectical, unscientific and theoretically wrong to regard the course of world history as smooth
and always in a forward direction, without occasional gigantic leaps back.

Further. National wars waged by colonies and semi-
colonies in the imperialist era are not only probable but
inevitable. About 1,000 million people, or *over half* of the
world's population, live in the colonies and semi-colonies
(China, Turkey, Persia). The national liberation movements
there are either already very strong, or are growing and
maturing. Every war is the continuation of politics by other
means. The continuation of national liberation politics in
the colonies will *inevitably* take the form of national wars
against imperialism. Such wars *might* lead to an imperialist war of the present "great" imperialist powers, but on the
other hand they might not. It will depend on many factors.

Example: Britain and France fought the Seven Years'
War for the possession of colonies. In other words, they
waged an imperialist war (which is possible on the basis
of slavery and primitive capitalism as well as on the basis
of modern highly developed capitalism). France suffered
defeat and lost some of her colonies. Several years later
there began the national liberation war of the North American States against Britain alone. France and Spain, then
in possession of some parts of the present United States,
concluded a friendship treaty with the States in rebellion
against Britain. This they did out of hostility to Britain,
i.e., in their own imperialist interests. French troops
fought the British on the side of the American forces. What
we have here is a national liberation war in which imperialist rivalry is an auxiliary element, one that has no serious
importance. This is the very opposite to what we see in the

war of 1914-16 (the national element in the Austro-Serbian War is of no serious importance compared with the all-determining element of imperialist rivalry). It would be absurd, therefore, to apply the concept imperialism indiscriminately and conclude that national wars are "impossible". A national liberation war, waged, for example, by an alliance of Persia, India and China against one or more of the imperialist powers, is both possible and probable, for it would follow from the national liberation movements in these countries. The transformation of such a war into an imperialist war between the present-day imperialist powers would depend upon very many concrete factors, the emergence of which it would be ridiculous to guarantee.

Third, even in Europe national wars in the imperialist epoch cannot be regarded as impossible. The "epoch of imperialism" made the present war an imperialist one and it inevitably engenders new imperialist wars (until the triumph of socialism). This "epoch" has made the policies of the present great powers thoroughly imperialist, but it by no means precludes national wars on the part of, say, small (annexed or nationally-oppressed) countries *against* the imperialist powers, just as it does not preclude large-scale national movements in Eastern Europe. Junius takes a very sober view of Austria, for example, giving due consideration not only to "economic" factors, but to the peculiar political factors. He notes "Austria's intrinsic lack of cohesion" and recognises that the "Hapsburg monarchy is not the political organisation of a bourgeois state, but only a loose syndicate of several cliques of social parasites", and that "the liquidation of Austria-Hungary is, from the historical standpoint, only the continuation of the disintegration of Turkey and, at the same time, a requirement of the historical process of development". Much the same applies to some of the Balkan countries and Russia. And if the "great" powers are altogether exhausted in the present war, or if the revolution in Russia triumphs, national wars and even victorious national wars, are quite possible. Practical intervention by the imperialist powers is *not* always feasible. That is one point. Another is that the superficial view that the war of a small state against a giant is hopeless should be countered by the observation that even a hopeless war is a war just the same. Besides, certain factors operating within the "giant" countries —the outbreak of revolution, for example —can turn a "hopeless" war into a very "hopeful" one.

We have dwelt in detail on the erroneous proposition that "national wars are no longer possible" not only because it is patently erroneous from the theoretical point of view — it would certainly be very lamentable if the "Left" were to reveal a light-hearted attitude to Marxist theory at a time when the establishment of the Third International is possible only on the basis of unvulgarised Marxism. But the mistake is very harmful also from the standpoint of practical politics, for it gives rise to the absurd propaganda of "disarmament", since it is alleged that there can be no wars except reactionary wars. It also gives rise to the even more ludicrous and downright reactionary attitude of indifference to national movements. And such an attitude becomes chauvinism when members of the "great" European nations, that is, the nations which oppress the mass of small and colonial peoples, declare with a pseudo-scientific air: "national wars are no longer possible"! National wars *against* the imperialist powers are not only possible and probable; they are inevitable, *progressive* and *revolutionary* *though* of course, to be *successful*, they require either the concerted effort of huge numbers of people in the oppressed countries (hundreds of millions in our example of India and China), or a *particularly* favourable conjuncture of international conditions (e.g., the fact that the imperialist powers cannot interfere, being paralysed by exhaustion, by war, by their antagonism, etc.), or the *simultaneous* uprising of the proletariat against the bourgeoisie in one of the big powers (this latter eventuality holds first place as the most desirable and favourable for the victory of the proletariat).

It would be unfair, however, to accuse Junius of indifference to national movements. At any rate, he remarks that among the sins of the Social-Democratic parliamentary group was its silence on the death sentence passed on a native leader in the Cameroons on charges of "treason" (evidently he attempted to organise an uprising against the war). Elsewhere Junius especially emphasises (for the benefit of the Legiens, Lensches and the other scoundrels who are still listed as "Social-Democrats") that colonial peoples must be regarded as nations along with all the others. Junius clearly and explicitly states: "Socialism recognised the right of every nation to independence and freedom, to independent mastery of its destinies"; "international socialism recognises the right of free, independent and equal nations, but it is only socialism that can create such nations, and only it can realise the right of nations to self-determination. And this socialist slogan," Junius justly remarks, "serves, like all other socialist slogans, not to justify the existing order of things, but to indicate the way forward, and to stimulate the proletariat in its active revolutionary policy of transformation" (pp. 77-78). It would be a grave mistake indeed to believe that all the German Left Social-Democrats have succumbed to the narrow-mindedness and caricature of Marxism now espoused by certain Dutch and Polish Social-Democrats who deny the right of nations to self-determination even under socialism. But the *specific*, Dutch-Polish, roots of *this* mistake we shall discuss elsewhere.

Another fallacious argument is advanced by Junius on the question of defence of the fatherland. This is a cardinal political question during an imperialist war. Junius has strengthened us in our conviction that our Party has indicated the only correct approach to this question; the proletariat is opposed to defence of the fatherland in this imperialist war *because* of its predatory, slave-owning, reactionary character, *because* it is possible and necessary to oppose to it (and to strive to convert it into) civil war for socialism. Junius, however, while brilliantly exposing the imperialist character of the present war as distinct from a national war, makes the very strange mistake of trying to drag a national programme into the *present*, *non*-national, war. It sounds almost incredible, but there it is.

The official Social-Democrats, both of the Legien and of the Kautsky stripe, in their servility to the bourgeoisie (who have been making the most noise about foreign "invasion" in order to deceive the mass of the people as to the imperialist character of the war), have been particularly assiduous in repeating this "invasion" argument. Kautsky, who now assures naïve and credulous people (incidentally, through Spectator, a member of the Russian Organising Committee) that he joined the opposition at the end of 1914, continues to use this "argument"! To refute it, Junius quotes extremely instructive examples from history, which prove that "invasion and class struggle are not contradictory in bourgeois history, as official legend has it, but that one is the means and the expression of the other". For example, the Bourbons in France invoked foreign invaders against the Jacobins; the bourgeoisie in 1871 invoked foreign invaders against the Commune. In his *Civil War in France*, Marx wrote:

"The highest heroic effort of which old society is still capable is national war; and this is now proved to be a mere governmental humbug, intended to defer the struggle of classes, and to be thrown aside as soon as that class struggle bursts out into civil war."[99]

"The classical example for all times," says Junius, referring to 1793, "is the Great French Revolution." From all this, he draws the following conclusion: "The century of experience thus proves that it is not a state of siege, but relentless class struggle, which rouses the self-respect, the heroism and the moral strength of the mass of the people, and serves as the country's best protection and defence against the external enemy."

Junius's practical conclusion is this: "Yes, it is the duty of the Social-Democrats to defend their country during a great historical crisis. But the grave guilt that rests upon the Social-Democratic Reichstag group consists in their having given the lie to their own solemn declaration, made on August 4, 1914, 'In the hour of danger we will not leave our fatherland unprotected'. They *did* leave the fatherland unprotected in the hour of its greatest peril. For their first duty to the fatherland in that hour was to show the fatherland what was really behind the present imperialist war; to sweep away the web of patriotic and diplomatic lies covering up this encroachment on the fatherland; to proclaim loudly and clearly that both victory and defeat in the present war are equally fatal for the German people; to resist to the last the throttling of the fatherland due to the state of siege; to proclaim the necessity of immediately arming the people and of allowing the people to decide the question

of war and peace; resolutely to demand a permanent ses-
sion of the people's representatives for the whole duration
of the war in order to guarantee vigilant control over the
government by the people's representatives, and control
over the people's representatives by the people; to demand
the immediate abolition of all restrictions on political
rights, for only a free people can successfully defend its
country; and finally, to oppose the imperialist war programme, which is to preserve Austria and Turkey, i.e.,
perpetuate reaction in Europe and in Germany, with the
old, truly national programme of the patriots and democrats
of 1848, the programme of Marx, Engels and Lassalle—the
slogan of a united, Great German Republic. This is the
banner that should have been unfurled before the country,
which would have been a truly national banner of liberation, which would have been in accord with the best traditions of Germany and with the international class policy
of the proletariat.... Hence, the grave dilemma—the
interests of the fatherland or the international solidarity of
the proletariat—the tragic conflict which prompted our
parliamentarians to side, 'with a heavy heart', with the
imperialist war, is purely imaginary, it is a bourgeois
nationalist fiction. On the contrary, there is complete
harmony between the interests of the country and the class
interests of the proletarian International, both in time of
war and in time of peace; both war and peace demand the
most energetic development of the class struggle, the most
determined fight for the Social-Democratic programme."

This is how Junius argues. The fallacy of his argument
is strikingly evident, and since the tacit and avowed
lackeys of tsarism, Plekhanov and Chkhenkeli, and perhaps
even Martov and Chkheidze, may gloatingly seize upon
Junius's words, not for the purpose of establishing
theoretical truth, but for the purpose of wriggling, covering
up their tracks and throwing dust into the eyes of the
workers, we must in greater detail elucidate the *theoretical*
source of Junius's error.

He suggests that the imperialist war should be "opposed"
with a national programme. He urges the advanced class to
turn its face to the past and not to the future! In France,
in Germany, and in the whole of Europe it was a *bourgeois-*

democratic revolution that, *objectively*, was on the order of the day in 1793 and 1848. Corresponding to this *objective* historical situation was the "truly national", i.e., the national *bourgeois* programme of the then existing democracy; in 1793 this programme was carried out by the most revolutionary elements of the bourgeoisie and the plebeians, and in 1848 it was proclaimed by Marx in the name of the whole of progressive democracy. *Objectively*, the feudal and dynastic wars were then opposed by revolutionary-democratic wars, by wars for national liberation. This was the content of the historical tasks of that epoch.

At the present time, the *objective* situation in the biggest advanced states of Europe is different. Progress, if we leave out for the moment the possibility of temporary steps backward, can be made only in the direction of *socialist* society, only in the direction of the *socialist revolution*. From the standpoint of progress, from the standpoint of the progressive class, the imperialist bourgeois war, the war of highly developed capitalism, can, *objectively*, be opposed only with a war *against* the bourgeoisie, i.e., primarily civil war for power between the proletariat and the bourgeoisie; for *unless* such a war is waged, serious progress is *impossible*; this may be followed—only under certain special conditions—by a war to defend the socialist state against bourgeois states. That is why the Bolsheviks (fortunately, very few, and quickly handed over by us to the *Prizyv* group) who were ready to adopt the point of view of conditional defence, i.e., defence of the fatherland on condition that there was a victorious revolution and the victory of a republic in Russia, were true to the *letter* of Bolshevism, but betrayed its *spirit*; for being drawn into the imperialist war of the leading European powers, Russia would *also* be waging an imperialist war, even under a republican form of government!

In saying that the class struggle is the best means of defence against invasion, Junius applies Marxist dialectics only half way, taking one step on the right road and immediately deviating from it. Marxist dialectics call for a concrete analysis of each specific historical situation. It is true that class struggle is the best means of defence against invasion *both* when the bourgeoisie is overthrowing feudalism, and when the proletariat is overthrowing the bourgeoisie. Precisely because it is true with regard to *every* form of class oppression, it is *too general*, and therefore, *inadequate* in the present *specific* case. Civil war against the bourgeoisie is *also* a form of class struggle, and only this form of class struggle would have saved Europe (the whole of Europe, not only one country) from the peril of invasion. The "Great German Republic", had it existed in 1914-16, would *also* have waged an *imperialist* war.

Junius came very close to the correct solution of the problem and to the correct slogan: civil war against the bourgeoisie for socialism; but, as if afraid to speak the whole truth, he turned *back*, to the fantasy of a "national war" in 1914, 1915 and 1916. If we examine the question not from the theoretical angle but from the purely practical one, Junius's error remains just as evident. The whole of bourgeois society, all classes in Germany, including the peasantry, were *in favour* of war (in all probability *the same* was the case in Russia—at least a majority of the well-to-do and middle peasantry and a very considerable portion of the poor peasants were evidently under the spell of bourgeois imperialism). The bourgeoisie was armed to the teeth. Under such circumstances to "proclaim" the programme of a republic, a permanent parliament, election of officers by the people (the "armed nation"), etc., would have meant, *in practice*, "*proclaiming*" *a revolution* (with the *wrong* revolutionary programme!).

In the same breath Junius quite rightly says that a revolution cannot be "made". Revolution was on the order of the day in the 1914-16 period, it was hidden in the depths of the war, was *emerging* out of the war. This should have been "*proclaimed*" in the name of the revolutionary class, and *its* programme should have been fearlessly and fully announced; socialism is impossible in time of war without civil war against the arch-reactionary, criminal bourgeoisie, which condemns the people to untold disaster. Systematic, consistent, practical measures should have been planned, which *could be carried out no matter at what* pace the revolutionary crisis might develop, and which would be in line with the maturing revolution. These measures are indicated in our Party's resolution: (1) voting against war credits;

(2) violation of the "class truce"; (3) creation of an illegal
organisation; (4) fraternisation among the soldiers; (5)
support for all the revolutionary actions of the masses.*
The success of *all* these steps *inevitably* leads to civil war.

The promulgation of a great historical programme was
undoubtedly of tremendous significance; not the old national German programme, which became obsolete in 1914,
1915 and 1916, but the proletarian internationalist and
socialist programme. "You, the bourgeoisie, are fighting
for plunder; we, the workers of *all* the belligerent countries,
declare war upon you for, socialism"—that's the sort of
speech that should have been delivered in the parliaments on
August 4, 1914, by socialists who had not betrayed the
proletariat, as the Legiens, Davids, Kautskys, Plekhanovs,
Guesdes, Sembats, etc., had done.

Evidently Junius's error is due to two kinds of mistakes
in reasoning. There is no doubt that Junius is decidedly
opposed to the imperialist war and is decidedly *in favour*
of revolutionary tactics; and all the gloating of the Plekhanovs over Junius's "defencism" cannot wipe out this
fact. Possible and probable calumnies of this kind must be
answered promptly and bluntly.

But, first, Junius has not completely rid himself of the
"environment" of the German Social-Democrats, even the
Leftists, who are afraid of a split, who are afraid to follow
revolutionary slogans to their logical conclusions.** This
is a false fear, and the Left Social-Democrats of Germany
must and *will* rid themselves of it. They *are sure to do so*
in the course of their struggle against the social-chauvinists. The fact is that they are fighting against *their own*
social-chauvinists resolutely, firmly and *sincerely*, and
this is the tremendous, the fundamental difference in prin-

---

* See present edition, Vol. 21, "The Conference of the R.S.D.L.P.
Groups Abroad."—*Ed.*

** We find the same error in Junius's arguments about which is
better, victory or defeat? His conclusion is that both are equally bad
(ruin, growth of armaments, etc.). This is the point of view not of
the revolutionary proletariat, but of the pacifist petty bourgeoisie.
If one speaks about the "revolutionary intervention" of the proletariat—of this both Junius and the theses of the *Internationale* group
speak, although unfortunately in terms that are too general—one
must raise the question from *another* point of view, namely: (1) Is

ciple between them and the Martovs and Chkheidzes, who, with one hand (*à la* Skobelev) unfurl a banner bearing the greeting, "To the Liebknechts of All Countries", and with the other hand tenderly embrace Chkhenkeli and Potresov!

Secondly, Junius apparently wanted to achieve something in the nature of the Menshevik "theory of stages", of sad memory; he wanted to *begin* to carry out the revolutionary programme from the end that is "more suitable", "more popular" and more acceptable to the *petty bourgeoisie*. It is something like a plan "to outwit history", to outwit the philistines. He seems to say, surely, nobody would oppose a *better* way of defending the real fatherland; and the real fatherland is the Great German Republic, and the best defence *is* a militia, a permanent parliament, etc. Once it was accepted, that programme would automatically lead to the next stage—to the socialist revolution.

Probably, it was reasoning of this kind that consciously or semi-consciously determined Junius's tactics. Needless to say, such reasoning is fallacious. Junius's pamphlet conjures up in our mind the picture of a *lone* man who has no comrades in an illegal organisation accustomed to thinking out revolutionary slogans to their conclusion and systematically educating the masses in their spirit. But this shortcoming—it would be a grave error to forget this—is not Junius's personal failing, but the result of the weakness of *all* the German Leftists, who have become entangled in the vile net of Kautskyite hypocrisy, pedantry and "friendliness" for the opportunists. Junius's adherents have managed, *in spite* of their isolation, to *begin* the publication of illegal leaflets and to start the war against Kautskyism. They will succeed in going further along the right road.

Written in July 1916
Published in *Sbornik*
Sotsial-Demokrata No. 1,
October 1916
Signed: *N. Lenin*

Published according to
the text in *Sbornik*

"revolutionary intervention" possible without the risk of defeat? (2) Is it possible to scourge the bourgeoisie and the government of one's *own* country without taking that risk? (3) Have we not always asserted, and does not the historical experience of reactionary wars prove, that defeats help the cause of the revolutionary class?

THE DISCUSSION ON SELF-DETERMINATION SUMMED UP

Issue No. 2 of the *Herald* (*Vorbote* No. 2, April 1916), the Marxist journal of the Zimmerwald Left, published theses for and against the self-determination of nations, signed by the Editorial Board of our Central Organ, *Sotsial-Demokrat*, and by the Editorial Board of the organ of the Polish Social-Democratic opposition, *Gazeta Robotnicza*. Above the reader will find a reprint of the former* and a translation of the latter theses.[100] This is practically the first time that the question has been presented so extensively in the international field: it was raised only in respect of Poland in the discussion carried on in the German Marxist journal *Neue Zeit* twenty years ago, 1895-96, before the London International Socialist Congress of 1896, by Rosa Luxemburg, Karl Kautsky and the Polish "independents" (champions of the independence of Poland, the Polish Socialist Party), who represented three different views.[101] Since then, as far as we know, the question of self-determination has been discussed at all systematically only by the Dutch and the Poles. Let us hope that the *Herald* will succeed in promoting the discussion of this question, so urgent today, among the British, Americans, French, Germans and Italians. Official socialism, represented both by direct supporters of "their own" governments, the Plekhanovs, Davids and Co., and the undercover defenders of opportunism, the Kautskyites (among them Axelrod, Martov, Chkheidze and others), has told so many lies on this question that for a long time there will inevitably be efforts, on the one hand, to maintain

---

* See pp. 143-56 of this volume.—*Ed.*

silence and evade the issue, and, on the other, workers' demands for "direct answers" to these "accursed questions". We shall try to keep our readers informed of the struggle between the trends among socialists abroad.

This question is of specific importance to us Russian Social-Democrats; the present discussion is a continuation of the one that took place in 1903 and 1913[102]; during the war this question has been the cause of some wavering in the thinking of Party members; it has been made more acute by the trickery of such prominent leaders of the Gvozdyov or chauvinist workers' party as Martov and Chkheidze, in their efforts to evade the substance of the problem. It is essential, therefore, to sum up at least the initial results of the discussion that has been started in the international field.

It will be seen from the theses that our Polish comrades provide us with a direct answer to some of our arguments, for example, on Marxism and Proudhonism. In most cases, however, they do not answer us directly, but indirectly, by opposing *their* assertions to ours. Let us examine both their direct and indirect answers.

1. SOCIALISM AND THE SELF-DETERMINATION OF NATIONS

We have affirmed that it would be a betrayal of socialism to refuse to implement the self-determination of nations under socialism. We are told in reply that "the right of self-determination is not applicable to a socialist society". The difference is a radical one. Where does it stem from?

"We know," runs our opponents' reasoning, "that socialism will abolish every kind of national oppression since it abolishes the class interests that lead to it...." What has this argument about the *economic* prerequisites for the abolition of national oppression, which are very well known and undisputed, to do with a discussion of *one* of the forms of *political* oppression, namely, the forcible retention of one nation within the state frontiers of another? This is nothing but an attempt to evade political questions! And subsequent arguments further convince us that our judgement is right: "We have no reason to believe that in a socialist society, the nation will exist as an economic and political unit. It will in all probability assume the character of a cultural and linguistic unit only, because the territorial division of a socialist cultural zone, if practised at all, can be made only according to the needs of production and, furthermore, the question of such a division will naturally not be decided by individual nations alone and in possession of full sovereignty [as is required by "the right to self-determination"], but will be *determined jointly* by all the citizens concerned...."

Our Polish comrades like this last argument, on *joint* determination instead of *self*-determination, so much that they repeat it *three times* in their theses! Frequency of repetition, however, does not turn this Octobrist and reactionary argument into a Social-Democratic argument. All reactionaries and bourgeois grant to nations forcibly retained within the frontiers of a given state the right to "determine jointly" their fate in a common parliament. Wilhelm II also gives the Belgians the right to "determine jointly" the fate of the German Empire in a common German parliament.

Our opponents try to evade precisely the point at issue, the only one that is up for discussion—the right to secede. This would be funny if it were not so tragic!

Our very first thesis said that the liberation of oppressed nations implies a dual transformation in the political sphere: (1) the full equality of nations. This is not disputed and applies only to what takes place within the state; (2) freedom of political separation.* This refers to the demarcation of state frontiers. This *only* is disputed. But it is precisely this that our opponents remain silent about. They do not want to think either about state frontiers or even about the state as such. This is a sort of "imperialist Economism" like the old Economism of 1894-1902, which argued in this way: capitalism is victorious, *therefore* political questions are a waste of time. Imperialism is

---

* See p. 143 of this volume.—*Ed.*

victorious, *therefore* political questions are a waste of time! Such an apolitical theory is extremely harmful to Marxism.

In his *Critique of the Gotha Programme*, Marx wrote: "Between capitalist and communist society lies the period of the revolutionary transformation of the one into the other. There corresponds to this also a political transition period in which the state can be nothing but the revolutionary dictatorship of the proletariat."[103] Up to now this truth has been indisputable for socialists and it includes the recognition of the fact that the *state* will exist until victorious socialism develops into full communism. Engels's dictum about the *withering away* of the state is well known. We deliberately stressed, in the first thesis, that democracy is a form of state that will also wither away when the state withers away. And until our opponents replace Marxism by some sort of "non-state" viewpoint their arguments will constitute one big mistake.

Instead of speaking about the state (which *means*, about the demarcation of its *frontiers!*), they speak of a "socialist cultural zone", i.e., they deliberately choose an expression that is indefinite in the sense that all state questions are obliterated! Thus we get a ridiculous tautology: if there is no state there can, of course, be no question of frontiers. In that case the *whole* democratic-political programme is unnecessary. Nor will there be any republic, when the state "withers away".

The German chauvinist Lensch, in the articles we mentioned in Thesis 5 (footnote),* quoted an interesting passage from Engels's article "The Po and the Rhine". Amongst other things, Engels says in this article that in the course of historical development, which swallowed up a number of small and non-viable nations, the "frontiers of great and viable European nations" were being increasingly determined by the "language and sympathies" of the population. Engels calls these frontiers "natural".[104] Such was the case in the period of progressive capitalism in Europe, roughly from 1848 to 1871. Today, these democratically determined

---

* See p. 150 of this volume.—*Ed.*

frontiers are more and more often being *broken down* by
reactionary, imperialist capitalism. There is every sign
that imperialism will leave its successor, socialism, a heri-
tage of *less* democratic frontiers, a number of annexations in
Europe and in other parts of the world. Is it to be supposed
that victorious socialism, restoring and implementing full
democracy all along the line, will refrain from *democratically* demarcating state frontiers and ignore the "sympathies" of the population? These questions need only be stated
to make it quite clear that our Polish colleagues are sliding
down from Marxism towards imperialist Economism.

The old Economists, who made a caricature of Marxism,
told the workers that "only the economic" was of importance
to Marxists. The new Economists seem to think either that
the democratic state of victorious socialism will exist without frontiers (like a "complex of sensations" without matter)
or that frontiers will be delineated "only" in accordance
with the needs of production. In actual fact its frontiers
will be delineated democratically, i.e., in accordance with
the will and "sympathies" of the population. Capitalism
rides roughshod over these sympathies, adding more obsta-
cles to the rapprochement of nations. Socialism, by organising production *without* class oppression, by ensuring the
well-being of *all* members of the state, gives *full play* to the
"sympathies" of the population, thereby promoting and
greatly accelerating the drawing together and fusion of
the nations.

To give the reader a rest from the heavy and clumsy
Economism let us quote the reasoning of a socialist writer
who is outside our dispute. That writer is Otto Bauer, who
also has his own "pet little point" —"cultural and national
autonomy" —but who argues quite correctly on a large number
of most important questions. For example, in Chapter 29
of his book *The National Question and Social-Democracy*,
he was doubly right in noting the use of national ideology
to cover up *imperialist* policies. In Chapter 30, "Socialism
and the Principle of Nationality", he says:

"The socialist community will never be able to include
whole nations within its make-up by the use of force.
Imagine the masses of the people, enjoying all the blessings
of national culture, taking a full and active part in legisla-

tion and government, and, finally, supplied with arms — would it be possible to subordinate such a nation to the rule of an alien social organism by force? All state power rests on the force of arms. The present-day people's army, thanks to an ingenious mechanism, still constitutes a tool in the hands of a definite person, family or class exactly like the knightly and mercenary armies of the past. The army of the democratic community of a socialist society is nothing but the people armed, since it consists of highly cultured persons, working without compulsion in socialised workshops and taking full part in all spheres of political life. In such conditions any possibility of alien rule disappears."

This is true. It is *impossible* to abolish national (or any other political) oppression under capitalism, since this *requires* the abolition of classes, i.e., the introduction of socialism. But while being based on economics, socialism cannot be reduced to economics alone. A foundation —socialist production —is essential for the abolition of national oppression, but this foundation must *also* carry a democratically organised state, a democratic army, etc. By transforming capitalism into socialism the proletariat creates the *possibility* of abolishing national oppression; the possibility becomes *reality* "only" —"only"! —with the establishment of full democracy in all spheres, including the delineation of state frontiers in accordance with the "sympathies" of the population, including complete freedom to secede. And this, in turn, will serve as a basis for developing the *practical* elimination of even the slightest national friction and the least national mistrust, for an accelerated drawing together and fusion of nations that will be completed when the state *withers away*. This is the Marxist theory, the theory from which our Polish colleagues have mistakenly departed.

2. IS DEMOCRACY "PRACTICABLE" UNDER IMPERIALISM?

The old polemic conducted by Polish Social-Democrats against the self-determination of nations is based entirely on the argument that it is "impracticable" under capitalism. As long ago as 1903 we, the *Iskra* supporters, laughed at this argument in the Programme Commission of the Second

Congress of the R.S.D.L.P., and said that it was a
repetition of the distortion of Marxism preached by the
(late lamented) Economists. In our theses we dealt with
this error in particular detail and it is precisely on this
point, which contains the theoretical kernel of the whole
dispute, that the Polish comrades did not wish to (or could
not?) answer *any* of our arguments.

To prove the economic impossibility of self-determination
would require an economic analysis such as that used to
prove the impracticability of prohibiting machines or introducing labour-money, etc. No one has even attempted to
make such an analysis. No one will maintain that it has
been possible to introduce "labour-money" under capitalism
"by way of exception" in even one country, in the way it
was possible for one small country to realise this impracticable self-determination, even without war or revolution,
"by way of exception", in the era of the most rabid imperialism (Norway, 1905).

In general, political democracy is merely one of the
possible *forms* of superstructure *above* capitalism (although
it is theoretically the normal one for "pure" capitalism).
The facts show that both capitalism and imperialism develop
within the framework of *any* political form and subordinate
them *all*. It is, therefore, a basic theoretical error to speak of
the "impracticability" of *one* of the forms and of *one* of the
demands of democracy.

The absence of an answer to these arguments from our
Polish colleagues compels us to consider the discussion
closed on this point. To make it graphic, so to say, we made
the very concrete assertion that it would be "ridiculous"
to deny the "practicability" of the restoration of Poland
today, making it dependent on the strategic and other
aspects of the present war. No reply was forthcoming!

The Polish comrades simply *repeated* an obviously incorrect assertion (§ II, 1), saying that "in questions of the
annexation of foreign territories, forms of political democracy are pushed aside; sheer force is decisive.... Capital
will never allow the people to decide the question of their
state frontiers...". As though "capital" could "allow the
people" to select *its* civil servants, the servants of imperialism! Or as though weighty decisions on important demo-

cratic questions, such as the establishment of a republic in place of a monarchy, or a militia in place of a regular army, were, *in general*, conceivable without "sheer force". Subjectively, the Polish comrades want to make Marxism "more profound" but they are doing it altogether unsuccessfully. *Objectively*, their phrases about impracticability are opportunism, because their tacit assumption is: this is "impracticable" without a series of revolutions, in the same way as democracy *as a whole*, *all* its demands taken together, is impracticable under imperialism.

Once only, at the very end of § II,1, in the discussion on Alsace, our Polish colleagues abandoned the position of imperialist Economism and approached the question of one of the forms of democracy with a concrete answer and not with general references to the "economic". And it was precisely this approach that was wrong! It would, they wrote, be "particularist, undemocratic" if *some* Alsatians, without asking the French, were to "impose" on them a union with Alsace, although part of Alsace was German-oriented and this threatened war!!! The confusion is amusing: self-determination presumes (this is in itself clear, and we have given it special emphasis in our theses) freedom to *separate* from the oppressor state; but the fact that *union* with a state presumes the consent of *that state* is something that is "not customarily" mentioned in politics any more than the "consent" of a capitalist to receive profit or of a worker to receive wages is mentioned in economics! It is ridiculous even to speak of such a thing.

If one wants to be a Marxist politician, one should, in speaking of Alsace, attack the German socialist scoundrels for not fighting for Alsace's freedom to secede and attack the French socialist scoundrels for making their peace with the French bourgeoisie who want to annex the whole of Alsace by force—and both of them for serving the imperialism of "their own" country and for fearing a separate state, even if only a little one—the thing is to show *how* the socialists who recognise self-determination would solve the problem in a few weeks without going against the will of the Alsatians. To argue, instead, about the horrible danger of the French Alsatians "forcing" themselves on France is a real pearl.

3. WHAT IS ANNEXATION?

We raised this question in a most definite manner in our theses (Section 7).* The Polish comrades did *not* reply to it: they evaded it, insisting (1) that they are against annexations and explaining (2) why they are against them. It is true that these are very important questions. But they are questions of *another kind*. If we want our principles to be theoretically sound at all, if we want them to be clearly and precisely formulated, we cannot *evade* the question of what an annexation is, since this concept is used in our political propaganda and agitation. The evasion of the question in a discussion between colleagues cannot be interpreted as anything but desertion of one's position.

Why have we raised this question? We explained this when we raised it. It is because "a protest against annexations is nothing but recognition of the right to self-determination". The concept of annexation usually includes: (1) the concept of force (joining by means of force); (2) the concept of oppression by another nation (the joining of "*alien*" regions, etc.), and, sometimes (3) the concept of violation of the *status quo*. We pointed this out in the theses and this did not meet with any criticism.

Can Social-Democrats be against the use of force in general, it may be asked? Obviously not. This means that we are against annexations not because they constitute force, but for some other reason. Nor can the Social-Democrats be for the *status quo*. However you may twist and turn, annexation is *violation of the self-determination* of a nation, it is the establishment of state *frontiers contrary to the will of the population*.

To be against annexations *means* to be in favour of the right to self-determination. To be "against the forcible retention of any nation within the frontiers of a given state" (we deliberately employed this slightly changed formulation of the same idea in Section 4 of our theses,** and the Polish comrades *answered* us with *complete* clarity at the beginning of their § I, 4, that they "are against the

---

* See pp. 152-53 of this volume.—*Ed.*
** See p. 147 of this volume.—*Ed.*

forcible retention of oppressed nations within the frontiers of the annexing state") —is *the same* as being in favour of the self-determination of nations.

We do not want to haggle over words. If there is a party that says in its programme (or in a resolution binding on all —the form does not matter) that it is against annexations,* against the forcible retention of oppressed nations within the frontiers of *its* state, we declare our complete agreement in principle with that party. It would be absurd to insist on the *word* "self-determination". And if there are people in our Party who want to change *words* in this spirit, who want to amend Clause 9 of our Party Programme, we should consider our differences with *such* comrades to be anything but a matter of principle!

The only thing that matters is political clarity and theoretical soundness of our slogans.

In verbal discussions on this question—the importance of which nobody will deny, especially now, in view of the war —we have met the following argument (we have not come across it in the press): *a protest against* a known evil does not necessarily mean recognition of a positive concept that precludes the evil. This is obviously an unfounded argument and, apparently, as such has not been reproduced in the press. If a socialist party declares that it is "against the forcible retention of an oppressed nation within the frontiers of the annexing state", it is *thereby committed to renounce retention by force* when it comes to power.

We do not for one moment doubt that if Hindenburg were to accomplish the semi-conquest of Russia tomorrow and this semi-conquest were to be expressed by the appearance of a new Polish state (in connection with the desire of Britain and France to weaken tsarism somewhat), something that is quite "practicable" from the standpoint of the economic laws of capitalism and imperialism, and if, the day after tomorrow, the socialist revolution were to be victorious in Petrograd, Berlin and Warsaw, the Polish socialist government, like the Russian and German socialist governments, would renounce the "forcible retention" of, say, the

---

* Karl Radek formulated this as "against old and new annexations" in one of his articles in *Berner Tagwacht*.

Ukrainians, "within the frontiers of the Polish state". If there were members of the *Gazeta Robotnicza* Editorial Board in that government they would no doubt sacrifice their "theses", thereby disproving the "theory" that "the right of self-determination is not applicable to a socialist society". If we thought otherwise we should not put a comradely discussion with the Polish Social-Democrats on the agenda but would rather conduct a ruthless struggle against them as chauvinists.

Suppose I were to go out into the streets of any European city and make a public "protest", which I then published in the press, against my not being permitted to purchase a man as a slave. There is no doubt that people would have the right to regard me as a slave-owner, a champion of the principle, or system, if you like of slavery. No one would be fooled by the fact that my sympathies with slavery were expressed in the negative form of a protest and not in a positive form ("I am for slavery"). A political "protest" is *quite* the equivalent of a political programme; this is so obvious that one feels rather awkward at having to explain it. In any case, we are firmly convinced that on the part of the Zimmerwald Left, at any rate —we do not speak of the Zimmerwald group as a whole since it contains Martov and other Kautskyites —we shall not meet with any "protest" if we say that in the Third International there will be no place for people capable of separating a political protest from a political programme, of counterposing the one to the other, etc.

Not wishing to haggle over words, we take the liberty of expressing the sincere hope that the Polish Social-Democrats will try soon to formulate, officially, their proposal to delete Clause 9 from our Party Programme (which is also *theirs*) and also from the Programme of the International (the resolution of the 1896 London Congress), as well as *their own* definition of the relevant political concepts of "old and new annexations" and of "the forcible retention of an oppressed nation within the frontiers of the annexing state".

Let us now turn to the next question.

4. FOR OR AGAINST ANNEXATIONS?

In § 3 of Part One of their theses the Polish comrades declare very definitely that they are against any kind of annexation. Unfortunately, in § 4 of the same part we find an assertion that must be considered annexationist. It opens with the following ... how can it be put more delicately?... the following strange phrase:

"The starting-point of Social-Democracy's struggle against annexations, against the forcible retention of oppressed nations within the frontiers of the annexing state is *renunciation of any defence of the fatherland* [the authors' italics], which, in the era of imperialism, is defence of the rights of one's own bourgeoisie to oppress and plunder foreign peoples...."

What's this? How is it put?

"The starting-point of the struggle against annexations is renunciation of *any* defence of the fatherland...." But any national war and any national revolt can be called "defence of the fatherland" and, until now, has been *generally* recognised as such! We are against annexations, *but*... we mean by this that we are against the annexed waging a war *for* their liberation from those who have annexed them, that we are against the annexed revolting to liberate themselves from those who have annexed them! Isn't that an annexationist declaration?

The authors of the theses motivate their ... strange assertion by saying that "in the era of imperialism" defence of the fatherland amounts to defence of the right of one's own bourgeoisie to oppress foreign peoples. This, however, is true *only* in respect of an imperialist war, i.e., in respect of a war *between* imperialist powers or groups of powers, when *both* belligerents not only oppress "foreign peoples" but are fighting a war *to decide* who shall have a *greater share* in oppressing foreign peoples!

The authors seem to present the question of "defence of the fatherland" very differently from the way it is presented by our Party. We renounce "defence of the fatherland" in an *imperialist* war. This is said as clearly as it can be in the Manifesto of our Party's Central Committee and in the Berne resolutions* reprinted in the pamphlet *Socialism and War*, which has been published both in German and French. We stressed this *twice* in our theses (footnotes to Sections 4 and 6).** The authors of the Polish theses seem to renounce defence of the fatherland *in general*, i.e., *for a national war as well*, believing, perhaps, that in the "era of imperialism" national wars *are impossible*. We say "perhaps" because the Polish comrades have *not* expressed this view in their theses.

Such a view is clearly expressed in the theses of the German *Internationale* group and in the Junius pamphlet which is dealt with in a special article.*** In addition to what is said there, let us note that the national revolt of an annexed region or country against the annexing country may be called precisely a revolt and not a war (we have heard this objection made and, therefore, cite it here, although we do not think this terminological dispute a serious one). In any case, hardly anybody would risk denying that annexed Belgium, Serbia, Galicia and Armenia would call their "revolt" against those who annexed them "defence of the fatherland" *and would do so in all justice*. It looks as if the Polish comrades are *against* this type of revolt on the grounds that there is *also* a bourgeoisie in these annexed countries which *also* oppresses foreign peoples or, more exactly, could oppress them, since the question is one of the "*right* to oppress". Consequently, the given war or revolt is not assessed on the strength of its *real* social content (the struggle of an oppressed nation for its liberation from the oppressor nation) but the possible exercise of the "*right* to oppress" by a bourgeoisie which is at present itself oppressed. If Belgium, let us say, is annexed by Germany in 1917, and in 1918 revolts to secure her liberation, the Polish comrades will be against her revolt on the grounds that the Belgian bourgeoisie possess "the right to oppress foreign peoples"!

---

* See present edition, Vol. 21, "The War and Russian Social-Democracy", "The Conference of the R.S.D.L.P. Groups Abroad".—*Ed.*

** See pp. 149 and 150 of this volume.—*Ed.*

*** See p. 305 of this volume.—*Ed.*

There is nothing Marxist or even revolutionary in this argument. If we do not want to betray socialism we *must* support *every* revolt against our chief enemy, the bourgeoisie of the big states, provided it is not the revolt of a reactionary class. By refusing to support the revolt of annexed regions we become, objectively, annexationists. It is precisely in the "era of imperialism", which is the era of nascent social revolution, that the proletariat will today give especially vigorous support to any revolt of the annexed regions so that tomorrow, or simultaneously, it may attack the bourgeoisie of the "great" power that is weakened by the revolt.

The Polish comrades, however, go further in their annexationism. They are not only against any revolt by the annexed regions; they are against *any* restoration of their independence, even a peaceful one! Listen to this:

"Social-Democracy, rejecting all responsibility for the consequences of the policy of oppression pursued by imperialism, and conducting the sharpest struggle against them, *does not by any means favour the erection of new frontier posts in Europe or the re-erection of those swept away by imperialism*" (the authors' italics).

Today "imperialism has swept away the frontier posts" between Germany and Belgium and between Russia and Galicia. International Social-Democracy, if you please, ought to be against their re-erection in general, whatever the means. In 1905, "in the era of imperialism", when Norway's autonomous Diet proclaimed her secession from Sweden, and Sweden's war against Norway, as preached by the Swedish reactionaries, did not take place, what with the resistance of the Swedish workers and the international imperialist situation—Social-Democracy ought to have been against Norway's secession, since it undoubtedly meant "the erection of new frontier posts in Europe"!!

This is downright annexationism. There is no need to refute it because it refutes itself. No socialist party would risk taking this stand: "We oppose annexations in general but we sanction annexations for Europe or tolerate them once they have been made"....

We need deal only with the theoretical sources of the error that has led our Polish comrades to such a patent...

"impossibility". We shall say further on why there is no reason to make exceptions for "Europe". The following two phrases from the theses will explain the other sources of the error:

"Wherever the wheel of imperialism has rolled over and crushed an already formed capitalist state, the political and economic concentration of the capitalist world, paving the way for socialism, takes place in the brutal form of imperialist oppression...."

This justification of annexations is not Marxism but Struveism. Russian Social-Democrats who remember the 1890s in Russia have a good knowledge of this manner of distorting Marxism, which is common to Struve, Cunow, Legien and Co. In another of the theses (II, 3) of the Polish comrades we read the following, specifically about the German Struveists, the so-called "social-imperialists":

(The slogan of self-determination) "provides the social-imperialists with an opportunity, by demonstrating the illusory nature of that slogan, to represent our struggle against national oppression as historically unfounded sentimentality, thereby undermining the faith of the proletariat in the scientific validity of the Social-Democratic programme...."

This means that the authors consider the position of the German Struveists "scientific"! Our congratulations.

One "trifle", however, brings down this amazing argument which threatens to show that the Lensches, Cunows and Parvuses are *right* in comparison to us: it is that the Lensches are consistent people in their own way and in issue No. 8-9 of the chauvinist German *Glocke*—we deliberately quoted it in our theses—Lensch demonstrates *simultaneously* both the "scientific invalidity" of the self-determination slogan (the Polish Social-Democrats apparently believe that *this* argument of Lensch's is irrefutable, as can be seen from their arguments in the theses we have quoted) *and* the "scientific invalidity" of the slogan against annexations!!

For Lensch had an excellent understanding of that simple truth which we pointed out to those Polish colleagues who showed no desire to reply to our statement: there is no difference "either political or economic", or even logical, between the "recognition" of self-determination and the "protest" against annexations. If the Polish comrades regard the arguments of the Lensches against self-determination to be irrefutable, there is one *fact* that has to be accepted: the Lensches also use *all* these arguments to oppose the struggle against annexations.

The theoretical error that underlies all the arguments of our Polish colleagues has led them to the point of becoming *inconsistent annexationists*.

5. WHY ARE SOCIAL-DEMOCRATS AGAINST ANNEXATIONS?

In our view the answer is obvious: because annexation violates the self-determination of nations, or, in other words, is a form of national oppression.

In the view of the Polish Social-Democrats there have to be *special* explanations of why we are against annexations, and it is these (I, 3 in the theses) that inevitably enmesh the authors in a further series of contradictions.

They produce two reasons to "justify" our opposition to annexations (the "scientifically valid" arguments of the Lensches notwithstanding):

First: "To the assertion that annexations in Europe are essential for the military security of a victorious imperialist state, the Social-Democrats counterpose the fact that annexations only serve to sharpen antagonisms, thereby increasing the danger of war...."

This is an inadequate reply to the Lensches because their chief argument is not that annexations are a military necessity but that they are *economically* progressive and under imperialism mean concentration. Where is the logic if the Polish Social-Democrats in the same breath recognise the progressive nature of *such* a concentration, refusing to re-erect frontier posts in Europe that have been swept away by imperialism, and protest *against* annexations?

Furthermore, the danger of *what* wars is increased by annexations? Not imperialist wars, because they have other causes; the chief antagonisms in the present imperialist war are undoubtedly those between Germany and Britain, and between Germany and Russia. These antagonisms have nothing to do with annexations. It is the danger of *national*

wars and national revolts that is increased. But how can one
declare national wars to be *impossible* in "the era of
imperialism", on the one hand, and then speak of the "danger" of national wars, on the other? This is not logical.

The second argument: Annexations "create a gulf between
the proletariat of the ruling nation and that of the oppressed
nation... the proletariat of the oppressed nation would
unite with its bourgeoisie and regard the proletariat of the
ruling nation as its enemy. Instead of the proletariat waging
an international class struggle against the international
bourgeoisie it would be split and ideologically corrupted...".

We fully agree with these arguments. But is it logical to
put forward simultaneously two arguments on the same
question which cancel each other out. In §3 of the first
part of the theses we find the above arguments that
regard annexations as causing a *split* in the proletariat,
and next to it, in §4, we are told that we must oppose the
annulment of annexations already effected in Europe and
favour "the education of the working masses of the oppressed
and the oppressor nations in a spirit of solidarity in struggle".
If the annulment of annexations is reactionary "sentimentality", annexations *must not* be said to create a "gulf"
between sections of the "proletariat" and cause a "split",
but should, on the contrary, be regarded as a condition for
the *bringing together* of the proletariat of different nations.

We say: In order that we may have the strength to
accomplish the socialist revolution and overthrow the bourgeoisie, the workers must unite more closely and this close
union is promoted by the struggle for self-determination,
i.e., the struggle against annexations. We are consistent.
But the Polish comrades who say that European annexations
are "non-annullable" and national wars, "impossible", defeat
themselves by contending "against" annexations with the
use of arguments *about* national wars! These arguments
are to the effect that annexations *hamper* the drawing
together and fusion of workers of different nations!

In other words, the Polish Social-Democrats, in order to
contend against annexations, have to draw for arguments on
the theoretical stock *they themselves* reject in principle.

The question of colonies makes this even more obvious.

6. IS IT RIGHT TO CONTRAST "EUROPE" WITH THE COLONIES IN THE PRESENT QUESTION?

Our theses say that the demand for the immediate liberation of the colonies is as "impracticable" (that is, it cannot be effected without a number of revolutions and is not stable without socialism) under capitalism as the self-determination of nations, the election of civil servants by the people, the democratic republic, and so on—and, furthermore, that the demand for the liberation of the colonies is nothing more than "the recognition of the right of nations to self-determination".

The Polish comrades have not answered a single one of these arguments. They have tried to differentiate between "Europe" and the colonies. For Europe alone they become inconsistent annexationists by refusing to annul any annexations once these have been made. As for the colonies, they demand unconditionally: "Get out of the colonies!"

Russian socialists must put forward the demand: "Get out of Turkestan, Khiva, Bukhara, etc.", but, it is alleged, they would be guilty of "utopianism", "unscientific sentimentality" and so on if they demanded a similar freedom of secession for Poland, Finland, the Ukraine, etc. British socialists must demand: "Get out of Africa, India, Australia", but not out of Ireland. What are the theoretical grounds for a distinction that is so patently false? This question cannot be evaded.

The chief "ground" of those opposed to self-determination is its "impracticability". The same idea, with a nuance, is expressed in the reference to "economic and political concentration".

Obviously, concentration *also* comes about with the annexation of colonies. There was formerly an economic distinction between the colonies and the European peoples — at least, the majority of the latter—the colonies having been drawn into *commodity* exchange but not into capitalist *production*. Imperialism changed this. Imperialism is, among other things, the export of *capital*. Capitalist production is being transplanted to the colonies at an ever increasing rate. They cannot be extricated from dependence on European finance capital. From the military standpoint,

as well as from the standpoint of expansion, the separation
of the colonies is practicable, as a general rule, only under
socialism; under capitalism it is practicable only by
way of exception or at the cost of a series of revolts and
revolutions both in the colonies and the metropolitan
countries.

The greater part of the dependent nations in Europe are
capitalistically more developed than the colonies (though
not all, the exceptions being the Albanians and many
non-Russian peoples in Russia). But it is just this that
generates greater resistance to national oppression and
annexations! Precisely because of this, the development of
capitalism is *more secure* in Europe under any political
conditions, including those of separation, than in the colonies.... "There," the Polish comrades say about the colonies
(I, 4), "capitalism is still confronted with the task of developing the productive forces independently...." This is even
more noticeable in Europe: capitalism is undoubtedly developing the productive forces more vigorously, rapidly and
independently in Poland, Finland, the Ukraine and Alsace
than in India, Turkestan, Egypt and other straightforward
colonies. In a commodity-producing society, no independent
development, or development of any sort whatsoever, is
possible without capital. In Europe the dependent nations
have both *their own* capital and easy access to it on a wide
range of terms. The colonies have no capital of *their own*,
or none to speak of, and under finance capital no colony
can obtain any except on terms of political submission.
What then, in face of all this, is the significance of the demand
to liberate the colonies immediately and unconditionally?
Is it not clear that it is more "utopian" in the vulgar, cari-
cature-"Marxist" sense of the word, "utopian", in the sense
in which it is used by the Struves, Lensches, Cunows,
with the Polish comrades unfortunately following in their
footsteps? Any deviation from the ordinary, the commonplace,
as well as everything that is revolutionary, is here
labelled "utopianism". But revolutionary movements of
all kinds—including national movements—are more possible, more practicable, more stubborn, more conscious and
more difficult to defeat in Europe than they are in the
colonies.

Socialism, say the Polish comrades (I, 3), "will be able to give the underdeveloped peoples of the colonies *unselfish cultural aid without ruling* over them". This is perfectly true. But what grounds are there for supposing that a great nation, a great state that goes over to socialism, will not be able to attract a small, oppressed European nation by means of "unselfish cultural aid"? It is the freedom to secede *"granted"* to the colonies by the Polish Social-Democrats that will attract the small but cultured and politically *exacting* oppressed nations of Europe to union with great socialist states, because under socialism a great state will mean so many hours *less* work a day and so much more *pay* a day. The masses of working people, as they liberate themselves from the bourgeois yoke, *will gravitate* irresistibly towards union and integration with the great, advanced socialist nations for the sake of that "cultural aid", provided yesterday's oppressors do not infringe on the long-oppressed nations' highly developed democratic feeling of self-respect, and provided they are granted equality in everything, including state construction, that is, experience in organising "their own" state. Under capitalism this "experience" means war, isolation, seclusion, and the narrow egoism of the small privileged nations (Holland, Switzerland). Under socialism the working people themselves will nowhere consent to seclusion merely for the above-mentioned purely economic motives, while the variety of political forms, freedom to secede, and experience in state organisation — there will be all this until the state in all its forms withers away — will be the basis of a prosperous cultured life and an earnest that the nations will draw closer together and integrate at an ever faster pace.

By setting the colonies aside and contrasting them to Europe the Polish comrades step into a contradiction which immediately brings down the whole of their fallacious argument.

7. MARXISM OR PROUDHONISM?

By way of an exception, our Polish comrades parry our reference to Marx's attitude towards the separation of Ireland directly and not indirectly. What is their objection?

References to Marx's position from 1848 to 1871, they say, are "not of the slightest value". The argument advanced in support of this unusually irate and peremptory assertion is that "at one and the same time" Marx opposed the strivings for independence of the "Czechs, South Slavs, etc."[105]

The argument is so very irate because it is so very unsound. According to the Polish Marxists, Marx was simply a muddlehead who "in one breath" said contradictory things! This is altogether untrue, and it is certainly not Marxism. It is precisely the demand for "concrete" analysis, which our Polish comrades insist on, *but do not themselves apply*, that makes it necessary for us to investigate whether Marx's different attitudes towards different concrete "national" movements did not spring from *one and the same* socialist outlook.

Marx is known to have favoured Polish independence in the interests of *European* democracy in its struggle against the power and influence —or, it might be said, against the omnipotence and predominating reactionary influence —of tsarism. That this attitude was correct was most clearly and practically demonstrated in 1849, when the Russian serf army crushed the national liberation and revolutionary-democratic rebellion in Hungary. From that time until Marx's death, and even later, until 1890, when there was a danger that tsarism, allied with France, would wage a reactionary war against a *non-imperialist* and nationally independent Germany, Engels stood first and foremost for a struggle against tsarism. It was for this reason, and exclusively for this reason, that Marx and Engels were opposed to the national movement of the Czechs and South Slavs. A simple reference to what Marx and Engels wrote in 1848 and 1849 will prove to anyone who is interested in Marxism in real earnest and not merely for the purpose of brushing Marxism aside, that Marx and Engels at that time drew a clear and definite *distinction* between "whole reactionary nations" serving as "Russian outposts" in Europe, and "revolutionary nations", namely, the Germans, Poles and Magyars. This is a fact. And it was indicated *at the time with incontrovertible* truth: in 1848 revolutionary nations fought for liberty, whose principal enemy was tsarism, whereas the Czechs, etc., were in fact reactionary nations, and outposts of tsarism.

What is the lesson to be drawn from this concrete example which must be analysed *concretely* if there is any desire to be true to Marxism? Only this: (1) that the interests of the liberation of a number of big and very big nations in Europe rate higher than the interests of the movement for liberation of small nations; (2) that the demand for democracy must not be considered in isolation but on a European—today we should say a world—scale.

That is all there is to it. There is no hint of any repudiation of that elementary socialist principle which the Poles forget but to which Marx was *always* faithful—that no nation can be free if it oppresses other nations. If the concrete situation which confronted Marx when tsarism dominated international politics were to repeat itself, for instance, in the form of a few nations starting a socialist revolution (as a bourgeois-democratic revolution was started in Europe in 1848), and *other* nations serving as the chief bulwarks of bourgeois reaction—then we too would have to be in favour of a revolutionary war against the latter, in favour of "crushing" them, in favour of destroying all their outposts, no matter what small-nation movements arose in them. Consequently, instead of rejecting any examples of Marx's tactics—this would mean professing Marxism while abandoning it in practice—we must analyse them concretely and draw invaluable lessons for the future. The several demands of democracy, including self-determination, are not an absolute, but only a *small part* of the general-democratic (now: general-socialist) *world* movement. In individual concrete cases, the part may contradict the whole; if so, it must be rejected. It is possible that the republican movement in one country may be merely an instrument of the clerical or financial-monarchist intrigues of other countries; if so, we must *not* support this particular, concrete movement, but it would be ridiculous to delete the demand for a republic from the programme of international Social-Democracy on these grounds.

In what way has the concrete situation changed between the periods of 1848-71 and 1898-1916 (I take the most important landmarks of imperialism as a period: from the

Spanish-American imperialist war to the European imperialist war)? Tsarism has manifestly and indisputably ceased
to be the chief mainstay of reaction, first, because it is
supported by international finance capital, particularly
French, and, secondly, because of 1905. At that time the
system of big national states—the democracies of Europe—
was bringing democracy and socialism to the world in spite
of tsarism.* Marx and Engels did not live to see the period
of imperialism. The system now is a handful of imperialist "Great" Powers (five or six in number), each oppressing
other nations: and this oppression is a source for artificially
retarding the collapse of capitalism, and artificially supporting opportunism and social-chauvinism in the imperialist nations which dominate the world. At that time, West-
European democracy, liberating the big nations, was
opposed to tsarism, which used certain small-nation movements for reactionary ends. Today, the socialist proletariat,
split into chauvinists, "social-imperialists", on the one
hand, and revolutionaries, on the other, is confronted by an
alliance of tsarist imperialism and advanced capitalist,
European, imperialism, which is based on their common
oppression of a number of nations.

Such are the concrete changes that have taken place in
the situation, and it is just these that the Polish Social-
Democrats ignore, in spite of their promise to be concrete!
Hence the concrete change in the *application* of the same
socialist principles: *formerly* the main thing was to fight
"against tsarism" (and against certain small-nation move-

---

* Ryazanov has published in Grünberg's *Archives of the History
of Socialism* (1916, I) a very interesting article by Engels on the
Polish question, written in 1866. Engels emphasises that the proletariat
must recognise the political independence and "self-determination"
("right to dispose of itself" [These words are in English in the original.—*Ed.*]) of the great, major nations of Europe, and points to the
absurdity of the "principle of nationalities" (particularly in its
Bonapartist application), i.e., of placing any small nation on the same
level as these big ones. "And as to Russia," says Engels, "she could
only be mentioned as the detainer of an immense amount of stolen
property [i.e., oppressed nations] which would have to be disgorged
on the day of reckoning."[106] Both Bonapartism and tsarism *utilise*
the small-nation movements for *their own* benefit, *against* European
democracy.

ments that *it* was using for undemocratic ends), and for the greater revolutionary peoples of the West; the main thing *today* is to stand against the united, aligned front of the imperialist powers, the imperialist bourgeoisie and the social-imperialists, and *for* the utilisation of *all* national movements against imperialism for the purposes of the socialist revolution. The *more purely* proletarian the struggle against the general imperialist front now is, the more vital, obviously, is the internationalist principle: "No nation can be free if it oppresses other nations".

In the name of their doctrinaire concept of social revolution, the Proudhonists ignored the international role of Poland and brushed aside the national movements. Equally doctrinaire is the attitude of the Polish Social-Democrats, who *break up* the international front of struggle against the social-imperialists, and (objectively) help the latter by their vacillations on the question of annexations. For it is precisely the international front of proletarian struggle that has changed in relation to the concrete position of the small nations: at that time (1848-71) the small nations were important as the potential allies either of "Western democracy" and the revolutionary nations, or of tsarism; now (1898-1914) that is no longer so; today they are important as one of the nutritive media of the parasitism and, consequently, the social-imperialism of the "dominant nations". The important thing is not whether one-fiftieth or one-hundredth of the small nations are liberated before the socialist revolution, but the fact that in the epoch of imperialism, owing to objective causes, the proletariat has been split into two international camps, one of which has been corrupted by the crumbs that fall from the table of the dominant-nation bourgeoisie—obtained, among other things, from the double or triple exploitation of small nations—while the other cannot liberate itself without liberating the small nations, without educating the masses in an anti-chauvinist, i.e., anti-annexationist, i.e., "self-determinationist", spirit.

This, the most important aspect of the question, is ignored by our Polish comrades, who do *not* view things from the key position in the epoch of imperialism, the standpoint of the division of the international proletariat into two camps.

Here are some other concrete examples of their Proudhonism: (1) their attitude to the Irish rebellion of 1916, of which later; (2) the declaration in the theses (II, 3, end of § 3) that the slogan of socialist revolution "must not be overshadowed by anything". The idea that the slogan of socialist revolution can be "overshadowed" by *linking* it up with a consistently revolutionary position on all questions, including the national question, is certainly profoundly anti-Marxist.

The Polish Social-Democrats consider our programme "national-reformist". Compare these two practical proposals: (1) for autonomy (Polish theses, III, 4), and (2) for freedom to secede. It is in this, and in this alone, that our programmes differ! And is it not clear that it is precisely the first programme that is reformist and not the second? A reformist change is one which leaves intact the foundations of the power of the ruling class and is merely a concession leaving its power unimpaired. A revolutionary change undermines the foundations of power. A reformist national programme does *not* abolish *all* the privileges of the ruling nation; it does *not* establish complete equality; it does *not* abolish national oppression *in all its forms*. An "autonomous" nation does not enjoy rights equal to those of the "ruling" nation; our Polish comrades could not have failed to notice this had they not (like our old Economists) obstinately avoided making an analysis of *political* concepts and categories. Until 1905 autonomous Norway, as a part of Sweden, enjoyed the widest autonomy, but she was not Sweden's equal. Only by her free secession was her equality manifested *in practice* and proved (and let us add in parenthesis that it was this free secession that created the basis for a more intimate and more democratic association, founded on equality of rights). As long as Norway was merely autonomous, the Swedish aristocracy had *one* additional privilege; and secession did not "mitigate" this privilege (the essence of reformism lies in *mitigating* an evil and not in destroying it), but *eliminated* it *altogether* (the principal criterion of the revolutionary character of a programme).

Incidentally, autonomy, as a reform, differs in principle from freedom to secede, as a revolutionary measure. This is unquestionable. But as everyone knows, in practice a reform is often merely a step towards revolution. It is autonomy that enables a nation forcibly retained within the boundaries of a given state to crystallise into a nation, to gather, assess and organise its forces, and to select the most opportune moment for a *declaration* ... in the "Norwegian" spirit: We, the autonomous diet of such-and-such a nation, or of such-and-such a territory, declare that the Emperor of all the Russias has ceased to be King of Poland, etc. The usual "objection" to this is that such questions are decided by wars and not by declarations. True: in the vast majority of cases they are decided by wars (just as questions of the form of government of big states are decided, in the vast majority of cases, only by wars and revolutions). However, it would do no harm to reflect whether *such* an "objection" to the political programme of a revolutionary party is logical. Are we opposed to wars and revolutions *for* what is just and beneficial to the proletariat, *for* democracy and socialism?

"But we cannot be in favour of a war between great nations, in favour of the slaughter of twenty million people for the sake of the problematical liberation of a small nation with a population of perhaps ten or twenty millions!" Of course not! And it does not mean that we throw complete national equality out of our Programme; it means that the democratic interests of *one* country must be subordinated to the democratic interests of *several and all* countries. Let us assume that between two great monarchies there is a little monarchy whose kinglet is "bound" by blood and other ties to the monarchs of both neighbouring countries. Let us further assume that the declaration of a republic in the little country and the expulsion of *its* monarch would in practice lead to a war between the two neighbouring big countries for the restoration of that or another monarch in the little country. There is no doubt that all international Social-Democracy, as well as the really internationalist section of Social-Democracy in the little country, *would be against substituting a republic for the monarchy* in this case. The substitution of a republic for a monarchy is not an absolute, but one of the democratic demands, subordinate to the interests of democracy (and still more, of course, to those of the socialist proletariat) as a whole. A case like this would in all probability not give rise to the slightest

disagreement among Social-Democrats in any country. But
if any Social-Democrat were to propose on *these* grounds
that the demand for a republic be deleted altogether from
the programme of international Social-Democracy, he would
certainly be regarded as quite mad. He would be told that
after all one must not forget the elementary logical difference
between the *general* and the *particular*.

This example brings us, from a somewhat different angle,
to the question of the *internationalist* education of the
working class. Can such education—on the necessity and
urgent importance of which differences of opinion among the
Zimmerwald Left are inconceivable—be *concretely identical*
in great, oppressor nations and in small, oppressed nations,
in annexing nations and in annexed nations?

Obviously not. The way to the common goal—complete
equality, the closest association and the eventual *amalgamation of all* nations—obviously runs along different routes
in each concrete case, as, let us say, the way to a point in
the centre of this page runs left from one edge and right,
from the opposite edge. If a Social-Democrat from a great,
oppressing, annexing nation, while advocating the amalgamation of nations in general, were for one moment to forget
that "his" Nicholas II, "his" Wilhelm, George, Poincaré,
etc., *also stand for amalgamation* with small nations (by
means of annexations)—Nicholas II for "amalgamation"
with Galicia, Wilhelm II for "amalgamation" with Belgium,
etc.—such a Social-Democrat would be a ridiculous doctrinaire in theory and an abettor of imperialism in practice.

In the internationalist education of the workers of the
oppressor countries, emphasis must necessarily be laid on
their advocating freedom for the oppressed countries to
secede and their fighting for it. Without this there can be
no internationalism. It is our right and duty to treat every
Social-Democrat of an oppressor nation who *fails* to conduct
such propaganda as a scoundrel and an imperialist. This
is an absolute demand, even where the *chance* of secession
being possible and "practicable" before the introduction of
socialism is only one in a thousand.

It is our duty to teach the workers to be "indifferent"
to national distinctions. There is no doubt about that.
But it must not be the indifference of the *annexationists.*

A member of an oppressor nation must be "indifferent" to whether small nations belong to *his* state *or to a neighbouring* state, or to themselves, according to where their sympathies lie: without such "indifference" he is *not* a Social-Democrat. To be an internationalist Social-Democrat one must *not* think only of one's own nation, but place *above it* the interests of all nations, their common liberty and equality. Everyone accepts this in "theory" but displays an annexationist indifference in practice. There is the root of the evil.

On the other hand, a Social-Democrat from a small nation must emphasise in his agitation the *second* word of our general formula: "voluntary *integration*" of nations. He may, without failing in his duties as an internationalist, be in favour of *both* the political independence of his nation and its integration with the neighbouring state of X, Y, Z, etc. But in all cases he must fight *against* small-nation narrow-mindedness, seclusion and isolation, consider the whole and the general, subordinate the particular to the general interest.

People who have not gone into the question thoroughly think that it is "contradictory" for the Social-Democrats of oppressor nations to insist on the "freedom to *secede*", while Social-Democrats of oppressed nations insist on the "freedom to *integrate*". However, a little reflection will show that there is not, and cannot be, any *other* road to internationalism and the amalgamation of nations, any other road *from the given* situation to this goal.

And now we come to the *specific* position of Dutch and Polish Social-Democrats.

8. THE SPECIFIC AND THE GENERAL IN THE POSITION OF THE DUTCH AND POLISH SOCIAL-DEMOCRAT INTERNATIONALISTS

There is not the slightest doubt that the Dutch and Polish Marxists who oppose self-determination are among the best revolutionary and internationalist elements in international Social-Democracy. How *can* it be then that their theoretical arguments as we have seen, are a mass of errors? There is not a single correct general argument, nothing but imperialist Economism!

It is not at all due to the especially bad subjective quali-
ties of the Dutch and Polish comrades but to the *specific*
objective conditions in their countries. Both countries are:
(1) small and helpless in the present-day "system" of great
powers; (2) both are geographically situated between tre-
mendously powerful imperialist plunderers engaged in the
most bitter rivalry with each other (Britain and Germany;
Germany and Russia); (3) in both there are terribly strong
memories and traditions of the times when they *themselves*
were great powers: Holland was once a colonial power
greater than England, Poland was more cultured and was
a stronger great power than Russia and Prussia; (4) to this
day both retain their privileges consisting in the oppression of other peoples: the Dutch bourgeois owns the very
wealthy Dutch East Indies; the Polish landed proprietor
oppresses the Ukrainian and Byelorussian peasant; the
Polish bourgeois, the Jew, etc.

The particularity comprised in the combination of these
four points is not to be found in Ireland, Portugal (she
was at one time annexed to Spain), Alsace, Norway, Finland, the Ukraine, the Lettish and Byelorussian territories
or many others. And it is this very peculiarity that is the
real essence of the matter! When the Dutch and Polish
Social-Democrats reason against self-determination, using
general arguments, i.e., those that concern imperialism in
general, socialism in general, democracy in general, national
oppression in general, we may truly say that they wallow
in mistakes. But one has only to discard this obviously
erroneous *shell* of general arguments and examine the *essence*
of the question from the standpoint of the *specific* conditions
obtaining in Holland and Poland for their particular position to become *comprehensible* and quite legitimate. It may
be said, without any fear of sounding paradoxical, that
when the Dutch and Polish Marxists battle against self-
determination they do not say quite what they mean, or,
to put it another way, mean quite what they say.*

---

* Let us recall that *all* the Polish Social-Democrats *recognised*
self-determination *in general* in their Zimmerwald declaration,
although their formulation was slightly different.

We have already quoted one example in our theses.* Gorter is against the self-determination of *his own* country but *in favour* of self-determination for the Dutch East Indies, oppressed as they are by "his" nation! Is it any wonder that we see in him a more sincere internationalist and a fellow-thinker who is closer to us than those who recognise self-determination *as* verbally and hypocritically as Kautsky in Germany, and Trotsky and Martov in Russia? The general and fundamental principles of Marxism undoubtedly imply the duty to struggle for the freedom to secede for nations that are oppressed by "one's own" nation, but they certainly do not require the independence specifically of Holland to be made a matter of paramount importance — Holland, which suffers most from her narrow, callous, selfish and stultifying seclusion: let the whole world burn, we stand aside from it all, "we" are satisfied with our old spoils and the rich "left-overs", the Indies, "we" are not concerned with anything else!

Here is another example. Karl Radek, a Polish Social-Democrat, who has done particularly great service by his determined struggle for internationalism in German Social-Democracy since the outbreak of war, made a furious attack on self-determination in an article entitled "The Right of Nations to Self-Determination" (*Lichtstrahlen* [107] — a Left Radical monthly prohibited by the Prussian censor, edited by J. Borchardt —1915, December 5, Third Year of Publication, No. 3). He quotes, incidentally, *only* Dutch and Polish authorities in his support and propounds, amongst others, the argument that self-determination fosters the idea that "it is allegedly the duty of Social-Democrats to support any struggle for independence".

From the standpoint of *general* theory this argument is outrageous, because it is clearly illogical: first, no democratic demand can fail to give rise to abuses, unless the specific is subordinated to the general; we are not obliged to support either "any" struggle for independence or "any" republican or anti-clerical movement. Secondly, *no* formula for the struggle against national oppression can fail to suffer from

* See p. 150 of this volume.—*Ed.*

the *same* "shortcoming". Radek himself in *Berner Tagwacht*
used the formula (1915, Issue 253): "Against old and new
annexations." Any Polish nationalist will legitimately
"deduce" from this formula: "Poland is an annexment,
I am against annexations, *i.e.*, I am for the independence
of Poland." Or I recall Rosa Luxemburg saying in an
article written in 1908,[108] that the formula: "against national
oppression" was quite adequate. But any Polish nationalist would say—*and quite justly*—that annexation is *one*
of the forms of national oppression, *consequently*, etc.

However, take Poland's *specific* conditions in place of
these general arguments: her independence *today* is "impracticable" without wars or revolutions. To be in favour of an
all-European war merely for the sake of restoring Poland
is to be a nationalist of the worst sort, and to place the
interests of a small number of Poles above those of the
hundreds of millions of people who suffer from war. Such,
indeed, are the "Fracy" (the Right wing of the P.S.P.)[109]
who are socialists only in word, and compared with whom
the Polish Social-Democrats are a thousand times right. To
raise the question of Poland's independence *today*, with
the *existing* alignment of the *neighbouring* imperialist powers,
is really to run after a will-o'-the-wisp, plunge into narrow-
minded nationalism and forget the necessary premise of an
all-European or at least a Russian and a German revolution. To have put forward in 1908-14 freedom of coalition
in Russia as an independent slogan would also have meant
running after a will-o'-the-wisp, and would, objectively,
have helped the Stolypin labour party (now the Potresov-
Gvozdyov party, which, incidentally, is the same thing).
But it would be madness to remove freedom of coalition
in general from the programme of Social-Democracy!

A third and, perhaps, the most important example. We
read in the Polish theses (III, end of §2) that the idea of an
independent Polish buffer state is opposed on the grounds
that it is an "inane utopia of small impotent groups. Put
into effect, it would mean the creation of a tiny fragment of
a Polish state that would be a military colony of one or
another group of Great Powers, a plaything of their military
or economic interests, an area exploited by foreign capital,
and a battlefield in future wars". This is all very *true*

when used as an argument *against* the slogan of Polish independence *today*, because even a revolution in Poland alone would change nothing and would only divert the attention of the masses in Poland from *the main thing* — the connection between their struggle and that of the Russian and German proletariat. It is not a paradox but a fact that today the Polish proletariat as such can help the cause of socialism and freedom, *including the freedom of Poland*, only by *joint* struggle with the proletariat of the neighbouring countries, against the *narrow Polish* nationalists. The great historical service rendered by the Polish Social-Democrats in the struggle against the nationalists cannot possibly be denied.

But these same arguments, which are true from the standpoint of Poland's *specific* conditions in the *present* epoch, are manifestly untrue in the *general* form in which they are presented. So long as there are wars, Poland will always remain a battlefield in wars between Germany and Russia, but this is no argument against greater political liberty (and, therefore, against political independence) in the periods between wars. The same applies to the arguments about exploitation by foreign capital and Poland's role as a plaything of foreign interests. The Polish Social-Democrats cannot, at the moment, raise the slogan of Poland's independence, for the Poles, as proletarian internationalists, can do *nothing* about it without stooping, like the "Fracy", to humble servitude to *one* of the imperialist monarchies. But it is *not* indifferent to the Russian and German workers whether Poland is independent, or they take part in annexing her (and that would mean educating the Russian and German workers and peasants in the basest turpitude and their consent to play the part of executioner of other peoples).

The situation is, indeed, bewildering, but there is a way out in which *all* participants would remain internationalists: the Russian and German Social-Democrats by demanding for Poland unconditional *"freedom* to secede"; the Polish Social-Democrats by working for the unity of the proletarian struggle in both small and big countries without putting forward the slogan of Polish independence for the given epoch or the given period.

9. ENGELS'S LETTER TO KAUTSKY

In his pamphlet *Socialism and Colonial Politics* (Berlin, 1907), Kautsky, who was then still a Marxist, published a letter written to him by Engels, dated September 12, 1882, which is extremely interesting in relation to the question under discussion. Here is the principal part of the letter.

"In my opinion the colonies proper, i.e., the countries occupied by a European population—Canada, the Cape, Australia—will all become independent; on the other hand, the countries inhabited by a native population, which are simply subjugated—India, Algeria, the Dutch, Portuguese and Spanish possessions—must be taken over for the time being by the proletariat and led as rapidly as possible towards independence. How this process will develop is difficult to say. India will perhaps, indeed very probably, make a revolution, and as a proletariat in process of self-emancipation cannot conduct any colonial wars, it would have to be allowed to run its course; it would not pass off without all sorts of destruction, of course, but that sort of thing is inseparable from all revolutions. The same might also take place elsewhere, e.g., in Algeria and Egypt, and would certainly be the best thing *for us*. We shall have enough to do at home. Once Europe is reorganised, and North America, that will furnish such colossal power and such an example that the semi-civilised countries will of themselves follow in their wake; economic needs, if anything, will see to that. But as to what social and political phases these countries will then have to pass through before they likewise arrive at socialist organisation, I think we today can advance only rather idle hypotheses. One thing alone is certain: *the victorious proletariat can force no blessings of any kind upon any foreign nation without undermining its own victory by so doing*. Which of course by no means excludes defensive wars of various kinds...." [110]

Engels does not at all suppose that the "economic" alone will directly remove all difficulties. An economic revolution will be a stimulus to *all* peoples to *strive* for socialism; but at the same time revolutions—against the socialist state—and wars are possible. Politics will inevitably adapt themselves to the economy, but not immediately or smoothly, not simply, not directly. Engels mentions as "certain" only one, absolutely internationalist, principle, and this he applies to *all* "foreign nations", i.e., not to colonial nations only: to force blessings upon them would mean to undermine the victory of the proletariat.

Just because the proletariat has carried out a social revolution it will not become holy and immune from errors and weaknesses. But it will be inevitably led to realise this truth by possible errors (and selfish interest —attempts to saddle others).

We of the Zimmerwald Left all hold the same conviction as Kautsky, for example, held before his desertion of Marxism for the defence of chauvinism in 1914, namely, that the socialist revolution is quite possible *in the very near* future —"any day", as Kautsky himself once put it. National antipathies will not disappear so quickly: the hatred —and perfectly legitimate hatred —of an oppressed nation for its oppressor *will last* for a while; it will evaporate only *after* the victory of socialism and *after* the final establishment of completely democratic relations between nations. If we are to be faithful to socialism we must even now educate the masses in the spirit of internationalism, which is impossible in oppressor nations without advocating freedom of secession for oppressed nations.

10. THE IRISH REBELLION OF 1916

Our theses were written before the outbreak of this rebellion, which must be the touchstone of our theoretical views.

The views of the opponents of self-determination lead to the conclusion that the vitality of small nations oppressed by imperialism has already been sapped, that they cannot play any role against imperialism, that support of their purely national aspirations will lead to nothing, etc. The imperialist war of 1914-16 has provided *facts* which refute such conclusions.

The war proved to be an epoch of crisis for the West-European nations, and for imperialism as a whole. Every crisis discards the conventionalities, tears away the outer wrappings, sweeps away the obsolete and reveals the under-lying springs and forces. What has it revealed from the standpoint of the movement of oppressed nations? In the colonies there have been a number of attempts at rebellion, which the oppressor nations, naturally did all they could to hide by means of a military censorship. Nevertheless, it is known that in Singapore the British brutally suppressed a mutiny among their Indian troops; that there were attempts at rebellion in French Annam (see *Nashe Slovo*) and in the German Cameroons (see the Junius pamphlet*); that in Europe, on the one hand, there was a rebellion in Ireland, which the "freedom-loving" English, who did not dare to extend conscription to Ireland, suppressed by executions, and, on the other, the Austrian Government passed the death sentence on the deputies of the Czech Diet "for trea-son", and shot whole Czech regiments for the same "crime".

This list is, of course, far from complete. Nevertheless, it proves that, *owing* to the crisis of imperialism, the flames of national revolt have flared up *both* in the colonies and in Europe, and that national sympathies and antipathies have manifested themselves in spite of the Draconian threats and measures of repression. All this before the crisis of imperialism hit its peak; the power of the imperial-ist bourgeoisie was yet to be undermined (this may be brought about by a war of "attrition" but has not yet hap-pened) and the proletarian movements in the imperialist countries were still very feeble. What will happen when the war has caused complete exhaustion, or when, in one state at least, the power of the bourgeoisie has been shaken under the blows of proletarian struggle, as that of tsarism in 1905?

On May 9, 1916, there appeared in *Berner Tagwacht*, the organ of the Zimmerwald group, including some of the Leftists, an article on the Irish rebellion entitled "Their Song Is Over" and signed with the initials K. R.[111] It described the Irish rebellion as being nothing more nor less than a "putsch", for, as the author argued, "the Irish question was an agrarian one", the peasants had been pacified by reforms, and the nationalist movement remained

---

* See pp. 305-19 of this volume.—*Ed.*

only a "purely urban, petty-bourgeois movement, which, notwithstanding the sensation it caused, had not much social backing".

It is not surprising that this monstrously doctrinaire and pedantic assessment coincided with that of a Russian national-liberal Cadet, Mr. A. Kulisher (*Rech*[112] No. 102, April 15, 1916), who also labelled the rebellion "the Dublin putsch".

It is to be hoped that, in accordance with the adage, "it's an ill wind that blows nobody any good", many comrades, who were not aware of the morass they were sinking into by repudiating "self-determination" and by treating the national movements of small nations with disdain, will have their eyes opened by the "accidental" coincidence of opinion held by a Social-Democrat and a representative of the imperialist bourgeoisie!!

The term "putsch", in its scientific sense, may be employed only when the attempt at insurrection has revealed nothing but a circle of conspirators or stupid maniacs, and has aroused no sympathy among the masses. The centuries-old Irish national movement, having passed through various stages and combinations of class interest, manifested itself, in particular, in a mass Irish National Congress in America (*Vorwärts*, March 20, 1916) which called for Irish independence; it also manifested itself in street fighting conducted by a section of the urban petty bourgeoisie *and a section of the workers* after a long period of mass agitation, demonstrations, suppression of newspapers, etc. Whoever calls *such* a rebellion a "putsch" is either a hardened reactionary, or a doctrinaire hopelessly incapable of envisaging a social revolution as a living phenomenon.

To imagine that social revolution is *conceivable* without revolts by small nations in the colonies and in Europe, without revolutionary outbursts by a section of the petty bourgeoisie *with all its prejudices*, without a movement of the politically non-conscious proletarian and semi-proletarian masses against oppression by the landowners, the church, and the monarchy, against national oppression, etc.—to imagine all this is to *repudiate social revolution*. So one army lines up in one place and says, "We are for socialism", and another, somewhere else and says, "We are for imperialism", and that will be a social revolution! Only those who hold such a ridiculously pedantic view could vilify the Irish rebellion by calling it a "putsch".

Whoever expects a "pure" social revolution will *never* live to see it. Such a person pays lip-service to revolution without understanding what revolution is.

The Russian Revolution of 1905 was a bourgeois-democratic revolution. It consisted of a series of battles in which *all* the discontented classes, groups and elements of the population participated. Among these there were masses imbued with the crudest prejudices, with the vaguest and most fantastic aims of struggle; there were small groups which accepted Japanese money, there were speculators and adventurers, etc. But *objectively*, the mass movement was breaking the back of tsarism and paving the way for democracy; for this reason the class-conscious workers led it.

The socialist revolution in Europe *cannot be* anything other than an outburst of mass struggle on the part of all and sundry oppressed and discontented elements. Inevitably, sections of the petty bourgeoisie and of the backward workers will participate in it—without such participation, *mass* struggle is *impossible*, without it *no* revolution is possible—and just as inevitably will they bring into the movement their prejudices, their reactionary fantasies, their weaknesses and errors. But *objectively* they will attack *capital*, and the class-conscious vanguard of the revolution, the advanced proletariat, expressing this objective truth of a variegated and discordant, motley and outwardly fragmented, mass struggle, will be able to unite and direct it, capture power, seize the banks, expropriate the trusts which all hate (though for different reasons!), and introduce other dictatorial measures which in their totality will amount to the overthrow of the bourgeoisie and the victory of socialism, which, however, will by no means immediately "purge" itself of petty-bourgeois slag.

Social-Democracy, we read in the Polish theses (I, 4), "must utilise the struggle of the young colonial bourgeoisie against European imperialism *in order to sharpen the revolutionary crisis in Europe*". (Authors' italics.)

Is it not clear that it is least of all permissible to contrast Europe to the colonies in *this* respect? The struggle of the oppressed nations *in Europe*, a struggle capable of going all the way to insurrection and street fighting, capable of breaking down the iron discipline of the army and martial law, will "sharpen the revolutionary crisis in Europe" to an infinitely greater degree than a much more developed rebellion in a remote colony. A blow delivered against the power of the English imperialist bourgeoisie by a rebellion in Ireland is a hundred times more significant politically than a blow of equal force delivered in Asia or in Africa.

The French chauvinist press recently reported the publication in Belgium of the eightieth issue of an illegal journal, *Free Belgium*.[113] Of course, the chauvinist press of France very often lies, but this piece of news seems to be true. Whereas chauvinist and Kautskyite German Social-Democracy has failed to establish a free press for itself during the two years of war, and has meekly borne the yoke of military censorship (only the Left Radical elements, to their credit be it said, have published pamphlets and manifestos, in spite of the censorship)—an oppressed civilised nation has reacted to a military oppression unparalleled in ferocity by establishing an organ of revolutionary protest! The dialectics of history are such that small nations, powerless as an *independent* factor in the struggle against imperialism, play a part as one of the ferments, one of the bacilli, which help the *real* anti-imperialist force, the socialist proletariat, to make its appearance on the scene.

The general staffs in the current war are doing their utmost to utilise any national and revolutionary movement in the enemy camp: the Germans utilise the Irish rebellion, the French—the Czech movement, etc. They are acting quite correctly from their own point of view. A serious war would not be treated seriously if advantage were not taken of the enemy's slightest weakness and if every opportunity that presented itself were not seized upon, the more so since it is impossible to know beforehand at what moment, where, and with what force some powder magazine will "explode". We would be very poor revolutionaries if, in the proletariat's great war of liberation for socialism, we did not know how to utilise *every* popular movement against *every single* disaster imperialism brings in order to intensify and extend the crisis. If we were, on the one hand, to repeat in a thousand keys the declaration that we are "opposed" to all national oppression and, on the other, to describe the heroic revolt of the most mobile and enlightened section of certain classes in an oppressed nation against its oppressors as a "putsch", we should be sinking to the same level of stupidity as the Kautskyites.

It is the misfortune of the Irish that they rose prematurely, before the European revolt of the proletariat had *had time* to mature. Capitalism is not so harmoniously built that the various sources of rebellion can immediately merge of their own accord, without reverses and defeats. On the other hand, the very fact that revolts do break out at different times, in different places, and are of different kinds, guarantees wide scope and depth to the general movement; but it is only in premature, individual, sporadic and therefore unsuccessful, revolutionary movements that the masses gain experience, acquire knowledge, gather strength, and get to know their real leaders, the socialist proletarians, and in this way prepare for the general onslaught, just as certain strikes, demonstrations, local and national, mutinies in the army, outbreaks among the peasantry, etc., prepared the way for the general onslaught in 1905.

11. CONCLUSION

Contrary to the erroneous assertions of the Polish Social-Democrats, the demand for the self-determination of nations has played no less a role in our Party agitation than, for example, the arming of the people, the separation of the church from the state, the election of civil servants by the people and other points the philistines have called "utopian". On the contrary, the strengthening of the national movements after 1905 naturally prompted more vigorous agitation by our Party, including a number of articles in 1912-13, and the resolution of our Party in 1913 giving a precise "anti-Kautskian" definition (i.e., one that does not tolerate purely verbal "recognition") of the *content* of the point.*

---

* See present edition, Vol. 19, pp. 427-29.—*Ed.*

It will not do to overlook a fact which was revealed at that early date: opportunists of various nationalities, the Ukrainian Yurkevich, the Bundist Liebman, Semkovsky, the Russian myrmidon of Potresov and Co., all spoke *in favour* of Rosa Luxemburg's arguments *against* self-determination! What for Rosa Luxemburg, the Polish Social-Democrat, had been merely an incorrect theoretical generalisation of the *specific* conditions of the movement in Poland, became *objective* opportunist support for Great-Russian imperialism when actually applied to more extensive circumstances, to conditions obtaining in a big state instead of a small one, when applied on an international scale instead of the narrow Polish scale. The history of *trends* in political thought (as distinct from the views of individuals) has proved the correctness of our programme.

Outspoken social-imperialists, such as Lensch, still rail both against self-determination and the renunciation of annexations. As for the Kautskyites, they hypocritically recognise self-determination—Trotsky and Martov are going the same way here in Russia. *Both of them*, like Kautsky, say they favour self-determination. What happens in practice? Take Trotsky's articles "The Nation and the Economy" in *Nashe Slovo*, and you will find his usual eclecticism: on the one hand, the economy unites nations and, on the other, national oppression divides them. The conclusion? The conclusion is that the prevailing hypocrisy remains unexposed, agitation is dull and does not touch upon what is most important, basic, significant and closely connected with practice —one's attitude to the nation that is oppressed by "one's own" nation. Martov and other secretaries abroad simply preferred to forget —a profitable lapse of memory! — the struggle of their colleague and fellow-member Semkovsky against self-determination. In the legal press of the Gvozdyovites (*Nash Golos*) Martov spoke *in favour* of self-determination, pointing out the indisputable truth that during the imperialist war it does not *yet* imply participation, etc., but evading the main thing —he also evades it in the illegal, free press! —which is that *even in peace time* Russia set a world record for the oppression of nations with an imperialism that is much more crude, medieval, economically backward and militarily bureaucratic. The Russian Social-

Democrat who "recognises" the self-determination of nations more or less as it is recognised by Messrs. Plekhanov, Potresov and Co., that is, without bothering to fight for the freedom of secession for nations oppressed by tsarism, is *in fact* an imperialist and a lackey of tsarism.

No matter what the subjective "good" intentions of Trotsky and Martov may be, their evasiveness objectively supports Russian social-imperialism. The epoch of imperialism has turned all the "great" powers into the oppressors of a number of nations, and the development of imperialism will inevitably lead to a more definite division of trends in this question in international Social-Democracy as well.

Written in July 1916
Published in October 1916
In *Sbornik Sotsial-Demokrata* No. 1
Signed: *N. Lenin*

Published according to
the *Sbornik* text

NOTES

[1] Written in 1915. In early 1916, Lenin, while in Berne, sent the manuscript to Maxim Gorky for the *Parus* Publishers, but it did not appear at that time. It was published in Petrograd in 1917 by *Zhizn i Znaniye*.

The material for the book—variants of the plan and statistical extracts from the U.S. Census reports for 1900 and 1910—was published in *Lenin Miscellany XIX* in 1932.

Lenin did not realise his intention of writing the second part of the book, which was to have dealt with Germany.   p. 13

[2] *Zavety* (Behests)—a legal literary and political monthly of a Socialist-Revolutionary orientation; published in Petersburg from April 1912 to July 1914.   p. 17

[3] Karl Marx, *Capital*, Vol. III, Moscow, 1959, pp. 600.   p. 22

[4] *Zemstvo*—so-called local self-government bodies headed by the nobility. They were set up in the central gubernias of Russia in 1864. Their powers were restricted to purely local economic affairs (hospitals, roads, statistics, insurance, etc.), and they were subordinated to the provincial governors and the Minister of the Interior, who could overrule any decisions the government found undesirable.   p. 60

[5] *Manilov*—a character in Gogol's *Dead Souls*, who had a very fertile imagination and loved to talk; a prattling self-complacent dreamer.   p. 84

[6] Kautsky's pamphlet, *Der Weg Zur Macht* (The Way to Power), published in Berlin in 1909.   p. 106

[7] *Die Neue Zeit* (New Times)—the journal of the German Social-Democratic Party, published in Stuttgart from 1883 to 1923. In 1885-95, it carried some articles by Engels, who often gave advice to its editors and sharply criticised them for any departures from Marxism. Beginning with the late nineties, after Engels's death, it made a regular practice of publishing articles by revisionists. During the First World War, it adopted a Centrist, Kautskyite stand, and supported the social-chauvinists. p. 106

[8] The article was written by Lenin in German and published in January 1916 in the first issue of the theoretical organ of the Zimmerwald Left, the magazine *Vorbote* (Herald). Earlier, Lenin had written an article in Russian under the same title; it was first

published in the magazine *Proletarskaya Revolutsia* (Proletarian Revolution) No. 5 (28) in 1924, and is included in Volume 21 of the present edition, where the text is not quite identical with the one in *Vorbote*.   p. 108

⁹ *The Quadruple Alliance*—the imperialist alliance of Britain, France, Russia and Italy, which in 1915 withdrew from the Dreibund and joined the Triple Entente.   p. 108

¹⁰ An opportunist trend in German and international Social-Democracy hostile to Marxism. It emerged in Germany at the end of the 19th century, and got its name from Eduard Bernstein, a German Social-Democrat, who tried to revise Marx's revolutionary theory on the lines of bourgeois liberalism. Among his supporters in Russia were the legal Marxists, the Economists, the Bund and the Mensheviks.   p. 112

¹¹ *Sozialistische Monatshefte* (Socialist Monthly)—the chief organ of the German Social-Democratic opportunists and an organ of international opportunism; during the First World War it took a social-chauvinist stand; published in Berlin from 1897 to 1933. p. 112

¹² Members of the Fabian Society, a British reformist organisation founded in 1884; it got its name from the Roman commander, Fabius Maximus (d. 203 B.C.), surnamed Cunctator, that is, the Delayer, for his tactics of harassing Hannibal's army without risking a pitched battle. Most of the Society's members were bourgeois intellectuals: scholars, writers, politicians (such as Sidney and Beatrice Webb, Bernard Shaw, Ramsay MacDonald, etc.); they denied the need for the class struggle of the proletariat and a socialist revolution, and insisted that the transition from capitalism to socialism lay only through petty reform and a gradual transformation of society. Lenin said it was "an *extremely opportunist* trend" (see present edition, Vol. 13, p. 358). In 1900, the Fabian Society was affiliated to the Labour Party. Fabian socialism is one of the ideological sources of the Labour Party policy.

During the First World War, the Fabians took a social-chauvinist stand. For Lenin's description of the Fabians, see "British Pacifism and the British Dislike of Theory" (present edition, Vol. 21).   p. 113

¹³ Founded in 1900 as an amalgamation of trade unions, socialist organisations and groups to seat workers' representatives in Parliament (Committee for Labour Representation). In 1906, it took the name of Labour Party. Trade-unionists are automatically members of the Party provided they pay membership dues. It is headed by an Executive Committee which together with the Trade Union General Council and the Executive Committee of the Co-operative Party constitute the so-called National Labour Council. The Co-operative Party and the I.L.P. are corporate members of the Labour Party.

Initially a working men's party (it was subsequently joined by considerable numbers of petty-bourgeois elements), the Labour

Party is opportunist in ideology and tactics. Since its emergence its leaders have been conducting a policy of class collaboration with the bourgeoisie. "The Labour Party is an out-and-out bourgeois party, for although it does consist of workers it is led by reactionaries—the worst reactionaries who operate in the spirit of the bourgeoisie...." (See present edition, Vol. 31, "Speech on the Membership in the British Labour Party, Delivered on August 6, 1920, at the Second Congress of the Communist International".) During the First World War, its leaders took a social-chauvinist stand.

Labour Governments (1924, 1929, 1945 and 1950) have conducted the policy of British imperialism. Dissatisfaction with the leadership's policy among the British working people has led to a Left-wing trend in the Party opposing the leadership's official policy. p. 113

[11] *The Independent Labour Party* (I.L.P.) is a reformist organisation founded by the leaders of the "new trade unions" in 1893, during the upswing in the strike movement and the working-class movement for independence from the bourgeois parties. The I.L.P. included members of the "new trade unions" and a number of old ones, and also intellectuals and petty-bourgeois elements influenced by the Fabians. The Party was headed by Keir Hardie. From the outset it took a bourgeois-reformist stand, concentrating on the parliamentary forms of struggle and parliamentary deals with the Liberal Party. Lenin said it was "in practice an opportunist party which has always depended on the bourgeoisie" (see present edition, Vol. 29, "The Tasks of the Third International").

At the outbreak of the First World War, the I.L.P. issued an anti-war manifesto, but soon slid down to social-chauvinist positions. p. 113

[15] *The British Socialist Party* was founded in Manchester in 1911 by a merger of the Social-Democratic Party with other socialist groups. It spread Marxist ideas and was a party that was "not opportunist and was *really* independent of the Liberals" (see present edition, Vol. 19, p. 273). But its small membership and weak ties with the masses lent it a somewhat sectarian character. During the First World War, a struggle broke out within it between the internationalist trend (William Gallacher, Albert Inkpin, John McLean, Theodore Rothstein, and others) and the social-chauvinist trend led by Hyndman. Some in the internationalist trend took a Centrist stand on a number of issues. In February 1916, a group of B.S.P. members founded *The Call*, a newspaper which played a great part in rallying the internationalists. The B.S.P. annual conference at Salford in April 1916 condemned the social-chauvinist stand of Hyndman and his supporters, and they left the Party.

The B.S.P. welcomed the Great October Socialist Revolution. Its members took a leading part in the British working people's movement in defence of Soviet Russia against foreign intervention. In 1919, the majority of its local organisations (98 against 4) voted in favour of joining the Communist International. Together with the Communist Unity Group, the B.S.P. played the decisive role in founding the Communist Party of Great Britain. At the first unity congress held in 1920, the overwhelming majority of local B.S.P. organisations joined the Communist Party. p. 113

[16] *Nasha Zarya* (Our Dawn)—a legal monthly of the Menshevik liquidators published in Petersburg from January 1910 to September 1914. It was the liquidators' centre in Russia. With the outbreak of the First World War the journal took a social-chauvinist stand. p. 113

[17] *Organising Committee* (O.C.)—the Mensheviks' governing centre, formed at the August conference of Menshevik liquidators and all anti-Party groups and trends in 1912. p. 113

[18] *Shiroki* (Broad) *Socialists*—an opportunist trend within the Bulgarian Social-Democratic Party. p. 113

[19] *Preussische Jahrbücher* (Prussian Yearbook)—a conservative monthly of the German capitalists and landowners published in Berlin from 1858 to 1935. p. 114

[20] Friedrich Engels, "Zur Kritik des sozial-demokratischen Programmentwurfes 1891" (published in *Die Neue Zeit*, Jg. XX, 1901, B. II, No. 1). p. 114

[21] Marx and Engels, *Selected Correspondence*, Moscow, 1955, p. 537. p. 116

[22] Engels's letter to Friedrich Albert Sorge of November 11, 1893. (No English translation available.) p. 116

[23] *The Zimmerwald Left* was formed by Lenin at the first socialist conference of internationalists at Zimmerwald, Switzerland, in early September 1915; it was, Lenin said, the first step in the development of the internationalist movement against the war. The Bolsheviks, led by Lenin, were the only group within the Zimmerwald Left to take a consistently correct stand. The group also included a number of inconsistent internationalists, whose mistakes Lenin criticised in "The Junius Pamphlet", and "The Discussion of Self-Determination Summed Up" (see pp. 305-19, 320-60 of this volume). p. 118

[24] A weekly founded in 1891. From 1893 it was an organ of the I.L.P.; from 1922, it was called the *New Leader*, and since 1946 it has been known as the *Socialist Leader*. p. 119

[25] *Berner Tagwacht* (Berne Reveille)—the organ of the Social-Democratic Party of Switzerland, published in Berne from 1893. In 1909-18, it was edited by R. Grimm. At the outbreak of the First World War, it carried articles by Liebknecht, Mehring and other Left-wing Social-Democrats. From 1917 the newspaper gave open support to the social-chauvinists. The paper's present stand on the key domestic and foreign policy issues coincides with that of bourgeois newspapers. p. 119

[26] Written by Lenin for the enlarged meeting of the International Socialist Commission (I.S.C.) in Berne which was held on February 5-8, 1916. It adopted several of Lenin's points but under the pressure of the Right-wingers rejected his proposal for "international unification of socialists opposing war and nationalism". It set the Second International Socialist Conference for April 24, 1916. The document had no title, the present one having been supplied by the Institute of Marxism-Leninism, C.C. C.P.S.U. p. 121

[27] The *I.S.C.* was the executive of the Zimmerwald group elected at the Zimmerwald Conference in September 1915. p. 121

[28] The R.S.D.L.P. Central Committee submitted proposals to the Second Socialist Conference on all the key items of the agenda. For the draft proposals written by Lenin, see pp. 169-79 of this volume. p. 121

[29] Written during the enlarged meeting of the I.S.C. in Berne. It was discussed and adopted. p. 122

[30] This speech was delivered at an international rally during the enlarged meeting of the I.S.C. in Berne. p. 123

[31] Adopted by the Zimmerwald Conference of internationalists in September 1915 (see present edition, "First Step", Vol. 21). p. 123

[32] The newspaper of the American socialists founded in Girard, Kansas, in 1895. While not officially connected with the American Socialist Party, the newspaper spread socialist ideas and was very popular among the workers. p. 125

[33] *La Bataille* (The Battle)—the organ of the French anarchist syndicalists, published in Paris from 1915 to 1920 in place of *La Bataille Syndicaliste*, which was closed down in September 1915; during the First World War, took a chauvinist stand. p. 127

[34] *Vorwärts* (Forward)—a daily, the Central Organ of the German Social-Democratic Party, published in Berlin from 1891 in accordance with a resolution of the Party's Halle Congress as a continuation of the *Berliner Volksblatt* (Berlin People's Newspaper), which had been published from 1884. On its pages Engels fought every manifestation of opportunism. In the late nineties, after Engels's death, the paper fell into the hands of the Party's Right wing and regularly printed articles by opportunists. It gave a biased account of the struggle against opportunism and revisionism within the R.S.D.L.P., supported the Economists, and after the Party split, the Mensheviks. During the years of reaction, *Vorwärts* published Trotsky's slanderous articles but refused to print refutations by Lenin and the Bolsheviks or fair accounts of the state of affairs in the Party.

During the First World War, it took a social-chauvinist stand. After the Great October Socialist Revolution it engaged in anti-Soviet propaganda. It was published in Berlin until 1933. p. 127

[35] *War industries committees* were set up in Russia in 1915 by imperialist Big Business. In its efforts to control the workers and

spread defencist sentiments among them, the bourgeoisie attached "workers' groups" to these committees which were to exhort the masses to increase munitions output. The Mensheviks were active in this pseudo-patriotic undertaking. The Bolsheviks successfully boycotted them with the aid of the majority of the workers. p. 128

[36] Founded in 1902. In 1905, the F.S.P. and the Socialist Party of France founded the United Socialist Party, which included all socialist parties and groups (Guesdists, Blanquists, Jaurèsists, etc.). The leadership of the F.S.P. passed into the hands of socialist-reformists (led by Jaurès), who constituted the majority. During the First World War, it took a social-chauvinist stand, its parliamentary group voted for war credits, and its members were in the bourgeois government. The F.S.P. split at its Tours Congress, December 25-30, 1920; the majority formed the Communist Party of France, while the Right-wing opportunist minority, led by Léon Blum, left the Congress and formed their own party, retaining the old name of the French Socialist Party.

The resolution motioned by Bourderon at the F.S.P. Congress in December 1915 was rejected by a majority. At that time, Bourderon belonged to the Right wing of the Zimmerwald group.
p. 128

[37] It was published in French as a leaflet in Geneva. p. 130

[38] The Menshevik magazine, *The International and the War*, only one issue of which was published in late 1915. p. 131

[39] *Die Internationale Sozialistische Kommission zu Bern. Bulletin* — the I.S.C. organ from September 1915 to January 1917. It was published in English, French, and German. There were six issues in all. p. 131

[40] The Menshevik group in the Fourth State Duma. p. 131

[41] *Luch* (The Ray)—a legal daily of the Menshevik liquidators, published in Petersburg from September 1912 to July 1913; financed from funds donated by *"rich friends from among the bourgeoisie"* (Vol. 20, p. 368). p. 131

[42] Legal Menshevik newspapers published in Petrograd: *Utro* (Morning), in August 1915; and *Rabocheye Utro* (Workers' Morning), in October-December 1915. p. 132

[43] *Sovremenny Mir* (The Contemporary World)—a literary, scientific and political monthly published in Petersburg from 1906 to 1918. Among its contributors were Mensheviks, including Plekhanov. Bolsheviks also contributed to the magazine during the bloc with the Plekhanov group of pro-Party Mensheviks and in early 1914. In March 1914, it carried Lenin's article "Socialism Demolished Again" (see present edition, Vol. 20, p. 187).

During the First World War the magazine was an organ of the social-chauvinists. p. 132

[44] *Nashe Slovo* (Our Word)—a Menshevik-Trotskyist daily, published in Paris from January 1915 to September 1916, in place of *Golos* (Voice).   p. 132

[45] *Prizyv* (The Call), published in Paris between 1915 and 1917 by a social-chauvinist group of Mensheviks and Socialist-Revolutionaries.   p. 135

[46] The conference was organised by the Socialist-Revolutionaries in Petrograd in July 1915. It adopted a resolution calling for active support of tsarism in the war.   p. 135

[47] In Turgenev's prose poem "An Everyday Rule to Follow". p. 136

[48] *Sotsial-Demokrat* (Social-Democrat)—the Central Organ of the R.S.D.L.P., an illegal newspaper published from February 1908 to January 1917, a total of 58 issues. The first was published in Russia, and the rest abroad, first in Paris, then in Geneva. Under a R.S.D.L.P. Central Committee decision, its Editorial Board was composed of Bolsheviks, Mensheviks and Polish Social-Democrats.

It carried more than 80 articles and notes by Lenin, who worked to make the Editorial Board conduct a consistent Bolshevik line. Some of the editors (Kamenev and Zinoviev) took a conciliatory attitude to the liquidators and tried to thwart the implementation of Lenin's line. The Mensheviks Martov and Dan, while hampering the work of the Central Organ's Editorial Board, openly defended the liquidators in their factional newspaper, *Golos Sotsial-Demokrata* (The Voice of a Social-Democrat). Lenin's resolute struggle against the liquidators finally forced Martov and Dan to resign from the Editorial Board in June 1911. From December 1911, the newspaper was edited by Lenin.

At the outbreak of the First World War, after an interval of one year, Lenin succeeded in resuming its publication. Issue No. 33 of *Sotsial-Demokrat*, dated November 1, 1914, carried a manifesto of the R.S.D.L.P. Central Committee, which was written by Lenin. His articles in the newspaper during the war were outstanding in implementing the Bolshevik Party's strategy and tactics on war, peace, and revolution, and in exposing overt and covert social-chauvinists and rallying the internationalist elements in the international working-class movement.   p. 137

[49] The name given by workers to the Menshevik liquidators who adapted themselves to the Stolypin regime, accepted it and tried to obtain the tsarist government's permission to set up a legal "labour" party, at the price of having to abandon the Programme and tactics of the R.S.D.L.P.   p. 138

[50] Lenin said it was "Octobrist" because it dove-tailed with the stand of the counter-revolutionary Octobrist Party.

Octobrists or the *League of October Seventeenth* was a counter-revolutionary party of big merchants and industrialists and big landowners who ran their estates on capitalist lines. It was formed in November 1905. The Octobrists supported the tsar's Manifesto of October 17, 1905 and gave full backing to his government's domestic and foreign policy. They were led by the industrialist A. Guchkov and landed proprietor M. Rodzyanko.   p. 139

51 A frame-up trial instituted in 1894 by reactionary royalist circles among the French militarists against Dreyfus, a Jewish officer of the General Staff, who was falsely accused of espionage and high treason. A court martial sentenced him to life imprisonment. The public movement for a review of the case took the form of a fierce struggle between the republicans and the royalists and led to his eventual release in 1906.

Lenin said the Dreyfus case was "one of the many thousands of fraudulent tricks of the reactionary military caste".   p. 145

52 The incident was caused by the brutality of a Prussian officer towards Alsatians in Zabern, Alsace, in November 1913, and resulted in a burst of indignation among the local, mainly French, population against the Prussian militarists (see Lenin's article "Zabern" in the present edition, Vol. 19, pp. 513-15).   p. 145

53 Marx's letters to Engels of November 2 (no English translation available) and November 30, 1867 (Marx and Engels, *Selected Correspondence*, Moscow, 1955, pp. 234-37).   p. 146

54 For a critique of Renner and Bauer's reactionary idea of "cultural and national autonomy" see Lenin's "Cultural and National Autonomy" (present edition, Vol. 19) and "Critical Remarks on the National Question" (Vol. 20).   p. 147

55 Karl Marx, "Konfidentielle Mitteilung", quoted from the manuscript kept in the archives of the Institute of Marxism-Leninism of the C.C. C.P.S.U.   p. 149

56 Friedrich Engels, "Der Prager Aufstand", in *Neue Rheinische Zeitung* No. 18, June 18, 1848.   p. 149

57 Marx's proposition on the Irish question was stated in his letters to Kugelmann on November 29 and to Engels on December 10, 1869 (Marx and Engels, *Selected Correspondence*, pp. 276-78 and pp. 279-81). Lenin quotes from Marx's letter to Engels on November 2, 1867 (no English translation available).   p. 149

58 *Die Glocke* (The Bell)—a magazine published in Munich and later in Berlin from 1915 to 1925 by the social-chauvinist Parvus (A. L. Helfand), a member of the German Social-Democratic Party.   p. 150

59 Friedrich Engels, "Der demokratische Panslawismus". Lenin used *Aus dem literarischen Nachlass von Karl Marx, Friedrich Engels und Ferdinand Lassalle*, hrsg. von Franz Mehring, Stuttgart, 1902, Bd. III, S. 246-64, in which the author of the article is not named.   p. 150

[60] The resolution was on the national question; it was written by Lenin and adopted by the meeting of the R.S.D.L.P. Central Committee and Party officials, which was held at Poronin, near Cracow, on October 6-14, 1913. For reasons of secrecy it was known as the "Summer" or "August" Meeting. For the text of the resolution, see Vol. 19, pp. 427-29.   p. 154

[61] *Gazeta Robotnicza* (Workers' Gazette)—the illegal organ of the Warsaw Committee of the Social-Democratic Party of Poland and Lithuania, published from May to October 1906. Its publication was resumed in 1912 and continued until January 1916. Parallel committees were established after the split among the Polish Social-Democrats in 1912: there were two Warsaw Committees and two organs of the same name, one published by the supporters of the Executive Committee in Warsaw and the other, by the Opposition Warsaw Committee in Cracow. The Opposition Warsaw Committee published two issues, Nos. 24 and 25 (with supplement), in Zurich in 1915-16.   p. 157

[62] This refers to the Brussels "Unity" Conference, July 16-18, 1914, called by the Executive Committee of the International Socialist Bureau (I.S.B.) for an exchange of opinion on the prospects of reuniting the R.S.D.L.P. The following were represented: R.S.D.L.P. Central Committee (Bolsheviks); Organising Committee (Mensheviks); Plekhanov's Unity group; the *Vperyod* group; the Bund; the Social-Democrats of the Latvian Territory; the Social-Democrats of Lithuania; the Polish Social-Democrats; the Polish Social-Democratic Opposition; the Polish Socialist Party (The Left wing). The I.S.B. Executive was represented by Vandervelde, Huysmans, Kautsky, Nemetz and others. Long before the Conference, the I.S.B. leaders made a secret arrangement with the liquidators on joint action against the Bolsheviks.

Lenin and the Bolsheviks were aware of the real aims pursued by the organisers of the Conference, but deemed it necessary to attend, because a refusal to do so would not have been understood by the workers of Russia. The R.S.D.L.P. Central Committee sent its delegation—I. F. Armand (Petrova), M. F. Vladimirsky (Kamsky) and I. F. Popov (Pavlov). Lenin briefed the delegates, wrote the report, gave detailed instructions, and provided them with the necessary material, documents and facts exposing the opportunism of the Menshevik liquidators and their allies. Lenin was living in Poronin and directed the delegation from day to day by his advice and instructions.

The R.S.D.L.P. Central Committee report was delivered by Armand. The I.S.B. leaders would not let her read the full text and she had to summarise only a part of the report and set out the Bolsheviks' terms for unity, which the Mensheviks and the leaders of the Second International met with cries and threats against the Bolsheviks. Kautsky, on behalf of the I.S.B., motioned a unity resolution, asserting that there were no substantial contradictions within the Russian Social-Democratic Party which could be an obstacle to unity. He was supported by Plekhanov and the representatives of the O.C., who fiercely attacked Lenin and the C.C. delegation. Rosa Luxemburg also took an erroneous stand and joined Plekhanov, Vandervelde, Kautsky and the others who supported the amalgamation of the Bolsheviks and the Mensheviks. Since the Conference was not empowered to adopt any resolutions—it was to confine itself to an exchange of opinion— the Bolsheviks and the Latvian Social-Democrats refused to take part in the voting, but the resolution was passed by a majority.

The Bolsheviks, led by Lenin, refused to abide by the decisions of the Brussels Conference and exposed the true aims of the "unifiers" before the international proletariat. The opportunist leaders of the Second International failed to eliminate the Bolshevik Party. p. 157

[63] After the Menshevik *K. A. Gvozdyov*—a policy of collaborating with the imperialist bourgeoisie. p. 159

[64] *L. Tyszka* (Jogiches), was a leader of the Polish Social-Democrats, at times unprincipled and vacillating in his political activity. During the First World War he joined the internationalists; worked with Rosa Luxemburg and Karl Liebknecht to found the Spartacus League in Germany; in March 1919 was arrested and killed in prison. For a characteristic of Tyszka, see Lenin's "The Split among the Polish Social-Democrats" (present edition Vol. 18), "Would-be Uniters", "Coteries Abroad and Russian Liquidators" (Vol. 19), *et. al.* p. 160

[65] The Second International Socialist Conference held in Kienthal, Switzerland, on April 24-30, 1916.

It was attended by 43 delegates from 10 countries—Austria, France, Germany, Italy, Norway, Poland, Portugal, Serbia, Switzerland and Russia. A delegate from Britain and a delegate from the Secretariat of the Youth International attended as guests. The delegates of the Indepenent Labour Party of Britain, the United States, Bulgaria, Rumania, Greece, and Sweden were refused passports and were unable to attend. Some Left-wing bodies delegated their powers to other parties: the Social-Democrats of the Latvian Territory transferred their credentials to the R.S.D.L.P. Central Committee; the delegate of the Dutch Lefts, H. Roland-Holst, to the Territorial Executive of the Social-Democrats of the Kingdom of Poland and Lithuania.

Russia was represented at the Conference by three R.S.D.L.P. Central Committee delegates headed by Lenin, two delegates from the Menshevik O.C. and three delegates from the Left Socialist-Revolutionaries. From Germany there were seven delegates from the Centrist Haase-Ledebour group, two delegates from the *Internationale* group and one from the Bremen Left-wing radicals. Italy was represented by seven delegates; France, by three Centrists and one syndicalist (Guilbeaux); Poland, by four, and Switzerland, by five.

The Conference discussed the following questions: (1) the struggle to end the war; (2) the attitude of the proletariat to questions of peace; (3) agitation and propaganda; (4) parliamentary activities; (5) mass struggle; and (6) convocation of the International Socialist Bureau.

Lenin started making extensive preparations for the Second International Socialist Conference immediately after the enlarged meeting of the International Socialist Committee in Berne (February 5-9, 1916). Without waiting for the Conference to be called officially, he sent to all the Bolshevik sections abroad and Left-wing socialists in various countries a letter, written with his participation, about the enlarged I.S.C. meeting and the convocation of the Conference, pointing to the need for immediate preparations for it and the election of delegates. His "Proposals Submitted by the Central Committee of the R.S.D.L.P. to the Second Socialist Conference" were also circulated for discussion among all Bolshevik organisations and among Left-wing Social-Democrats in France, Germany, Britain, Switzerland, Italy, Holland, Norway, Sweden and other countries. In some of his letters Lenin stressed that the Bureau of the Zimmerwald Left should prepare a report and theses for the Conference and hold a number of Left-wing meetings before and during the Conference.

As a result of the work done by Lenin and the Bolsheviks, the Left wing at the Conference was stronger than at Zimmerwald. It was joined by the delegate of the International Socialists of Germany group, two delegates of the *Internationale* group, the French syndicalist Guilbeaux, the representative of the Serbian Social-Democrats, Kaclerović, and the Italian socialist Giacinto Serrati. Thus, the Zimmerwald Left, which had 12 delegates at the Kienthal Conference, on some points obtained from 12 to 19 votes, or almost one-half. This reflected the shift to internationalism in the international working-class movement. During the Kienthal Conference, Lenin called several meetings of the Left to discuss "The Proposals Submitted by the Central Committee of the R.S.D.L.P. to the Second Socialist Conference". He rallied the Left-wing forces for joint and organised action at the Conference against its Kautskyite majority. The Zimmerwald Left worked out and laid before the Conference a draft resolution on the question of peace, which contained Lenin's key propositions. To avoid complete exposure, the Right-wing majority at the Conference was forced to follow the Left on a number of questions, but continued to oppose the break with the social-chauvinists.

Lenin took an active part in the Conference: he was a member of the commission on the convocation of the I.S.B., spoke several times, talked with delegates and exchanged notes with them at the sittings.

The struggle centred on the convocation of the I.S.B.; the Left got in an addendum to the resolution, which censured the activity of the I.S.B. but did not reject the possibility of its convocation, to the effect that in the event of its being convened an enlarged International Socialist Committee was to be called to discuss joint action by the representatives of the Zimmerwald group. The Conference adopted a resolution on the struggle for peace and an "Appeal to the Peoples Being Ruined and Slaughtered".

In view of the vote for war credits cast by the minority of the French parliamentary group, the Zimmerwald Left tabled a motion stating that such acts are incompatible with socialism and the anti-war struggle. Lenin said the Kienthal Conference was a step forward, although it failed to adopt the key Bolshevik propositions on turning the imperialist war into civil war, the defeat of one's own imperialist government, and the establishment of the Third International. It helped to crystallise and rally the internationalist elements on the ideological foundation of Marxism-Leninism. On the initiative of Lenin and the Bolsheviks, these elements subsequently constituted the nucleus of the Communist (Third) International.   p. 161

[66] *Arbeiter Zeitung* (Workers' Newspaper)—a daily, the Central Organ of the Austrian Social-Democrats, published in Vienna from 1889. During the First World War it took a social-chauvinist stand. Lenin called it the newspaper of the "Viennese traitors to socialism".

It was closed down in 1934 and resumed publication in 1945 as the Central Organ of the Socialist Party of Austria.   p. 165

[67] *Nash Golos* (Our Voice)—a social-chauvinist Menshevik newspaper, published in Samara in 1915 and 1916.   p. 166

[68] *The International Socialist Bureau* (I.S.B.) was the permanent executive and information body of the Second International located at Brussels. It was founded by a decision taken at the Paris Congress of the Second International (1900). It consisted of two delegates from each national party, and was to meet four times a year, the Executive Committee of the Belgian Labour Party being charged with its direction in between sessions. Vandervelde was its Chairman, and Huysmans, its Secretary. Lenin was a member of the Bureau, as a representative of the R.S.D.L.P., from 1905. From June 1914, on Lenin's proposal, M. M. Litvinov was appointed to represent the R.S.D.L.P. Central Committee. When the First World War broke out the I.S.B. became a pliable tool in the hands of the social-chauvinists.   p. 169

[69] A congress of the Dutch Social-Democratic Party held at Arnhem on January 8-9, 1916.   p. 173

[70] See "The United States of Europe Slogan" in the present edition, Vol. 21.   p. 173

[71] *Avanti!* (Forward!)—a daily, the Central Organ of the Italian Socialist Party, founded in December 1896. During the First World War it was inconsistently internationalist, and retained its ties with the reformists. It is now the Central Organ of the Italian Socialist Party.   p. 174

[72] An I.S.C. "Appeal to All Affiliated Parties and Groups", adopted unanimously by the enlarged meeting of the I.S.C. in Berne on February 5-9, 1916. The delegation of the R.S.D.L.P. Central Committee, led by Lenin, stated that it regarded the Appeal as a step forward as compared with the decisions of the First International Socialist Conference at Zimmerwald but did not find it satisfactory on all points. The Appeal was published in No. 3 of the I.S.C. *Bulletin* on February 29, 1916, and in No. 52 of *Sotsial-Demokrat* on March 25, 1916.　　　　　　　　　　p. 178

[73] The official I.S.C. statement dated September 29, 1915, and published in No. 2 of the I.S.C. *Bulletin* on November 27, 1915, which said, contrary to the decisions of the First Zimmerwald Conference, that the I.S.C. was prepared to consider itself dissolved as soon the I.S.B. resumed its activities at The Hague. This was helping to restore the Second International.　　　　　　　　　p. 178

[74] A group of German Left-wing Social-Democrats which emerged during the First World War. Its organ, *Lichtstrahlen* (Rays of Light), was published in Berlin from 1913 to 1921. The I.S.D. openly opposed war and opportunism and took the most consistent stand in Germany on separation from the social-chauvinists and Centrists. Borchardt, representing the group at the Zimmerward Conference, alone of the 10 German delegates signed the draft resolution and draft manifesto of the Zimmerwald Left. Soon after the Conference, the Bureau of the Zimmerwald Left was informed that the I.S.D. group had joined it, and this was reported in *Internationale Flugblatt* (International Leaflets) No. 1. The group had no extensive ties with the masses and soon broke up.　　　　　　　　　　　　　　　　　　　　　　p. 180

[75] G. V. Chicherin.　　　　　　　　　　　　　　　　　　　　p. 180

[76] A magazine founded by Lenin and published by the Editorial Board of *Sotsial-Demokrat* jointly with G. L. Pyatakov and E. B. Bosch, who financed it; Bukharin was one of the editors. Only one (double) issue was published. It carried, apart from the article "The Honest Voice of a French Socialist", two other articles by Lenin: "The Collapse of the Second International" and "Imperialism and Socialism in Italy".

The publication plan was worked out by Lenin in the spring of 1915. The organisational meeting of the Editorial Board was held under his guidance. Lenin planned to make *Kommunist* an international organ of the Left-wing Social-Democrats, but it soon transpired that there were grave contradictions between the Editorial Board and Bukharin, Pyatakov and Bosch, which were aggravated after the publication of the No. 1-2 issue. The Bukharin-Pyatakov-Bosch group took an incorrect stand on a number of points of principle in the Party's Programme and tactics—the right of nations to self-determination, the role of democratic demands and the minimum programme in general, etc.—and tried to make use of the magazine for factional purposes. On the Edito-

13*

rial Board Lenin fought the Bukharin-Pyatakov-Bosch group, exposed their anti-Bolshevik views and factional activities, and sharply criticised the conciliatory attitude to the group on the part of G. Y. Zinoviev and A. G. Shlyapnikov.

In view of the group's anti-Party attitude, the *Sotsial-Demokrat* Editorial Board declared, on Lenin's proposal, that it considered it impossible to continue publication. Lenin wrote the draft resolution of the R.S.D.L.P. Central Committee terminating the publication of *Kommunist*. The Central Committee Bureau in Russia, having heard a report on the contradictions on the *Kommunist* Editorial Board, declared its full solidarity with the Editorial Board of the Central Organ, *Sotsial-Demokrat*, and expressed the wish that "all publications of the Central Committee should be edited on lines strictly in conformity with the Central Committee's policy adopted before the outbreak of war". From October 1916, the Editorial Board of *Sotsial-Demokrat* began publication of *Sbornik Sotsial-Demokrata*. p. 180

[77] This article first appeared in *Voprosy Strakhovania* (Insurance Questions), 1916, No. 5, that was intermittently published in Petersburg from October 1913 to March 1918. During the First World War, it was the only legal Bolshevik periodical in Petersburg. It fought not only for workers' insurance, but also for full-blooded Bolshevik slogans: the eight-hour day, confiscation of big landed estates and a democratic republic. p. 182

[78] Engels, "The Role of Violence in History", in *Die Neue Zeit* (1895/96, Vol. 1) under the title, "Gewalt und Oekonomie bei der Herstellung des neuen Deutschen Reiches" ("Violence and the Economy in the Establishment of the New German Empire"). p. 184

[79] *Russkoye Znamya* (Russian Banner)—a reactionary newspaper, organ of the Union of the Russian People, published in Petersburg from November 1905 to 1917. p. 184

[80] Written in Zurich in January-June 1916.

Lenin began to take note of new developments in capitalism long before the outbreak of the First World War. In several of his writings from 1895 to 1913—"Draft and Explanation of a Programme for the Social-Democratic Party" (1895-96); "The War in China" (1900); "The Lessons of the Crisis" (1901); "Review of Home Affairs" (1901); "Concentration of Production in Russia" (1912); "The Growth of Capitalist Wealth" (1913); "Backward Europe and Advanced Asia" (1913); "The Historical Destiny of the Doctrine of Karl Marx" (1913); "Concerning Certain Speeches by Workers' Deputies" (1912), and others — Lenin pointed out and analysed some characteristic aspects of the imperialist epoch— the concentration of production and the growth of monopoly; the export of capital; the struggle for new markets and spheres of influence; the internationalisation of economic relations; the parasitism and decay of capitalism; the growth of contradictions between labour and capital and the sharpening of the class struggle; and the creation of the material conditions for the transition to socialism. He devoted special attention to exposing predatory colonial policy, the fight for a division and redivision of the world, and the preparation of imperialist wars of aggrandisement. In his article, "Marxism and Revisionism", written in 1908, he came out against the attempts to revise Marxism and undermine it from inside under the pretext of amending and correcting the theory, in particular, Marx's theory of crises. Lenin wrote: "The forms, the sequence, the picture of particular crises changed, but crises remained an inevitable component of the capitalist system. While uniting production, the cartels and trusts at the same time, and in a way that was obvious to all, aggravated the anarchy of production, the insecurity of existence of the proletariat and the oppression of capital, thereby intensifying class antagonisms to an unprecedented degree. That capitalism is heading for a break-down—in the sense both of individual political and economic crises and of the complete collapse of the entire capitalist system—has been made particularly clear, and on a particularly large scale, precisely by the new giant trusts" (see present edition, Vol. 15, pp. 35-36).

Lenin kept abreast of all the latest writings on capitalism, as will be seen from his review of Hobson's *The Evolution of Modern Capitalism*. In August 1904, Lenin began a translation of Hobson's *Imperialism*, the manuscript of which has not yet been found.

It was on the outbreak of the First World War that Lenin undertook a comprehensive study of the monopoly stage of capitalist development. This was required by the working-class revolutionary struggle in Russia and other capitalist countries. In order to provide correct leadership for the revolutionary movement and combat the ideology of imperialist reaction and the reformist policy of conciliation with imperialists, it was necessary to "see one's way in the key economic question without a study of which there was no understanding of the assessment of modern war or modern politics, namely: the economic essence of imperialism".

Lenin must have started his close study of the writings on imperialism in mid-1915, when he was in Berne, for his first indexes of literature, plans, extracts, notes and summaries date to that period. The preparatory materials for *Imperialism, the Highest Stage of Capitalism* (*Notebooks on Imperialism*) make up about 800 printed pages. They contain extracts from 148 books (including 106 in German, 23 in French, 17 in English, and 2 translations into Russian), and 232 articles (of them 206 in German, 13 in French, and 13 in English) from 49 periodicals (34 German, 7 French and 8 English).

In early January 1916, Lenin accepted an order for a book on imperialism from the legal *Parus* Publishers, founded in Petrograd in December 1915. Lenin wrote to Maxim Gorky on December 29, 1915 (January 11, 1916): "I am getting down to the writing of a pamphlet on imperialism" (see present edition, Vol. 35). In the early part of February 1916, he left Berne for Zurich, where

he continued to collect and work on materials on imperialism.
He worked at the Zurich Cantonal Library and ordered books from
other towns.

On June 19 (July 2), 1916 Lenin wrote to M. N. Pokrovsky,
who was then living in France and editing for *Parus* a series of
pamphlets about West-European countries during the First World
War: "Today, I sent you a manuscript by registered mail" (see
present edition, Vol. 35). The manuscript, which was mailed with
the letter, did not reach Pokrovsky, and another copy had to be
sent. Besides, the publishers suggested that the finished manuscript should be shortened from eighty to fifty pages, but Lenin
objected because "it is absolutely impossible to cut it down once
again and squeeze it into fifty pages" (ibid.).

When the book reached the publishers, Menshevik elements
among the management deleted from the book parts sharply
criticising Kautsky and Martov, and made corrections in the text
which not only distorted Lenin's style but also his ideas. Thus,
Lenin's terms *pererastaniye* (capitalism *growing into* imperialism)
was altered to *prevrashcheniye* (transformation); *reaktsionny kharakter* (*reactionary nature* of the theory of ultra-imperialism) to
otstaly kharakter (backward character), etc. In mid-1917, the book
was published under the title *Imperialism, the Latest Stage of
Capitalism* (*A Popular Outline*) with a preface by Lenin, dated
April 26, 1917.   p. 185

[81] This preface was first published under the title "Imperialism and
Capitalism" in *Communist International* No. 18, dated October
1921.   p. 189

[82] A Centrist party set up at an inaugural congress at Gotha in April
1917. Owing to the revolutionary upswing, which was greatly
intensified by the bourgeois-democratic revolution in Russia in
February 1917, the opportunist leadership of the Social-Democratic
Party of Germany was losing ground among the rank and file.
To overcome their discontent, divert attention from the revolutionary struggle and prevent the establishment of a revolutionary
working-class party, the Centrist leaders tried to set up a party
which would give them continued control of the masses. It was
intended to make the Independent Social-Democratic Party of
Germany such a party. The Independents used Centrist phrases
to cover up their call for unity with the social-chauvinists and
desertion of the class struggle. The bulk of the party consisted of
the Kautskyite Labour Commonwealth.

The Spartacus group remained in the party for a time but
was organisationally and politically independent, continuing
its illegal work and struggle to rid the masses of the influence of
Centrist leaders. In 1918, the Spartacus League withdrew from the
Independent Party and became the core of the Communist Party
of Germany.

In October 1920, a split took place at the congress in Halle.
In December 1920, a considerable part of the Independent S. D.
Party merged with the Communist Party of Germany. The Right-

wing elements formed a separate party and took the old name of
I.S.D.P.G., which existed until 1922.   p. 193

[83] *The Spartacists* — members of a revolutionary organisation of
German Left-wing Social-Democrats; formed in January 1916 under
the leadership of Karl Liebknecht, Rosa Luxemburg, Franz Mehring,
Clara Zetkin, J. Marchlewski, L. Jogiches (Tyszka) and Wilhelm
Pieck. In April 1915, Luxemburg and Mehring founded *Die
Internationale*, a magazine which rallied the main group of the Left-
wing Social-Democrats of Germany. From 1916, the *Internationale*
group, apart from the political leaflets they had been printing
since 1915, began the illegal publication and circulation of
Political Letters which were signed Spartacus (issued regularly
until October 1918); this gave the group its name of Spartacus
League. They conducted revolutionary propaganda among the
masses, organised massive anti-war action, led strikes, exposed
the imperialist nature of the world war and the treachery of the
opportunist Social-Democratic leaders. But they made serious
theoretical and political mistakes: they denied the possibility of
national liberation wars in the imperialist epoch, they took an
inconsistent stand on the slogan of turning the imperialist war
into a civil war, underestimated the role of the proletarian party
as the vanguard of the working class, underestimated the peasantry
as the ally of the proletariat and were afraid to break with the
opportunists. Lenin repeatedly criticised their mistakes (see "The
Junius Pamphlet", "A Caricature of Marxism and 'Imperialist
Economism'", etc.).

In April 1917, the Spartacus League joined the Centrist
I.S.D.P.G. (see Note 82), but remained organisationally independent. During the revolution in Germany in November 1918, they
issued their own programme (December 14) and broke with the Independents. On December 30, 1918-January 1, 1919, they founded
the Communist Party of Germany.   p. 193

[84] In the present edition, the author's references and notes are given
as footnotes.   p. 196

[85] Karl Marx, *Capital*, Vol. III, Moscow, 1959, p. 593.   p. 216

[86] These occurred during the widespread establishment of joint-
stock companies in the early seventies, which was accompanied by
all manner of fraudulent operations by bourgeois businessmen,
who were making a great deal of money, and by wild speculation
in real estate and securities.   p. 218

[87] *Frankfurter Zeitung* (Frankfort Newspaper)—a German bourgeois newspaper published in Frankfort-on-Main from 1856.
                                                          p. 220

[88] G. V. Plekhanov.   p. 228

[89] *Produgol*—an abbreviation for the Russian Society for Trade in
Mineral Fuel of the Donets Basin, founded in 1906. *Prodamet*—
Society for Marketing Russian Metallurgical Goods.   p. 232

[90] The exposure in France in 1892-93 of incredible abuses, corruption of politicians, officials and the press bribed by the French Panama Canal company. p. 237

[91] Marx and Engels, *Selected Correspondence*, Moscow, 1955, pp. 132-33. p. 283

[92] The Menshevik S. M. Nakhimson. p. 289

[93] Karl Marx, *Capital*, Vol. III, Moscow, 1959, pp. 117-18. p. 290

[94] *Boxer* (more precisely: I Ho T'uan) *Rebellion*—a popular anti-imperialist uprising in China in 1899-1901 organised by the I Ho Ch'üan (Righteous Harmony Fists) society, which later became known as I Ho T'uan (Alliance for Righteous Harmony). It was ruthlessly crushed by an expeditionary corps of the imperialist powers under the command of the German General Waldersee, with the German, Japanese, British, American and Russian imperialists taking part. China was forced to sign the Peking (Final) Protocol which turned her into a semi-colony of the foreign imperialists. p. 296

[95] Rosa Luxemburg. p. 305

[96] The all-Germany conference of Left-wing Social-Democrats held at Karl Liebknecht's home in Berlin on January 1, 1916. The conference adopted the theses of the *Internationale* group which were worked out by Rosa Luxemburg. p. 305

[97] *Bremer Bürger-Zeitung* (Bremer Citizens' Newspaper)—a daily, the organ of the Bremen group of German Social-Democrats. It was published from 1890 to 1919; in 1914-15, it was in fact an organ of the German Left-wing Social-Democrats; in 1916 it fell into the hands of the Kautskyites. p. 307

[98] *Volksfreund* (People's Friend)—a daily Social-Democratic newspaper, founded in Brunswick in 1871; in 1914 and 1915 it was the organ of the German Left-wing Social-Democrats, but in 1916 it fell into the hands of the Kautskyites. p. 307

[99] Marx and Engels, *Selected Works*, Vol. I, Moscow, 1958, p. 540. p. 314

[100] The theses were compiled by the Editorial Board of *Gazeta Robotnicza* and published in *Sbornik Sotsial-Demokrata* No. 1 in October 1916. p. 320

[101] For an assessment of the three views on Poland's independence, see Lenin's article, "The Right of Nations to Self-Determination" (Vol. 20). p. 320

[102] The 1903 discussion on the R.S.D.L.P. draft Programme, later adopted at the Party's Second Congress [see "Material for the Preparation of the Programme of the R.S.D.L.P.", "Concerning the Statement of the Bund", "On the Manifesto of the Armenian Social-Democrats", "Does the Jewish Proletariat Need an 'Independent Political Party'?", and "The National Question in Our Programme" (see present edition, Vol. 6)], and the 1913 discus-

sion on cultural and national autonomy between the Bolsheviks on the one hand, and, the liquidators, Trotskyites and Bundists on the other (see "The National Programme of the R.S.D.L.P.", present edition, Vol. 19 and "Critical Remarks on the National Question" and "The Right of Nations to Self-Determination", Vol. 20). p. 321

[103] Marx and Engels, *Selected Works*, Vol. II, Moscow, 1955, pp. 32-33. p. 323

[104] See pamphlet by Engels, *Po und Rhein*, Section IV, M/E/L, Zur deutschen Geschichte, Bd. II, 1, S. 689 (no English translation available). p. 323

[105] Friedrich Engels, "Der demokratische Panslawismus", in *Neue Rheinische Zeitung* Nos. 222 and 223, February 15 and 16, 1849 (no English translation available). p. 340

[106] See article by Engels, "What Have the Working Classes to Do with Poland?", Section II, in *Commonwealth*, of March 24 and 31 and May 5, 1866. p. 342

[107] *Lichtstrahlen* (Rays of Light)—a monthly, the organ of the Left-wing Social-Democrats of Germany, edited by Borchardt. It appeared in Berlin irregularly from 1913 to 1921. p. 349

[108] Rosa Luxemburg's article, "The National Question and Autonomy", in Nos. 6, 7, 8-9, 10, 12 and 14-15 of the magazine *Przegląd Socjaldemokratyczny* (Social-Democratic Review) for 1908 and 1909. p. 350

[109] The Right wing of the Polish Socialist Party, a petty-bourgeois nationalist party founded in 1892. p. 350

[110] Marx and Engels, *Selected Correspondence*, Moscow, 1955, p. 423. p. 352

[111] Karl Radek. p. 354

[112] *Rech* (Speech)—a daily, the Central Organ of the Cadet Party published in Petersburg from February 1906; closed down by the Petrograd Soviet's Revolutionary Military Committee on October 26 (November 8), 1917; publication continued under another title until August 1918. p. 355

[113] *Libre Belgique* (Free Belgium)—an illegal journal of the Belgian Labour Party, Brussels (1915-18). p. 357

THE LIFE AND WORK
OF
V. I. LENIN

Outstanding Dates
(December 1915-July 1916)

1915

December 1915-   Lenin lives in Berne, Switzerland.
late January
1916

Mid-December 1915 Lenin holds a meeting of Social-Democrat
internationalists to discuss preparations for the
Second International Socialist Conference.

December 29,   Lenin sends Maxim Gorky the manuscript of
1915 (January 11, his book, *New Data on the Laws Governing the*
1916)   *Development of Capitalism in Agriculture*, for
publication in Petrograd.

December 29,   Lenin works on his *Imperialism, the Highest*
1915-June 19,   *Stage of Capitalism* at the Berne and Zurich
1916 (January   libraries.
11-July 2, 1916)

December 1915   Lenin writes a preface to Bukharin's pamphlet,
Imperialism and the World Economy.

In a letter to the Geneva section of the Bolsheviks Lenin points out the need for a special resolution condemning the Mensheviks' fraudulent
elections to the "workers' groups" under the
war industries committees in Petrograd.

December 1915-   Lenin is editor of the R.S.D.L.P.'s Central Organ,
January 1917   *Sotsial-Demokrat.*

1916

January 2 (15)   Lenin directs the sitting of the Zimmerwald Left
Bureau to discuss the representation of the Dutch
Left-wing Social-Democrats on the Bureau, and
the publication of *Vorbote* (Herald) as the organ of
the Zimmerwald Left.

January 12 (25)   Lenin directs the sitting of the Zimmerwald Left
Bureau to discuss measures in connection with the
forthcoming publication of the first issue of *Vorbote*.

January, later   Lenin's article "Opportunism and the Collapse of
than 12 (25)   the Second International" is published in *Vorbote*
No. 1.

January 17 (30)	Lenin writes a letter of instructions to the Zurich section of the Bolsheviks about the work to be done among young people in view of the forthcoming meeting of the International Socialist Bureau of Youth Organisations.
January 23-26 (February 5-8)	Lenin takes part in the work of the enlarged meeting of the I.S.C. in Berne, writes the draft resolution on the convocation of the Second International Socialist Conference and the terms of representation.
January 26 (February 8)	Lenin speaks at an international meeting in Berne on the imperialist war and the tasks facing the proletariat.
January 28 (February 10)	Lenin writes the letter, "The Tasks of the Opposition in France".
January 28 or 29 (February 10 or 11)	Lenin leaves Berne for Zurich.
January- February	Lenin writes his theses, "The Socialist Revolution and the Right of Nations to Self-Determination", which are published in *Vorbote* No. 2, in April 1916.
February 3 (16)	Lenin sends the Bolshevik sections abroad a communication on the enlarged meeting of the I.S.C. held on January 23-26 (February 5-8); he instructs them to start immediate preparations to mobilise the forces of the Zimmerwald Left for the elections to the Second International Socialist Conference scheduled for April.
February 4 (17)	In Zurich, Lenin reads his paper, "Two Internationals".
February 5 (18)	Lenin's article, "Have the O.C. and the Chkheidze Group a Policy of Their Own?", is published in *Sotsial-Demokrat* No. 50.
February 13 (26)	In Zurich, Lenin reads his paper, "The 'Terms of Peace' in Connection with the National Question".
February 16 (29)	Lenin's articles, "Peace Without Annexations and the Independence of Poland as Slogans of the Day in Russia", and "Wilhelm Kolb and Georgy Plekhanov", are carried in *Sotsial-Demokrat* No. 51.
February 17 (March 1)	In Geneva, Lenin reads his paper, "The 'Terms of Peace' in Connection with the National Question".
February 27 (March 11)	Lenin issues instructions to stop publication of *Kommunist* in view of the anti-Party position of the Bukharin-Pyatakov group, who tried

to use the journal for their own factional ends, and plans the publication of *Sbornik Sotsial-Demokrata*, under the editorship of the R.S.D.L.P. Central Organ, *Sotsial-Demokrat*.

February-March	Lenin writes his "Letter from the Committee of Organisations Abroad to the Sections of the R.S.D.L.P."
End of February-March	Lenin writes the "Proposals Submitted by the Central Committee of the R.S.D.L.P. to the Second Socialist Conference" (theses), has them translated into German and French and circulates them among the Bolshevik sections abroad and the Left-wing internationalists of various countries. The theses are published in the I.S.C. *Bulletin* No. 4, on April 9 (22).
End of February-April	Lenin writes his article "Split or Decay?".
March 6 (19)	In a letter to A. M. Kollontai in Norway, Lenin asks her to have *Internationale Flugblatt* No. 1, carrying the draft resolution and manifesto of the Zimmerwald Left, translated into English and published in Norway, and to take measures to circulate it in America, Britain, Sweden, Norway and other countries.
	Lenin sends his theses, "The Socialist Revolution and the Right of Nations to Self-Determination", to Norway to allow Swedish and Norwegian Left-wing socialists to study them.
March 12 (25)	Lenin's article, "The Peace Programme", is carried by *Sotsial-Demokrat* No. 52.
March-June	In his works and letters to Bolsheviks abroad, Lenin exposes the anti-Party views of the Bukharin-Pyatakov group on the key questions of Marxist theory and tactics, and their double-dealing in respect of the Party centre. He also exposes the double-dealing of Zinoviev, who in fact supports the Bukharin-Pyatakov group.
April 5 (18)	Lenin delivers his report, "The Immediate Tasks of the Social-Democrats in Russia", at a joint meeting of the Zurich section of the Bolsheviks with Polish and Latvian Social-Democrat internationalists.
April 11-17 (24-30)	Lenin takes part in the work of the Second International Socialist Conference in Kienthal, organises and rallies its Left, directs the commission on resolutions (criticising the pacifism and activity of the I.S.B.) and secures their adoption.

April, not earlier than 16 (29)	Lenin makes an outline of an article or report on the results of the Second International Socialist Conference.
May 20 (June 2)	In Geneva, Lenin reads his paper, "Two Trends in the International Working-Class Movement".
May 31 (June 13)	Lenin's article, "German and Non-German Chauvinism", is printed in *Voprosy Strakhovania* No. 5 (54)
May-July	In letters to Left-wing Social-Democrat internationalists in the Scandinavian countries, Lenin gives directives on preparations for a conference of socialists of the neutral countries and defines the tactics of the Left-wing delegates.
June 19 (July 2)	Lenin completes his work on *Imperialism, the Highest Stage of Capitalism*, and mails the manuscript to the *Parus* Publishers.
Between July 4 and 7 (17 and 20)	Lenin goes to live at Flums, a mountain village near Zurich.
July 12 (25)	Lenin's mother, M. A. Ulyanova, dies in Petrograd.
First half of July	Lenin writes his articles, "The Junius Pamphlet", and "The Discussion on Self-Determination Summed Up". Both are published in *Sbornik Sotsial-Demokrata* No. 1, in October 1916.

В. И. ЛЕНИН

СОЧИНЕНИЯ
ТОМ 22

На английском языке

Printed in the Union of Soviet Socialist Republics